TEACHERS,
STUDENTS
AND PEDAGOGY

TEACHERS, STUDENTS AND PEDAGOGY:

Selected Readings and Documents in the History of Canadian Education

Douglas O. Baldwin

Fitzhenry & Whiteside

Teachers, Students and Pedagogy:
Selected Readings and Documents in the History of Canadian Education

Copyright © 2008 Douglas O. Baldwin

Fitzhenry and Whiteside Limited
195 Allstate Parkway
Markham, Ontario L3R 4T8

In the United States:
311 Washington Street,
Brighton, Massachusetts 02135

www.fitzhenry.ca   godwit@fitzhenry.ca

Library and Archives Canada Cataloguing in Publication
Teachers, students and pedagogy : readings and documents in the history of Canadian education / ed. Douglas O. Baldwin.
Includes bibliographical references.

ISBN 1-55244-100-8

1. Education—Canada—History. I. Baldwin, Douglas, 1944-
   LA411.T42 2007   370.971   C2007-904753-X

Fitzhenry & Whiteside acknowledges with thanks the Canada Council for the Arts, and the Ontario Arts Council for their support of our publishing program. We acknowledge the financial support of the Government of Canada through the Book Publishing Industry Development Program (BPIDP) for our publishing activities.

Design by Fortunato Design Inc.

Cover image courtesy: Ministry of Education, Archives of Ontario, I0021549
Classroom with teacher's office in back, Horner Avenue School, Long Branch, 1916

Printed and bound in Canada

1 3 5 7 9 10 8 6 4 2

TABLE OF CONTENTS

Introduction		vii
Chapter 1:	**Educating Girls and Native Peoples in New France**	1
	Documents	18
Chapter 2:	**Pioneer Education to 1840**	26
	Documents	48
Chapter 3:	**Teaching as a Career for Women**	55
	Documents	73
Chapter 4:	**Curriculum and Pedagogy in the Mid-Nineteenth Century**	77
	Documents	96
Chapter 5:	**Rural School Teachers**	113
	Documents	127
Chapter 6:	**Gender and Domestic Science**	136
	Documents	155
Chapter 7:	**The Goals of Physical Education**	162
	Documents	180
Chapter 8:	**High School Culture Between the Wars**	188
	Documents	211
Chapter 9:	**Native Education**	229
	Documents	250
Chapter 10:	**Growing Up: 1914-1960**	262
	Documents	296
Chapter 11:	**Teaching Teachers**	309
	Documents	327
Chapter 12:	**The Ideal Curriculum**	336
	Documents	342
Chapter 13:	**Assessment and Accountability**	357
	Documents	363
Acknowledgements		375
Endnotes		378

Introduction

Formal education is one of the few aspects of life that virtually every Canadian has in common. Between the ages of approximately 5 and 16, we spend six hours a day, ten months a year, in a classroom. It is here that many youth (whom politicians and the general public declare to be our most precious resource) have significant defining life experiences. Yet, Canada's educational system is often in turmoil. Teachers' strikes, work-to-rule, low achievement results, funding cuts, back-to-work legislation, accountability, and standardized testing are everyday news. As public confidence in our educational system wanes, Canadians wonder what happened and what needs to be done. Although this collection does not claim to provide the "solution," it offers an historical perspective for some of the more important issues in the history of Canadian education.

To learn about the past is to discover that life was not always as it is today, and that it need not remain the same in the future. The best way to demonstrate the need for changing contemporary ideas, methods, and institutions is to show that the original rationale for their existence no longer applies. The writing of history is not a harmless exercise. In 213 BC, for example, the emperor of China ordered that all histories written about China before his reign be burned. The "Burning of the Books," he wrote, was to prevent historians from studying "the past in order to criticize the present age." German philosopher G.W.F. Hegel's famous comment that "peoples and governments have never learned anything from history," is somewhat cynical, but it is true that the "lessons" of the past have not always been heeded. It is difficult to disagree with Greek philosopher Sophocles' belief that "a sensible person judges the present by past events."

Historians are products of their time. The topics they choose to research are generally what their society finds interesting and relevant. Since historians usually suffer both from too much and too little information, they must reconstruct and interpret the past by selecting what they believe to be the most significant material. This task is more akin to the work of the painter than to that of the photographer, and the result is a likeness rather than an exact duplication. "Facts" are not always facts. As British historian E.H. Carr wrote, "Facts are like fish swimming about in a vast and sometime inaccessible ocean: and what the historian catches will depend partly on chance, but mainly on what parts of the ocean he chooses to fish in and what tackle he chooses to use, these two factors of course being determined by the kind of fish he wants to catch."[1]

The history of Canadian education has mimicked the general trends in historical writing. Prior to the late 1960s, most history writing was "whiggish" in nature. Historians focused on great men and their heroic deeds, which were usually political, economic, or military in nature. Thanks to these altruistic men, history was a record of continuous improvement in which class, gender, and ethnic conflicts were minimized. When the history of Canadian education was discussed, it was usually only when it impinged on politics, as in the case of the Manitoba Schools debate at the end of the nineteenth century. Those few historians who discussed the history of Canadian education chronicled the evolution of public education from pioneer times to the present in a laudatory tone. Statistics showing increases in the number of students, teachers, books, and schools charted the vigorous growth of education under the leadership of great men like Egerton Ryerson, who initiated centrally-controlled, free, and compulsory education. Few writers reflected on these changes, questioned their efficacy, or investigated the motives of their promoters.[2]

In the late 1960s, the rise of feminist and New-Left historical writing sparked interest in family, gender, the working class, and underprivileged groups in society. This "new" social history critically examined the motives and actions of "the great men," often employing sophisticated quantitative methods and model-building, and eschewing traditional narrative history. Influenced by Michael B. Katz at the Ontario Institute for Studies in Education, the new "revisionist" historians of education believed that the educational system was simply a reflection of the inequalities in the larger society, and that schools served to buttress the social order. Some historians asserted that the goal of "heroic" school promoters of the past was to socialize rather than educate. These "social control" historians portrayed a hierarchical educational system run by white, Anglo-Saxon, capitalist, middle-class men that deliberately sought to perpetuate the existing racist and class-based social order—a system that had remained fundamentally unchanged ever since.

The social control school had its critics. "Moderate revisionists," for example, believed that although the system had its flaws, society had benefited from universal, free education. As schools became an ideological battleground in the 1970s, the history of education emerged from the periphery of scholarly work to become an exciting and stimulating field of study. Empirical research methodologies and new sets of questions on such topics as literacy, gender, school attendance, and curricula raised new questions and provoked intense debates.

By the 1980s, the views of proponents of social control were criticized as being too simplistic and deterministic. New researchers (and some old social controllers) discovered that parents and local communities were often directly involved in educational reforms and that the central educational bureaucracies were frequently sensitive to local needs. Educational policies were a product of negotiations between the centre and the periphery, rather than an imposition from the top down. The revisionists were also accused of characterizing the ruling class as more homogeneous than it actually was, in both composition and ideology. In addition, studies in gender, ethnic, and working-class history indicated that such groups were not passive recipients of top-down decrees, but were often active participants.

The field of educational history gradually widened as its complexity became apparent. Regional studies replaced national works as researchers explored more limited topics in greater detail. Some of the best articles were reproduced in anthologies devoted to Western Canada, British Columbia, women, or the Native Peoples. Not only were issues of gender, race, ethnicity, power, and class investigated, but the field of inquiry was also expanded to include such non-formal educational settings as the family, apprenticeship, libraries, mechanics' institutes, and Sunday schools. In 1989, E.G. Finley's *Education in Canada: A Bibliography* listed over 14,000 entries in two volumes. That year, the Canadian History of Education Association transformed its newsletter into a biannual journal, *Historical Studies in Education*, and sponsored regular conferences. A recent volume of this journal included a bibliography of approximately 600 articles written in the 1990s. The history of education had come of age.

Today, articles by historians of education can be found in journals relating to economics, to medicine, Native studies, art, and political history. Whereas earlier historians studied the makers of educational policies, and later researchers examined education from the viewpoint of ethnicity, class and gender, more recent writers have turned their attention to the actual experiences of teachers and school children, the culture of the classroom, and the ways in which adults of different eras conceptualised childhood.

The Readings

How can we make sense of the scholarship on the history of education in Canada, especially in light of the explosion of interest in this subject during the past several decades? The articles and primary documents that follow focus on three broad themes that are at the core of education. The readings on teachers explore who became teachers, how they were trained, and what their experiences were in various parts of the country, in different time periods. The articles on pedagogy investigate changing methodologies and curricula, and the reasons behind these changes. The material on student experiences seeks to understand how young people of differing ethnic and social backgrounds responded to the classroom experience. For each topic there are many excellent articles from which to choose, with new ones being published almost every month. What follows is my own personal selection, informed by several years of weekly seminar discussions with Acadia University students taking courses on the history of Canadian education.

Further Reading

The best guide to the literature on the history of Canadian education is in the annual bibliographies published in *Historical Studies in Education*. In 1999 (vol. 11, no. 2) this journal printed a bibliography of the "works related to" the history of education from 1980 to 2000. This source, which promises to be updated regularly, can also be found at http://www.edu.uwo.ca/hse/index.html. For earlier bibliographies, see Alan H. Child, "The History of Canadian Education: A Bibliographic Note," *Histoire Sociale* (November 1971); Micheline Dumona, et al., "Bibliographie sur l'histoire de l'éducation des filles au Québec," *Resources for Feminist Research/Documentation sur la recherche féministe*, vol. 14, no. 2 (July 1985); Susan Gelman and Alison Prentice, eds. *The History of Gender and Teaching: A Selected Bibliography of English Language Published Sources* (Toronto, 1990); Valerie Giles, *Annotated Bibliography of Education History in British Columbia* (Victoria, 1992); and Neil Sutherland, et al., *Contemporary Canadian Childhood and Youth: A Bibliography* (Westport, Conn., 1992). For bibliographies on Native education see, Kathy Vermette, "Bibliography of First Nations Pedagogy," in Marie Battiste, Jean Barman eds. *First Nations Education in Canada: The Circle Unfolds* (Vancouver, 1995), and Katherine Graham, et al., *Public Policy and Aboriginal Peoples, 1965-1992*, vols.1 and 4 (Royal Commission on Aboriginal Peoples, 1996).

Since education is a provincial responsibility, provincial history journals such as *Acadiensis, Ontario History, Saskatchewan History*, and *BC Studies* regularly publish articles on the history of education. *Education Canada, Atlantis, History of Education Quarterly, McGill Journal of Education*, and *Canadian and International Education* are also worth consulting. The most readily available primary sources are provincial annual reports of departments of education. Each report includes curricula, inspectors' reports, and statistics on students, teachers, and courses. Printed compilations of primary documents include J.G. Hodgins, *The Documentary History of Education in Upper Canada from the Passing of the Constitutional Act in 1791 to the Close of Doctor Ryerson's Administration of the Education Department in 1876* (Toronto, 1894-1910); Douglas Lawr and Robert Gidney, eds. *Educating Canadians: A Documentary History of Public Education* (Toronto, 1973); and Alison L. Prentice and Susan E. Houston, eds. *Family, School and Society in Nineteenth-Century Canada* (Toronto, 1975). For archival guides see: Patrick A. Dunae, *The School Record: A Guide to Government Archives Relating to Public Education in British Columbia, 1852-1946* (Victoria, 1992); and Diana Moore and Andrea Schwenke, *New Brunswick Schools: A Guide to Archival Sources* (Fredericton, 1992).

For the historiography of the history of education see: Paul Axelrod, "Historical Writing and Canadian Education from the 1970s to the 1990s," *History of Education Quarterly*, 36/1 (Spring 1996); Chad Gaffield, "Children, Schooling, and Family Reproduction in Nineteenth-Century Ontario," *Canadian Historical Review*, 72/2, (1991); Harvey Graff, "Towards 2000: Poverty and Progress in the History of Education," *Historical Studies in*

Douglas O. Baldwin

Education 3 (Fall, 1991); Eric W. Ricker, "Historians and the Study of Educational Policy: An Overview," in Eric W. Ricker and B. Anne Wood, eds., *Historical Perspectives on Educational Policy in Canada: Issues, Debates and Case Studies* (Toronto, 1995); Neil Sutherland and Jean Barman, "Out of the Shadows: Retrieving the History of Urban Education and Urban Childhood in Canada," in Ronald K. Goodenow and William E. Marsden, eds., *The City and Education in Four Nations* (Cambridge, 1992); and J. Donald Wilson, "Some Observations of Recent Trends in Canadian Educational History," in J.D. Wilson ed., *An Imperfect Past: Education and Society in Canadian History* (Vancouver, 1986).

This book is dedicated to four future students—my grandchildren, Riley, Cole, Chase, and Ella.

Chapter One:
Educating Girls and Native Peoples in New France

Following Samuel de Champlain's settlement in Quebec City in 1608, population growth proceeded slowly as few people in France were willing to emigrate to New France. In 1627, there were less than 100 European settlers and by 1663 the population had increased to a mere 2,500 people. Thanks to early marriages, large families, and low mortality rates, by the time of the British Conquest in 1759-60, approximately 70,000 French Canadians lived in New France. This was a relatively young community. The average family had between five and six children, and most individuals did not survive beyond the age of 45.

Religion played a major role in the life of New France. France was a Catholic country, and almost everyone in the colony was a Roman Catholic. The priests cared for the people from baptism to marriage to death. They advised, comforted, warned, and helped the people of New France in a variety of ways. Since clergymen were among the few educated people in the colony, and as the church had considerable financial resources, priests were very influential. Jesuit missionaries worked among the Aboriginal Peoples and acted as translators. Female Catholic orders taught Native children, looked after the poor, the crippled, the sick, and the homeless. The church's job was also to ensure that the people lived moral lives and it sought to regulate everything from clothing styles and entertainment to what was thought and said. Most people, however, did not always do what the priests wanted them to do.

The French believed that their own ways were superior to the Aboriginal People and attempted to turn them into good Roman Catholics who dressed and acted like the French. In 1615, three Récollect missionaries came to New France to Christianize the Native Peoples. When the Native Peoples resisted all proselytizing efforts, the Jesuits, a more organized and zealous missionary organization, took over in 1627. To encourage converts, the missionaries provided Christian Natives with cheaper goods, presents, and guns. In return, the Natives had to agree to be baptized, accept Catholic views on sex, marriage and divorce, give up all good luck charms, and not participate in their traditional feasts and celebrations.

To more thoroughly convert the younger generation, the Jesuits opened a boarding school for Native boys. However, the rigid curriculum was irrelevant to their needs, and the alien concepts of time, order, competitiveness, and punishments caused most Native boys to run away. To instruct Native girls, the

Jesuits asked the Ursuline nuns to open a girls' boarding school in 1639. This task fell to Marie Guyart (Marie de l'Incarnation), whose activities are discussed in the following article.

After a religious experience as a child, Marie wanted to follow her visions and join a convent and become a nun. Her parents, however, insisted she marry, which she did at age 17. Two years later, her husband died, leaving Marie with a young baby. To make ends meet, she operated her brother-in-law's transport business, where her activities included grooming horses and keeping the accounts. When her son turned eleven, despite his pleas, Marie placed him with relatives and became an Ursuline nun. Marie de l'Incarnation now dedicated her life to God. Many religious orders at this time believed that suffering was an essential element of holy life, but Marie sometimes carried it to extremes. She wore shirts with knots and thorns in them, slept on a hair mattress that kept her awake much of the night, and awakened early to flay herself with whips made of leather tongs or nettles. Marie also deliberately scorched her skin with fire to share in Jesus' sufferings on the cross.

At the convent, Marie read the *Jesuit Relations* (reports written by Jesuits in New France about their experiences) and had a dream in which the Virgin Mary beckoned her to Quebec to evangelize Native girls. In 1639, Marie and a few other nuns sailed to Quebec. Her talents in business proved valuable to the success of the school. Marie oversaw the construction of the convent, and when fire destroyed this building, she raised the money to rebuild it. She learned both Iroquoian and Algonquin and compiled several dictionaries in these languages. When she died in Quebec in 1672, at the age of seventy-three, Marie had written more than 13,000 letters that detailed missionary activity and Aboriginal customs.

Although education was generally left to the Catholic Church, there were some lay school masters. These individuals travelled from place to place and peddled their expertise for room and board and a small fee. Recently arrived from France, these young males hoped to use their teaching skills as a stepping stone to other jobs.

Since most teachers, religious and lay, had been trained in France and used French textbooks (there were no printing presses, booksellers, or lending libraries in New France) colonial education mirrored that in France. But it was not a carbon copy, as the Native Peoples modelled different habits, and traditional French education was not crucial to farming, fishing, or the fur trade. In 1760, the colony supported approximately eighty teachers. Male Catholic orders operated three schools, and female orders ten schools.

In the article reproduced below, Nadia Fahmy-Eid examines the importance of social rank, gender, and ethnicity in the educational system of New France. Shaped by the metropolitan imperatives of church and state, the curriculum of New France was designed to produce the "ideal" woman. For additional information on schooling in Quebec see: Micheline Dumont, *Girls' Schooling in Quebec, 1639-1960* (Ottawa: CHA Historical Booklet, 1990); Roger Magnuson, *Education in New France* (Montreal, 1992); "Jesuit Pedagogy and the Wilderness Classroom in 17th-Century Canada," *Canadian Journal of Native Education* 17, 1 (1990); and Cornelius Jaenen, *The Role of the Church in New France* (Toronto, 1966).

The Education of Girls by the Ursulines of Quebec During the French Regime[3]

The education of girls by the Ursulines of Quebec was based primarily on the philosophy that prevailed in French metropolitan society in the seventeenth and eighteenth centuries. In France and New France, the education of girls was based on a specific definition of their role in society and consequently differed markedly from that of boys. Also, both societies were divided according to social rank and income, which were determining factors in the kind of education a girl would receive. In the colony the education of girls by the Ursulines was unique because society was further divided along ethnic lines—French and Indian.

This discussion will be limited to elementary school education since secondary schooling was not available to girls in either France or New France. In the colony, only the College of the Jesuits in Quebec offered higher education.

Philosophy of the Education of Girls

Although in New France no central organization was responsible for subject matter, pedagogy, or grade levels, the curriculum of the elementary school—*petite école* as it was then known—was fairly uniform. This uniformity was possible because the program was drawn from homogeneous philosophical and pedagogical sources and was limited in content. Besides the catechism, the girls were taught to read, write, and, in the language of the time, *jeter*—count with the use of *jetons* or tokens (usually old copper pennies). At this level, the education offered to girls and boys was almost the same. However, it should be noted that the curriculum for girls invariably included the teaching of "woman's" work (which will be discussed later).

Religion was the cornerstone of the education offered by the *petite école*, the "school of the popular classes." Since salvation was of paramount importance, boys and girls received the same religious instruction. In New France girls were sent to school mostly around the time of their First Communion. As in most Catholic societies of the Western world at the time, secular education was secondary to religious instruction, the method favoured to Christianize the masses. In fact, the many treatises on education written in the sixteenth and seventeenth centuries often lamented the ignorance of the masses, referring less to their illiteracy than to their ignorance of basic religious truths and the corresponding moral precepts. Church-approved pedagogical guides and educational manuals circulated freely between France and the colony. The colony's strong ties with the motherland largely explain their similar educational philosophies.

In Quebec the Ursulines and the Sisters of the Congregation of Notre-Dame had much the same objectives for girls' education as their French counterparts. The writings of Marie de l'Incarnation revealed that the Christianization of Indian girls and the religious education of French girls were of utmost importance. In his letters of authorization written in 1676 to the Sisters of the Congregation of Notre-Dame, the Bishop of Quebec, Monsignor de Laval, reiterated: "... one of the best means to ensure our congregation's devotion, and the best manner to preserve and augment our parishioners' piety is by providing children with instruction and a good education; knowing that the Lord has blessed our Sister Bourgeoys and her companions ... we have authorized and authorize the establishment of the religious order of the said Bourgeoys and the novices who have joined her or who will join her in the future, permitting them to live together as a community."

While religious instruction was stressed more for young girls, it was also available to boys. However, only girls were taught domestic arts. Here, too, the teachers in New France merely followed the general educational philosophy of the time; the education of girls, particularly those of the popular classes in seventeenth- and eighteenth-century France, focused primarily on domestic skills, especially needlework. The following pedagogical treatises written by Catholic educators in Louis XIV's France are unanimous about the importance of the domestic work of women: De Fénelon, *Traité de l'éducation des Filles*, 1687; Abbé Claude Fleury, *Traité du choix et de la méthode des études*, 1689; Charles Rollin (rector of the Université de Paris in 1694), *Traité des études*, 1726. Accordingly, the curriculum, which minimized academics and emphasized the teaching of household arts, was eminently suited to the nature and social role of women. It should be noted that daughters of the nobility were taught more refined skills. For example, Madame de Maintenon, the founder of St. Cyr, taught her students embroidery, lacework, and so on. However, these students were in the minority, as were the convent boarders of l'Assomption, Sacré-Coeur, or the Ursulines of both France and the colony. For most of the students of the petites écoles, instruction in domestic arts, including needlework, provided early training for their future in a society where roles and tasks were defined according to class and gender. In addition to the teaching of catechism, reading, and writing, the Augustines' curriculum in France emphasized: "For the good of our young girls ... as well as for the families they will one day raise ... they must learn to sew and do the different kinds of woman's work." The constitution of the Ursulines of Rouen stated the importance of teaching girls to "sew and carry out other honest tasks appropriate to their sex." The Ursulines of Quebec also stressed this kind of education. In her writings Marie de l'Incarnation explained that besides catechism, reading, writing, and basic arithmetic, the nuns felt it important to teach the girls "all the tasks peculiar to their sex, all that a girl should know."[4] In fact, Monsignor Laval confirmed that the Sisters of the Congregation of Notre-Dame "raised little girls in the fear of God and taught them good Christian morals. They also taught them to read, write and carry out other tasks of which they were capable."

Thus, the educational philosophies in both the colony and France were inspired by the same sources. In Quebec the philosophy was shaped by the church's guidelines of strict orthodoxy and by some central ideas which held that, fundamentally, young girls should become good Christians first and then be groomed for the future roles assigned to them by society—mothers and housewives. As will be discussed later, these roles varied little, regardless of the social class of the pupils.

Programs

The educational policies and objectives of the program offered by the *petites écoles* in New France were directly related to the socioeconomic factors which determined whether a pupil attended school as a boarder (*pensionnaire*) or as a day student (*externe*), and to the French/Indian ethnic factor which was peculiar to this frontier society. Tuition for boarders varied with the "class" of the institution and the clientele. The cost associated with this kind of education was prohibitive for the popular classes because girls of rural and urban working-class families made a twofold contribution to the household: domestic and financial. As such, not only did the families have to pay for their daughters' education, they also had to be prepared to do without this dual contribution. Consequently, girls of modest means could only be day students, paying little or no tuition for this kind of education. Clearly, the division between boarders and day-pupils was directly linked to social class, and the education offered to each group differed as a result.

With respect to this division, a perfect analogy between schools in New France and the motherland is impossible because of the unique circumstances surrounding the colony's existence. Within the colonial perspective of the time, demand from France dictated production in the colony, thus preventing New France from fully exploiting its resources and filling its coffers. What riches the colony had were more uniformly distributed than in France, and social classes were less sharply defined. Generally, life in this frontier society was difficult and great fortunes were few. This economic reality precluded high tuition fees for girls' boarding schools. In fact, the cost of education remained low throughout the French regime and decreased further in the years following the Conquest. In addition to the colony's unique socioeconomic situation, its geography—the distance between home and school, the harshness of the climate, and the short growing season—at times made boarding school the only viable form of education for girls in rural areas. Yet, during the French regime there were but nine convents in the countryside: five were founded in the seventeenth century, four in the eighteenth century. These convents, run by the Sisters of the Congregation of Notre-Dame, usually lodged two or three nuns, but it is unclear whether they were all teachers. Neither these modest institutions nor their alternatives, such as the missions set up in several rural parishes, could bridge the gap between urban and rural education. This disparity may be viewed as a new distinction, or as an extension of the boarder versus day-pupil division and further explains the qualitative and quantitative differences in the content and level of programs offered to girls in New France.

Furthermore, the ethnic variable (previously discussed) is linked to the unique circumstances surrounding the colony's existence and is reflected in the different educational programs offered to French and Indian girls. Lastly, the make-up of the teaching community also influenced the educational programs for girls in New France. Depending on the provisions of their respective constitutions (cloistered order for the Ursulines, or secular order for the Sisters of Notre-Dame, who enjoyed relatively unrestricted movement) and the human and socioeconomic geography of their apostolate, the religious communities of New France each tended to offer somewhat different programs of education. This tendency became more pronounced with time, lasting until the beginning of the nineteenth century.

Education of Indian Girls

From the start, Indian girls—Huron, Algonquin, Montagnais and some Iroquois—were taught separately from French girls. Around 1668 the Crown ordered the integration of the two groups; the results of the experiment were unconvincing, and this attempt at assimilating the Indians was short-lived. The annals of the convent confirm that "by the end of the year (1668), only one little Savage remained at the seminary in Quebec, and our sisters went back to teaching in separate groups."

The curriculum and methods used to teach native girls were different for day-pupils and boarders, also called seminarians. Furthermore, the boarding students who attended school for only five to six months of the year (usually during the hunting season) were considered "temporary" pupils and were offered an educational program that differed from their "permanent" counterparts. However, most of the students were day-pupils and received only religious instruction; a small minority learned to read and write. The chronicles of the Ursulines, as well as letters written by Marie de l'Incarnation, attest to the heterogeneous nature of the day-pupils. From different Indian nations and social ranks, this varied and ever-changing group of men and women of all ages had different motivations for coming to the convent. The nuns knew very well that most often these "heathens" came to them for material aid rather than salvation: In 1641, Mother Marie de l'Incarnation spoke of "eight hundred visits from Savages whom we succored as best we could."[5] That same year she wrote: "There are times when the Savages almost die of hunger. They sometimes go three or four leagues [fifteen to twenty kilometres] to find miserable wood berries or wretched roots that we could scarcely suffer in our mouths. We are so afflicted at seeing them in such starvation that we scarcely dare look at them. Judge for yourself whether it is possible not to strip oneself of everything on these occasions."[6] The need for sustenance was even more pronounced in the winter when the ranks of the needy included old people who could not join in the hunt. "If they were not cared for at that time they would die of hunger in the cabins,"[7] the Venerable Mother stated. The education offered to these "makeshift" students was minimal. The annals of the Ursulines recount that "they [the nuns] did not object to the frequent visits of these good Savages, who suffered from such hunger. The sisters' charity was twofold: they had them pray to God, gave them food and sent them on their way with an encouraging word." Further on, the chronicler continues: "During this period, around 1662, 70 to 80 Huron girls came to class every day, just like our day-pupils. After having them say their prayers, sing hymns and recite the catechism, we explained and taught Christian doctrine. We then gave them *sagamité* [a popular native dish made of black prunes, bread, maize, Indian meal, and suet or lard]." The nuns understood that they could not separate material aid from spiritual guidance, the first often a precondition for the second. This concept was explained by the founder of the Ursulines, who in one of her letters described a "feast" for a large group of natives: "This is how we win souls to Jesus Christ, we entice them with the promise of sustenance." She continued on the subject: "After instruction and prayers we feast them according to their fashion."[8] At the end of the letter she concluded: "It is a singular consolation to us to deprive ourselves of all that is most necessary in order to win souls to Jesus Christ."[9]

Both day-pupils and "temporary" seminarians received religious instruction in their native tongues, which the Ursulines had to learn. Studying under Father Le Jeune, Mother Marie de l'Incarnation and Mother Sainte-Croix learned Algonquin, and Mother Saint-Joseph learned Huron. In 1640 Mother Marie wrote: "We study the Algonquin tongue, which is very difficult." The following year she added: "... there are many thorns in learning a speech so contrary to ours ... the desire to speak does much."[10] Evidently, this "desire to speak" was a strong motivating force for Marie de l'Incarnation: her proficiency in Algonquin, and subsequently in Iroquois, was such that she composed works in both languages. She elaborated: "As these matters are very difficult, I am resolved that before my death I shall leave as much writing as I can. Between the beginning of last Lent and Ascension Day, I wrote a big book in

Algonkin [sic] about sacred history and holy things, and also an Iroquois dictionary and an Iroquois catechism that is a treasure. Last year I wrote a big dictionary in the French alphabet; I have another in the Savage alphabet."[11]

To prepare the temporary boarders, who remained at the school a few months (sometimes just a few days) for baptism or communion, the nuns enlisted the help of the permanent boarders. In a way, "the oldest and most educated" became the religious instructors of the newcomers, responsible for "welcoming these temporary boarders. They had to explain the doctrine of Jesus Christ using the question and answer method used in the instruction of catechism, interpret holy pictures and tell them stories to hold their attention." On this subject, Father Le]eune wrote: "There is one girl; not more than eight years old, who teaches the younger ones, helps them examine their conscience and teaches them to never hide a sin."[12]

The educators also endeavoured to teach these temporary boarders household arts. "I have begun to show them needlework," wrote Madame de la Peltrie in 1640. That same year, the Jesuit Relations adds: "They are wonderfully clever in performing all their little tasks and the small household duties that we teach them."[13] This kind of instruction, in addition to the teaching of catechism, was clearly an attempt to introduce the girls to a certain way of life—to Western mores.

Following the Crown's directive to assimilate the natives, the colonial educators for a while went beyond proselytizing and added a cultural dimension to their program. The first Mother Superior of the Ursulines, who along with the other nuns was sceptical of this ambitious but unrealistic program, commented with a touch of humour: "A Frenchman would more easily become savage than a Savage a Frenchman." She continued on the subject of the native boarders: "... of a hundred that have passed through our hands we have scarcely civilized one."[14]

Certainly, assimilation was somewhat more successful with permanent than with temporary boarders. However, the scarcity of quantitative data makes it difficult to determine who these permanent boarders were. Sporadic information exists as to their number and the circumstance of admission, but there is little on the duration of their stay. For example, the annals of the convent tell us that "in the month of August, Father Raguenau brought us eight seminarians. In this same month of August 1650, came to us Elizabeth Astache of the Algonquin nation. After having been at the seminary for some time, she died." The founder of the Ursulines merely commented that there were "just as many temporary as permanent boarders." In 1654 she noted: "We have some Huron girls that the Reverend Fathers have judged suitable to be reared by us as French girls ..."[15]

The following year, she wrote of the Iroquois: "Their ambassadors ... admired our Savage seminarists [sic] when they heard them singing the praises of God in three different tongues. They were delighted to see them so well reared in the French way." Later, still on the subject of the Iroquois ambassadors, Mother Marie added: "They got singular pleasure from seeing and hearing our seminarists [sic], among others a little Huron of ten or eleven years whom we are rearing as a French girl. She can read, write, and sing in three tongues—namely Latin, French, and Huron."[16] Without specifying the number, Marie de l'Incarnation again wrote: "We have assimilated several savage girls, Huron and Algonkin [sic], who later married Frenchmen and were happy together." However, she explained that "nonetheless, we only assimilated a few poor orphan girls in our care, and those whose parents wished their daughters to be reared in this manner."

Various reasons accounted for a boarder's "permanent" status: young Indian girls entrusted or "given to" the Ursulines by the Jesuit Fathers, young orphaned girls taken in by the nuns, young girls or young ladies seeking or offered sanctuary from undesirable fiancés, husbands, or suitors, and so forth. The permanent boarders also varied in age; Marie de l'Incarnation confirmed that "in the case of Savage girls, we take them at all ages."[17] According to the records, the nuns took in "babies who not only required care during the day but kept the nuns awake at night." The chronicler continues: "In 1643 Mother Marie de Saint-Joseph took in a frail little creature a few months old, brought to the parlor by a poor, disconsolate mother." The Relation by Father Vimont (a Jesuit) also speaks of the nuns taking care of "three little orphans who needed a wet-nurse." The data, however, indicate that babies in the seminary were the exception and that the Indian boarders ranged from five to twelve years old. One could well imagine the difficulty these children had in adapting to such a completely different milieu and way of life. Still, records of that time are replete with examples of the native boarders' piety and devotion. While very few became the object of a hagiographic biography like Thérèse, the Huron girl, the letters of Marie de l'Incarnation as well as the Jesuit Relations are filled with testimonials and anecdotal accounts of the pious and exemplary behaviour of the native boarders. They write of Marie Amiskouevan, whose "docility, modesty, and obedience could make one believe she was a well-bred French girl," and of Marie-Magdeleine Abatenau, who "at age seven, does everything she is told with such good behaviour and good grace one would take her for a girl of rank."[18] Marie-Ursule Gamitiens was five or six years old and "is no sooner awake than she prepares herself to pray to God. She says her rosary during Mass and sings hymns in her Savage tongue."[19] Marie de l'Incarnation wrote that Agnes Chabdikouechich, "who has made very great progress ... in the knowledge of the mysteries and, as well, in good manners, spoke and wrote with ease not only her native tongue but also French .... She was so devout, we thought to bring her into our Order, but she died in the woods, book in hand, praying to God."[20]

It is primarily the zeal with which the Indian seminarians prayed and their promptness to confess and do penance that elicited glowing testimonials in their regard. They were praised for being docile and obedient. Marie de l'Incarnation wrote the following to her son, who seemed incredulous at the exemplary behaviour of so many Indians: "If our Savages are as perfect as I tell you? ... There are Savages as there are Frenchmen. Among them there are the more and less devout, but generally speaking, they are more devout than the French."[21]

Despite this piety and devoutness which the educators mentioned so often, few native girls seemed to have had the religious calling. The chronicler of the Ursulines comments: "There are about eight young girls who, according to our Mother Superiors could have become nuns and who would have devoted their lives to God but for the accidents which Providence failed to prevent. The two Savage girls who became nuns at the Congregation around 1685 both died young, and the same fate befell those who became sisters of the Hôtel-Dieu at Quebec." It is unclear whether these "accidents" happened by chance or because the young Native girls had difficulty adapting to a singular and specific way of life for which their original culture had in no way prepared them. Though few in number, historical records do speak of the unhappiness that some Indian boarders felt at having been forcibly transplanted into such a foreign environment. In a letter to a "lady of rank," Marie de l'Incarnation wrote of the difficulties the sisters experienced in getting their first boarder to adapt to her new life. This ten-year-old Indian girl was yet another of Madame de la Peltrie's godchildren: "The first Savage seminarist [sic] that was given to us, Marie Negabamat by name, was so used to running in the woods that we lost all hope of keeping her in the seminary. The Reverend Father Le Jeune, who had persuaded her father to give her to us, sent two older Christian girls with her. These remained with her for some time in order to settle her, but to no avail, for she fled into the woods four days later, after tearing to pieces a dress we had given her."[22] The founder also wrote that "there are still others that go off by some whim or caprice; like squirrels, they climb our palisade, which is high as a wall, and go to run in the woods."[23]

Although other seminarians who resented being separated from their families expressed their will to leave in less spectacular ways, they were no less determined. Such was the case with seven-year-old Nicole Assepanse, about whom Marie de l'Incarnation wrote: "This girl has a mind so open that she is as capable of instruction as a girl of twenty. She was only five months in the seminary and was able to recount the principal points of our Faith and knew the catechism and Christian practices perfectly.... The girl nevertheless could not leave her mother whose only child she was, but she said, 'Though I wish to go, it is not because I lack for anything. I eat as much as I wish, the virgins give me fine clothes and love me very much, but I cannot leave you.'"[24]

Yet, for those Indian girls whose protests led to depression or ill-health, the first Mother Superior realized that there was no point in keeping them "by force or by entreaties,"[25] explaining, "Others are here only as birds of passage and remain with us only until they are sad, a thing the Savage nature cannot suffer; the moment they become sad, their parents take them away lest they die."[26]

The end of the seventeenth century was characterized by steadily declining Indian enrollment. While no single cause seems to have been at the root of this decline, the following reasons may provide some explanation: the moving of Indian nations away from Quebec, the taking over of Indian missions by the Sisters of the Congregation of Notre-Dame (a non-cloistered, hence more mobile congregation), and the realization that the long-term goal of assimilating Indian girls was a failure. In her writings, the chronicler of the Ursulines, after mentioning the presence at the convent of the "last Indian girls to form a separate class after 1700," states that "around 1725, the Indian boarders had all but disappeared." In fact, it was around this time that the Ursulines, when taking their vows, ceased to mention the instruction of Indian girls.

The Education of French Girls

Day-Pupils

"It was first as day-pupils that French young ladies attended the school of the Ursulines when the sisters lived in the Lower Town," reports the Order's annalist. To explain the raison d'être of a day-school, she specifies: "In the Institute of Ursuline Nuns, a day-school that does not charge tuition is deemed as essential as a boarding school, for it affords poor and rich alike the opportunity to benefit from education." Not only was the day-school system ideally suited to the children of poor families, it also provided a solution to the overcrowding in the "Louvre," the name the nuns had jokingly given their small house on the quay.

The absence of day-school records makes it difficult to establish the annual enrollment of day-pupils. While there are some quantitative data on boarders, the information available on day-pupils is based primarily on general accounts which refer to the school population as a whole, that is, to both day-pupils and boarders. In 1652 Marie de l'Incarnation described how "the day after our arrival in Quebec, French and Savage girls alike were brought to us in great numbers so that we could educate them in good morals and piety."[27] On the subject of French girls, the founder of the Ursulines commented in 1664, "There is not one that does not pass through our hands."[28] Four years later she wrote, "I do not know the number of externs [day-pupils] for in winter the snow obliges them to remain at home. We have those of Upper Town and Lower Town. The French bring their daughters from a distance of sixty leagues [300 kilometres]."[29]

The chronicler of the Ursulines wrote that in 1687 there were about 50 day-school pupils. Additionally, records indicate that at the beginning of the eighteenth century there were more day—pupils than boarders, who numbered 55 to 60.

Marie de l'Incarnation painted the moral and psychological profile of day-girls as follows: "These girls are docile, they have good sense, and they are firm in the good when they know it."[30] She explained, however, that she could not look after their moral welfare quite as well as if "they were cloistered." Evidently, because they were more numerous and transient than boarders, day-pupils were not as closely supervised. As was previously discussed, day-girls were taught reading, writing, and counting, but the emphasis was on religious instruction. One may assume that day-pupils were entitled to the same kind of education as short-term boarders. According to the founder, the school-mistresses had to apply themselves strenuously to teach those boarders in one year "reading, writing, calculating, the prayers, Christian habits, and all a girl should know."[31] Although this education would be considered minimal by today's standards, it reflected to a large extent the attitudes of the time—an era that expected little of girls, especially those of modest means.

Boarders

Three years after their arrival in New France, the Ursulines finally had their own convent. Built for them in the Upper Town in 1642, this building housed a residence for the nuns and a separate boarding school for French and Indian girls. Both the founder of the Ursulines and the chroniclers used different terms to designate schools for French and Indian students: "boarding school" for French girls and "seminary" for Indian girls.

At the time, the Ursuline convent was the only educational institution for girls in the colony; however, extraordinary circumstances forced the boarding school to close on several occasions. A fire which destroyed the convent closed the school from December 1650 to June 1652 and forced the Ursulines to seek shelter at the Hôtel-Dieu for three weeks. They then moved into Madame de la Peltrie's house next door to the ravaged convent. A second fire closed the school again in October 1686; the convent was restored with the help of the colonists and reopened its doors in November 1687. The siege of Quebec by the English in the fall of 1687 again forced the boarding school to close, this time for more than a year. During this time, the Ursulines provided asylum to refugees, thus creating a situation which the chronicler of the Ursulines describes as follows: "Not only was our house filled with lay people, but our classroom for day-pupils became cluttered with furniture and goods; it served to store the belongings of those who had brought them."

Save these few short interruptions, the boarding school had an unbroken existence, even after the Conquest in 1760. According to the annals of the convent, "eighteen to twenty French girls" comprised the first group to attend the boarding school. Their names, moreover, were inscribed in the registers of the time. While there is more statistical information on boarders than on day-pupils, the data are sporadic at best. Thus, one must resort to estimates in order to paint a general picture of student enrollment during that time. Over the years, various factors influenced enrollment. In 1668 the desperate financial situation of the Ursulines forced Mother Marie to send some boarders home: "We are limited to sixteen French girls and three Savages."[32] The following year she wrote about enrollment to a nun at Tours: "The colony has grown, and now we usually have 20 to 30 boarders." As the population increased, so did the number of students. The Ursuline chronicler records that "around 1700 there were on average 60 boarders," and that "in 1793 there were still 40 boarders despite the small-pox epidemic that ravaged Quebec." Was the chronicler correct in concluding that "the number of boarders was constantly on the rise?" In fact, in 1750 the nuns had to open another class to accommodate the increasing number of students. However, a comparison of the chronicles' figures between 1641 and 1719 indicates a total of 1,206 boarders, or an annual average of twelve, thus confirming that the increase was not constant but varied considerably.

From its inception the boarding school kept a School Register for French and Indian Girls which paints a picture of the geographical and social origins of the boarders. According to this register (rather difficult to decipher), kept until 1717, the majority came from Quebec. However, a significant minority came not only from surrounding parishes (Île d'Orléans, Château Richer, Neuville, and so on) but also from greater distances, such as Trois-Rivières. Marie de l'Incarnation sometimes mentioned that they also had boarders from Montreal, notwithstanding the Sisters of the Congregation of Notre-Dame's active presence in that town.

Just as their geographic origins were diverse, so too were the boarders' social origins: the registers for the two decades following the opening of the boarding school reveal that of the 81 families whose daughters studied under the Ursulines, 9 belonged to the nobility, 41 to the bourgeoisie and 31 to the lower class (commonly referred to as *petites gens*). The annals stressed that only the social elite attended the boarding school: "This is confirmed by the names that grace our registers—magistrates, interpreters well-versed in Savage tongues, doctors, merchants and businessmen of all kinds.... Note too, the names of illustrious and valiant officers." According to the chronicler, these girls of such gentle birth had to behave in a manner befitting their class and as such "not allow themselves to be swayed by the appeal of life's transitory honours or crushed by its tribulations, but always behave as paragons of Christian virtue."

This glowing description of the young girls attending the boarding school contrasts with Mother Marie's rather negative perception of their undisciplined behaviour. She expressed these feelings in some of her letters; for example, she wrote the following to her son in 1652: "... the French girls would be real brutes without the education they receive from us and need even more than the

Savages...."[33] Some fifteen years later, the founder seemed not to have changed her mind about these students and reiterated: "Thirty girls give us more work in the boarding school than sixty would in France."[34]

It seems that young girls in France were more conservative than their counterparts in the colony. Based on Marie de l'Incarnation's accounts, the sociogeographic setting of New France was conducive to more liberal ways of thinking and behaving. Certain situations and sociogeographic characteristics peculiar to this frontier society constituted in the eyes of the nuns a definite source of "moral disorder." As the founder wrote in one of her letters, circumstances at times made it necessary for some parents to leave their daughters at home in the care of men (family, friends, neighbours, or hired help). In a letter to her son she described this kind of situation: "Great care is taken in this country with the instruction of the French girls, and I can assure you that if there were no Ursulines they would be in continual danger for their salvation. The reason is that there are a great many men, and a father and mother who would not miss Mass on a feast-day or a Sunday are quite willing to leave their children at home with several men to watch over them. If there are girls, whatever age they may be, they are in evident danger, and experience shows they must be put in a place of safety. In a word, all I can say is the girls in this country are for the most part more learned in several dangerous matters than those of France."[35]

Nonetheless, the nuns must have been generally satisfied with the education they provided, and the changes that they were able to bring about in the behaviour of their students, for in the same letter in which Mother Marie expressed her concerns, she also affirmed: "Our Reverend Fathers and Monsignor our Prelate [Bishop Laval] are delighted with the education we give the young girls. They let our girls receive communion as soon as they are eight years old, finding them as well instructed as they could be."[36] The Jesuit Fathers echoed such testimonials on various occasions, as did Father Raguenau in the Relation of 1651: "Experience teaches us that the girls who have been with the Ursulines feel the benefit of their stay there throughout their lives, and that in their households the fear of God reigns more than elsewhere, and they bring up their children much better therein."[37] Seventeen years later, in the Relation of 1668, Father Le Mercier also stated: "The Ursuline Mothers have had so great success in the instruction of the girls who have been confided to them ... that in visiting the households of Canada, and each house in particular, it is very easy to distinguish, by the Christian education of the children, the mothers who have come out of Ursuline houses from those who have not had that advantage."[38]

To complete the social profile of the clientele of boarders, one must go beyond the moral assessment and value judgements of life in the colony and examine the financial dimension: the cost of attending boarding school. Some students remained for a year or more; others for a few months, just long enough to prepare for First Communion. The Mother Superior wrote: "... several board with us for only a short while.... Some of them are left with us by their parents till they are of an age to be provided, either for the world or for religion."[39] The annual boarding fee, which varied with the length of stay, was approximately 120 livres and appears to have remained constant throughout the French regime. This must have been a major expense for many colonial families since at the end of the 1660s, 120 livres represented the yearly wages of a "skilled worker." However, the Ursulines designed a sliding scale of boarding fees in light of the economic hardships in the colony, which were more pronounced during the seventeenth century, a period characterized by frequent wars and financial instability. Mother Marie de l'Incarnation frequently wrote of the harsh reality of the country's poverty—a reality that she and her companions had to come to terms with. One of the hardships was the scarcity of money in circulation in the colony. The Company of One Hundred Associates, with its barter policy, preferred the colonists to pay in kind—in this case, pelts—rather than with money. Consequently, the nuns often found themselves having to accept payment in kind for part of or even the entire boarding costs. The chronicles of the community contain several examples of this form of payment, such as the fee paid in 1646 for a Mademoiselle C. (whose name the chronicler discreetly withholds, referring to her as "belonging to one of the country's prominent families").

Received January 13	3 ½ cords of firewood
Received March 6	4 cords of firewood
Received March 13	1 12-pound pot of butter
Received November 13	1 fattened pig, 1 barrel of peas, one barrel of salted eels

Despite this kind of arrangement, which should have compensated for the scarcity of money in circulation, many families still could not afford their daughters' tuition. In a letter dated September 1660, Mother Marie wrote of this problem, noting that it cost more to educate French girls than Indian girls: "The expenses at the Seminary are many, not because we have many Savage boarders but because we receive many French girls whose parents do not have the means to pay their daughters' board. And we must say that the French girls cost us by far much more to feed and care for than do the Indian girls. God is the Father of us all, and we must hope that he will help us to help them."

This help came in the form of bursaries (*fondations*) provided by generous benefactors, notably Madame de la Peltrie, who was the foremost contributor in the community. Her donations, earmarked for total or partial payment of some tuition fees, alone represented 3,405 livres, or 41 percent of all the bursaries granted between 1641 and 1662. In 1660 Madame de la Peltrie, commonly referred to as "our Mother and benefactress" by the chronicler of the

Ursulines, established six 100-livre bursaries for the education of poor girls, to be granted upon her death. The Jesuits were just as important a source of funds, since between 1652 and 1660 they contributed 3,330 livres, or 40.2 percent of all tuition fees paid until that date. In 1660 Monsignor de Laval became the third highest contributor with 535 livres or 18.5 percent of all the *fondations* established until 1662. By contrast, the state's contribution (disbursed by the governors, d'Ailleboust of Coulonges and Voyer of Argenson) was but a meagre 20 livres.

However, the generosity of the benefactors depended more on the recipients' social standing than on their true financial needs; consequently, moneys were not distributed equitably. Thus, of the 81 families who received grants for their daughters between 1642 and 1662, nine were of the noble class and received larger bursaries than families of the bourgeoisie. Accordingly, the families of eight of these nine school-age girls were able to pay for the education of their daughters. The bursaries received by 41 bourgeois families allowed them to pay for the education of only 51 of their 105 school-age daughters. During this same period, the *petites gens*—labourers and small land owners—received bursaries for only 33 of their 73 girls. While allowing more girls to attend boarding school, this system of grants did not resolve the social inequities in education. Although boarding school was not the exclusive domain of the nobility and bourgeoisie, girls from the popular classes were a minority. To a large extent, this reality explains the enriched—perhaps more refined—program that was available only to boarding students.

The scattered accounts in the Ursuline chronicles reveal that while the nuns taught a more advanced program of French to boarding students, they were also concerned with teaching grammar to day-pupils. The chronicler of the Order at Trois-Rivières recounts the extent to which grammar books were scarce before and after the Conquest: "Grammar books were so rare that the day-school only had one; it was placed on a desk in the middle of the room, opened to a page held in place by a wood frame. Each student took turns to learn the lesson of the day, and only the schoolmistress was allowed to turn the pages of the treasured book." Still, it is difficult to assess just how extensive the girls' knowledge of grammar was, since the chronicles (for both Quebec and Trois-Rivières) are vague on this subject.

Little information is available on the teaching of what was known as "art and decorative art" during this period. Clearly, the nuns excelled in this area, whether in needlework, embroidery on silk or bark (most often used to decorate altars), or the gilding of statues, tabernacles, or reliquaries. The annals speak of Jeanne Le Ber, a girl of gentle birth, who, following the example of the nuns, showed such an affinity for the arts of embroidery and gilding that she "soon equalled her teachers." Hers was probably not an isolated case, and most of the young girls who stayed long enough at the boarding school likely learned these arts.

While little is known about the grammar and art programs taught to boarding students, there is some evidence that the program as a whole was more complete and "refined" than the one available to day students (who were not only more transient than boarders but also non-paying). It bears repeating that most of these boarders came from prominent families; consequently, not only did they have to become good Christians but they also had to live up to the requirements and social standards of their elite class. Thus, the chronicler at Trois-Rivières justifies the greater emphasis on teaching the girls to behave and think in a certain way than on the depth and breadth of the program. In fact, she relates on the subject: "We did not seek to impart to these girls tremendous knowledge—this was not appropriate for women—but sought to instill in them that refined way of thinking, that wondrous ability to make good conversation, the gift of good letter-writing, all these things which, after virtue, make up a good education and a refined woman." The Quebec annalist adds that the nuns felt the need "to accustom the girls to speak correctly and with ease, to present themselves gracefully, and to learn, as the rule states, the morals of the most honest and virtuous Christians who live honourably in the world."

Behind this educational program one finds a portrait of the ideal future woman as envisioned and expected by society in a given era and social milieu. In order to create this female ideal who was both graceful and articulate, the teaching of theatre was considered the method of choice: reciting in public, verbal sparring matches, recitals, poems, and pastorals (short plays of religious and moral nature). The boarders performed on special occasions such as religious feasts, end-of-year award ceremonies, or receptions for distinguished guests. The chronicler of Quebec explains the context and objectives of these kinds of oratorical exercises: "It is a practice in our classrooms that with the advent of certain holidays, and especially at Christmas time, we have the children learn a pastoral or other religious play by heart, not only to develop their memories and fill their minds with good things but also to develop graceful carriage and gestures. Each child has a role in these exercises. We try, as much as possible, to accommodate the personalities and tastes of the young girls."

It would be interesting to examine some of these theatrical exercises more closely. Although replete with *naïveté*, they merit attention less for their intrinsic literary qualities than for their educational purposes and the cultural framework in which they were written.

The education of girls in New France was based on a specific definition of women. Upon closer examination, it is clear that several socialization models influenced women. Both the ethnic (French/Indian) and social class (boarders/day pupils) variables contributed to the definition of these models and influenced their application. However, whether instruction was provided to French or Indian girls, day pupils or boarders, whether it was academic or socioreligious, the education of girls under the Ursulines of Quebec had one common characteristic: it was based on a general concept of women, their nature as well as their place and role in society. This concept existed at a particular time in history (the Old Regime) and in the geopolitical context of a frontier society that faced unique material challenges: the economic constraints of the colony's resources and production, and a harsh climate. Compared to the schooling available to girls in France and boys in the colony, the Ursuline community offered girls a unique kind of education.

* * * * *

Documents for Chapter One

To what degree do the first four documents below support the conclusions/observations of the previous article regarding the purpose of education, the supply of teachers, gendered education, availability of schools, and general interest in education? Document 5 describes education in Quebec in 1950—to what extent had the goals, the curriculum, pedagogy, teachers, and gendered ideas changed during the intervening two centuries?

1) ETIENNE CHARON'S PETITION TO THE KING, 1718

Etienne Charon very humbly recalls to Your Majesty that in the letters patent dated April 5, 1694, Louis XIV founded a hospital on the island of Montreal under the supervision of a *Communauté de Maîtres d'Ecole* for the maintenance and succour of indigent cripples and old people, and for raising and educating young boys according to the faith and for teaching them a trade. Etienne Charon further recalls that Your Majesty has been informed of the great benefit which the Colony of Canada has derived from the establishment and the great amount of good work done by the *Soeurs de la Congrégation*, who number almost one hundred, in educating young girls in rural parishes. Your Majesty, by mean of the letters patent dated February 1718, would have confirmed those letters patent of Louis XIV concerning the establishment of said hospital. In order to increase the number of schoolteachers who take care of the hospital and in order to render them capable of educating the young boys from rural areas in Our Holy Faith and capable of preventing these boys from joining the Indians, of civilizing the young boys and of making them better suited to serve the Colony, Your Majesty has granted to the schoolteachers 3000 pounds payable each year by the farmers of the Colony ....

* * * * *

2) MEMORANDUM TO THE MINISTER OF MARINE FROM GOVERNOR VAUDREUIL AND INTENDANT BEGON, OCTOBER 1718

... If the council will kindly allow us to explain our feelings concerning this change, we shall be honoured to point out that the education now being proposed for the young boys of this colony is merely a pretext since there are already schools for them maintained by the Jesuits in Quebec City and by the seminary in Montreal. Furthermore, in remote areas located along the two shores of the St. Lawrence River and the Gulf of St. Lawrence, the habitants are not clustered in villages, but, rather, are spread out on the same lines according to the area of the land they were given. Thus, the school-teachers are not capable of carrying out the boys' education. This education could consist only of catechisms, held by the priest on holidays and Sundays.

* * * * *

3) DECREE BY THE CONSEIL d'ETAT, 3 MARCH 1722

It is hereby decreed by the King in Council on this third day of March, seventeen hundred and twenty-two that by His Majesty's orders the general hospital founded in Ville-Marie to maintain 8 teachers by means of an amount of three thousand pounds granted yearly by His Majesty to this hospital. The hospital shall enter into whatever agreement it may deem suitable with these teachers regarding the amount of 375 pounds allocated to each of them. Anything left from the 375 pounds after the teachers have been paid shall revert to the hospital.

His Majesty wishes that these teachers maintained by Him teach at their schools free of charge. He has heard the report and duly considered all the facts. He has also had the advice of the Duc d' Orléans [Regent of France]. Thus, His Majesty has ordered and orders that the eight teachers thus provided with funds shall maintain local schools free of charge in accordance with the provisions of said decree without demanding anything from the parents of the young boys they will educate.

However, His Majesty has no intention of restricting the charitable donations the inhabitants of Canada may wish to contribute to the hospital in view of their children's education ....

* * * * *

4) GIRLS' EDUCATION, 1752[1]

These sisters (80 in number and 30 of whom are in the city while the others are spread out in the villages) are to be found away from the banks of the river and the gulf on the seigneurial estates. They are attracted there to educate girls. The usefulness of the sisters seems obvious, but the evil they create acts like a slow poison which tends to depopulate the countryside. An educated girl acts up, is affected, wants to settle in the city, must get a merchant for a husband and considers the social status of her birth to be beneath her dignity.

*   *   *   *   *

5) EDUCATION IN QUEBEC (1951)[2]

Catholics being in the majority, they established a century ago a school system in accordance with their faith and respecting that of the Protestant minority. It is unlike almost any other as it provides for a dual system of state public schools based on religious belief.

Briefly, education comes under two committees, one Catholic, the other Protestant. Each committee has jurisdiction over the schools of its faith. The Catholic committee is constituted by all the bishops of the province ex officio and an equal number of lay members appointed by the government. These committees plan the curriculum, approve textbooks, draw up regulations for their schools, and make recommendations to the government on school policy. A Department of Education supervises the working of the whole system.

At the local level, school boards, formed of five members elected by ratepayers, impose and collect property taxes, engage and pay teachers, maintain schools. A minority dissenting from the faith of the majority may elect its own trustees and have its own schools.

School expenses are paid from local taxes and Government grants, these being shared between Catholic and Protestant in proportion to school population. Such public financing of denominational education gives satisfaction to all and has brought a century of peace between the two groups.

Besides the public schools, there are a large number of private and residential schools maintained by religious orders. The whole school system is definitely oriented towards humanistic training, with emphasis on spiritual and moral values. It aims to develop men and women of character, able citizens, concerned with livelihood, but more with the good life.

Moral Education

Catholicism provides a philosophy of education, which is, of course, followed in the schools. According to this philosophy, religion is the primary function of Catholic schools. Catholics believe that what man most needs to know is how to attain a happy future life, therefore the school must include religious training, this being the core of educational content.

Religion cannot be dissociated from morals. Morality implies conformity to the will of God as expressed by Christ. There is thus a moral code, authoritative, universal, unchanging, obligatory. Religion offers the strongest sanctions impelling the individual to conform to these standards and to practise virtue. It teaches that every good deed has its reward, every wrong one its punishment. To the convinced believer, the hope of eternal happiness and the fear of eternal suffering provide the highest motivation and may mould a whole life. Indeed, for centuries, the Catholic doctrine has engendered countless saints and heroes and borne fruit in innumerable lives of self-sacrifice and devotion. The church has been rightly called the Supreme Character Builder, whose methods, however, are too little known. It has always devoted full attention to moral education. Modern educational literature and practice often ignore the responsibilities of the school in training character, but this deficiency could never be reproached to the Catholic Church.

Character may be defined here as conduct according to Christian morality. The objectives of character education are the spiritual advancement of the individual and therefore of the group, a sound knowledge of right and wrong, full self-realization, moral excellence.

Training of the will is a primary element in character education. There can be no character without self-denial, sacrifice, effort, a fact that modern education tends sometimes to overlook. Like intellectual and physical aptitudes, the will must be trained and gradually perfected. Habit formation, emotional control, and worthy ideals are other basic elements of character education.

Teaching Methods

A detailed review of teaching methods would be impossible here. Reference will be made only to what is more peculiar to Quebec schools. Generally speaking, methods of teaching religion are about the same in all Catholic schools. The school day opens with prayers and catechism, the lesson lasting half an hour. The teaching is carried out by a regular teacher, who, in half the cases, is a Brother or a Sister, a member of a religious Order. In many schools, the parish priest comes once a month for supervision. At the time of Solemn Communion, he himself teaches in church, during a full month, the pupils who are called. The *curé is* also an official visitor of the public schools in his parish.

The first aim of the teacher is to have the child understand to the limit of his ability the matter which is presented to him. The teacher begins the explanation with a story, usually taken from the life of Christ. Use of pictures, discussions, exercises, is made. After the lesson has been well explained, children are questioned in the teacher's own words; they are then asked to memorise a formula. The lesson ends by a practical application, a specific conduct assignment, a resolution, the stressing of a life value.

A detailed syllabus is traced for each grade; in Grades X–XII, apologetics and church history are taught. Questions on religion are asked in all official examinations. Moreover, definite guidance on moral training is given. Duties to God, others, and self are outlined. Actions are suggested for each theological and moral virtue. As to charity, for instance, the following are listed among others, with indication of the grades in which they are more particularly recommended: give little pleasures to your parents; help aged persons in crossing streets or from falling on ice; show your satisfaction in a companion's success; try to see the qualities rather than the defects of people around you; do your share in group work; do not tease others unduly; seek occasions to help others; take great care of your health, etc. Besides, in the monthly report to parents, character deficiencies that may occur are noted.

To classroom teaching is added the teaching in church, also prayers, the Mass, the sacraments, sermons, good deeds, and the whole atmosphere of the school, the presence of the crucifix and religious pictures, the teacher's personality and example.

Our schools, like all Catholic schools, give due importance to discipline, considered one of the most effective means of character development, provided it is meaningful, constructive, and tends to self-discipline. The beginning of discipline is obedience. The nature of the child makes authority necessary. Observance of regulations is expected, and it must be said that indiscipline is not a problem, as it appears to be in some other school systems. It may be added that there is no co-education at the secondary level.

In most schools sports are well organised, but no particular use is made of them for character training, more effective means being available. Thrift is promoted by many school banks, where children deposit their savings. Manual training is taught especially for its formative values: orderly habits, thoughtful planning, exactitude, self-expression, respect for labour.

Residential Schools

Character training is particularly fostered by the large number of private residential boys' and girls' schools, located throughout the province and attended by some 12 per cent of the school population, a larger proportion than in most countries. It is a well-established custom in many families to send their children to these schools, maintained by priests or religious Orders. Indeed, numerous parents favour these institutions on account of the sound moral training they give.

The educative values of good residential schools are well known. Character training cannot be neglected there, neither can it be left to the home. Living during ten months of the year in a community of 200-500 fellow students cannot fail to mould character. Regulations must be obeyed, and the daily routine of these houses would be found austere by many. Rising is at 5:30 or 6, then Mass, study, breakfast. Classes start at 8 and fill four or five hours of the day.

Personal study requires about the same number of hours. The day is interspersed by prayers, chapel, and occasionally a sermon. Improper literature is forbidden. Discipline is somewhat exacting, but the trend is definitely towards an increasing measure of student government. In the classical colleges (leading to the B.A. and professional studies), most students choose among the priest teachers a 'spiritual director' whom they consult freely for spiritual and moral advice and who often acts as guidance counsellor. The education given alike in these colleges to future priests, and to future members of the professions, contributes greatly to the happy relations between church leaders and the people.

It may be added that the school curriculum includes the study of ethics; in public schools, rudiments are given in Grade XII, while a more thorough study is part of the two-year course of philosophy in classical colleges. This latter course, which lasts one year, covers the nature and source of ethics, free will, law (eternal, natural, human, divine), conscience, family, parenthood, society, authority, the State, Communism, etc.

Catholic Youth Movement

A development of recent years in a great number of schools is the Catholic Action movement, *la Jeunesse Étudiante Catholique* (Catholic Student Youth). The movement aims to make students more actively participating in their own religious education. Boys and girls practise religion by living it in school. It is an application, with a social bias, of the activity programme to religious and moral training. When students wish to improve the quality of group life, they soon learn that changing others must begin with themselves and that Christianity is a call to dynamic living rather than a set of prohibitions. Catholic Action aims at the same moral objectives as the school, but it provides a new way to attain them.

The J.E.C. works mainly through extra-curricular activities: sports, games, leisure, school paper, co-operative, discussion clubs, student council, etc. Students have thus numerous occasions to work for the common good, to practise charity and other virtues. In each school, the movement is supervised by a chaplain who acts as adviser. A central office co-ordinates activities and publishes a monthly.

The J.E.C. has brought about excellent results in every school where it has been established. It has revitalised faith, developed responsibilities, initiative, and social-mindedness, stimulated leadership, and incidentally favoured intellectual achievement. Besides the J.E.C., other associations, such as the Boy Scouts, Girl Guides, 4-H Clubs, Children of Mary, Catholic Rural and Working Youth, contribute also to character development during school years or in the immediate years afterwards.

Girls' Education

A feature of our school system is the preparation of girls for family life. Marriage is the career followed eventually by most women, and it is felt that the school should not ignore it.

Through all grades, the curriculum seeks to build a truly feminine mentality, which is considered more important than domestic skills; it endeavours to inculcate respect for family life, it exalts the beauty of the home, its virtues, its unique function in society. In school, girls learn sewing, cooking, home maintenance. Half a day a week in each grade is allocated to these subjects. Moreover, some secondary schools, which receive special grants for that purpose, devote particular attention to household science. In Grades VIII and IX, the course, while being still predominantly academic, gives more time to the duties of a housewife. The superior schools of Household Science, of which there are thirty-six, emphasise still more, in Grades X, XI, and XII, the preparation for family life, to which they devote about two-thirds of their time. These schools have done remarkable work and induced much favourable comment. The curriculum includes, besides religion, French and arithmetic, child and adolescent psychology, child care, family education, science as related to the home, cooking, dressmaking, interior decoration, weaving. The students, organised into family groups, undertake in turn housekeeping, budgeting, shopping, preparation of meals, evening parties, etc., all these activities being carried out so as to promote the best family spirit.

Vocational Schools

Unlike academic schools, technical schools are undenominational, however, a Catholic chaplain is attached to each such school and a short course on religion is given each week, non-Catholic students being dispensed from attendance. A recent innovation in the new apprenticeship centres, which train for various manual trades, may be worth mentioning here.

As the law required moral instruction, school authorities looked for literature especially adapted to this class of trainees and different from the usual lessons, but could not find any, either in French or in English. A chaplain then decided to prepare a suitable course himself. The course deals in a broad way with the human and moral aspects of work: the individual, marriage, family, citizenship, labour, wages, rights and duties of workers and employers, social legislation, the moral law and economics, etc.

For teaching purposes, the class is divided in groups of four or five, with a leader who has previously received special instruction. The discussion goes on for half an hour around one of the topics of the course. All groups reassemble for the last half-hour, for further discussion under the teacher's guidance. Each topic is summarised in an attractive booklet. These booklets have proved best-sellers in their field, and the course has worked great improvement among the men.

Conclusion

Much remains to be said on moral education in Quebec, but perhaps the above would serve as a general view of the matter.

Sir Richard Livingstone, in his pungent little book, *Education for a World Adrift*, deplores in modern teaching the absence of a true philosophy of life, a spiritual element, a moral standard. This guiding principle French-Canadians always had. They have a common faith, a common culture, common standards of conduct. For them, religion and morals are one, spiritual values are foremost. The knowledge and practice of religion is for them the core of education and life, which must inspire the whole educational process. They may not always live up to the ideals of their doctrine, but on the whole they have remained faithful, they have retained a way of life that gives primacy to spiritual and moral values which may serve as an example to the world.

The eminent English historian, Arnold Toynbee, wrote recently: "I suspect that the coming people in the Americas may be the French-Canadians" (*The World Review*, March, 1949, page 12). This prediction may appear debatable, but it indicates the opinion of a keen student of civilisation that this people holds values and standards that have proven their worth in the course of history. Their moral education has undoubtedly been a signal contribution to this achievement.

*   *   *   *   *

1 Louis Franquet, *Voyages et memoires sur le Canada* (Quebec, 1889), 31-32.
2 Charles Bilodeau, "Quebec Education," in *The Year Book of Education, 1951* (London, England: University of London Institute of Education, 1951), pp. 395, 397-402.

Chapter Two:
Pioneer Education to 1840

Pioneer life in English Canada was arduous. Everything was new and strange, and it was easy to become discouraged and homesick. Clearing land was brutally hard. Pioneers had to fell trees that sometimes towered as high as fifteen-story buildings, and then remove the stumps. Homes had to be built, firewood cut, seeds planted, livestock cared for, wheat threshed, furniture made, meals cooked, and children raised. Most people earned their living by farming, fishing, lumbering, or by a combination of all three. As late as 1851, only about 15% of Canadians lived in urban communities of 1,000 or more. Because the settlers needed all the help they could get to perform chores around the farm, they often kept their children at home rather than send them to school.

The state took little interest in education prior to 1840 or so, and education was neither compulsory nor free. There was virtually no government control over teacher training, textbooks, or curriculum. Initially, all schools were privately run (religious denominations founded their own schools) and were paid for by tuition fees.

Wealthy parents hired tutors from Great Britain, or several families shared a tutor, who might be the local clergyman's wife or another educated woman. For many women, teaching was an alternative to marriage and provided financial independence and personal satisfaction.

In Upper Canada, the first government initiative was the creation of grammar schools (roughly the equivalent of high schools).[40] The 1807 Grammar School Act created one grammar school in each of the colony's eight districts. These schools charged admission fees, were controlled by the Anglican Church, and taught a classical curriculum to students intending to advance to university or enter the professions. Although the government provided an annual grant of 100 pounds towards each teacher's salary, it made no provision for inspection and grammar schools generally operated independent of government control. By 1839, there were twelve grammar schools in the colony with about 300 students.

In 1816, Upper Canada established common schools to provide a basic education. The government provided 25 pounds per teacher, but the elected school boards were responsible for raising money through taxes, erecting a school house, hiring and firing teachers, determining the curriculum and the textbooks, and setting school regulations. The trustees' only requirements were to ensure that teachers were British subjects and submit an annual report to the Board of Education appointed by the Lieutenant Governor.

Most pioneer schools were crude log buildings heated by open fireplaces. As late as 1850, nearly half of Upper Canada's rural schools were one-room structures that measured approximately 20 by 24 feet. Students sat on backless benches, used outdoor privies, and drank from a common pail of water. Classes met only six months a year and the curriculum consisted of little more than the three R's. Girls learned the various domestic skills considered important for their future roles as wives and mothers. Later in the pioneer period, the daughters of the middle and upper classes received instruction in languages (to improve their conversational skills), dancing and music (to entertain guests), and such "ornamental subjects" as needlework.

Although the following article is over thirty years old, it provides an excellent insight into the state of education in Upper Canada and a good model of how to develop and argue a point of view. Additional sources on pioneer education include: Jane Errington, "Ladies and Schoolmistresses: Educating Women in Early Nineteenth-Century Upper Canada," *Historical Studies in Education*, 6, 1 (Spring, 1994); Harry Smaller, "Teachers and Schools in Early Ontario," *Ontario History*, 85, 4 (December, 1993); Jean Barman, "Beginnings: The Emergence of Educational Structures in 19th Century British Columbia," in Gillian Creese and Veronica Strong-Boag, eds., *British Columbia Reconsidered: Essays on Women* (Vancouver, 1992); Robert Carney, "Going to School in Upper Canada," in E. Brian Titley ed., *Canadian Education: Historical Themes and Contemporary Issues* (Calgary, 1990); and G. Davies, "Private Education for Women in Early Nova Scotia: 1784-1894," *Atlantis* 20, 1 (Fall-Winter, 1995).

* * * * *

Elementary Education in Upper Canada: A Reassessment[41]

In her book on Upper Canada published in 1838, Anna Jameson was sharply critical of the state of education in the colony. Ignorance and indifference to educational improvement, she asserted, were rampant. Many members of the assembly "could not read, and many more could not spell"; she was informed, moreover, that "in the distant townships, not one person in twenty or thirty could read or write, or had the means of attaining such knowledge." Her own small attempt to change things met only rebuff; "cold water was thrown upon me from every side—my interference in any way was so visibly distasteful, that I gave my project up ..."[1]

Mrs. Jameson's opinions on the state of education in Upper Canada were neither new nor singular. The literature of the period is crowded with familiar comments to the same effect. In the early 1820s, E.A. Talbot had claimed that "the great mass of the people ... are completely ignorant even of the rudiments of the most common learning."[2] A year after Mrs. Jameson's book was published, Lord Durham wrote that "even in the most thickly peopled districts there are but few schools, and those of a very inferior character; while the more remote settlements are almost entirely without any".[3] Many contemporaries agreed. The witnesses who appeared before Mackenzie's committee on grievances were nearly unanimous on the inadequacy of the common schools.[4] The sorry state of education was a frequent subject of discussion in the newspapers.[5] And more than one serious critic argued that between 1815 and 1839 the condition of the schools had actually become worse rather than better.[6]

Such pessimism about the state of education in Upper Canada was common enough; but it was never a unanimous verdict. Indeed, it was contested by a variety of observers throughout the colony's history. As early as 1810 a correspondent to the *Kingston Gazette* had declared that schools "are numerous in every part of the country."[7] Writing at the same time as E.A. Talbot, John Howison, a British visitor, thought that while provision for higher education was sadly lacking, "schools, at which the essential branches are taught, exist in the most secluded parts of the Province ...."[8] In the early thirties, Isaac Fidler, an English clergyman living near Thornhill, remarked that "education in country places is not so far advanced as in towns ... yet I am greatly mistaken if there are many persons in Canada who cannot read and write, if we except poor immigrants from Europe".[9] The *Kingston Chronicle* agreed: "there is scarcely a hamlet in Upper Canada where the schoolmaster may not be found ...."[10] In 1839 the same newspaper flatly rejected the charges made by Mrs. Jameson,[11] as did a correspondent in the *Brockville Recorder*:

> verily, Mr. Editor, our sympathising neighbours across the St. Lawrence have their Mrs. Trollope, and we good ignorant souls, have our Mrs. Jameson .... I assert, and I have some means of knowing ... that even in the "distant townships" there is not one in five who cannot read and write, and in my own township of Augusta there is not one in ten, who cannot read fluently and write legibly; and if there are exceptions, they are, as the *Kingston Chronicle* justly observes, composed of persons not born in the Province.[12]

There was, then, both a pessimistic and an optimistic view of the state of education in Upper Canada. Over the years, however, it has generally been the pessimistic version that has found its way into the historical literature. Even when historians have rejected the extreme claims of Talbot or Mrs. Jameson, they have still tended to agree with contemporary critics that the provision of basic education in the colony was inadequate and needed to be improved. It is the purpose of this article to offer a reassessment of that interpretation, and to suggest first, that there was far more schooling available than has generally been recognized, and thus the optimists were closer to the truth than the pessimists;

secondly, that judgements about the quality of schooling must be made within the context of contemporary educational expectations; and third, that the pessimistic viewpoint tells us far more about the expectations of the school reformers of the 1830s and '40s than it does about the expectations of those who actually created and maintained the schools.

Upper Canada possessed a variety of ways for passing on literacy and learning from one generation to the next. The most familiar means was through the schools that received financial aid from the government under the terms of the Common School Act of 1816—schools that, to borrow an English phrase, I shall call "grant-aided". Because the trustees were required to report regularly to the legislature, we have been left with a substantial body of sources on the grant-aided schools, including the school reports and statistics published in the Legislative Journals—sources that were often reprinted in the newspapers and quoted in speeches and books by contemporaries.

These sources, it must be emphasized, refer almost exclusively to the grant-aided schools; but they have too often been used as though they account for all of the basic schooling available in the colony. Though the grant-aided schools are obviously an important component in any evaluation of the availability of elementary education, they were only one of the means of obtaining literacy and learning. There were also a large number of common schools not recorded in the government statistics because they did not receive the government grant—schools I shall call "non-aided." And the day school, aided or non-aided, was only one of the ways in which children acquired the rudiments of an English education. Neither the non-aided schools nor the other institutions of basic education have received the attention they deserve.

There is no means of measuring in any exact way the number of non-aided schools. But there is a substantial amount of evidence to suggest that, from 1816 until the early 1840s, the non-aided schools were as numerous, or nearly so, as those that received government aid. The information contained in the returns to Robert Gourlay's questionnaire to the people of Upper Canada is particularly valuable. Gourlay's informants were requested to provide statistics on the number of schools in their townships. In some cases their replies can be matched up with complete school reports for the same year, from the District Boards of Education. Where this is possible, far more schools turn up in the former lists than the latter. In the London District, for example, nineteen schools received the government grant, but thirty-six are listed in the Gourlay returns; in the Gore District it was nine as opposed to thirty-seven; in Niagara, thirty as opposed to forty-six; in the Western District, ten as opposed to forty. The same discrepancies appear in other parts of the colony.[13]

A variety of sources confirm the existence of this gap between the total number of schools and the total number of grant-aided schools, not only for the early years of the Act of 1816, but throughout the period it was in force.

John Strachan, a close observer of the colony's educational development, noted the discrepancy repeatedly. In 1819 he remarked that some thirty-five hundred children were in grant-aided schools "besides a great number of schools of a similar description to which the bounty of government cannot be extended."[14] In the mid-twenties he wrote that "the Schools supported by Subscribers are perhaps not fewer in number than those established by Law."[15] A remarkable number of more specific examples support Strachan's view. The Home District Board of Education reported in 1819 that twenty schools had received the grant and "many others ... from various irregularities have not yet been recognized."[16] The township and town of Sandwich reported in 1829 that it had two grant-aided schools; but in a select committee report of 1830, a witness mentioned that the town had five schools, with three more in the rural parts of the township.[17] Toronto provides an extreme example. The city had only one school listed in the returns for 1838; yet three years later The Church estimated that Toronto had some forty non-aided schools.[18] As late as 1846, Egerton Ryerson claimed that only half the children attending day schools in Toronto were in government-aided schools.[19]

The existence of these non-aided schools is also confirmed by the large number of teachers who at one time or another registered complaints about being excluded from the government grant. In 1841, for example, a teacher in the Home District petitioned the legislature for redress, declaring that he had taught school for several years but had not received his share of the grant because he was not a British subject.[20] In York, Thomas Appleton and Alexander Stewart, both of whom had their grants cut off in the early twenties, continued to teach in the town until at least the end of the decade.[21] Such examples can easily be mutiltiplied.[22]

The difference between the number of grant-aided and total common schools has also been noted by students of local history. J.A. Bannister, for example, in his careful study of the schools of Norfolk County, found that "the location of each of the schools [reported to the government during the 1820s] can be fixed with tolerable accuracy. ...Yet there is no reference to any [grant-aided common] school in the vicinity of Vittoria though for a decade it had been the judicial centre of the London District, and was by far the most important town at that time." But there are, he adds, local records that give scattered evidence of schools in Vittoria throughout the 1820s. "Dover Mills [Port Dover] was another of the thriving centres of population for which no school is mentioned in the reports;" yet here again there were schools in existence from 1810 onwards.[23]

At a time when many communities were new and poor and thus in need of the government grant, the existence of so many rural non-aided schools calls for some explanation. In part it was due to the terms of the Act of 1816 itself. Grant-aided schools were required to remain open for six months of the year and to have at least twenty children in attendance. Some schools could not meet one or the other of these conditions and were consequently refused the grant by the boards of education.[24]

More important in limiting the number of grant-aided schools than the Act itself, however, was the way in which it was administered. The government had imposed a maximum grant for each district, and an upper limit on the amount paid to any one teacher. Beyond that, distribution policy lay with the District Boards of Education. For years in the Home District it was a matter of policy to restrict the number of grant-aided schools on the grounds that a few well-paid teachers would produce better schools than a multitude of badly-paid and hence incompetent ones.[25] The Western District Board of Education followed a somewhat similar policy, giving the maximum individual grant the law allowed to a relatively small number of well-paid teachers. Inevitably such policies meant a limited number of grant-aided schools, and a large number of precariously-financed, non-aided schools, especially in the back townships.[26] In other parts of the colony, the grant was divided, increasingly minutely, among all the teachers who applied for it, and this too contributed to the number of non-aided schools. After 1820, when the total government grant was reduced by two-thirds, individual payments might amount to as little as five pounds or less annually. To receive their grant, teachers had to appear before members of the district boards. And since it was often a long way to the district town, and many of the boards met on rare, irregular, and frequently unpublicized occasions, some teachers simply never bothered to make the effort required to receive such small sums.[27] There were, as well, teachers who failed to obtain the their grants through ignorance of the law or misadventure of various kinds.[28] For a variety of reasons, then, there were always a substantial number of schools in the rural areas of the colony that existed without the government grant and thus do not show up in the colony's school statistics.

The presence of non-aided schools in the towns and villages is easier to explain. A larger and more compact population, and the availability of hard currency, attracted a steady flow of teachers prepared to risk opening private venture schools—that is, schools where the teacher had no contractual agreement with a group of subscribers and hence no salary guarantee before he began teaching, something that few teachers in rural areas would risk. Outside of York and Kingston, these private venture schools were probably rare before the middle twenties; after that they could be found in increasing numbers throughout urban Upper Canada.

Because of the volume and variety of the sources that have survived, Toronto provides some of the best examples of the number and longevity of these private venture schools. Between 1815 and 1846 the city newspapers and directories contain notices for fifty-eight of them. From the late twenties, they always outnumbered, by a substantial margin, the grant-aided schools: the *York*

Commercial Directory of 1833-34 lists nineteen of them; *Brown's Toronto ... Directory* of 1846-47 lists twenty-four—in comparison to four and fifteen grant-aided schools respectively. Forty of the private venture schools either did not survive more than a year or so, or left no record of their survival. Eighteen of them can be shown to have existed three years or more—a reasonable test of the efficiency and the economic viability of a non-aided school.

A few of these schools were exclusive. Two or three of them—all female academies—catered to the elite of Toronto and the province at large; board and education at Mrs. Cockburn's school, opened in 1817 and still running in 1846, could cost as much as twenty pounds a quarter year.[29] Other schools served the sons and daughters of the middling ranks of society, charging fees about the same as those of the district grammar schools.[30] But most of the private venture schools were inexpensive. The majority of them, as *The Church* put it in 1841, taught the children of "the humbler classes" and charged fees similar to those charged in the rural common schools.[31] Nearly all of the private venture schools began with the three Rs, and some of them were surprisingly large. Thomas Caldicott's Academy had some eighty students, and the Bay Street Academy usually had a hundred or more.[32]

Toronto, however, was not alone in being well provided with private venture schools. In Kingston, forty-eight can be traced between 1815 and 1846; continuity over three years or more can be demonstrated in eleven cases.[33] A long list could be made of the private venture schools—sometimes with proof of continuity, sometimes not—throughout the thirties and early forties in Brockville, Sandwich, Perth, Cobourg, Niagara, London, Prescott, Cornwall, Grimsby, and other Upper Canadian towns and villages.[34]

There were other kinds of schools in the colony that do not show up in the government statistics. Two joint-stock institutions—the Bath and Grantham academies—offered the elementary subjects at prices comparable to the grant-aided schools, and both had a majority of their pupils in the elementary departments: in 1832, for example, the Grantham Academy had some ninety pupils, only eight of whom were advanced enough to be studying the classics.[35] There was, as well, the Methodist-operated Upper Canada Academy, with a student population in the late thirties of between eighty and a hundred; it, too, took pupils only beginning to learn their letters.[36] And to this list must be added the Upper Canada Central School, an institution that was grant-aided but, because of its separate sources of financing, was never included in the school statistics. The Central School was, in fact, the largest school in the province, with an enrolment that often exceeded three hundred in the thirties and early forties.[37]

Day schools, however, were not the only way children in Upper Canada learned their letters. Some received most of their schooling at home. The English sociologist, Frank Musgrove, has recently pointed out that in Britain in the first third of the nineteenth century, domestic education was still a preferred means of educating children among many middle-class parents.[38] Judging by the number of advertisements for governesses and tutors in Upper Canadian newspapers, it was apparently preferred by many parents in the colonies as well. Sometimes two or three families would hire a teacher to attend a group of children in one of their homes—John Macaulay's daughter began her education this way.[39] Sometimes an educated woman—in many cases a clergyman's wife—would accept a few carefully selected children to educate with her own family.[40] Sometimes a tutor or a governess was hired by a single family.[41] Private tuition of this sort might be expensive or it might not. In 1835, the Solicitor General was prepared to offer what he described as a "liberall salary" to obtain a suitable governess for his two daughters, and Adam Fergusson must have gone to considerable expense to bring a tutor out from Scotland for his sons;[42] but modestly prosperous parents were more likely to be looking for some-one "to whom a comfortable *Home* is more an object than mere salary" and they could, apparently, expect to find applicants who would demand less than the cost of sending their children to a boarding school.[43]

With few exceptions, all day schools, aided or non-aided, charged tuition fees, while the cost of domestic education, unless carried out by a child's parents, would equal or exceed the cost of school fees. What happened, then, to the child whose parents could not afford school fees, who lived out of reach of a day school, or who were too uneducated themselves to tutor their own children? Some of these children were assured of the essentials of literacy through the terms of their apprenticeship indentures which, for younger boys, often required their masters to send them to school for a short time.[44] Others could take advantage of the urban evening schools established "for the accommodation of youth, whose other engagements may prevent their attendance during business hours."[45] The evening schools tended to specialize in practical subjects like commercial arithmetic, bookkeeping, and penmanship, but the regular inclusion of the three Rs in their advertisements suggests, as well, that there was a steady demand for even the most elementary training from young people already at work.[46]

For those who could not attend a day school, however, the most accessible means of learning to read, and more rarely to write, was the Sunday school— and institution that appeared in Upper Canada immediately after the War of 1812, and by the thirties was common throughout the colony, urban and rural areas alike.[47] The primary purpose of the Sunday school was religious training. But for Protestants, making a child "wise unto salvation" meant, among other things, enabling him to read his Bible. Thus the Sunday school had, of necessity, to teach children to read if it was not done elsewhere. There was, as well, a more mundane reason for teaching reading: the success of the pedagogical techniques used by the Sunday schools depended on it, as the following comments by George Ryerson demonstrate.

The teacher [Ryerson wrote in 1826] after noting ... the absentees, etc., proceeds to hear the weekly tasks of scripture, Catechisms, etc., asking questions on them and giving explanations and enters in his book an account of the Chapter, Verse, etc. They then instruct them in some Catechism or other useful subject for some time .... The teacher then receives their Tracts and questions them respecting their contents, and gives them a fresh tract. To each child of the reading classes a tract is given, commonly of those published by the London Tract society; these are selected not only with a view to the instruction of the child but also with a reference to the circumstances, the character or the vices of its parents .... The next Sunday the tract is returned ... and another given. The teacher then gives to each child who is present in proper time, one ticket (pasteboard with a verse of Scripture printed on it) and one ticket for every twenty verses of Scripture or questions of Catechisms, properly and distinctly recited. To these tickets which are all committed to memory before returned, we attach the nominal value of one-tenth of a penny, and they are redeemed by a present of useful little books of the value of the tickets received.[48]

Thus for both religious and pedagogical reasons, the Sunday schools began their work, when necessary, by teaching the children to read. There must have been many children throughout Upper Canada, who, like the Rev. John Carroll, acquired much of the little formal learning they had at a Sunday school where, as he puts it, "in those days, we did spell as well as read and we learned much relative to the meaning of words ...."[49] In Kingston, in 1825, for example, the Sunday school at St. George's Church began with the "elements of education" so that "many children who did not know the alphabet, are spelling and reading with tolerable ease."[50] In Trafalgar township, a school of seventy students included "general reading lessons" and spelling as a regular part of its weekly timetable.[51] A Methodist preacher stationed at Guelph reported in 1842 that his Sunday school had seventy-five pupils, many of whom "have no other opportunity of learning to read, and therefore the institution is of great importance."[52]

There are enough reports of illiteracy in the colony to suggest that at least some children went without any schooling at all. One common reason for this, at a time when the individual parent bore the cost of most forms of schooling, was poverty. The recognition that poverty and illiteracy went hand in hand was, indeed, a spur to the establishment and maintenance of some schools. One of the subsidiary purposes of the Sunday schools was always, as the Toronto Methodists put it, "to impart intellectual instruction ... to those children whose parents are too poor to afford them the advantages of a week day school."[53] And the attempt to establish charity or free schools in the larger towns testifies to the existence of parents who could pay school fees. William Macaulay's description of the function of the Central School in Toronto is illuminating on this point: it was, he wrote in 1839, "most useful in educating, in a limited way, great numbers of the poorer class of children in this City, who otherwise would be brought up in the lowest depths of ignorance"; the school should be maintained, he added, "for the instruction of the inferior and indigent part of the population, in the first elements of learning."[54] In a similar vein, the editor of the *Kingston Chronicle* urged his fellow citizens to establish an infant school in order to confer "a gratuitous education upon the multitude of friendless, and in some cases fatherless objects, that are to be perpetually met with in our streets."[55]

In rural areas, individual poverty was only one factor that limited access to schooling. In a new or thinly settled township, schooling might be unavailable even to the modestly prosperous. Roads, for example, could be as crucial as money in securing accessibility: "it appears to me," the Rev. John Roaf remarked in the late thirties, "that the prevalence of Education in a neighbourhood depends much more upon the opening of roads ... than upon any gratuity made directly to its schools."[56] Moreover, even in the midst of educational plenty, an isolated community might still go without. West Gwillimbury, for example, had several schools in 1830; yet a petition signed by twenty-nine residents of the township stated that they were "totally without the means of affording to their children the smallest portion of education, by reason of the want of a schoolmaster within any reasonable distance ... and are consequently desirous of having a school established in their immediate neighbourhood."[57] Occasionally, there was no school simply because members of a small community disagreed on the religious affiliation of the teacher, on the site of the schoolhouse, or on some other contentious issue.[58]

That some children went without any schooling at all, however, should not be allowed to obscure the fact that schooling in one form or another was widely available. As early as 1817, according to the Gourlay returns, nearly all reporting townships had a school, and where the population was large enough or scattered enough to warrant it, most townships had several.[59] Despite a temporary setback after 1820 when the government grant was sharply reduced, the grant-aided common schools grew steadily from 1816 until, in the late 1830s, there were more than eight hundred of them, scattered over nearly every township in the province.[60] To these means of education must be added the substantial number of non-aided schools in both town and country, and the variety of other ways in which Upper Canadian children learned their letters.

It might be argued, indeed, that we should accept the opinion of the optimists for no other reason than that the pessimists' case is so susceptible to refutation. To acquiesce in E.A. Talbot's verdict is to doubt the authenticity of the school reports of the early 1820s, including those for the district in which he lived; it is to assume, moreover, that all the schools reported in the Gourlay returns had either disappeared by 1824 or had never existed in the first place. And ignoring the non-aided schools altogether for the moment, the existence of grant-aided schools in nearly every township of the colony by the late thirties, including many in the newest and most remote, is in itself enough to raise doubts about Lord Durham's knowledge of the subject and Anna Jameson's judgement. Other pessimistic sources are no less suspect. William Lyon Mackenzie, attempting to score political points, charged in 1831 that "in the most populous country townships in the Home District there is not at this time of year more than one school of ten scholars, although the number of persons between six and sixteen is over 600!"[61] "This time of year" was, in fact, a time when no rural youngster old enough to help at home would ever be found in school. Or another example: in November 1838, Egerton Ryerson was asserting that because of the "monopolizing" educational policy of the Family Compact, most of the population was "growing up in ignorance". Three months later he flatly rejected the same charge when made by Mrs. Jameson, who, he claimed, was grossly misinformed: "the schoolhouses in every settled township of the Province are so many proofs and monuments of the estimate of education by the inhabitants, and of their desire to confer its advantages upon their children ...."[62]

There is, however, a difference between saying that schooling was widely available and that it actually reached most children. The former point has been examined at some length; but can anything be deduced about the latter point? Given the fact that no accurate count of the number of schools is possible, and that there is no systematic way to examine literacy rates through sources drawn directly from the period, it might be best to leave the latter question unanswered, or merely to indicate the number of contemporary observers who believed that literacy was widespread. For those who are prepared to accept the reliability of mid-nineteenth century census data, however, there is one significant piece of quantitative evidence that confirms the optimists' case. The census of 1861 required each householder to indicate the number of persons *over* twenty years of age within that household who were illiterate. The returns show an astonishingly high literacy rate—somewhere around ninety per cent—for most areas of Upper Canada. The significant point for the argument here, however, is that the census question dealt only with those over twenty years of age. A quick survey of the enumerators' returns for sample rural and urban areas shows that literacy was almost universal for those born in Upper Canada; and most of those counted would have received their schooling *before* the 1840s—or at least before the full impact of the Ryersonian school reforms began to be felt.

This general conclusion, that most Upper Canadian children growing up before the 1840s had at least attained literacy, is confirmed by a systematic study of the same census data for one urban community by a member of the O.I.S.E. Canadian History Project. Mr. Harvey Graff has found that in Hamilton, literacy among the native-born was nearly universal, though older people were somewhat less likely to be literate than younger ones.[63] If the census data is even roughly reliable, then it suggests that the opinion of the optimists was fully justified: schooling was wide-spread and, in one form or another, it reached most Upper Canadian children.

But, the skeptical reader murmurs, the question of quantity is not the most important one; what really perturbed the contemporary critics of Upper Canadian education was its quality. In a memorial to the legislature in 1835, for example, Mahlon Burwell declared that the people of the colony were "at this moment totally uneducated." What he meant, however, was not that there were no schools but that the schools were inferior in character. "The little instruction given to the children," he continued, "has no influence over their morals—does nothing to open or expand their intellectual faculties, much less to direct them in their conduct of life—English reading imperfectly taught, something of writing, and the first five rules of Arithmetic, which the teachers we employ are seldom able to explain, make up the meager sum total of what the rising generation learn at our Common Schools."[64] His criticism was echoed by a succession of politicians, newspaper editors, clergymen and other observers of the schools.[65] The teachers, they claimed, were inadequate; the pupils attended irregularly; schooling rarely lasted more than three or four years and in many cases only a few months; and children learned little more than the three Rs. As an anonymous writer put it in the *Monthly Review* in 1841,

> if the defects of the system are so obvious and glaring when tried by ordinary rules, how much more so when judged by the high standards of what education, even in Common Schools, ought to be! On this point public opinion wants raising to a higher standard than generally prevails. To be taught a little reading, writing and arithmetic, is not education in any correct acceptation of the term. This neither develops the faculties of the mind, nor implants a little of the means of doing so. It merely enables a man to perform the very lowest part of his duties in business, or as a social being, but the highest parts of those duties are not even noticed. The sentient being is so far from having its faculties cultivated, that it is never even taught their names—it is so far from receiving any intellectual training, that in the vast majority of cases the scholar leaves school without having learned a single fact in relation to his mind and its various powers. Education stops short at the very threshold of the temple that it ought to fill with glory.[66]

"Public opinion wants raising" indeed. This was the voice of the educational reformer speaking—the voice of a growing number of public men in the thirties and early forties who were increasingly convinced that universal schooling, guided by the hand of government, was an essential prerequisite for the political, economic, and social well being of society.[67] It was the voice of Anna Jameson, with the Cousin report on the achievements of Prussian education tucked under her arm, of Egerton Ryerson, stuffed full of the education mania from his reading of the leading English and American journals, of the Rev. William Bell, peddling the notion that the Scottish normal schools held the key to the improvement of teaching in Upper Canada, of a host of others caught up in one of the great panaceas of the age of improvement.[68] But it was not necessarily the voice of the people who built and maintained the schools. And what the critics and reformers called flaws and weaknesses, can, if examined from another perspective, be seen as perfectly comprehensible aspects of a pattern of schooling that fitted naturally into the larger context of family life and work.

Parents, for example, seem to have had a relatively clear idea of what should be taught in school, though it differed sharply from the more grandiose conceptions of the school reformers. Take the following striking statement of purposes drawn up by the subscribers to a school in Norfolk County:

We the undersigned being deeply impressed with the necessity and utility of giving our children an education, by which they will be enabled to read the word of God and transact their own business— And being desirous and anxious of having a school taught for that desirable purpose—Therefore we mutually agree to engage C.D. Shiemerhorn to teach said school ... Said Shiemerhorn is to teach the different branches of *reading, writing, Arithmetic* and E*nglish Grammar* if all are required ...[69]

The ends were clear and the means were limited. Schooling would enable a child to read his Bible and get on in the world; the three Rs were sufficient to enable him to do so.

Time and time again—in the school reports, in advertisements and teachers' contracts, in memoirs—the same purposes are restated. A teacher's contract from Grantham township requires him to teach "Spelling, Reading, Writing, Arithmetic, to maintain good order" and to "suppress all immoral habits and practices among his pupils."[70] A contract from Ameliasburgh binds the master "to teach Reading, Writing and Arithmetic, if required."[71] An advertisement for a teacher by a group of school trustees in the Bathurst District says that "as liberal wages will be given, none need apply but such as can teach English Grammar well, besides the other branches usually required in Common Schools".[72] At a time when local people had unqualified control of what was to be taught, these contracts and advertisements reflect with rare accuracy the things they wanted from the school. As Canniff Haight put it, "in those days most of the country youth ... were content if they learned to read and write, and to wade through figures as far as the Rule of Three. Of course there were exceptions ... but generally this was the extent of the aspiration of the rising generation, and it was not necessary for the teacher to be profoundly learned to lead them as far as they wished to go."[73]

Haight's comment raises a second point. School reformers and well-educated members of the boards of education might complain regularly about the quality and the remuneration of teachers, but the people who ran the schools evidently felt differently. In the Niagara District, according to the secretary of the board of education, teachers' salaries were "so low as not to induce men of sufficient qualifications generally to engage in the humble and ill-requited duties"; yet, he continued, "after the approval and appointment [of teachers] by the trustees, the board have not rejected teachers however incompetent from a regard to the wishes of their employers ...."[74] Teachers were ill-paid not simply because of the limited financial means of many rural, neighbourhoods, but because of the limited purposes to be achieved. The school may have been a necessary institution, but it was not, as Haight points out, one that required expensive skills or great learning in the teacher.

Reformers often referred to irregularity of attendance as one of the major defects of the common schools. Seen from the family's point of view, however, it has a different meaning. Irregularity of attendance, wrote one school commissioner in 1842, was due "in some instances ... to the carelessness, indifference, or possibly poverty of the parents but it is more often caused by their [the children's] services being required at home."[75] Schooling, however valuable it might be deemed by parents, was something to be fitted in with the other needs of the family—the work of the farm, of the workshop, or the home. Being a pupil was a part of growing up, but it was not the child's only, or even primary, role.

The seasonal pattern of school attendance was also determined by the routine of family life. Throughout the rural areas there were two distinct school terms. Children too young to help with the family work and to cope with bad weather and the winter snow were usually sent to school only in the summer months; for older members of the family the pattern was reversed. As a correspondent to the *Kingston Herald* put it, "in almost all the country places in Western Canada, the common schools in the summer season are seldom attended by others, than children from *3 ½ years ... to 12 or 13 years of age*. Few or no adults of either sex can attend. But in the winter season, the reverse takes place, the younger children are withdrawn, and the elder ones *from 16 to nearly 30 years of age attend.*"[76]

Surveying what they took to be the inadequacies of the schools, the educational reformers were often quick to lay the blame for such conditions on the ignorance and indifference of parents and trustees. But it must be remembered that every common school in the colony was the product of voluntary sacrifice. No law required a child to attend school, no schoolhouse had to be built, no teacher had to be paid. The fact that many local people did not see the school in the same light as the educational reformers does not mean they were indifferent to schooling. The majority of the urban private venture schools survived because parents of the "humbler classes", as *The Church* called them, were prepared to pay tuition fees. The same is true of the non-aided schools in the rural parts of the province. And the fact that the government aided some common schools does not lessen significantly the pre-eminent role of local initiative, though it undoubtedly lessened its burdens. In new townships, or in poor or isolated neighbourhoods, government aid was probably decisive in keeping a school open: every grant-aided school in a given district received the same amount, of financial aid, and the smaller the number of families involved in supporting a school, the more important the role of the grant would be.[77] But in most cases the government grant was not the main sustaining force. The cost of erecting and maintaining the schoolhouse was borne by the local community or by the parents of the children who attended that school. The grant could be applied only to teachers' salaries, but it was never anticipated that it would cover the whole of that salary, most of which, in fact, was met by tuition fees agreed upon by the teacher and the parents concerned. The common schools of Upper Canada were not "government schools" though the government provided financial aid to some of them; they were the products of local initiative and they reflected local needs.

It must be remembered too that schooling was not cheap. According to the Gourlay report, tuition fees in the rural schools in 1817 averaged ten shillings a quarter year for each pupil. There is no evidence that the cost fell significantly until the Common School Act of 1841 increased the size of the grant, introduced property taxation, and set the maximum fee at one shilling three pence a month.[78] The degree of voluntarism involved in creating the schools and the cost of maintaining them are both proofs against shallow charges of indifference and ignorance.[79]

It was voluntarism, moreover, that accounts for the institutional variety that characterized Upper Canadian educational provision. So long as schooling was primarily the responsibility of the family, parents used whatever means available to attain their ends. Some could afford tutors and governesses. Some used the urban private venture schools. Others had to create a school by co-operative effort. And some had access only to the charity school or the Sunday school. The variety of colonial schooling, however, was not simply an ad hoc response to frontier conditions; it was the typical way in which the educational needs of most people were met at the time, not only in Upper Canada but in America and Britain.[80] And educational "improvement" would come, not as some students of the subject would have it, from the natural course of a society maturing from a pioneer to a settled state, but from a new and compelling ideology of schooling that was emerging in the middle decades of the nineteenth century on both sides of the Atlantic. The Upper Canadian educational reformers of the 1830s were among its harbingers in North America.

One final point. Occasionally there are those who point out that no matter how many schools existed, they were still not numerous enough to accommodate all children between the ages of five and sixteen; and thus, in the final analysis, educational provision in Upper Canada was both quantitatively and qualitatively inadequate. The premise is correct but the conclusion is inappropriate. Contemporaries often used the ages between five and sixteen to indicate the years within which schooling should take place, and, often enough, advanced educational reformers wanted all children in school long enough to learn more than the three Rs. But no one suggested that all children should attend school between five and sixteen years inclusive; that is an idea that belongs to a later period. And attempts to judge Upper Canadians by a standard of attendance and enrolment which, in fact, was hardly attained in Ontario in the 1930s, let alone a century earlier, is a particularly flagrant form of historical whiggism.

What, then, can be said about the state of schooling in Upper Canada? It was characterized by a variety of institutions, by limited purposes, by voluntarism, and by the high degree of responsibility borne by the family. For children in isolated sections of a settled township, in new townships, or for the urban poor, schooling of any kind might be hard to come by. But for most children the means to attain literacy existed and most children did in fact attain it. Beyond that, the level of schooling became a highly individual matter, for it was parents themselves who decided how long their children would attend school, by whom they would be taught, and what subjects.

The educational reformers, however, were riding the wave of the future. The Ontario school system that took shape in the middle decades of the nineteenth century first undermined and then destroyed the traditional character of Upper Canadian educational provision. With larger grants and an improved administrative system, the number of non-aided schools that catered to the "humbler classes" declined sharply as these schools transformed themselves into grant-aided institutions. At the same time, "private" schooling began to take on a new meaning—to denote a conscious (and expensive) rejection of the state system. The power given after 1846 to the central educational authority ended effective parental control over the qualifications of teachers and the content of the curriculum. The purposes of schooling became increasingly "public" ones—schools existed to serve the political, economic and social needs of the state and the society. The duty of government expanded with the expansion of purposes: it was no longer enough to assist local effort—the aim of the Act of

1816; governments would increasingly require local effort, and, in 1871, demand that every child attend school. The new dispensation was introduced, no doubt, with the best of intentions, and justified in the name of progress and humanity. In the process, variety, voluntarism, and the primary responsibility of the family for the education of the child became, in Peter Lazlett's evocative phrase, a part of "the world we have lost".

NOTES

1 Anna Jameson. *Winter Studies and Summer Rambles in Canada ...* (London, 1838), Vol. I, 34-5.

2 E.A. Talbot, *Five Years' Residence in the Canadas ...* (London, 1824), Vol. II, 116.

3 C.P. Lucas. ed., *Lord Durham's Report ....* (Oxford. 1912), Vol. II, 184-5.

4 Journals of the Legislative Assembly of Upper Canada [J.L.A.], 1835, Appendix No. 21. 7th Report on Grievances, Appendix to the 7th Report: Examination of Subjects.

5 For example, see the *Brockville Recorder*, 29 Dec. 1836; *Christian Guardian*, 28 Aug. 1839; *Upper Canada Herald*, 10 Dec. 1839.

6 See the *Brockville Recorder*, 14 Oct. 1836, and Public Archives of Canada [P.A.C.] RG5. Al.Vol. 14, I.G. Booth to Harrison. 26 Nov. 1839.

7 *Kingston Gazette*, 30 Oct. 1810.

8 John Howison, *Sketches of Upper Canada ...* (Edinburgh, 1821), p. 260.

9 Isaac Fidler, *Observations on Professions, Literature, Manners and Emigration ...* (London, 1833), p. 329.

10 *Kingston Chronicle*, 7 Dec. 1833.

11 Quoted in the *Upper Canada Herald*, 12 Feb. 1839. Similarly see the *Christian Guardian*, 20 Feb. 1839: *Kingston Chronicle*, 13 Apr. 1839.

12 *Brockville Recorder*, 28 Feb. 1839.

13 Compare the complete set of township returns and summary statistics in Robert Gourlay, *Statistical Account of Upper Canada* (London, 1822), Vol. I, and the school returns made by the boards of education in P.A.C., RG5, A1, Vol. 34 (London), Vol. 38 (Gore), Vol. 39 (Niagara), and P.A.C., RG5, B11, Vol. 1-2 (Western).

14 Quoted in J.G. Hodgins, ed. *Documentary History of Education in Upper Canada* (Toronto, 1893-1904) [D.H.E.], I, 154-8.

15 P.A.C., RG5, B1l, Vol. 3, Report of the General Board of Education, n.d. [1825 or 1826]. Similarly see J.L.A., 1829, Appendix: Report of the President of the General Board of Education.

16 P.A.C., RG5, Al, Vol. 44, Report of the Board of Education, Home District, 13 June 1819. Similarly see *ibid.*, Vol. 38. Report of the Board of Education. Ottawa District. n.d. [1816].

17 J.L.A., 1830, Appendix: Report ... on the Petition of the Trustees of the District School of the Western District; *ibid.*, Common School Reports, Western District.

18 See J.L.A., 1839, School Reports, 276-9; *The Church*, 7 Aug. 1841.

19 Quoted in F.A. Walker, *Catholic Education and Politics in Upper Canada* (Toronto, 1963).p.69.

20 J.L.A., 1841, 21 June 1841.

21 J.L.A., 1828, Appendix: Report of a Select Committee on the Petition of Thomas Appleton, Minutes of Evidence. That Stewart, like Appleton, continued to teach in York, see the *Niagara Gleaner*, 23 Jan. 1830.

22 See, for example, P.A.C., RG5, C1, Vol. 21, Papers relating to the Petition of David Walker, 6 Feb. 1840; *ibid.*, Vol. 75, James Walker to Harrison, 8 Dec. 1841; *ibid.*, RG5. B11, Vol. 1-2. Richard Leonard to Hillier, 24 July 1824; *ibid.*, Proudfoot Papers. John Cameron to Rev. William Proudfoot, 16 Jan. 1839; J.L.A., 1839. Appendix: School Reports, London District. 283-92; Public Archives of Ontario [P.A.O.], RG2, C-6-C, Elizabeth Twigg to Murray, 26 Dec. 1843.

23 J.A. Bannister, *Early Educational History of Norfolk County* (Toronto, 1926), pp. 118-22.

24 See, for example. P.A.C., RG5, A1, Vol. 38, Report of the Board of Education, Gore District, 2 Feb. 1818; *ibid.*, RG5, C1, Vol. 65, No 930, Petition of John Dwyer of Emily ..., 28 June 1841.

25 See G.W. Spragge, ed., *The John Strachan Letter Book, 1812-34* (Toronto, 1946), pp. 75-9; P.A.C., RG5, A1, Vol. 44, Report of the Board of Education for the Home District 13 June 1819.

26 See P.A.C., RG5, B11, Vol. 1-2, Report of the Board of Education of the Western District, n.d. [1818]; *ibid.*, RG5, C1, Vol. 72. No. 1760, Papers relating to the Board of Education, Western District, 1841. For an example of the non-aided schools in the western District, compare P.A.C., Society for the propagation of the Gospel in Foreign Parts [S.P.G.], MSS "C", Rev. T.B. Fuller to the Bishop of Montreal, 11 Oct. 1838; and J.L.A., 1839, Appendix: School Reports for 1838, p. 297.

27 See, for example, P.A.C., RG5, B11, Vol. 5, John Talbot to Colborne, 1 Aug. 1834.

28 For a spectacular example of nine year duration see P.A.C., RG5, B11, Vol. 1-2, Richard Leonard to Hillier, 24 July 1824. Similarly see P.A.C., RG5, A1; Vol. 55, I.H. Johnson to Maitland, 1 Jan. 1822; P.A.O., RG2, C-6-C, George Foster to Murray, 1 Mar. 1843.

29 The school was begun in 1817 by Mrs. Goodman (*Upper Canada Gazette*, 4 Sept. 1817), passed on to Mrs. Cockburn in 1821 (*York Weekly Post*, 26 Dec. 1821), and was still running in 1846 (*British Colonist*, 11 Aug. 1846). For a sampling of the expenses of sending a

daughter there in the late thirties see the school accounts in P.A.O., Roe Family Papers.

30 For example see the *Patriot*, 10 June 1834, and the *British Colonist*, 18 Aug. 1846 (Misses Winn); *Colonial Advocate*, 14 July 1831, and *British Colonist*, 28 Aug. 1846 (Misses McCord); *Patriot*, 13 Sept. 1839, and *British Colonist*, 13 Nov. 1846 (Mrs. Crombie).

31 *The Church*, 7 Aug. 1841. Fees for individual schools are usually given in their newspaper advertisements.

32 For Caldicott's school see the *Patriot*, 9 Aug. 1833, and *City of Toronto ... Commercial Directory ... 1837*. For the Bay Street Academy see the *Patriot*, 5 Jan. 1836, and the *British Colonist*, 11 Sept. 1846.

33 Based on a search of the *Kingston Gazette*, the *Kingston Chronicle*, and the *Upper Canada Herald*, between 1815 and 1846.

34 The relevant newspaper files are most useful but where there is no newspaper other sources are informative. In Cornwall, for example, a girls' school, open for ten years before 1839, turns up in P.A.C., RG5, A1, Vol. 225. Mrs. Blackwood to Arthur. 22 July 1839. Occasionally, where there is only a single source for a school, the proprietor will provide helpful historical information herself, as in the case of Mrs. O'Brian of Prescott, who in an advertisement thanked the public for "their patronage over the last eight years" and hoped it would continue. *Brockville Recorder*, 27 Jan. 1831.

35 On the Bath Academy see *Upper Canada Herald*, 6 Jan. 1830 and P.A.C., RG5, B11, Vol. 5, Petition of the President of the Bath School Society, Nov. 1836. On the Grantham Academy see P.A.C., RG5, B11, Vol. 4, Memorial of the Trustees ..., Nov. 3, 1832. One other joint-stock academy—the Ancaster Literary Institution—did receive the common school grant and would, therefore, be included in the educational statistics. See P.A.C., RG5, C1, Vol. 98, William Craigie to Bagot, 15 Nov. 1842.

36 See J.L.A., 1836-37, Appendix No. 68: Report of a Select Committee on the Petition of Rev. Mr. Richey: *Christian Guardian*, 1 Feb. 1837.

37 For its history see G.W. Spragge, "The Upper Canada Central School", *Ontario Historical Society Papers and Records*, XXXII (1937), 171-91.

38 Frank Musgrove, "Middle-class Families and Schools. 1780-1880," in P.W. Musgrave, ed. *Sociology, History, and Education: A Reader* (London, 1970), pp. 117-25.

39 See P.A.O., Macaulay Papers, John Macaulay to Ann Macaulay, 8 Nov. 1840. Similarly see William Canniff, *The Medical Profession in Upper Canada* (Toronto, 1894), pp. 317-18.

40 See, for example, the *Patriot*, 1 Dec. 1835; *The Church*, 26 Jan. 1839 and 5 Jan. 1844; *British Colonist*, 3 Aug. 1843 and 14 Aug. 1846.

41 See, for example, the *Patriot*, 25 Feb. 1834 and 26 June 1838: *Kingston*

Chronicle, 23 Apr. and 5 Oct. 1842; *The Church*, 17 July 1841 and 24 Aug. 1844.

42 See *The Albion* (New York), 6 June 1835; P.A.C., RG5, CI, Vol. 81, No. 2719, Fergusson to Harrison, 13 Jan. 1842.

43 *British Colonist*, 20 Nov. 1839; *The Church*, 4 May 1839. In Britain, at least, governesses' salaries were notoriously low. See M.J. Peterson, "The Victorian Governess," *Victorian Studies*, XIV, No. I (Sept. 1970), 11-12.

44 For some typical examples see P.A.C., McPherson Papers, Vol. I, four indentures dated 1840, 1842, 1845 and 1846.

45 *British Colonist*, 5 June 1846.

46 See, for example, *Niagara Gleaner*, 1 Oct. 1825; *Kingston Gazette*, 8 Sept. 1818; *Kingston Chronicle*, 22 Oct. 1826; *Hallowell Free Press*, 8 Nov. 1831.

47 See for example the *Christian Guardian*, 4 Sept. 1830 and 5 July 1843; *The Church*, 1 July, 5 and 19 Aug., and 2 Sept. 1837.

48 P.A.C., RG5, B11, Vol. 3, George Ryerson to Maitland, 9 June 1826.

49 J.W. Grant. ed., *Salvation! O The Joyful Sound* (Toronto, 1967), p. 86.

50 *Kingston Chronicle*, 11 Mar. 1825.

51 *Christian Guardian*, 19 Aug. 1835.

52 P.A.C., Methodist Missionary Society, Synod Minutes, Western District of Canada, Report of Sunday Schools, 1842.

53 *Christian Guardian*, 14 Jan. 1835. Similarly see the *Kingston Gazette*, 29 Mar. 1817; P.A.C., McDonald-Stone Papers, Vol. 4, Ephraim Webster to Mrs. S. Baker, 12 Mar. 1841.

54 P.A.C., RG5, B11, Vol. 5, Documents relating to ... the Accounts of the Central School: 1. Report of William Macaulay, 8 Aug. 1839.

55 *Kingston Chronicle*, 29 Oct. 1831. Similarly see the Colonial Advocate, 12 Nov. 1829, and the *British Colonist*, 18 Sept. 1839.

56 Quoted in D.H.E., III. 269. Similarly see P.A.C., RG5, Al, Vol. 96, Petition of the Township of Nelson ... 26 Oct. 1829.

57 P.A.C., RG5, B11, Vol. 4, Petition of the Inhabitants of ...West Gwillimbury, 20 May 1830. Similarly see the *Christian Guardian*, 23 July 1831; J.R. Godley, *Letters from America* (London, 1844), I, 210.

58 See, for example, P .A.C., S.P.G., X Series, X7, Mr. Blake's Statement, No.1, 28 Oct. 1840, p. 490; *ibid.*, Mr. Morse's Journal, No. 7, 21 Jan. 1841, pp. 513-14; *Bathurst Courier*, 10 July 1835.

59 Since there were no returns from some of the most economically advanced and heavily populated areas—very few replies were received from the Midland and Eastern Districts and none from the Home District—the number of schools reported in Gourlay's volume is probably somewhat less than representative. For the statistics see Gourlay, *Statistical Account*, Vol. 1.

60 School returns were printed annually as appendices to the J.L.A. from the late twenties but are rarely complete. Before that, scattered returns can be found in P.A.C., RG5, A1 and B11. A nearly complete set for the Eastern District which indicates the annual growth and the effects of the cutback of 1820 has survived in P.A.C., McGillivray Papers, Vol. 3, School Papers, 1816-31.

61 *Colonial Advocate*, 22 Sept. 1831.

62 *Christian Guardian*, 7 Nov. 1838 and 20 Feb. 1839.

63 Harvey I. Graff, "Towards a Meaning of Literacy: Literacy and Social Structure in Hamilton, Ontario, 1861," *History of Education Quarterly*, XII, No.3 (Fall 1972), 411-31.

64 J.L.A., 1835, Appendix No. 58, Memorial of M. Burwell on the Subject of Education.

65 See for example the *Gore Gazette*, 24 Mar., 21 Apr., and 26 May 1827; *Upper Canada Herald*, 24 Mar. 1835; *St. Catharines Journal*, 12 Nov. and 10 Dec. 1835; *Brockville Recorder*, 29 Dec. 1836; *Christian Guardian*, 24 Feb. 1836; *Western Herald* (Sandwich), 4 Sept. 1838.

66 Quoted in the *Christian Guardian*, 22 Sept. 1841.

67 Some of the more important aspects of this growing conviction are examined by Susan E. Houston, "Politics, Schools, and Social Change in Upper Canada", C.H.R., LIII, No. 3 (Sept. 1972), 249-71, and by R.D. Gidney, "Common School Improvement and Upper Canadian Public Opinion in the 1830s," *Social History*, April 1972.

68 See Anna Jameson, *Winter Studies ...*, Vol. 1, 34-5; *Canadian Christian Examiner and Presbyterian Review*, Vol. 2, No.3 (Mar. 1838). By the early thirties Ryerson was already well aware of the main currents of educational reform: see the *Christian Guardian*, 7 Dec. 1831.

69 Norfolk Historical Society Collection, Contract between Teacher and Subscribers dated 2 Oct. 1826, pp. 2761-2.

70 Niagara Historical Society Museum, Secord Papers, Articles of agreement between Richard H. Secord and the undersigned subscribers, n.d.

71 "The Bell and Laing School Papers," *Lennox and Addington Historical Society Papers and Records*, V (1914), 16-17. Similarly see P.A.O., Education Papers, John Lindsay Contracts; *ibid.*, Miscellaneous File.

72 *Bathurst Courier*, 12 June 1835.

73 Canniff Haight, *Life in Canada Fifty Years Ago ...* (Toronto, 1885), p. 157.

74 J.L.A., 1830, Appendix: Report of the Niagara District Board of Education.

75 P.A.O., RG2, F2, Report ... from No. 1 School Division, Burgess, 1842.

76 *Kingston Herald*, 14 Dec. 1841.

77 See for example P.A.C., RG5, A1, Vol. 51, Report of the Eastern District Board of Education, 7 Feb. 1821.

78 Tuition fees are usually given in the township returns in Gourlay, *Statistical Account*, Vol. 1. Payments in individual cases can be found in the teachers' contracts; see above fns. 69-71. For the law on school finance, see the Acts of 1816 and 1841 printed in D.H.E., I, 102-4, and IV, 48-55.

79 A point rarely acknowledged by any of the observers of Upper Canadian education with the notable exception of John Strachan, who repeatedly pointed out the degree of initiative shown by local people both before 1816 and after; for example, see G.W. Spragge, ed., *The John Strachan Letter Book*, p. 75.

80 For the United States, the classic statement of this argument is Bernard Bailyn, *Education in the Forming of American Society* (New York. 1960). Most recently, see Carl F. Kaestle, "Common Schools Before the 'Common School Revival': New York Schooling in the 1790s," *History of Education Quarterly*, XII. No. 4 (Winter 1972), 465-500. For summaries of the comparable British situation see J.W. Adamson, *English Education, 1789-1902* (Cambridge, 1930), especially Ch. I; E.G. West, *Education and the State* (London, 1965), Ch. 9; L.J. Saunders, *Scottish Democracy 1815-1840* (Edinburgh, 1950), 248ff.

*   *   *   *   *

Documents for Chapter Two

The following documents indicate the rudimentary nature of pioneer schools as well as society's expectations of teachers and students. To what extent do Documents 6 and 8 support Gidney's thesis in the previous chapter? Applying Gidney's optimistic and pessimistic interpretations to the Nova Scotia school commissioner's report for 1824 (Document 9), what information would an "optimist" use and what material would a "pessimist" select from this report? Based on Document 9, explain why the salaries of qualified teachers were so low, and why school attendance often dropped below 50%. Using Documents 7 and 10, compare pioneer school regulations to those of today's elementary schools.

6) NEWSPAPER ADVERTISEMENT FOR MISS RADCLIFFE'S SCHOOL, 1828[1]

TERMS

At Mrs. & the Miss RADCLIFFE'S School,
Niagara.
BOARDING with ordinary Tuition, including English Grammar, Geography with the use of Globes, History; Composition, Plain and Ornamental Needlework, &c, &c, &c,

	£ 6	0	0	Per Quarter
Writing & Ciphering, ... "	10	0		"
Day Scholars, (including Writing and Ciphering,) .... "	1 10	0		"
Music, ... "	1 10	0		"

Drawing, Velvet Painting, Artificial Flower & Card Work,
   charged separately.
No entrance money required.
No Pupil taken for any term less than six Months.
A quarters notice, or a quarters payment expected, previous to a
   pupil's leaving School.
No allowance for temporary absence. Each Lady to bring Bed &
   Bedding, Towels, Spoons, Knife & Fork, which will be returned.
Bills paid Quarterly.

7) RULES FOR OAKVILLE'S FIRST COMMON SCHOOL, UPPER CANADA, 1836[2]

1. School to be open at 9 o'clock a.m. and an intermission for fifteen minutes at ½ past Ten, and to be dismissed at 12 o'clock noon—to be called in at 2 o'clock p.m. an intermission for fifteen minutes at ½ past 3 p.m. and dismissed at 5 o'clock p.m.
2. Due regard to cleanliness, and the avoiding of all infectious diseases among the children in School such as the Itch and Whooping Cough, etc.
3. The pupils to be strictly required to observe good order at the intermission and noon hours, to avoid all screaming and useless noises, quarrelling, etc.
4. Good fires to be kept during all wet and damp days—
5. As all good children from their cradle are possessed by enquiring minds, that proper attention be given to all enquiries they may make relative to education in mildness, with an approbation of their conduct in so doing.
6. That swearing, calling of bad names be strictly forbidden.
7. That punctuality in attendance on the regular school hours be particularly required by the teacher, and also that his example in so doing be a sufficient warning to them—
8. That all pupils in the school do not be allowed to whisper and laugh during the school hours, and but one allowed to be out of school at a time, and not then without the consent of the teacher.
9. That the teacher be required to take a paternal as well as pedagogical care over all pupils placed under his tuition.
10. That the teacher requires each subscriber to the school to furnish his quota of firewood for the season and have it cut and properly piled for the use of the stove in said school house.

Some other minor laws are actually necessary which should be discretionary with the teacher by and with the advice and consent of the trustees.

*   *   *   *   *

8) THE HOUSEHOLD AS SCHOOL, 1839[3]

Thursday, January 24, 1839. This was school day; my new pupil is far in advance of the other children. My most distant scholars come twice a week. Mondays and Thursdays: the little ones likewise on a Wednesday, as they are close at hand, and it is worth while coming up for an hour ....

Tuesday, July 9, 1839. My school assembled in the afternoon, but we all felt the weather. I was sleepy, and the children were languid. I had a new scholar, a girl of ten or twelve years of age, not yet perfect in her letters. And now I think my number is up. When more come on I must turn some of the old ones off, unless I can introduce the mutual instruction system, or, as I cannot well extend my school hours, the benefit to each individual must be necessarily diminished by an increase of numbers. At present if the amount of good gained in a lesson is not very great, at any rate they are put into the way of learning, and rendered capable of improving themselves ....

Tuesday, December 3, 1839. I had my school today, but at present it consists only of my two oldest children. I do not regret it as these get a start from receiving more of my attention, whilst those I hope will not forget much who are at present kept away by bad roads and want of shoes. Schooling has been very light work for some time. First the harvest came, during which I had a very small attendance. Then the Regatta, which was a holiday. Afterwards potato-raising interfered a good deal, and now the roads ....

* * * * *

9) REPORT OF THE N.S. SCHOOL COMMISSIONERS, 1824

We add a list of such Masters as we know of being licenced, and also of such others as are general residents—None of these are constantly employed—At some periods, their respective neighbourhoods are scant of a *sufficiency of uneducated children* to form a school,—At other times, our resident masters are *undervalued* and *underbid* by itinerant strangers who offer to teach—Of these latter, some few have proved abandoned characters, *sufficiently specious* to deceive the ordinary class of settler, though, without any one solid literary qualification—Male and female instructors (not making teaching their steady profession) are occasionally engaged in neighbourhoods for a single season—These are often of the friends or relations of such neighbourhoods, disengaged (for the time) from more profitable employment—

To the third,]—fourth and fifth—[Questions]

The number of scholars attendant upon a school is very fluctuating—In the closest neighbourhoods, that, would be a very full school, which, should embrace, *during the most favorable seasons of the year,* from thirty five to forty scholars, including both sexes—, and *during some parts of the year* it must be expected to dwindle down to ten or fifteen—Children dwelling more than three miles from the school-house cannot well attend—Children of the poorer—and perhaps those of the next rising class of settlers, after the age of ten or twelve years cannot well be *spared from work*—If such improve in learning after that age it is by means of *Night-Schools*, kept *in time of Winter*—One or two neighbourhoods of our thickest settlement, may afford, within a sweep of three or four miles from a common centre, a constant annual list of sixty children (including both sexes and all ranks and degrees) between the age of four and twelve,—But, inferior health,—or the occasional want of decent cloathing [sic] are drawbacks form the school,—And so also are indifference, unsettled views,—domestic bustle, prejudices,—as well as, in some cases, *real poverty*, and in others, covetousness—subject, as every school is, to these deductions and considering that, the *maximum* of learning sought by the *generality* is no more than to read and write *indifferently*, and to cypher so far as to cast up pounds shilling & pence, it is not to be expected that, our best settled neighbourhoods could enable a school to average more than thirty scholars (boys with girls) by the Year ....

To the eighth and ninth
As before observed, none of our neighbourhoods have a constant or permanently established school—The settlers on the Town plot of Digby and at the mouth of Sissibou River come nearest to the accomplishment of this end—The whole Western District of Annapolis County might be cast into eleven school circuits of nearly equal magnitude and population—Each of these eleven would embrace an *extent of land* sufficient for a *very large* parish or township— In the present state of our settlements each one affords some central spot that is moderately populous—a regular school in each of these central positions would prove *more or less* beneficial to all the settlers, but least perhaps to the poorest—for our poorest settlers are nowhere to be found in a body, but detached and scattered on the out skirts [sic], upon new or barren tracts—The constant residence however of a sober, moral and orderly school-master, though possessing but slender literary qualifications, would be advantageously felt throughout the circuit—The decease of most *our elders* has left the *present race* of our inhabitants without any means of *benefiting by example*,—But, one *correct stationary man*, aided by the occasional visits and correspondence of the District Clergy, might strengthen the influence of the well disposed, and preserve something of just moral sentiment alive—

* * * * *

10) BY-LAWS OF THE UPPER CANADA ACADEMY, 1837[4]

In the Female Department, which is perfectly distinct, instruction will be given in all constituent parts of a superior English Education, and in French, Drawing and Embroidery.

Besides the ordinary routine of tuition, lectures on the Sciences and on other subjects of general utility, will be delivered; to which all Students susceptible of benefit from them will be admitted.

[The By-Laws for the regulation of students were strict.]

1. The hour of rising is, in summer, 5, and in the winter, 6—of retiring, 9, in the summer, and 10 in the winter. Morning and Evening Prayer in the Lecture Room, to be regularly attended with becoming reverence by all the Students.

2. As the foundation of that order is so essential in an Institution for the intellectual and moral training of youth, due respect and subordination to the Teacher and Officers of the Institution are imperative upon all placed under their tuition and care.

3. It is required that the conduct of the students be in all respects distinguished by moral propriety. All profane, obscene and indecent language; games of chance, and fighting or wrestling are among the grosser violations of the law.

4. All indecencies, such as writing upon the walls, loud speaking, whistling, or laughing within doors, playing in the halls or rooms, entering the house with dirty shoes, slovenliness of person or dress, rushing to or from meals, unbecoming conduct at table, and the odious practice of spitting on the floor, are strictly prohibited.

5. All who board in the Institution shall retire to their respective apartments immediately after tea, and occupy the evening in preparing their lessons for the subsequent day, or when these are dispatched, in improving reading or conversation. Permission will be very rarely granted to any to spend the evening out, and that only when it is known where and how they will occupy it, in which case they must always return before the 9 o'clock bell rings.

6. Each student will be held responsible for the appearance and furniture of his apartment, which he is to sweep out and clean every morning before breakfast, and in which he shall, at no time, indulge in or permit any boisterous or disorderly proceedings. No gossiping, unnecessary visiting, or assembling in groups in each others rooms, will by, any means, tolerated.

7. The front of the edifice is appropriated as a pace of exercise for the females—the rear, and playground, for the males. And more effectually to preclude all intercommunication between the sexes, their corresponding, conversing, or in any way, associating together, save in the case of brothers and sisters (and that by permission of the Principal or Preceptress) is expressly interdicted.

8. The Students shall all be present in their classrooms and under the eye of the Teacher during the hours of school, unless those, who, in consideration of the peculiar nature of their studies, obtain from the Principal, on the recommendation of the Teacher, the privilege of prosecuting them in their own apartments—a privilege, however, which will be accorded only to such as are known to be distinguished for habits of application and general good conduct.

9. None of the young ladies or gentlemen, entrusted by their parents to the

care of the Institution, are at liberty to go to the village, or to take excursions in the neighbourhood, to contract debts or to dispose of anything in their possession, without the concurrence of those upon whom its superintendence and direction devolves. It is confidently believed that it will be in perfect accordance with the views of the parents who sent their sons to this Institution, to treat as an offence, peculiarly revolting and ominous in youth—their using ardent spirits, or visiting taverns.

10. All letters to whomsoever written, by such as are placed there by their parents or guardians, must pass, on the female side through the hand of the Preceptress, and on the other through the Principal, for examination and approval. The first Monday in each month is the time appointed for writing letters—but whenever circumstances render a deviation from that time really necessary, an exemption will be readily granted.

11. All regular Students are required regularly to attend public worship on the Lord's Day, under the Ministry their parents may prefer. To prevent disorder, those attending the Wesleyan Chapel will walk together, the young gentlemen preceding the ladies, going and returning. Neither riding nor visiting for pleasure on the Sabbath, making the slightest disturbance, within doors, nor lounging about the premises, in a word, no species of conduct by which that hallowed day would be desecrated, will be connived at.

12. Day Scholars are not permitted to linger in, or about the Institution, after the regular hours of School. During the time of recess at noon should they not be required by their parents to go home to dinner, they may remain in their class room, or take exercises on the premises, but they are not to enter the rooms of resident Students in their absences. In case of their staying away, or attending irregularly, they will be required to produce a written apology from their parents.

13. It is expected and required of all that board in the Institution, that they will render the situation of the Steward and Stewardess, whose ordinary duties demand such unceasing labor and attention, as comfortable as they can, by studiously avoiding giving them any trouble additional to their daily operations, except in cases of extreme necessity. None of the Scholars are allowed to visit the Steward's residence, unless invited by them or the Stewardess, or sent by one of the Teachers. Immediately after meals all are to leave the Dining Hall.

14. As a cautionary expedient against fire, it is deemed highly necessary to require, that during the time fires are allowed in the rooms, the doors be left unlocked in the night, that the stove may be inspected by a person appointed for that purpose. Any Students detected in kindling fire, after the stove shall have been inspected, unless it be required by sudden indisposition, will forfeit by the first offence the comfort of fire in their rooms for one week, and by a repetition of it, the use of stoves altogether.

15. It is earnestly recommended to all within these walls to read a chapter of the Bible and offer prayer every morning and evening to Him who by his Apostle has said, "If any man lack wisdom, let him ask of God, who giveth to all men liberally and unabraideth not, and it shall be given him." Minor violations of these laws, all of which it is believed are salutary and reasonable, will elicit rebuke, or receive appropriate degrees of correction—grosser infractions of them, especially if persisted in after admonition, will subject the delinquent to the disgrace of expulsion.

A copy of these Regulations will be given to each student on entering; the acceptance of which will be considered as a pledge of compliance therewith.

* * * * *

1 *Niagara*, 9 December 1828.
2 Quoted in S. Houston and A. Prentice, *Schooling and Scholars in Nineteenth-Century Ontario* (Toronto: University of Toronto Press, 1988), 57-58.
3 Quoted in H.H. Langton, ed., *A Gentlewoman in Upper Canada: The Journals of Anne Langton.* Anne Langton was educated in Rome and Switzerland and later moved to her brother's farm near Sturgeon Lake, Upper Canada—about which she wrote, "I assure you there cannot well be a more unpoetical and unromantic existence than ours." Once their farm was established, she had more time for other interests, and Anne taught children in the district, wrote journals, and painted sketches of rural life.
4 Quoted in Marion Royce, "Methodism and the Education of Women in Nineteenth-Century Ontario," *Atlantis,* Vol. 3, No 2 (Spring 1978), 134-37.

Chapter Three:
Teaching as a Career for Women

By the middle of the nineteenth century, every colony but Canada East (Quebec) was moving towards greater state control over education. This included teacher training and certification, curriculum and textbooks, and school inspections. The first priority was trained, professional teachers. Normal schools (renamed teachers' colleges in Ontario in 1953) provided instruction in modern pedagogical ideas. These teaching techniques were then developed in model schools under the guidance of master teachers. The first normal schools were established in Toronto (1847), Fredericton (1848), and Truro (1855).

Since most prospective teachers had only ten or eleven years of schooling, normal schools taught the subject matter that the teachers would be required to cover once they acquired a teaching position. The students, depending upon how well they did in their examinations, qualified for a first, second, or third class license—and the corresponding salaries.

Initially, the authorities discouraged women from becoming teachers. However, since male teachers were in short supply, and as women were willing to accept less pay than men for equal work, and were not as liable to leave for better jobs, they were gradually accepted into the teaching ranks—especially in the lower grades where their perceived nurturing qualities and moral superiority were considered important. Male teachers were recognized for their acquired education and hard work, whereas females were accepted for their innate abilities as mothers and wives. In Nova Scotia, which allowed school boards to hire women as public school teachers in 1838, women were not allowed to write the examination for the first-class teacher's certificate until 1869. The Toronto Normal School provided separate entrances, classrooms, and corridors for males and females, and students were punished for talking to the opposite gender in and outside of class.

The following account of Annie Leake's career as a teacher in rural Nova Scotia provides an in-depth examination of one female teacher in this transition period. Using Leake's autobiography, Marilyn Färdig Whiteley explores her motivation in becoming a teacher, the new teacher-training programme, the problems of a rural, female teacher, and her attempts to cope with them.

Additional secondary sources on early teacher training and female teachers include: Janet Guildford, "'Separate Spheres': The Feminization of Public School Teaching in Nova Scotia, 1838-1880," *Acadiensis*, 22, 1 (Autumn, 1992); Alison Prentice, "'Friendly Atoms in Chemistry': Women and Men at Normal School in Mid-Nineteenth Century Toronto," in D. Deane, C. Read eds., *Old Ontario: Essays in Honour of J.M.S. Careless* (Toronto, 1990); and George D. Perry, "'The Grand Regulator': State Schooling and the Normal-School Idea in Nova Scotia, 1838-1855," *Acadiensis*, 32, 2 (Spring, 2003).

* * * * *

Annie Leake's Occupation: Development of a Teaching Career, 1858-1886[42]

In 1911, Annie Leake Tuttle wrote about a pivotal moment in her life, an incident that had occurred when she was seventeen:

> Sometime during the Spring of 1857 Miss Bessie Buckley our Preachers daughter, came running over to our home, asking, would I go with her down to the Presbyterian Church and hear Dr. Forrester of the Normal School Truro give a lecture .... I secured mother's consent, and went to this lecture, and it proved a turning point in my life. I there heard, or had the way set before me, whereby I could secure the coveted education and self support, if I could only become a School teacher. Oh! how I listened and I daresay prayed for help.[1]

Annie Leake was the fourth of thirteen children of Olevia Lockhart and Thomas Leake, who lived at Crossroads, two miles north of Parrsboro, Nova Scotia. Their farm and carpenter shop returned to them a meagre livelihood, and Annie at age ten had gone to live and work in the homes of first one uncle, and then a second. Her opportunities for schooling had been severely limited. Now, at seventeen, she was again living at home; she was a recent Methodist convert, hungry for more education, and anxious to be a contributor, rather than a burden, to the family economy.

Annie lived at a time of significant change in education in her native province: there was movement toward free graded schools employing trained teachers. John William Dawson, the first Superintendent of Education, had campaigned for the establishment of a normal school. The legislature agreed in 1854 to found a teacher-training institution that opened the following year in Truro. Meanwhile Dawson had resigned, and Alexander Forrester took over as Superintendent of Education in 1854, and as principal of the new Normal School.

Forrester worked untiringly to gain support for the professional education of teachers that would prepare them to work in a system of education intended to educate the child "as a whole: *i.e.,* physically, intellectually, moraly."[2] Patterned on the Training System of David Stow in Glasgow, it combined elements of the "Objective System" based on Pestalozzi with moral education grounded in the Bible. According to Forrester, training teachers for this work would raise the quality of education, increase the number of female teachers, and help to establish teaching as a permanent employment and indeed a profession.[3] Annie was one of the young women Forrester encouraged to enter teaching; unlike many, she became a "career" teacher.[4] For her, this new educational movement offered a significant new opportunity.

Annie Leake began to write her life story in 1906, long after her twenty-seven years of teaching were over. Annie had observed many changes in her lifetime, and she knew that the next generation could not picture the old ways unless she described them in detail. Thus her autobiography allows us to see through her eyes a major transition in the history of Canadian education. It shows the inadequacies of the old system under which she was educated. It also demonstrates the possibilities of the new, formalized system that offered a permanent, professional career for an ambitious and dedicated young woman.[5] It offers insight into the problems of one rural female teacher, and her strategies for coping with them, and, finally, it illustrates the career limitations faced by one woman at that time.

The life story of Annie Leake serves as a case study, illuminating many of the discussions concerning women who entered teaching, especially rural teaching, in the nineteenth century.[6] Especially significant is the insight the autobiography offers concerning Annie's motivation. In an article comparing the views of nineteenth-century male school reformers in New England with the private writings of female teachers from the same period and area, Jo Anne Preston identifies two common aspirations of these women: they wished to pursue their intellectual interests, and they desired good wages so that they might lead independent lives.[7] Annie Leake showed clearly and directly in her autobiography that teaching attracted her for the same reasons. Yet another element runs through the text, that of spiritual purpose, of her belief in a divine plan for her life. Teaching provided Annie with "the coveted education and self support," and "suited [her] temperament & ambition;" at the same time, it offered a deep satisfaction to an idealistic evangelical woman.

Annie's first contact with schooling came when she went as a young visitor to the nearby school. Her autobiography describes the log schoolroom with its immense fireplace, desk running around three sides, slab seats, and chair for the master. She

> was perched up, upon one of those slab seats, legs dangling in the air,
> & no support for my back. A boy stood not far away, with his back to
> the fire and a ruler in his hand. His duty was, to watch the scholars at
> their books, that they did not look off or raise their eyes from study. If
> one was so unfortunate to do so, the ruler was thrown at that one and
> they had to pick it up and carry it to the Master, to be slapped, and

then take the place, to watch others. I was not a timid child but I had fears, that day, until I found out that I was not counted in. But I went no more while that old fashioned Master had rule.

Annie's own schooling began when she was eight; the school had a teacher "a little more modern." He was Edward Vickery, later a member of the provincial parliament. Annie reported that in six months she was able to read in the New Testament, one of their few schoolbooks.[8] She studied for a year with Vickery, for six months with James Sproule who would later become her brother-in-law, and for a few weeks with a female teacher. This was Annie's primary period of schooling.

As Annie put it, her days of childhood ended when she was ten. Her uncle, Albert Lockhart, asked whether she could come and help in his home. She recognized her family's struggle to earn a livelihood, and went. Although she was living not far from her parents' home, she was far indeed from the life of her childhood as she worked nine months for her aunt and uncle, and did not attend school.

The next fall, another uncle, Christopher Lockhart, asked whether Annie could come help his wife. He was a Methodist minister stationed far away in Chatham, New Brunswick, but he promised "much better advantages ... in getting an education" than Annie could have at the farm near Parrsboro. That was the bait she needed, and Annie replied, "If I can go to School all the time I will go." The promise was not kept. Christopher's wife found Annie too useful, and treated her as a servant. Annie calculated that she attended school six months of the sixteen that she was in Chatham. Yet that short time had value. Davice Howe, the teacher, used the "monitorial system," assigning even someone as untaught as Annie "classes in the Alphabet to teach." Howe told her that she had the "teaching Gift." The girl whose previous accomplishments had been picking wild strawberries and mixing buckwheat pancakes had now been recognized as possessing a skill that would later provide her with her occupation.[9]

After more than a year in Chatham, Annie returned to her parents for a few months. Then, when she was thirteen, she assisted her Uncle Christopher in Aylesford, Nova Scotia. There was no school nearby, so she got her education "in the care of children and domestic science." She spent the following year helping her parents. By now she was "old enough to be useful." She wrote, "it was a busy household and my education was going on in many lines, but not at School."

About the time of her fifteenth birthday, she returned with her uncle to Aylesford with little expectation of schooling. Briefly, however, Annie had an opportunity:

Quite early in the Spring there was a School opened near, taught by a young lady, whom I think had received some training at Normal School Truro if it was so it was during the winter 1855, the year of opening, of that Institution. At least, she knew how to teach, and I was ready & eagar to learn. But alas I had only six weeks of the priviledge, Uncle was removed from Aylesford to Barington at the coming Conference.

In Barrington, Annie's frustration was acute: the good school there was too far for her nephew to walk to, so he and Annie attended a private school in an upstairs bedroom. Years later she wrote bitterly, "I felt it an injustice then, I feel it so still. Miss McDonald who taught the school was a lady as also was her mother Mrs. Crowell. But it was sewing, fancy work, some reading and writing, but Oh dear where was my arithmetic & grammar & spelling & history etc."

Recognizing the unlikelihood of getting an education in her uncle's household, and no longer willing to work there as a servant, Annie returned to her parents in June of 1856. Anxious about what she "was going to do with herself" in her parents' "already overcrowded home," she helped with the household work, and educated herself as best she could.

My father was a reader, and as there was a very good school library in Town father brought home such books as "Dick Astronomy" "Life of Columbus" etc. etc. I can see myself seated at a table in the common living room of the family, which was heated at this time by a cooking stove. On the table was one tallow candle, and by that father & I was reading & mother sewing often darning or patching the children's clothing. In addition to the reading I was also knitting socks or mittens for the children. There were six brothers to knit for at this time and all at home, so mother could not spare me time to read without knitting also. It was no very great hardship to me as I had learned to knit before I could remember, and my mind was on Search for knowledge.

It was while she was seventeen, and living at home, that Annie was converted. She had been brought up among Methodist influences, with one uncle a minister, her brother-in-law, James Sproule, a local preacher, and her Grandfather Lockhart an exhorter "especially gifted in Prayer." Yet Annie did not experience conversion until February, 1857. This was the turning point in her personal life. It also led to the development of her talents: when her grandfather travelled to lead prayer services, sometimes she went along to give her testimony. Thus she became accustomed to speaking in public.

Then in May, 1857 she heard Dr. Forrester when he came to Parrsboro on one of the speaking tours he made at the close of each Normal School term. He travelled to promote the cause of education, and listening to him, Annie saw a new option: she could become a trained teacher! This would satisfy her yearning for education, her restlessness under the discipline of her mother, and her desire to be self-supporting. Annie's statement that she "prayed for help" is no mere conventional language; she had undergone her conversion experience only three months earlier. In her autobiography she originally described Forrester's lecture as "the turning point" in her life, and then changed it to "a turning point." Annie affirmed the pivotal nature of the earlier conversion experience, but it was the second event that provided her with a specific aim. A teaching career as Forrester described it no doubt appeared especially suitable to the zealous convert because Forrester was a Presbyterian minister for whom religion played an important role in education. Now Annie knew what she wanted to do with herself.

But how? Annie had no money for Normal School. While Forrester had given her the dream, it was James Sproule who suggested the practical means. Annie could teach in order to send herself to Normal School. She failed in her first attempt to get a position, but a year later, in May, 1858, Sproule fitted up space in his home at West Brook for a schoolroom. Ten subscribers agreed to pay twenty shillings each for six months of education for their children, and Annie became a schoolteacher.[10]

Annie recognized how poorly trained she was. "But," she wrote, "I knew something of the 'Three R's.' So, in reading, spelling, multiplication [sic] table, and the fundamental rules of arithmetic I drilled my fifteen or twenty pupils successfully. At the same time I studied the English Grammar, some Geography & Arithmetic with my Brother in law." In November, after her first teaching term had ended, Annie obtained a Second Class Certificate. This allowed her a share in the provincial support given to certified teachers.[11] She taught at Apple River from December until April. Here she was anxious about her ability to govern the young men who came out of the lumber camps and into her classroom at the end of winter but, she wrote, "my fears were groundless, they conducted themselves as young Gentlemen, and were a help in the government of the younger ones."[12]

Then, at last, Annie was able to go to Truro as a student. It was a two-day journey by stagecoach from Parrsboro to Truro.[13] She arrived in May, 1859, three-and-a-half years after the opening of the Normal School. With the help of the Methodist minister, Annie found a boarding home, and began her studies. The school had a faculty of four. As its principal, Forrester gave instruction in education and in natural science. There was also a professor of English and classics, one of mathematics and natural philosophy, and one of music. The students observed and practised in the Model School that was a vital part of Stow's system of teacher teaming. Opened in 1857, it employed four teachers who supervised the education of about two hundred pupils.

Annie's autobiography acknowledges her deficiencies but also her determination:

They soon discovered that I had come to learn, and that I knew somewhat at least my ignorance. One difficulty I had then and have never been able to overcome, I was constitutionally a poor speller, a poor speller by inheritance, it belonged to the family. This hampered me a lot. I could do nothing scarcely taking notes, but I could comprehend, and my memory was good, so I could often give Dr. Forrester what he wanted from his yesterday's lecture when others with piles of notes were dumb. Then I had acquired the use of my voice, hearing it in Public without alarm, and truly I got through this first Term at Normal School wonderfully considering.

The plan of study was, in fact, arranged to accommodate those like Annie who arrived with gaps in their education: the first month of each term was devoted to a "thorough review of the work ... with a considerable variety of preliminaries."[14] At the end of the month, Forrester heard the students, and if necessary altered their classification before they began the regular session of nearly four months. Annie, at the end of her first term, was among those whose "deficiencies in scholarship when they entered" prevented them from reaching "the requisite attainments to entitle them to a Second Class Diploma."[15] She had, however, studied at her "first really good Public School," and she was thoroughly dedicated to the Model School methods of education taught there.

Her brother-in-law suggested that she teach in the village of New Canaan, where the people had recently built a new schoolhouse, but there was a problem:

They had arranged their desks all around the sides of the room according to ancient custom. But how could I manage a School according to Model School patern [sic] without the children seated facing me, and I standing upon a platform before them? So I had James Sproule call a meeting of the supporters of the School and lay the matter before them .... this School house was the only preaching place in this Section and the seats so arranged would be inconvenient for the congregation. But I pleaded my cause before these hardy sons of toil, and secured at least a compromise. The seats were arranged facing the teacher, but they were long seating, some six or more instead of only two.[16]

Thus Annie obtained some of the conditions necessary for teaching according to the new methods. She wrote, "So New Canaan had the advantage of my first putting into practice my instruction in 'The Normal School.'" However, she was not invited to continue beyond that one term. She explained, "I was too modern I imagine."

In the spring of 1860 she lived again in her sister's home, and taught nearby. Here, too, she attempted to teach as she had been taught: she closed the school with a public examination conducted as closely as possible "according to Normal Instruction." An elderly lady remarked to Annie at the close, "Oh! I suppose we could have done the same if we had 'Cheek enough.'"[17] Not everyone was ready for Annie's modern methods.

For a year she taught in Parrsboro, with three of her brothers and two of her sisters among her students. Then in November, 1861, she resumed going to the Normal School. She was part of a class of thirteen working toward a First Class Diploma.[18] In March of 1861, Annie proudly received the First Class Diploma which, unlike a local licence, entitled her to teach anywhere in Nova Scotia.

Annie taught until the following November at Athol in what she described as "a little old School house on the edge of a bank, where with what help I could secure I had knocked out the remains of the ceiling and had the inner roof white washed and the beams trimmed with spruce or fir boughts [sic]. This was another attempt to carry out the principles received at Normal School." The building could not be used for a school in winter, so she spent that season living once more in the home of her Uncle Christopher, now in Annapolis, where she took the place of a teacher attending Normal School.

Annie returned to Athol, where a cookhouse had been prepared as a school. It "had been roughly but comfortably seated according to improved ideas and there was a rough platform and a desk of some kind." With her father's help, Annie mounted maps that she obtained from Provincial Supply. On his lathe her father turned a good-sized wooden ball that she painted as a globe, and he turned and she painted one hundred and forty-four smaller balls; these they strung on wires to make a "ball frame," or abacus. School inspector James Christie lamented the lack of modern teaching equipment in Cumberland County: there were only four or five globes, and a few ball frames. Annie Leake, however, ensured that her school was well-prepared for the new methods, with a globe and an abacus of her own devising, and with an unabridged dictionary purchased with a gold piece she received from an aunt.[19]

Model School methods also required singing; Forrester quoted with approval the view that "to attempt to conduct an infant or primary school without music, is as impossible as to govern a nation without laws."[20] He regarded vocal music and physical exercise to be simultaneously "intellectual stimulants and moral sedatives."[21] Unfortunately Annie could not sing a note. At Athol, however, a friend came in to the school to teach songs. Another part of Forrester's method was "to give the Bible to the Children" in the form of Bible stories, precepts, and memory verses. This harmonized well with Annie's own beliefs, and she gave the lessons happily, hoping that they "left an impression at least they helped me to govern as far as I could by 'Moral Suasion.'" Thus in the equipment of the room and in her own teaching she was well prepared when Forrester himself paid a visit to her school. She wrote, "Everything was rough, but clean and brightened up as best we could. He was delighted, a perfect little Model School, was his Compliment and of course I was pleased."[22]

This "perfect little Model School" could not be used in the winter, however, and again Annie moved. A man from "The Brook," near Amherst, fitted up a vacant house as a school, secured students, and offered Annie the exceptional salary of four hundred dollars a year. She taught there two years, from the fall of 1863 to that of 1865. These were "the days before we had a School System, the last days of the old law:" The Free School Act of 1864 brought free public education to Nova Scotia, and the people in nearby Amherst were building a graded school to fulfil the requirements of the new law. Annie was ambitious to teach there. As a graduate of the Normal School, she was already among the better-qualified teachers in the province.[23] Annie felt, however, that if she wished to teach in the new school, she needed to prepare herself.

Thus Annie studied at the Branch Institution for Females of the Mount Allison Wesleyan Academy in Sackville, New Brunswick, from November, 1865 until the following May. The Academy offered a systematic course of "solid studies" that would prepare young women "to exert a moral influence, the stronger always for being associated with intellectual vigor."[24] Annie worked hard learning mathematics, French, and Latin. Although she could not attend for a second year in which she would have earned the Academy's Mistress of Liberal Arts degree, Annie left Sackville confident that she had made an investment in her future.

However, opposition to the new school legislation had been strong, and the citizens found ways in which to express their unhappiness:[25]

I returned to Amherst and taught in the old School during the Summer fully expecting to take the position, I had prepared myself for and made application. The people had been taxed to build the house, and when the time came to vote money for the teachers [sic] salaries the amount was not sufficient for the purpose. My application was received but the salary offered was so much less than I had been receiving ... that I rejected it, and at once made up my mind that I would leave Amherst. I wrote this rejection to the School authorities, at once after receiving it. I wrote also at once to Dr. Forrester telling him what I had done and why, and then packed my few belongings, and secured a passage in the Stage, that would take me to Parrsboro the next day. I often wonder since, where the courage came from, to do it, to throw myself out of what was considered the best position in my native country. I had of course asked Dr. Forrester, Principal of Normal School for a position, in some other part of the Province.

Annie knew well the distress of unemployment: many times she had wondered anxiously what she would do next. Yet the girl who once decided that she would no longer work as a servant for her uncle's wife had become a young woman who would not accept a position that offered an inadequate salary.[26]

In turning down the post and letting Forrester know of her needs, Annie Leake once again overcame her problems in the same way she had done this throughout her years as a teacher in rural Nova Scotia. Independent by nature, Annie managed her own career under what were often difficult circumstances. Yet she worked in co-operation with others and welcomed their aid. Just as she improved the school house at Athol "with what help [she] could secure," and worked the lathe with her foot while her father turned the one hundred and forty-four balls for the abacus, so she wrote letters and travelled and also accepted assistance from her brother-in-law, her uncle, and her mentor, in her search for teaching positions.[27]

Forrester was no longer the Superintendent of Education; in the reorganization that accompanied the new legislation, he had lost that position to retain only the post of Principal of the Normal School. Yet quickly and in an unexpected way he came to Annie's aid. He invited her to become head of the primary or infant department of the Model School in Truro. She told Forrester of her inability to sing, but he promised her assistance, and she accepted a position that she described as "far above my highest dreams at the time." She went on to record that perhaps her "highest motive in writing all this down is to show the wonderful Providence of 'Our Father' in thus helping me on from Step to Step in the work, He *wished* me to do."

For ten years Annie taught her young students and supervised the pupil-teachers, and sometimes conducted for Forrester the model Bible lessons that formed part of the training of the young teachers. Annie herself became a role model for the pupil-teachers. Many years later, one of them gave testimony in a newspaper interview: "We younger teachers looked upon Miss Leake as superior; and her silent influence upon us was for good. In any doubtful situation that arose, we would question ourselves and each other as to what Miss Leake would say of the matter."[28] After Forrester's death in April, 1869, John B. Calkin became Principal, and Annie continued to teach in the Model School.

Two items in Annie's scrapbook hint at her professional involvement while she worked in Truro. One is a letter written early in 1869 by T.H. Rand, who had succeeded Forrester as provincial Superintendent of Education. Rand acknowledged receiving from Forrester the manuscript of a "Phonic Primer" prepared by Annie. With Forrester's strong support, the phonic method of instruction was gaining favour. The *Nova Scotia Series* readers were supplanting the imported books that had been used throughout the region, but the new readers were not without their critics.[29] Nevertheless, Rand gave Annie's manuscript a less than warm reception:

Will you be so good as to give me a statement of the *specific plan* of your primer-& wherein it differs from other phonic primers. Also a brief explanation of the lines on the flyleaf.

If you specify what you deem the *merits* of your book, I shall be in a better position to examine it with the conviction that I am not overlooking any of its merits.[30]

There is no further record of Annie's attempt at textbook production, and no copy of her primer.

If Annie was discouraged in this attempt to establish herself as a professional, she must have found more pleasing a letter from J. Parsons sent later that year. He asked her to write a paper to be read at the Educational Association's annual convention. He explained:

We wish to bring more of the practical into our deliberations and must look to the Teachers to perform the work. *Order and Management in the Primary Department of a Graded School* is what we felt would be interesting and beneficial, and one with which you are familiar. We want a paper that will open the subject for discussion without necessarily settling every difficulty raised.[31]

The report of that meeting states that on 27 December, Parsons read an essay "written by a lady teacher .... The essay was well written and instructive, and abounded in practical suggestions for the training of the little ones."[32] Thus Annie Leake contributed anonymously and *in absentia* to the educational discussion of her day.

In 1873 she took a rest period of six months. During part of this time she visited a brother who had moved to Boston. She took with her a letter of introduction to the Superintendent of Public Schools so that "one of our most successful Primary School Teachers" might visit schools there.[33] In November, she returned to Truro with her salary increased fifty dollars to three hundred and fifty dollars a year. There she continued teaching until she received an unexpected visitor in December, 1876.

A new education act in Newfoundland for the first time gave money to the Methodists to be used for teacher training. The Methodist Church already ran an academy in St. John's, and it responded promptly to this opportunity. In October, George Milligan, the Superintendent of Methodist Schools, was authorized by the Board of Directors "to get a teacher (female) for the Normal School—at a Salary not exceeding $400 per annum."[34] This turned out to be more difficult than they expected. At a special meeting in December, Milligan made a proposition

that he would altho at personal inconvenience—proceed to the neighboring provinces forthwith—(his expenses being paid) and endeavor by such special effort to secure the services of the needed Teacher ... this proposition was agreed to by the Directors—as also discretionary powers if need be to advance $100 on the sum before named as the Salary of such Teacher.[35]

Thus, in December, Milligan arrived in Truro and called at the house where Annie was boarding. They talked for about half an hour, he offered the higher salary as he had been authorized to do, and Annie agreed to go to St. John's. In January she took charge of the new Model School.

According to Milligan's annual report, the school was in an "unpretending" but comfortable building, with the infant schoolroom on the ground floor, and the primary room on the second floor. "Both rooms," he wrote, "have American desks and chairs (to accommodate one hundred and twenty pupils), ample black-boards, maps, illustrated cards, a small globe, ball frames, a set of kindergarten toys, and other things suitable for an Infant or Primary school."[36] Annie's employer was supplying the type of equipment that Annie had once struggled to obtain.

To her dismay, however, she discovered about one hundred students waiting for her! An assistant was hired to help with the infant students, and Annie had charge of the primary class of at least seventy, and again supervised the pupil-teachers. At the end of the first year, Milligan reported, "The primary department in both divisions is conducted much to my satisfaction; and it is not saying too much for it, that it is truly a model school, and as personal visitation of similar Institutions in several countries enables me to know, that in elementary work it will compare favourably with them."[37]

Milligan's reports continued to wax enthusiastic, but the minutes of the Directors' meetings show that Annie was not always satisfied with the conditions. She complained about the uncleanly schoolrooms and the state of the water closets. She may not have complained formally about her salary although it remained the same, while members of the academy faculty and Annie's assistant received increases. In her autobiography, however, she lamented that the pay was much less generous than it had appeared because living expenses were so high in St. John's.[38] Yet she stayed ten years, working ten months each year, and sailing home to her family during the summer.

While she taught, Annie also continued her own education in a manner that had only recently become possible. She undertook the Chautauqua Literary and Scientific Circle directed home-reading programme. Growing out of the summer assemblies that began in 1874 at Chautauqua Lake, New York, for the training of Sunday-school teachers, this four-year correspondence course offered instruction in such areas as literature, history, and science. It was first offered in 1878, and Annie probably began her work two years later, for she completed it in 1884. Once more her thirst for education caused Annie to study; working among well-educated colleagues, she may also have welcomed the prestige of the Chautauqua Diploma.

In the summer of 1886, Annie found that her father's health was failing. She, the available daughter, resolved to aid her parents. When she returned to work, she also tendered her resignation. A committee asked her to reconsider. Annie described the scene:

> I do not forget the gentlemen of that Committee, the whole scene as I stood upon the platform and heard their plea I replied I have stood upon this platform for ten years, and really am tired, although I may not look so, but I would remain, only I promised my father that I would come home and stay with him while he lived. I said my parents brought up twelve children, and I am the only one who can go home to them, in this their time of need. Nothing more was said, my resignation was accepted, and a pupil of my own training was appointed in my place.

Part of the official version differs. According to the minutes, Annie consented at one point to reconsider her resignation, but then declined "as the Board had not offered her any financial inducement."[39] Annie's account made no mention of this, although she had felt overworked and underpaid. Concerning her departure from Truro, she had written that "one gets tired of working year after year in the same groove or I suppose I did." More than a century later we cannot determine what blend of fatigue, family duty, and financial frustration caused Annie's decision, but as the bells of St. John's rang in the new year of 1887, she waited aboard a steamer to sail for Nova Scotia. It had been almost thirty years since Forrester's lecture had suggested to Annie what she might do with herself. Annie had advanced in her career by working in a specialization which was seen as acceptable for women, teaching young children and training the teachers of young children.[40] Now, finally, she had left the classroom.

Annie's life was far from over. After her father's death, she spent five years in Victoria, British Columbia, as the first matron of a rescue home for Chinese prostitutes, an experience that called upon all of her skills in teaching and management. Then, two years after she left Victoria, she renewed acquaintance with Milledge Tuttle of Pugwash, Nova Scotia. They had talked of marriage when she was a young teacher, but his parents had interfered. Years later she observed philosophically, "I believe I was called to a mission much more suited to my temperament and ambition. That I had loved and could not 'put off the old love and put on the new' was a help to me in my occupation. I would have been a disappointed woman if I had not had my occupation which suited me exactly." Now Milledge was a widower. They married, and for seven years Annie occupied herself as wife and step-mother.

Then, in 1902, Milledge died. Annie considered returning to the classroom, but, she wrote, "was told and perhaps felt that I had better leave that work for those younger in years." For five years, she lived with friends and relatives. Then she entered the Old Ladies' Home in Halifax, not because she felt old, but because she needed a home.[41] She remained active for many years in Missionary Society and WCTU work, and died twenty-seven years after moving to Halifax, at the age of ninety-five.

Annie Leake Tuttle was one of the pioneering professionals for whom the educational reforms of the nineteenth century made room. Growing up with limited prospects for education or earning a livelihood, she seized the opportunity offered by Normal School training and became one of the new professional female teachers. Motivated by a longing for education and by a desire for financial and personal independence, she found satisfaction in an occupation that also gave scope for her idealism and her sense that Annie's divine Father had plans for her. After years of moving from one rural school to another, Annie worked as part of the teacher-training system and served as a role-model to young women. Her career was limited to the instruction of the less advanced students and of their teachers: we recognize this as a constraint. Yet we must acknowledge that to Annie, her attainments seemed far beyond her highest dreams; the frustration that she recognized and expressed in her autobiography was the difficulty of gaining continuous employment at adequate pay in properly equipped schools. Despite these difficulties, however, Annie Leake Tuttle was grateful for her opportunity to have her "occupation which suited [her] exactly."

NOTES

*An earlier version of this paper was presented at the meeting of the Canadian History of Education Association in October of 1990. I wish to thank Alison Prentice for encouraging me to look at the Annie Leake material from this perspective, and for giving the manuscript her remarkably thoughtful and helpful attention.

1 The autobiography of Annie Leake Tuttle and also her letters and scrapbooks are in the possession of the Reverend J. Ernest Nix of Mississauga, Ontario. I am grateful for the generous access which he and his family have given me to this remarkable collection, and for his gracious help and encouragement. Unless otherwise identified, all quotations are from the Annie Leake Tuttle autobiography. Spelling and style follow the original document.

2 Alexander Forrester, *The Object, Benefits and History of Normal Schools with the Act of Legislature of Nova Scotia Anent Normal School etc.* (Halifax: James Barnes, 1855), 3. Forrester discussed the merits of these

systems in *The Teacher's Text Book* (Halifax: A. and W. Mackinlay, 1867), esp. 316-19.

3 Forrester, *The Object*, 4-5. Forrester favoured the employment of young women in primary schools because of their "natural fitness, both mental and moral," for that work. Later, in *The Teacher's Text Book*, he reported the general opinion "that the infant and primary departments are best fitted for the female, whilst the head masterships, and the more advanced sections, are for the male" because of the "position of subordination and of dependence assigned" to females by "the law of nature and revelation" (566). For the attitudes of Dawson, Forrester, and then later J.B. Calkin toward women teachers, see Alison Prentice, "The Feminization of Teaching," in *The Neglected Majority*, ed. Susan Mann Trofimenkoff and Alison Prentice (Toronto: McClelland and Stewart, 1977), 53.

4 Wayne Fuller has noted that rural teachers in the United States were not generally as "career oriented" as most urban teachers: "The Teacher in the Country School," in *American Teachers: Histories of a Profession at Work*, ed. Donald Warren (New York: Macmillan, 1989), 109. However, in their discussion of why work as teachers became available for women in rural Ontario and Quebec in the mid-nineteenth century, Danylewycz, Light, and Prentice note the presence of a few "career" teachers in rural Ontario during the period when Annie was teaching in Nova Scotia: Marta Danylewycz, Beth Light, and Alison Prentice, "The Evolution of the Sexual Division of Labour in Teaching: Nineteenth Century Ontario and Quebec Case Study," in *Women and Education*, ed. Jane Gaskell and Arlene McLaren (Calgary: Detselig Enterprises Ltd., 1987), 43-44.

5 On the relationship of formalized school systems to the feminization of teaching in the United States, see John L. Rury, "Who Became Teachers?" in *American Teachers*, 19.

6 Alison Prentice and Marjorie R. Theobald provide an excellent summary of the current state of this discussion in "The Historiography of Women Teachers: A Retrospect," in their *Women Who Taught* (Toronto: University of Toronto Press, 1991), 3-33, and Prentice deals with many of the research questions in "Multiple Realities: The History of Women Teachers in Canada," in *Feminism and Education: A Canadian Perspective*, ed. Frieda Forman et al. (Toronto: Centre for Women's Studies in Education, 1990), 125-44.

7 Jo Anne Preston, "Female Aspiration and Male Ideology: School-teaching in Nineteenth-Century New England," in *Current Issues in Women's History*, ed. Arina Angerman et al. (London: Routledge, 1989), 177-78.

8 The use of the Bible for teaching reading and spelling was "all but entirely discontinued" by 1867 according to Alexander Forrester, who applauded the change. "To use it in this way, was fitted not only to despoil the

Sacred volume of that sacredness and reverence with which its perusal should always be associated, but to awaken in the minds of the young positive dislike and abhorrence to its truths" (*Teacher's Text Book,* 188).

9   The monitorial system was one of the educational methods which Forrester criticized in his *Teacher's Text Book,* 313-14. He recognized, however, that "it is well fitted to discover those who possess an aptness to teach, whose gifts might be more beneficially employed in teaching than in any other pursuit or calling."

10   Annie first attempted to gain employment for a summer term, and first succeeded for the summer a year later; she does not say whether she attempted to obtain a school during the winter, but that could have been more difficult. On the seasonal pattern of women's teaching, see Alison Prentice, "The Feminization of Teaching," 53.

11   Her share for the work she had done was £4.10.0, as it was also for the next term of teaching. Public Archives of Nova Scotia [PANS], School Papers: Parrsboro (RG14 Vol. 74), 1858, 1859.

12   Seasonal "resource frontier" work by young men is one of the factors noted by Danylewycz, Light, and Prentice as making a greater place for female teachers in some areas ("The Evolution of the Sexual Division of Labour in Teaching," 42).

13   School commissioners from the students' home districts were supposed to pay the travelling expenses of "every student duly recommended to the Normal School," but Annie Leake's petition to the Parrsboro board "was not allowed." Remarks by Forrester suggest that this was a matter of contention with other boards as well. PANS, School Papers: Parrsboro (RG14 Vol. 74), Nov. 1859; *Journal of Education and Agriculture for Nova Scotia* 1, 2 (Aug. 1858).

14   *Register and Circular with Brief History and Condition of the Normal School of Nova Scotia, 1862* (Halifax, 1862), 21.

15   *Journal of Education and Agriculture for Nova Scotia* 2, 4 (Oct. 1859).

16   In his *Teacher's Text Book,* Forrester described with approval the classroom arrangement required by Stows Training System: "With the children all arranged in parallel rows and their eyes directed toward their teacher, the sympathy of numbers operates far more powerfully, and so blends all their thoughts and sentiments into one, rendering, thereby, the intellectual and moral development of one, or more, beneficial to the whole" (319).

17   While school examinations were, for Annie, part of Model School practice, she must have been aware of the approved way of conducting them: Forrester recognized the evil of examinations characterized by "external pomp," and called for examinations to be "fair representations of the actual condition of the school" (Teacher's Text Book, 522-24).

18   The *Register and Circular ... of the Normal School* 24, listed requirements

which differed in a few respects for male and female students. While the five men in the class would be required "to demonstrate any Proposition in the First Four Books of Euclid" and to show mastery of the rules of mensuration and the elements of land surveying and navigation, the eight women were held responsible only for the first book of Euclid and the elements of practical mathematics.

19 PANS, *Annual Report of the Common, Superior, Academic and Normal and Model Schools in Nova Scotia*, by the Superintendent of Education, 1865. The following year he complained that very few teachers possessed that "almost indispensable aid for procuring knowledge," an unabridged dictionary. The system adopted by Forrester required the use of visible objects in teaching the young; for the importance of the ball-frame, see *Teacher's Text Book*, 395.

20 Ibid., 247.

21 *Register and Circular ... of the Normal School*, 20.

22 A much later article in the *Halifax Chronicle* indicates that Forrester's tour was one which Annie herself arranged for him at his request because she knew the district. She scheduled lectures at West Brook, Maccan, Athol, Advocate Harbor, Spencers Island, Port Greville, and Parrsboro, and he followed the strenuous plan, remarking to her, "You've worked me hard" (*Halifax Chronicle*, 29 Jan. 1927).

23 In 1865 the school inspector reported ninety licensed teachers in Cumberland county, of whom ten held a First Class rating; Annie was one of the two women in this select group. PANS, *Annual Report*, 1865.

24 *The Mount Allison Wesleyan Academy Catalogue and General Circular*, 1865, 33. Annie's report of her studies does not completely harmonize with the course of study listed in the circular. "Latin or French" is listed for study by the Junior Class, along with rhetoric and chemistry; algebra, geometry, and trigonometry are listed as Senior Class subjects. Yet Annie reported: "I finished what was then, their Course in Mathematics, and studied Latin and French." While the circular stated that "it is considered desirable, whether they remain long enough to finish the course or not, that the order of the studies prescribed should be followed as far as circumstances will permit," perhaps Annie's circumstances did not "permit." On the ideals and realities of this schooling, see John G. Reid, "The Education of Women at Mount Allison, 1854-1914,"*Acadiensis* 12, 2 (Spring 1983): 3-33.

25 G.P. Hennessey studied the records of the Board of Trustees for the meeting held October 16, 1865, and wrote, "At this meeting it was resolved to raise land and erection of a building, furniture etc., for an Academy and Grade Schools, also that four hundred dollars, be raised by subscription for the support of schools for the year. This latter shows how averse

the meeting was to taxation for educational purposes. An amendment to the first sum of six hundred dollars was voted down." Cumberland County Archives, Amherst—Education collection, G.P. Hennessey, "Education in Amherst."

26 According to the report of the trustees to the ratepayers' annual meeting of 1867 (quoted by Hennessey in "Education in Amherst"), three women served in the new building when it opened. The one teaching in the preparatory department received $280, the one in the intermediate department received $260, and the one in the primary department received $140. Even this rate of pay was significantly above the "very lowest" pay scale specified by the 1864 act.

27 Annie had no formal support structure like that available later in rural British Columbia, described by J. Donald Wilson in "'I am ready to be of assistance when I can': Lottie Brown and Rural Women Teachers in British Columbia," in *Women Who Taught*, 202-29.

28 *Halifax Chronicle*, 5 Feb. 1927.

29 Judith Ann Evans, "Too Many Cooks Spoil the Broth: School Readers from a Century Ago," *Nova Scotia Historical Review* 2, 1 (1982): 69-70.

30 Scrapbook of Annie Leake Tuttle.

31 Ibid.

32 *Journal of Education* 29 (Feb. 1870): 451.

33 Scrapbook of Annie Leake Tuttle.

34 Newfoundland Conference of the United Church of Canada Archives, Minutes, Board of Directors, Wesleyan Academy, 18 Oct. 1876.

35 Ibid., 4 Dec. 1876.

36 *Report of the Public Schools of Newfoundland for the Year Ended Dec. 31, 1876* (St. John's: Robert Winton, 1877),12.

37 *Report of the Public Schools of Newfoundland under Methodist Boards for the year ended December 31, 1878* (St. John's: Morning Chronicle Office, 1879), 21.

38 Annie's time in Newfoundland is the one period for which there are records of her complaints other than in her autobiography. It is clear that during her career she was sometimes frustrated by the conditions under which she had to work, and by the inadequacy of her salary. In St John's she also had difficulty finding a suitable place to board. Unlike the women whom Lottie Brown attempted to assist in British Columbia (Wilson, "I am ready to be of assistance"), she did not complain of hostility or loneliness, and unlike the writers of those letters studied by Jo Anne Preston ("Female Aspiration and Male Ideology," 179), she spoke only with affection of her students. Of course she was writing many years after the events she described, yet the differences in attitude may not be attributable solely to the gap in time: perhaps her idealistic motivation

and sense of providence coloured her experience, her memory, or both.

39 Newfoundland Conference Archives, Minutes, Board of Directors, Wesleyan Academy, 8, 9, and 15 Nov. 1886.

40 Geraldine Jonçich Clifford refers to college and university teaching and school administration in her discussion of gender patterns and the "career ladder" in education in the United States ("Man/Woman/Teacher: Gender, Family and Career in American Educational History," in *American Teachers*, 326-28). Annie Leake's move to Model School teaching and the supervision of pupil-teachers would appear to be an alternate form of career progress.

41 She was able to do this because she had saved enough from her earnings to purchase a government annuity which paid her two hundred dollars a year. The Home cost one hundred, leaving her one hundred "for Church and personal use."

*   *   *   *   *

Documents for Chapter Three

Martha Hamm Lewis was the first accredited female teacher in New Brunswick. The following account of her teaching career provides an insight into the problems and motivations of early Maritime female teachers. How does Lewis' career compare to that of Annie Leake? It might prove worthwhile to role play Lewis' entrance and exit from class (complete with veil and curtsy) to gain at least a partial idea of her situation at the Normal School. Analyze the statistics in Document 12. Conjecture why Lower Canada had a much higher proportion of female teachers than did the other colonies, and why the percentage of female teachers gradually increased. Using document 13, describe the ideal teacher.

11) MARTHA HAMM LEWIS GOES TO NORMAL SCHOOL, 1849[1]

In the year of grace 1849 Martha Hamm Lewis of Saint John, N. B., then in her early twenties, led the womanhood of this province in a great advance—none the less epoch-marking if, at the moment, few followed in her wake, and her quiet penetration of the serried ranks of Mandom apparently was little heralded for the great victory it was!...

Miss Lewis loved her books; she had herself been educated at home by private tutors and had attended boarding school. There was a Grammar School in Saint John, in Fredericton, and others too, in the growing towns of New Brunswick, as well as many smaller schools. ALL WERE BEING TAUGHT

BY BOYS AND MEN, even though in some places, where there was no "SELECT ACADEMY FOR YOUNG LADIES," little girls sometimes attended those schools with their brothers.

She was confident that she knew as much or more than those boys whom she heard of as year by year attending the Normal School now flourishing in Saint John, and who proudly a year later produced the credentials that set seal to their ability to instruct the young. Had she not even coached many of these young men while they were attending the Normal School classes?

WHY SHOULD A GIRL NOT BE ALLOWED TO DO THE SAME? WHY NOT HERSELF BECOME A LICENSED TEACHER?...

Martha Hamm Lewis wrote to the authorities of the Normal School asking for admission. Her application was promptly refused. She wrote again, and again more insistently. The refusal was repeated as steadily; but there was nothing said to show that existing laws forbade,—she was refused entirely on the grounds of custom, expediency, "impossibility."

Finally Miss Lewis wrote to the Lieutenant-Governor. Correspondence ensued. The Governor ruled that she was not ineligible; and the momentous hour came when an Order-in-Council was passed directing that Miss Lewis be admitted to the Normal School, her contention as to no disqualification under provincial laws being upheld. This grave decision, however, was accompanied by a warning that Miss Lewis could in no wise hold them responsible for any results that might follow!

On receiving this dictum Mr. Duval, Head of the Normal School, is reported to have been overwhelmed with his increased responsibilities and to have walked the floor o' nights. This new step took one's breath (in 1849)! It might well be subversive of all discipline at the School! How would it fare with those tender youths committed to his care when this hardy and forward young woman came amidst them?! In solemn conclave it was decided that if Miss Lewis must be admitted, certain safeguards must be rigidly imposed! She must enter the classroom ten minutes before the other students! She must sit alone at the back of the room! SHE MUST ALWAYS WEAR A VEIL! She must make her curtsy to the teacher and retire from the classroom five minutes before the lecture ended, and leave the premises without speaking to any of those susceptible youths, her fellow students!...

But the term passed with no untoward incident at the school. Everyone breathed more freely; and those who had sponsored her brave step were vindicated. The following term Miss Lewis was accompanied by a friend. After that it must have been much easier to overlook the scoffing comments that reached her at times. And how much easier to curtsy together!

In 1850 (the license is still extant), Miss Lewis was given her credentials to teach in the parish of Upham, and in 1853 was licensed afresh to teach in Saint John city.

* * * * *

12) THE FEMINIZATION OF TEACHING, 1851-1871[2]

SEX RATIOS AMONG COMMON OR PUBLIC SCHOOL TEACHERS IN LOWER AND UPPER CANADA, NOVA SCOTIA AND NEW BRUNSWICK, 1851-1871

		LOWER CANADA		UPPER CANADA		NOVA SCOTIA		NEW BRUNSWICK	
		No.	%	No.	%	No.	%	No.	%
1851	males	—	—	2,251	77.8	662	80.2	—	—
	females	—	—	726	22.2	163	19.8	—	—
1856	males	892	32.2	2,622	71.1	485	56.0	—	—
	females	1,877	67.8	1,067	28.9	381	44.0	—	—
1861	males	1,270	29.9	3,031	69.9	649	69.6	—	—
	females	2,980	70.1	1,305	30.1	283	30.4	—	—
1871	males	1,115	21.8	2,641	49.8	806	52.6	402	44.2
	females	4,005	78.2	2,665	50.2	726	47.4	507	55.8

13) PROGRAMME FOR THE EXAMINATION AND CLASSIFICATION OF TEACHERS OF COMMON SCHOOLS ... FOR UPPER CANADA, 1855[3]

N.B.—Candidates are not eligible to be admitted to examination, until they shall have furnished the examiners with satisfactory evidence of their strictly temperate habits and good moral character.

QUALIFICATIONS OF THIRD CLASS TEACHERS.[52]

Candidates for certificates as third class teachers are required:

1. To be able to read intelligibly and correctly any passage from any common reading book.
2. To be able to spell correctly the words of an ordinary sentence dictated by the examiners.

3. To be able to write a plain hand.
4. To be able to work readily, questions in the simple and compound rules of arithmetic, and in reduction and proportion, and to be familiar with the principle on which these rule depend.
5. To know the elements of English grammar, and to be able to parse any easy sentence in prose.
6. To be acquainted with the elements of geography, and the general outline of the globe.
7. To have some knowledge of school organization and the classification of pupils.
8. In regard to teachers of French or German, a knowledge of the French or German grammar may be substituted for a knowledge of the English grammar; and the certificates to the teachers expressly limited accordingly....

II. [1]—That no male student shall be admitted under eighteen years of age, nor a female student under the age of sixteen years. [2]—Those admitted must produce a certificate of good moral character, dated within at least three months of its presentation, and signed by the clergyman or minister of the religious persuasion with which they are connected; ... [4]—must sign a declaration of their intention to devote themselves to the profession of school-teaching, and that their object in coming to the Normal School is to qualify themselves better for the important duties of that profession.

*　*　*　*　*

1　"Martha Hamm Lewis Goes to Normal School in the Year of Grace 1849, As Narrated by Her Daughters," *The Educational Review* (October, 1931).
2　Alison Prentice, "The Feminization of Teaching in British North America and Canada, 1845-1875," *Social History/Histoire Sociale*, 8, 15 (May, 1975), 11.
3　Prescribed by the Council of Public Instruction for Upper Canada.
4　This was the lowest licence granted by the colony.

For a full-length study of Annie Leake Tuttle see *The Life and Letters of Annie Leake Tuttle: Working for the Best*, edited by Marilyn Färdig Whitley, published by Wilfred Laurier University Press, 1999.

Chapter Four:
Curriculum and Pedagogy in the Mid-Nineteenth Century

E arly nineteenth-century teachers relied for the most part upon learning techniques such as memorization and recitation, enforced by corporal punishment. Rural schools usually consisted of one room filled with students between the ages of 5 and 16 who possessed varying levels of skills, knowledge, and ability. To facilitate learning, many teachers separated students by age, ability, or probable occupation and then divided their time between each group. Individual students thus received the teacher's attention for only approximately one-third of the day, for the rest of the time pupils worked on assignments.

In an attempt to rectify this situation, some larger schools adopted the Bell System (also termed Monitorial or Lancastrian), first employed in Madras, India, for teaching orphaned British children. Following the French Revolution, this pedagogy gained widespread acceptance in Great Britain and later in British North America.

The Bell System enabled one teacher to control and teach a large number of children of varying abilities and ages. The teacher divided the pupils into sections by ability and selected the best students to act as monitors. Prior to class, the teacher instructed the monitors in that day's work, and the monitors taught the lesson as the teacher worked individually with other students. The Monitorial System was an inexpensive way of providing mass schooling in a time when there were few trained teachers and a marked lack of funds. (See Document 18).

By the middle of the nineteenth century a new, more optimistic, view of child behaviour led to less authoritarian ways of motivating children. Instead of demanding memorization, teachers were encouraged to promote active learning with a practical bent. Visual aids, like apples, might be employed to teach addition and division. Maps and globes were used in geography class. Exercises involving money, weights, and time helped mental arithmetic.

Textbooks are a valuable measure of official orthodoxy, as well as crucial educational tools—especially for new teachers. Since textbooks are authorized by the government, and often acknowledged as official canon by the teacher, students view them as the official, authentic, version of the world. These learning materials were frequently the first, and sometimes the only, books many elementary students read. They were thus the vehicle through which a child was introduced to contemporary social issues.

Textbook analysis reveals a society's social and political philosophies, exposing a hidden curriculum which includes attitudes on such matters as nationalism, gender, morality, and social harmony. Susan E. Houston and Alison Prentice, two of Canada's most prolific scholars of the history of education, investigated Ontario's provincially-approved textbooks and their role in socializing young people in "What One Might Teach and Another Learn," reproduced below.

Other useful secondary sources include: Harro Van Brummelen, "Shifting Perspectives: Early British Columbia Textbooks from 1872 to 1925," in *Schools in the West: Essays in Canadian Educational History*, ed. Nancy M. Sheehan, et al. (Calgary, 1986); James Love, "Cultural Survival and Social Control: The Development of a Curriculum for Upper Canada's Common Schools in 1846," *Histoire Sociale-Social History*, 15, 3 (1982); and Harry Smaller, "Teachers and Schools in Early Ontario," *Ontario History* 85, 4 (1993).

* * * * *

What One Might Teach and Another Learn[43]

How best to bring some semblance of order, some system, to common schooling in the province was the challenge Egerton Ryerson faced as he assumed the superintendency in 1844. The anarchy had become proverbial: virtually no two schools were alike; facilities were haphazard at best; the teachers untrained, pupils of all ages (and both sexes) generally were jumbled together and, worse still, each attended according to necessity or whim. From the very outset, school textbooks proved to be a key element in Ryerson's design for school improvement. The immediate target was American textbooks.

Undoubtedly, there were a number of American publications in circulation in the province, concentrated where late American settlement predominated (although the oft-repeated charge that American textbooks dominated the common school curriculum in the 1820s and 1830s is not easily substantiated). Nevertheless, allegations of the insidious political threat posed by numerous American imprints in the schools became commonplace after the rebellion activity of the late 1830s.

Virulent anti-American feeling was rife in certain circles, especially among Tories; moreover, a more temperate version of pro-British sentiment was instinctively shared by the tens of thousands of recent immigrants from the British Isles who had chosen to set down roots in this British North American colony in the previous decade. For all the objections to various details of Ryerson's administration over the years, few quarrelled with his 'leading idea': 'to render the educational system, in its various ramifications and applications, the indirect, but powerful instrument of British Constitutional Government.'

Thus there was a political argument to be made for replacing American schoolbooks, an argument that justified the introduction of a comprehensive textbook policy in the mid-1840s. To help set the stage, as of 1 January 1847, all *foreign* (that is, *American*) books were prohibited—with the exception of the as-yet-indispensable editions of Morse's *New Geography* and the desirable *Kirkham's English Grammar*.[1]

What could be put in their place? In retrospect one best appreciates the genius of Ryerson's policy on textbooks in the context of the overall structural weakness of the fledgling provincial school system. Imagine this small world as a chessboard and ask: what single move could accomplish *all* the following—compensate for inadequately trained teachers; classify pupils according to ability and prior knowledge; meet the challenge of endemic pupil-teacher mobility; minimize sectarian animosity; provide affordable and universally available reading material to families and local communities before the advent of a viable domestic book trade? *Answer*: prescribe the series of school readers published by the Irish Commissioners of National Education. Within a month of his official appointment in 1844, Ryerson tipped his hand and encouraged the Montreal publishing firm Messrs Armour and Ramsay in a scheme to reprint the Irish readers for Canadian use. After his year-long European tour he moved swiftly. He commended the readers in his influential 1846 report and, on his recommendation, the newly appointed Board of Education approved a prescribed list of textbooks for the common schools, composed entirely of twenty-six publications of the Irish commissioners' series, including the famous readers. Adoption of the new texts was voluntary: local school trustees retained the right to choose schoolbooks, but now they risked losing the government grant if they persisted with unauthorized texts. Although the board ordered Ryerson to tread softly and 'to recommend a delicate treatment of the subject' in any correspondence with school trustees, 'rather permitting such [unauthorized] books to fall into disuse than to exclude them altogether,' the impact of the legislation and board regulations was immediate and decisive. Within a year nearly one-half (1,317 of 2,727) of the common schools had adopted the Irish readers; at the height of their popularity in 1866, all but 54 of the province's more than 4,000 common schools had succumbed. Of course, no edict could instantly resolve the textbook muddle. Inevitably individual school trustees, teachers, and parents remained confused and, occasionally, simply adamantly opposed. But in this instance Ryerson's basic administrative strategy of encouraging voluntary local compliance with central policy initiatives was remarkably successful.[2]

The series of Irish readers and the Irish commissioners' other publications had two advantages over their competitors in the schoolbook field. For their time they were remarkably good, and they were very inexpensive. Cheapness, in this case, was clearly related to merit. The Irish commissioners had over the decades created a domestic demand for their books by a shrewd combination of regulation and marketing strategy. The result: attractively low prices—and from there the advantages of economies of scale in production and distribution multiplied. Regarded as superior to the ponderous and heavily religious publications used in schools catering to English working-class children, by the 1840s the Irish national series were the most popular school-books in the British Isles. The Irish commissioners deliberately fostered export sales by selling books at or near cost outside Ireland and by granting reprinting rights to independent foreign agents. It has been estimated that during the 1850s the commissioners exported almost as many books as they kept at home.

The special arrangements that Ryerson negotiated with the commissioners in 1846 were, on the Irish side, simply grist to the export mill; from the Canadian standpoint, however, they were extraordinary. Having devised an elaborate system of incentives to local publishers and booksellers, Ryerson improvised: to ensure that local schools throughout the province were supplied adequately and swiftly with books and other equipment, in 1850 he opened the Educational Depository, in essence a government-owned mail-order bookstore. Local school trustees thus had a choice: should the local book trade raise prices on the authorized Irish school texts, they could buy directly from the depository the edition that the education department imported directly from Dublin at cost.[3]

The decision to adopt the Irish national series for Ontario schools had a profound impact on generations of youngsters. Arguably, none of the much-publicized mid-century innovations—the legislative framework, the Normal School, the Educational Depository—was more important. For much of the century, school-books were *the* central feature of the common school. In rural schools especially, but, until very late, almost everywhere, the school-books available dictated the 'curriculum.' For two or more generations so few of the province's teachers had real professional training that when much else failed, as we know it frequently did, memorizing the textbook could pass the time and placate the school trustees on examination day. School-books were counted upon to convey the 'useful knowledge' necessary to deal with the practicalities of life and to provide an inkling of the standards of belief and behaviour expected by adult society.

The Irish readers were exceptionally effective on both counts. Typically, instructional books in the late eighteenth and early nineteenth centuries were self-contained and unrelated to each other. Lindley Murray's *The English Reader* is a prime example. A staple of the Upper Canadian common school through the 1830s and 1840s, Murray's *Reader* ran through scores of editions in England, Ireland, the United States, and Upper Canada between the 1790s and the 1840s. It was essentially a literary anthology, arranged as 'Narrative Pieces, Didactic Pieces, Argumentative Pieces, Descriptive Pieces, Pathetic Pieces, Dialogues, Public Speeches ... and Promiscuous Pieces.' Murray sampled some of the best, and most morally improving, examples of literary culture but catered very little to the ages of his readers. That the Irish readers did do. Conceived as an integrated sequential series, each reader built on the content of the previous one, increasing in difficulty as well as in volume of information. In effect, pedagogy became inseparable from content once the Irish readers were adopted. Children could pass from learning the alphabet to simple stories of biblical history to the elements of natural history and physical science and the principles of political economy. Ryerson's breathless characterization captures something of the scope:

> in the fourth and fifth books, the most important subjects of Physical Geography and Geology, of Jewish History and Political Economy, of General History and Chronology, of Vegetable and Animal Physiology, of Natural History, including elementary Mechanics, Astronomy, Hydrostatics, Pneumatics, Optics, Electricity, and Chemistry, are treated in a manner both attractive and scientific, and adapted to the intercourse and pursuits of life—the whole being interspersed with miscellaneous and poetic selections calculated to please the imagination, to gratify and improve the taste, and to elevate and strengthen the moral feeling.[4]

A true compendium of the latest Victorian intellectual enthusiasms! And that in large measure explains the extraordinary popularity of the Irish texts. For working-class school children, in Britain especially, the content of the Irish readers vastly extended the range of basic information available: it mattered little that very few youngsters would ever reach the fourth or fifth books. By comparison to the typical fare of the Bible, scripture lessons, and religious tracts, the Irish series appeared notably secular and its 'useful knowledge' proved so irresistible that the major school societies—Protestant and Roman Catholic—in England had produced their own versions, close copies of the Irish series, by the early 1860s. But *secular* in the sense of *non-religious* the Irish commissioners' books definitely were not. The Irish readers were intentionally (and conspicuously in their time) 'non-denominational' in that they had the approval of both Roman Catholic and Protestant authorities in Ireland (a critical point for Ryerson, which he would stress repeatedly as the debate over separate schools in Ontario quickened in the 1850s). Non-sectarian, nevertheless, was Christian; the world view presented to children by the Irish readers was carefully constructed around Christian conceptions of God and the duties owed to Him.[5]

The First Book of Lessons opened with a section of seven lessons 'designed merely to make the Child familiar with the *forms* of Letters;' the remaining lessons advanced through two-, three-, and four-letter one-syllable words, laying the groundwork of basic language skills. Dogs, cats, rats, and pigs made an early appearance, but so too, as one of the first sentences that children learned to read, did the adage *'To do ill is a sin.'* The message was swiftly enforced in subsequent lessons by 'If I sin, I am bad, Let me not sin, as bad men do' and 'It is a sin to do ill.' As the prefatory note to teachers recommended that their pupils be 'perfectly acquainted with one Lesson before they proceed with another' and that they 'exercise them as much as possible on the *meaning* of such words and sentences as admit of being defined and explained,' one can probably assume that the concepts of good, sin, and evil were drilled early in each child's school career.[6]

The Second Book of Lessons followed naturally; after a review of words of one syllable, experience in reading and spelling advanced via moral fables and biblical stories to the stage of fairly complicated words, such as *innumerable*, and the first principles of grammar. The illustrative stories exhibited the virtue of having been written for children, exploiting situations and terms they could relate to; but however simplified the vocabulary, the message was never ambiguous: the divine order of the universe was mirrored in civil society. In the tale of 'The Daw with the Borrowed Feathers,' in which a humble jackdaw is vain enough to want to dress like a peacock, the moral is made devastatingly clear: 'It is wisest and safest to pretend to nothing that is above our reach and our circumstances, and to aim at acting well in our own proper sphere rather than have the mere appearance of worth and beauty in the sphere which is designed for others.'[7] The corresponding selections of verse had no literary pretensions. The opening and closing lines of 'We Must Not Be Idle' still stir memories:

> How doth the little busy bee
> Improve each shining hour ....,
> For idle hands some mischief still
> Will ever find to do.

By the end of the *Second Book* it was assumed that youngsters had acquired basic reading skills. Nevertheless, the original step between the second and the third book—with its selections from contemporary literary figures such as William Wordsworth, Robert Southey, and Sir Walter Scott—proved sufficiently difficult that *A Sequel to the Second Book of Lessons* was interposed. The sequel, which was used in Ontario schools, caught the attention of William Sherwood Fox, a political science professor at Queen's University in 1932. Intrigued by the extent to which national character and national political culture might be attributed to the socializing effect of differing school curricula, Fox saw the 'balance, sanity, clarity and simplicity' of the Irish books as a glaring contrast to the extravagant jingoism of the comparable American classics, McGuffey's readers. Overall, he concluded, the 1859 Canadian edition of *A Sequel to the Second Book of Lessons* was 'one of the most remarkable common school textbooks I have ever seen.' Inevitably, after another half-century the perspective has shifted, and our judgment is less benign: it does not matter that the information is even more outdated with the passage of time, the moral preaching now seems obvious in ways it did not to Sherwood Fox in the 1930s. For example, one of the notable features of the *Sequel* was its beginning section devoted to a discussion of the principles of a sound education written in language children could understand. The prospective reader (typically nine or ten years of age) is asked to remember not being able to read or write, and then going to school for the first time and learning habits of cleanliness, order, respect, silence, and self-discipline—the things taught first 'because they are necessary to the peace and comfort of others, and therefore to the order of the school.' In a confidential tone the author reminds his reader: 'You know how disagreeable it is to sit by a dirty child.' Indeed! What ripples might such a remark cause in colonial schoolrooms in newly settled rural communities or burgeoning commercial centres? Might the behaviour of Miss Mary Ann Kennedy, a teacher at Victoria Street School in Toronto, be related somehow as she accused Mira and Faithful Murdrew, of 4 Bond Street, of being 'uncleanly in their persons' and told other children not to sit near them? She acted on 'hearsay,' as it turned out, and was duly reprimanded; but could some of her students have taken that particular lesson too much to heart? One cannot help but wonder.[8]

By the 1860s many common school students in Ontario would get into, if not through, the *Third Book*; markedly fewer got to the end of the *Fourth Book*; and the astronomy, hydrostatics, and pneumatics of the natural philosophy section of the *Fifth Book* found only a tiny audience, being remote from even the majority of teachers.[11] That being the case, the overall character of the intermediate-level readers takes on a particular importance, for these were among the last—and the most demanding—instructional materials to which ordinary mid-Victorian Ontarians would be exposed. Following the now-familiar format, the third and fourth books advanced instruction through increasingly sophisticated lessons in spelling, grammar, natural history, geography, and literary appreciation. *Third Book* teachers were advised to have their pupils memorize the best pieces of poetry and that they 'be taught to read and repeat them with due attention to pronunciation, accent and emphasis.' A single reading lesson might well combine instruction in a number of areas. One *Third Book* story about how glass is made introduced students to concepts such as *brittleness* and *transparency*, the geography of the Middle East (Syria and Sidon), the spelling of *manufactured*, and the details of the invention of glass. By the *Fourth Book* a selection about Linnaeus, the famed Swedish naturalist, cloaked a lesson on the Latin and Greek roots of English words ['What is the Latin root of *naturalist*? What is the first affix added to *natura*?'] in a discussion of the tripartite division of nature as animal, vegetable, and mineral.

In the late twentieth century even the physical size, printing, and illustrations of these little Victorian books seem quaint. Two contrary impressions of their content stand out: the factual material and information is eclectic and surprisingly contemporary, while aesthetic or literary values are largely ignored. In the critical sections of prose and poetry the selections were chosen for their didactic qualities rather than their stylistic merit. Almost none of the excerpts from the classics, ancient and modern, that had graced the early readers remained. To be sure, an obligatory smattering of Shakespeare survived (mostly as obscure stanzas from unnamed plays), along with a little Milton (the highlights of *Paradise Lost* proved irresistible), but in the company typically of the minor works of minor talents. No reasonable interest in near-contemporary authors could produce that end result naturally. Clearly the object was to cultivate the reader's moral, not aesthetic, sensibilities.

Culturally, then, elementary education was quite probably impoverished by reliance on the Irish readers. Certainly they offered predictable gruel when compared to the richness possible in earlier times when one might learn much of what the teacher happened to know, from whatever books could be mustered for the purpose. In other ways, however, as we have noted, the Irish readers brought the curriculum 'up-to-date.'

One of the most striking features of the *Third* and *Fourth* books of lessons was the introduction of current liberal economic theory in the form of lectures on political economy. The basic tenets of nineteenth-century *laissez-faire* doctrine, in considerable measure an apology for the class relations and political alignments of the emerging industrial capitalist economy, were promoted by the Irish series. The Reverend Richard Whately, the author of an 1833 tract for schools, *Easy Lessons on Money Matters for the Use of Young People*, somewhat unexpectedly became the Anglican archbishop of Dublin, an Irish education commissioner, and chief proponent of the Irish national series of textbooks. In the form of lectures on such topics as Money, Exchange and the Division of Labour, the *Easy Lessons* were reproduced in the Irish readers: the first four sections in the *Third Book*, the remaining six sections in the *Fourth Book*.[12]

In the 'unsubtle, pre-digested morality' of Whately's lectures (to borrow J.M. Goldstrom's phrase), the virtues of hard work, perseverance, and thrift were applauded; backsliding or lack of will invariably doomed one to poverty or worse. The forces fragmenting the traditional work processes of the self-employed craftsman or small producer were heralded as signs of civilization: 'when everyman does everything for himself everything is badly done,' *Third Book* readers were reminded.[13] Unfettered, the laws balancing supply and demand worked to the benefit of both worker and employer, and the seemingly glaring discrepancies between rich and poor were often deceptive. A long lesson in the *Fourth Book* on the rich and poor (and the 'cheering thought that no one is shut out from the hope of bettering his condition and providing for his children') included a story on the complex economic functions performed by a rich man as he employs others, buys objects, etc., etc. The conclusion was meant to be reassuring: 'the rich man, therefore, though he appears to have so much larger a share allotted to him, does not really consume it but is only the channel through which it flows to others. And it is by this means much better distributed than it would have been otherwise.'[14]

In truth, the Irish readers were saturated with a very specific social and political philosophy. Labelling a discrete section structured in a distinctive lecture format 'Political Economy and the Useful Arts' was a misleading editorial device, in that it implied that these values and this kind of material could be excluded from the curriculum by omitting the specified lessons. That was hardly the case. The importance of social harmony and the corresponding futility—indeed immorality—of radical social protest were common themes in even the earliest readers.[15] By contrast to the past, the present was characterized as a time of restless energy and striving after dreams. The economic (and social) system would prove a hard but just taskmaster to those who dared to grasp the nettle: various sagas of male achievement attested to that. A Birmingham entrepreneur, William Hutton, and the explorer Christopher Columbus, for example (whose stories appear in the *Sequel to the Second Book*), were both very poor but virtuous and persevering youths who gained wealth and respect. However farfetched such stories might have seemed when read in the Canadian countryside, they evidently appealed to Ontario educators. Toronto's local superintendent, for example, examined the city's common school children in the mid-1860s more often on these two biographical lessons than on any others in the *Sequel*.[16] More generally, the tenets of political economy accorded perfectly with the ideal of the common school as a place where the son of the manufacturer might sit next to the son of a doorman. Indeed, Ryerson, the chief publicist of that myth, wrote his own textbook version of Whately's *Easy Lessons* late in his career *as Elements of Political Economy or How Individuals and a Country Become Rich* (Toronto: Copp Clark 1877). With time the Irish readers became less exceptional.[17] Eventually, as some material became dated and factual inaccuracies were exposed, pressure mounted for Ryerson and the Council of Public Instruction to arrange for their replacement. On 4 January 1868, a new series of six books was authorized: the *Canadian National Series of Reading Books*, otherwise known as the 'Red Series' or the 'Ryerson Books.' Faithful to tradition, the new series responded to growing nationalist feeling by being in all essentials a made-in-Canada version of the Irish texts.[18]

Readers were the key element in the new common school curriculum for they provided the vehicle for instruction in reading, spelling, and grammar as well as more general knowledge. But they were not the only school-books. The basic elementary fare of the three Rs had, whenever possible, relied on books other than a reader and the Bible. Spelling books, English grammars, and arithmetics abounded in the common schools to the point of nuisance by the mid-1840s. Under pressure from the Board of Education's authorized list the number of these texts was trimmed, but uniformity throughout the province was never as critical a goal for Ryerson in the areas peripheral to reading. For writing (penmanship), geography, and history—even spelling, grammar, and arithmetic—the teacher's command of the subject matter and teaching skill mattered more than any single text. As Ryerson admitted in 1847 with reference to mathematics, he believed that 'the Teacher is the true, and the best, "arithmetic" for the Schools; and, if he cannot teach and illustrate its principles and rules without references to a particular Textbook, very little of the science of numbers will be learned in his school.'[19]

In the mid-1840s one arithmetic text, Francis Walkingame's *The Tutor's Assistant*, dominated the field, being used in over 42 per cent of the common schools. A late-eighteenth-century production, Walkingame's book went through countless editions over more than half a century. The 1818 Montreal edition (based on the fifty-first London edition) was widely used in the 1830s and reportedly until 1845 in Middlesex County, while an even later edition was reprinted in Picton in 1849.[20] Such longevity was feasible because the substance of arithmetic instruction changed very little over time: addition, subtraction, multiplication, division, vulgar fractions, decimals, square and cube roots— these and more were illustrated by examples and learned by memorizing rules and answering practice questions. Often the illustrations were eminently practical. From weights and measures the student advanced to details of basic business practice: the nature of bills of sale or how to calculate single and compound interest. Ryerson's major reservation about the various texts in current use in the 1840s related to the alien and necessarily somewhat abstract quality of the examples used to explain the various rules. Much more desirable to have illustrations 'selected from the statistics and commerce of the Country in which it [the textbook] might be used,' he observed in 1847. As he well knew, authorization of the two Irish arithmetics changed very little, for their examples were British. The situation became critical in the late 1850s when Canada switched to a decimal currency. Among the first Canadian texts authorized to supplement the Irish commissioners' publications were two new editions (1859 and 1860) of the Irish arithmetics now 'adapted to the decimal currency.' For students, substituting texts meant little more than that they were now drilled in converting pounds, shillings, and pence into dollars and cents, in addition to reducing days, hours, and minutes to seconds, miles to inches, and writing the current date in Roman numerals. Roman notation was so popular with Toronto teachers in the mid-1860s that members of the committee on school management protested that the pupils were 'not young Romans of the 2nd and 3rd century, but Anglo-Saxons living in an intensely practical age.'[21]

Allegations of impracticality were not limited to arithmetic classes. Controversy over spellers and the way in which spelling and reading were taught had been brewing for some time before Ryerson's intervention. The traditional spelling books that came under fire had often been little more than disembodied lists of combinations of syllables to be memorized and of words to be spelled, sometimes—but by no means always—followed by short definitions. Typically, little effort was made to introduce young students to words that might relate to the world with which they were familiar.[22] To try to teach spelling effectively while divorcing it from reading and comprehension appeared nonsensical to a new generation of educators. Ryerson, in his 1846 report, came out firmly on the side of the modernists. The Irish national readers were specifically designed to accomplish the task of teaching spelling through reading. A short list of new words to be learned prefaced each lesson text, which then set the words in context. As a deliberate statement on this point, the Irish series did not include a 'speller' as such. According to the Irish method (which Ryerson and the Normal School promoted), when students had advanced to a certain stage they were introduced to a supplementary book, *The Spelling-Book Superseded*, compiled by Robert Sullivan, master of the Dublin Normal School. Designed to help students with some of the anomalies of the English language, this 'little book' offered practical rules for spelling and pronunciation and, as well, explained how some words similar in sound differed in spelling (bough/bow); how words identically spelled could be pronounced differently (bow/bow); and how words spelled and pronounced alike could differ in meaning (bat,n./ bat,v.).[23]

English grammar, too, had its rules, which students diligently memorized and then practised by answering prepared exercises. The more senior students grappled with the Latin and Greek roots of words, prefixes, affixes, and suffixes, and the distinctions among phrases, clauses, and sentences; but for the majority the heart of grammar teaching remained *parsing*: the description of words in a sentence in terms of grammatical rules, as parts of speech, and in their relationship to one another. Accuracy became increasingly important as popular speech became standardized and mistakes in grammar and mispronunciations threatened to betray dubious social or ethnic origins. At the same time, educators continued to regard grammatical drill as a form of mental discipline by which students learned to think in an orderly fashion as well as to communicate effectively. Increasingly, too, after mid-century, emphasis shifted to the ability to write as well as to speak correctly. The grammar in the Irish series directed students to do their work almost entirely in writing, presuming at least some attention had been paid to acquiring the skill of writing or penmanship. Practice in forming arabic numerals and then letters on slate began as the alphabet was learned and, gradually, depending on the availability of school desks on which to write and paper or exercise sheets on which to practice, the student progressed from 'large' to 'small hand' to a 'bold free handwriting' that was as legible as print.[24]

The poverty of many mid-century schoolhouses affected all instruction to some degree, but the study of geography was especially hampered by the lack of blackboards, maps, globes, and pens and ink. As the Educational Depository supplied these items in large volume through the 1850s and early 1860s, geography became more widely studied; but a serious problem remained. British publications—even the Irish national series—typically focused on Britain as the centre of the world, neglecting the entire North American continent and ignoring the Canadas altogether. The most commonly used American texts, on the other hand, often appeared to promote republicanism, and Olney's *A Practical System of Popular Geography*, an attractively illustrated, outrageously chauvinistic political tract, aroused legitimate political concern in Canada. Convinced of the importance of geography, the Board of Education capitulated to popular interest in North America and permitted the continued use of the most neutral American text, Morse's *New Geography*, published in New York by Harper and Row. The weakness of the Irish texts, which had been authorized in 1846, was met temporarily in 1857 by John George Hodgins's *Geography and History of British North America and of the Other Colonies of the Empire*. While this, his first attempt, came under fire for gross inaccuracies, by 1865 Hodgins had produced a trio of Canadian texts that successfully supplanted both the American and the Irish geographies: *Lovell's General Geography*, *Lovell's Easy Lessons in General Geography*, and *History of Canada and of Other British North American Provinces*.[25]

Of all the subjects that Ryerson desired to see in the common school curriculum none approached the importance of religious instruction. 'The Christian religion should be the basis, and all pervading principle of it,' he wrote confidently in 1846; but at the same time, as a pioneer champion of Methodism he was not unaware of the depth to which sectarian feeling scarred communities throughout the province. The Irish example had attracted Ryerson from the outset precisely because it seemed to offer a resolution to sectarian differences; for there Roman Catholic and various Protestant church authorities had been able to collaborate in the establishment and regulation of the national schools. In the matter of regulations for religious instruction in the province's common schools, Ryerson followed the Irish precedent and consulted with a number of leading Protestant and Roman Catholic churchmen before drafting the regulations of 1846.[26] The mood was conciliatory, but the question remained: where in this provincial context might common ground be found? One risked denominational wrath by being too prescriptive, too authoritarian; on the other hand, diffidence only invited charges of promoting a 'godless' school system—an allegation that Ryerson personally could not tolerate. The ground he chose, in 1846, was the local school section: legislation was put in place to protect the freedom of conscience of any child whose parents objected to whatever form of religious instruction the local school trustees authorized. Similar assumptions underlay the 1850 legislation and regulations, but already the 'common ground' was shifting: religious instruction proved to be a bone of endless contention. Decisions about the extent and content of the observances depended on thousands of locally elected trustees, their personal convictions, doctrinal beliefs, and political connections with local ratepayers and parents; day to day, the knowledge and religious commitment of the teacher often determined the outcome.

By 1855 the education department was forced to retreat. The new common school regulations were made to conform to those recently devised for the grammar schools: neither assumed nor required anything, but recommended daily opening and closing exercises, which might incorporate non-denominational prayers, a reading from the Scriptures, and, ideally, the Lord's Prayer and the Ten Commandments. By 1857 the position of the local trustees was clarified further in that schoolhouses were to be made available once a week, out of school hours, to local clergy 'of any persuasion, or their authorized representatives' to offer religious instruction to pupils of their faith.[27] The new regulations reduced local tension by offering trustees, parents, and communities an avenue of retreat, with the result that by the 1860s there was enormous variety in the ways religious instruction was carried on. The teacher's responsibility, however, became less clear once religious instruction was replaced by moral lessons. Neil Campbell, who took over ss 7, Oro Township, in 1871, confided to his diary a sense of the difficulties teachers faced in trying to inculcate moral values: 'some teachers give moral lectures once a week &c, but few can do this who do not as it were preach to their pupils by uttering truisms and if you do you will soon lose the respect of your pupils and might as well be silent.'[28]

Egerton Ryerson had set an ambitious agenda for the province's common schools in 1846. 'What the child needs in the world he should doubtless be taught in the school,' he proposed, and the appropriate yardstick of need was to be neither the past nor the present 'but what ought to be, and what must be, if we are not to be distanced by other countries in the race of civilization.' His ideal 'system of common school instruction' included:

Reading, Writing, Drawing, Arithmetic, the English language, Music, Geography, elements of General History, of Natural History, of Physiology and Mental Philosophy, of Chemistry, Natural Philosophy, Agriculture, Civil Government & Political Economy.[29]

A flight of fancy, really, and easily ridiculed when many schools at the time he was writing were not unlike those in Dundas, where in 1850 'the amount of grammar, geography, dictionary and meanings taught ... [were] not worth mentioning; and as for history, composition, geometry, natural philosophy and the like, they were never thought of.'[30] By the 1860s a scaled-down version of Ryerson's blueprint had taken shape, owing in large measure to the Irish readers and the requirements set for the county board second-class teaching certificate held by approximately 48 per cent of common school teachers. To read 'with ease, intelligence and expression'; to write a 'bold free hand'; to know the principles of reading and pronunciation and the rules for teaching writing, 'Fractions, Involution, Evolution, and Commercial and Mental Arithmetic', as well as the common rules of orthography; to be able to parse, write grammatically with correct spelling and punctuation the substance of dictation, and be familiar with a school geography—these were the demands made of prospective teachers and, invariably, they shaped and limited what was taught in the individual schoolroom.[31]

That at least was the conclusion the Reverend James Fraser drew from his visit to the province's schools on behalf of the British Schools Inquiry Commission in the summer of 1865. Having arrived from the American leg of his journey in late July only to discover that many schools (including those in Hamilton) were already closed for the summer vacation, Fraser visited schools in Ottawa, Toronto, Clinton, and one or two other villages. So confident was he of his impression that 'they were characterized by a remarkable similarity of system, and the differences observable between them were differences of degree rather than kind,' that he doubted whether more examples would alter his opinion.

In effect it was all very familiar, much like ordinary English elementary schooling. In the range of subjects taught, for example, the best schools in Toronto equalled most English town schools in providing solid daily doses of an hour each of reading, arithmetic, writing, and grammar, supplemented by classes in geography and history, oddments of singing, drawing, and drill, and, where appropriate, higher mathematics such as algebra and Euclidean geometry. The lessons struck Fraser as long and, particularly in reading, pupils were expected to 'possess themselves of the matter of the lesson.' Quick answers were generally discouraged by giving students time 'for reflection and thought.'[32] The Irish readers provided the framework that carried the students from the most elementary to advanced work as the course of study became more elaborate at the stage of the fourth and fifth readers. By the end of the *First Book of Lessons* youngsters should have known the simple rules for addition and subtraction, perhaps the multiplication tables, how to print on the slate, and, if there were maps or a blackboard, perhaps a little geography. By the *Third Book* one was very likely to be writing with pen and ink and studying the elements of grammar, parsing easy sentences, and beginning world history and natural history. By the *Fourth Book* arithmetic lessons reached vulgar and decimal fractions and square roots, and geography now required an atlas as well as a textbook. Only with the *Fifth Book*, however, came the separate lessons in natural philosophy, algebra, mensuration, geometry, bookkeeping, or linear drawing with which to cap 'a thorough English education.'[33]

Instruction for girls had always differed somewhat from that for boys, but bigger schools and an enlarged curriculum accentuated the gender gap. The public debate in the 1860s over whether some subjects were appropriate for young women or whether girls were even capable of learning certain things related primarily to the issue of girls' attendance at grammar school. Common school practices elicited little discussion, but the incidence of sexual segregation and special treatment ranged in degrees from blatant to subtle. The education department encouraged explicit separation into single-sex classrooms or schools and, in the 1850s and 1860s, that became standard practice in town and city schools whenever space and teaching staff permitted. Typically, intermediate and senior boys' classes were taught by men; the girls' division by women (there was even an authorized Irish reader 'for the use of female schools'). The vast majority of youngsters, especially those in one-room country schools, experienced the differences as a matter of emphasis. One suspects that more frogs were caught by boys than girls for a natural history lesson, and certainly girls typically began needlework (which they brought from home) along with the alphabet. Even in Toronto schools, where boys and girls worked through the readers at the same pace, the local superintendent examined only boys on the *Second Book* lesson on cruelty to insects (section IV, lesson 5) while the tale of 'The Theft of the Golden Eagle' (about a stolen baby and a mother's bravery) was a favourite of the girls reading from the *Sequel*. By the senior division, boys studied bookkeeping, practical mensuration, and, perhaps, the first two or three books of Euclid; the girls, meanwhile, polished their crochet skills and did worsted work and embroidery instead of mathematics. Their accomplishments at plain and ornamental needlework, map and watercolour drawing, and penmanship were often displayed during midsummer and winter holidays.[34]

The introduction of military drill at the height of the American Civil War highlighted these obvious gender divisions. In December 1862 Ryerson urged all male common school teachers to start drill for boys over the age of ten years. Nothing too fancy was possible, he realized, for he could not count on the teachers' having any experience, but 'they might be taught to face right and left, to march, and to form fours deep.' In Toronto in 1863, under the tutelage of a prominent local citizen, Major R.B. Denison, the senior common school boys were drilled an hour a week; 'a few parents have objected,' the local superintendent honestly admitted, 'but generally the Drill has been equally acceptable and beneficial.'[35] Ryerson was convinced, as were many of his British and American contemporaries, that military drill provided an indispensable lesson in citizenship and patriotic duty, and in 1865 he even flirted with making military studies compulsory in the grammar schools. As the threat of military action receded, the moral value of drill came to the fore. Over the years educators and their publicists had lost few opportunities to applaud habits of obedience and discipline among school children. As the *Globe* once described it, the sight of children returning to their places 'as regularly and soberly as soldiers' was' the very best evidence that could be given of the healthy state of the school.' 'Nothing else is so well adapted to secure those habits,' Ryerson forecast in 1862, and that message was heard in the depth of Huron County where regular drill in ss 1, Howick, reputedly lent 'a tone of regularity to all the exercises of the school.'[36]

Enthusiasm for military drill proved short-lived and by 1870 had become virtually extinct even in the grammar schools.[37] But interest in the 'regularity of the movement and the aim at perfection on the part of every scholar,' that so pleased Cyrus Carroll about the Howick school children did not evaporate; it was transferred to gymnastic exercises for boys and a genteel form of calisthenics for girls. Vocal music was another special case, in that the teacher's interest and talent, much more than the availability of *Hullah's Music* textbook, determined whether it was taught. In most instances, however, subjects were added to, not dropped from, school curricula in these decades. As schoolhouses improved, maps, blackboards, and perhaps a globe or abacus appeared to make the study of geography, history, or mathematics something more than memorizing the textbook. In country schools there was often a battle to persuade parents to buy new textbooks (some expected a set to last at least a generation). But by the late 1860s, as additional texts were authorized along with the new Canadian readers, even rural teachers offered algebra, geometry, or bookkeeping occasionally.[38]

The Irish readers played such a central role in shaping a uniform curriculum for common schools across the province that one might expect their replacement to have caused at least a mild disruption. It did not. The Canadian series, authorized in 1866, took their place with scarcely a ripple. For all their additional Canadian content, the readers continued essentially unchanged, still primarily repositories of the 'useful knowledge' upon which public educators had placed great store since the 1820s. Even making allowances for the fact that some things cannot be counted and could not otherwise have been measured by the education department in its ceaseless documenting of the 'progress' of education, one retains the disquieting impression that for all its expansion in quantity, common school instruction did not become appreciably more generous, intellectually. Amid the accumulation of facts and memorizing of maxims there was precious little for the imagination.[39]

NOTES

3 'E.R. to Higginson, 30 Apr. 1845,' *DHE* vol., 5, 240; E. Ryerson, *Special Report on the Means which Have Been Adopted for the Establishment of a Normal School and for Carrying into Effect Generally the Common School Act* (Montreal 1847) 14-15; J. Donald Wilson, 'Common School Texts in Use in Upper Canada prior to 1845,' Bibliographical Society of Canada *Papers* 9 (1970) 36-53; Viola E. Parvin, *The Authorization of Textbooks for the Schools of Ontario, 1846-1950* (Toronto: University of Toronto Press 1965), 29; Bruce Curtis, 'Schoolbooks and the Myth of Curricular Republicanism: The State of the Curriculum in Canada West, 1820-1850,' *HS/SH* 32 (Nov 1983) 305-30; James H. Love, 'Anti-Americanism and Common School Education Reform in Mid-Nineteenth Century Upper Canada: The Niagara District as a Case Study' (PhD diss., University of Toronto 1978) and 'Cultural Survival and Social Control: The Development of a Curriculum for Upper Canada's Common Schools in 1846,' *HS/SH* 30 (Nov. 1982), 357-82

4 E. Ryerson, 'Circular Addressed to District Superintendents ... December 1846,' *DHE* vol. 6, 267; *A Brief History of Public and High School Textbooks Authorized for the Province of Ontario 1846-1889*, Prepared by the Education Department (Toronto: Warwick and Sons 1890); 'Proceedings of the Board of Education, Oct, 30, 1846,' *DHE* vol. 6, 245; *ARUC* (1847) *DHE* vol. 7, 162; George L. Parker, *The Beginnings of the Book Trade in Canada* (Toronto: University of Toronto Press 1985) 112 ff. An inventory of the books actually used in the common schools across the province could be compiled on the basis of information surviving in manuscript form for the period 1855-70 in the local superintendents' annual reports, RG2 F-3-B.

5 Donald H. Akenson, *The Irish Education Experiment: The National System of Education in the Nineteenth Century* (London: Routledge and Kegan Paul 1970), 227-30; Dianna S. Cameron, 'John George Hodgins and Ontario Education, 1844-1912' (MA diss., University of Guelph 1976) 113-15; J.M. Goldstrom, *The Social Content of Education, 1808-1870: A Study of the Working Class School Reader in England and Ireland* (Shannon: Irish University Press 1972); also 'The Content of Education and the Socialization of the Working Class Child, 1830-1860,' in Phillip McCann, ed., *Popular Education and Socialization in the Nineteenth Century* (London: Methuen 1977), 93-109; 'Proceedings of the Board of Education Oct. 9, 1846,' *DHE* vol., 6, 242-5

6 *JEUC* 1 (Nov. 1848) 337; Curtis, 'Schoolbooks and the Myth of Curricular Republicanism,' 328; William Sherwood Fox, 'School Readers as an Educational Force: A Study of a Century of Upper Canada,' *Queen's Quarterly* 39 (1932), 688-703

7 Goldstrom, *The Social Content of Education*; Ruth Miller Elson, *Guardians of Tradition: American Schoolbooks of the Nineteenth Century* (Lincoln: University of Nebraska Press 1964)

8 *The First Book of Lessons for the Use of Schools* (Montreal and Toronto: James Campbell 1867), sect. 2, lessons 6, 7, 10

9 *The Second Book of Lessons for the Use of Schools* (London 1858), sect. 4, lesson 11

10 Fox, 'School Readers'; *A Sequel to the Second Book of Lessons for the Use of Schools* (1864) 13; reprinted in Parvin, *Authorization of Textbooks* 27; TBEHC, James Porter Diary, vol. 4, 10 May 1872

11 In Hamilton in 1868, 3.7 per cent of students in the common school system were in Book 5; in Toronto in 1875 the figure was 5 per cent; cf. 'E. Ryerson to the Provincial Secretary 18 Mar. 1872,' *DHE* vol. 24, 210-11. See also R.D. Gidney and W.P.J. Millar, 'From Voluntarism to State Schooling: The Creation of the Public School System in Ontario,' *CHR* 66 (Dec. 1985), table 3, 473.

12 J.M. Goldstrom, 'Richard Whately and Political Economy in School Books, 1833-1880,' *Irish Historical Studies* 15 (1966), 133-46; also *The Social Content of Education* 83-5; and 'The Content of Education and the Socialization of the Working Class Child,' 102-3

13 *The Third Book of Lessons for the Use of Schools* (Toronto 1851), sect. 3, lesson 10

14 *The Fourth Book of Lessons for the Use of Schools* (Montreal: R. and A. Hiller 1853), 229

15 Compare *First Book* sect. 3, lesson 22; *Second Book* sect. 2, lessons 8, 11; sect. 3, lessons 5, 7; sect. 4, lessons 1, 6.

16 Sharon Dyas, 'The World View Presented to Children of Toronto Schools, 1862-67' (Ms, Department of History, York University 1978), an analysis of vols. 2 and 3 of James Porter's diary

17 C.F. Elson, *Guardians of Tradition*, and Goldstrom, 'The Content of Education and the Socialization of the Working Class Child.'

18 Parvin, *Authorization of Textbooks,* 39-40; *A Brief History,* 7

19 *ARUC* (1847) *DHE* Vol. 7, 162-3; Curtis, 'Schoolbooks and the Myth of Curricular Republicanism'

20 Wilson, 'Common School Texts,' 41, 46-7; 1,162 of the 2,727 common schools reported using Walkingame's arithmetic, *ARUC* (1847) *DHE* vol. 7, 163. See also W.B. Gray, 'The Teaching of Mathematics in Ontario, 1800-1941' (DPAED diss., University of Toronto 1948), chs. 2, 3

21 J.H. Sangster, *National Arithmetic in Theory and Practice: Designed for the Use of Canadian Schools* (Montreal: Lovell 1859); *Series of National Schoolbooks. First Book of Arithmetic: For the Use of Schools*, rev. ed., Adapted to the New Decimal Currency (Toronto: Robert McPhail 1860);

Parvin, *Authorization of Textbooks*, 38-9; *Annual Report of the Local Superintendent ... Toronto* (1865), 50;TBEHC, James Porter Diary, vol. 3, Mar. 1866

22 C.F. Elson, *Guardians of Tradition* 2, and Bruce Curtis, 'The Speller Expelled: Disciplining the Common Reader in Canada West, 1846-50,' *Canadian Review of Sociology and Anthropology* 22 (Aug. 1985), 346-68

23 E. Ryerson 'Report on a System of Public Elementary Instruction for Upper Canada,' *DHE* vol. 6, 170-1; Robert Sullivan, *The Spelling-Book Superseded; Or, a New and Easy Method of Teaching the Spelling, Meaning, Pronunciation and Etymology of All the Difficult Words in the English Language with Exercises on Verbal Distinctions*, 18th ed. (Dublin 1850)

24 Alison Prentice, *The School Promoters; Education and Social Class in Mid-Nineteenth Century Upper Canada* (Toronto: McClelland and Stewart 1977), 76-9; C.E. Phillips, 'The Teaching of English in Ontario, 1800-1900' (D PAED diss., University of Toronto 1935); Margaret Hoddinott, 'On the Teaching of Writing in Upper Canada in the First Half of the Nineteenth Century' (Ms, Department of History, York University 1985). There were no desks for *Second Book* pupils in Toronto until 1874 (*ARUC* [1874] App. B, 84).

25 E. Ryerson, 'Public Elementary Instruction,' *DHE* vol. 6, 182-5; *JEUC* 18 (June 1865), 96; 'E.R. to Chas. Coburn, Pennsylvania,' *DHE* vol. 19, 67-9; Parvin, *Authorization of Textbooks*, 33-4, 38-9; *A Brief History*, 8; A.G. Croal, 'The History of the Teaching of Science in Ontario, 1800-1900' (D PAED diss., University of Toronto 1940), chs. 2, 3; E.J. Quick, 'The Development of Geography and History Curricula in the Elementary Schools of Ontario, 1846-1966' (D Ed diss., University of Toronto 1967), chs. 2, 3

26 *DHE* vol. 6, 193, 299-300

27 *ARUC* (1847) *DHE* vol. 7, 165; *ARUC* (1857) 18-21; R.D. Gidney and D.A. Lawr, 'Bureaucracy *vs.* Community?: The Origins of Bureaucratic Procedures in the Upper Canadian School System,' *Journal of Social History* 13 (Spring 1980), 445, 449-50; W.D. Edison Matthews, 'The History of the Religious Factor in Ontario Elementary Education' (D PAED diss., University of Toronto 1950), 103-5

28 Simcoe County Archives, Neil J. Campbell Ms (Diary and school census ss 7, Oro Township) 82; *Fraser Report*, 293 ff, and see especially 248-51, in which Fraser reproduces all mention of religious instruction in 152 local superintendents' reports for 1863.

29 E. Ryerson, 'Public Elementary Instruction,' *DHE* vol. 6, 193

30 *ARUC* (1850), App. A, 156

31 'Minimum Qualifications for Second Class Teachers, 1850,' *DHE* vol. 9, 220. On 31 Dec. 1858 the Council of Public Instruction officially pre-

scribed a course of study for each of the three divisions in the common
school, *DHE* vol. 14, 63-4.

32 *Fraser Report*, 206, 241, 242
33 Toronto Board of School Trustees, *Report of the Past History and Present
Condition of the Common or Public Schools of the City of Toronto* (Toronto
1859) 58-63, 108-25; *Annual Report of the Local Superintendent* ...
Toronto (1875) table H; 'Nineteen Years' Progress of the Hamilton City
Schools, 1850-1869,' in J. George Hodgins, ed., *Schools and Colleges of
Ontario, 1792-1910* (Toronto 1911), vol. 1, 75-6; *ARUC* (1868)
London, App. A, 108-11; Rev. George Blair, *Address to the School Trustees,
Parents and Common School Teachers of the County of Durham C.W.*
(Bowmanville 1866); Honora M. Cochrane, ed., *Centennial Story: The
Board of Education for the City of Toronto 1850-1950* (Toronto 1950)
34 Prentice, *The School Promoters*, 152-3; Dyas, 'The World View Presented
to Children'; Toronto Board, *Report of the Past History and Present
Condition* 61; Cochrane, *Centennial Story* 43, 45
35 *DHE* vol. 17, 236; *ARUC* (1863) 18-19; ibid. App. A, 151; *DHE* vol.
18, 93
36 *Globe* 14 Nov. 1853; *ARUC* (1866) App. A, 46; also Pt 1, 26
37 'Report and Suggestions with Respect to the County Grammar (now
High) Schools of Ontario for the Year 1870,' *DHE* vol. 22, 246
38 Reminiscences, *DHE* vol. 28: George Peters 275; Hugh Lucas 277; Ellen
Bowes 261
39 Bruce Curtis, 'Curricular Change and the Red Readers: History and
Theory' (Paper presented at the Goodson Seminar, University of Western
Ontario, 2-3 Oct. 1986). *C.F. David Vincent, Bread, Knowledge and
Freedom: A Study of Nineteenth Century Working Class Autobiography*
(London: Methuen 1982)

*   *   *   *   *

Documents for Chapter Four

The following documents reveal the moral and religious values that were considered important at mid-nineteenth century. Of course, the views expressed in
textbooks tell us more about the official values of the time than how widespread they were. The first document (14) outlines the goals of the most widely used textbook in British North America. The Murray Readers were mentioned in the previous article. To what extent do today's beliefs differ from
those expressed in the Murray Readers? The following two documents are
extracts from school inspectors' reports. The report for the County of Durham
(16) provides an eyewitness account of teaching methods in the third quarter
of the nineteenth century. How did the education system benefit from the

involvement of school inspectors? Document 17 reveals the teachers' responsibilities and the Board of Trustees' attitude towards teachers. The final document (18) illustrates the Bell method of teaching large numbers of students. Role play either the instruction to begin the day, teaching the letters A and B, or the question and answer section, and comment on the effectiveness of this teaching strategy.

14) PREFACE TO THE MURRAY READER, 1830[1]

Many selections of excellent matter have been made for the benefit of young persons. Performances of this kind are of so great utility, that fresh productions of them, and new attempts to improve the young mind, will scarcely be deemed superfluous, if the writer make his compilation instructive and interesting, and sufficiently distinct from others.

The present work, as the title expresses, aims at the attainment of three objects: to improve youth in the art of reading; to meliorate their language and sentiments; and to inculcate some of the most important principles of piety and virtue.

The pieces selected, not only give exercise to a great variety of emotions, and the correspondent tones and variations of voice, but contain sentences and members of sentences, which are diversified, proportioned, and pointed with accuracy. Exercises of this nature are, it is presumed, well calculated to teach youth to read with propriety and effect. A selection of sentences, in which variety and proportion, with exact punctuation, have been carefully observed, in all their parts as well as with respect to one another, will probably have a much greater effect, in properly teaching the art of reading, than is commonly imagined. In such constructions, every thing is accommodated to the understanding and the voice; and the common difficulties in learning to read well are obviated. When the learner has acquired a habit of reading such sentences, with justness and facility, he will readily apply that habit, and the improvements he has made, to sentences more complicated and irregular, and of a construction entirely different.

The language of the pieces chosen for this collection has been careful regarded. Purity, propriety, perspicuity, and in many instances, elegance of diction, distinguish them. They are extracted from the works of the most correct and elegant writers. From the sources whence the sentiments are drawn, the reader may expect to find them connected and regular, sufficiently important and impressive, and divested of every thing that is either trite or eccentric. The frequent perusal of such composition naturally bends to infuse a taste for this species of excellence; and to produce a habit of thinking, and of composing, with judgment and accuracy.

That this collection may also serve the purpose of promoting piety and virtue, the Compiler has introduced many extracts, which place religion in the most amiable light; and which recommend a great variety of moral duties, by the excellence of their nature and the happy effects they produce. These subjects are exhibited in a style and manner which are calculated to arrest the attention of youth; and to make strong and durable impressions on their minds.

The Compiler has been careful to avoid every expression and sentiment, that might gratify a corrupt mind, or, in the least degree, offend the eye or ear of innocence. This he conceives to be peculiarly incumbent on every person who writes for the benefit of youth. It would indeed be a great and happy improvement in education, if no writings were allowed to come under their notice, but such as are perfectly innocent; and if on all proper occasions, they were encouraged to peruse those which tend to inspire a due reverence for virtue, and an abhorrence of vice, as well as to animate them with sentiments of piety and goodness. Such impressions deeply engraven on their minds, and connected with all their attainments, could scarcely fail of attending them through life, and of producing a solidity of principle and character, that would be able to resist the danger arising from future intercourse with the world.

The Author has endeavoured to relieve the grave and serious parts of his collection, by the occasional admission of pieces which amuse as well as instruct. If, however, any of his readers should think it contains too great a proportion of the former, it may be some apology to observe, that in the existing publications designed for the perusal of young persons, the preponderance is greatly on the side of gay and amusing productions. Too much attention may be paid to this medium of improvement. When the imagination, of youth especially, is much entertained, the sober dictates of the understanding are regarded with indifference; and the influence of good affections is either feeble, or transient. A temperate use of such entertainment seems therefore requisite, to afford proper scope for the operations of the understanding and the heart.

The reader will perceive, that the Compiler has been solicitous to recommend to young persons, the perusal of the sacred Scriptures, by interspersing through his work some of the most beautiful and interesting passages of those invaluable writings. To excite an early taste and veneration for this great rule of life is a point of so high importance, as to warrant the attempt to promote it on every proper occasion.

To improve the young mind, and to afford some assistance to tutors, in the arduous and important work of education, were the motives which led to this production. If the Author should be so successful as to accomplish these ends, even in a small degree, he will think that his time and pains have been well employed, and will deem himself amply rewarded.

*　*　*　*　*

15) MORALITY IN UPPER CANADIAN COMMON SCHOOLS, 1853[2]

Section 5. Constitution and Government of Schools in respect to Religious and Moral Instruction.

As Christianity is the basis of our whole system of elementary education, that principle should pervade it throughout. Where it cannot be carried out in mixed schools to the satisfaction of both Roman Catholics and Protestants, the law provides for the establishment of separate schools. And the Common School Act, fourteenth section, securing individual rights as well as recognizing Christianity, provides, "That in any Model or Common School established under this Act, no child shall be required to read or study in or from any religious book, or to join in any exercise of devotion or religion, which shall be objected to by his or her parents or guardians: Provided always, that within this limitation, pupils shall be allowed to receive such religious instruction as their parents or guardian shall desire, according to the general regulations which shall be provided according to law."

In the section of the Act just quoted, the principle of religious instruction in the schools is recognized, the restriction within which it is to be given is stated, and the exclusive right of each parent and guardian on the subject is secured, without any interposition from Trustees, Superintendents, or the Government itself.

The common school being a day, and not a boarding school, rules arising from domestic relations and duties are not required; and as the pupils are under the care of their parents and guardians on Sabbaths, no regulations are called for in respect to their attendance at public worship.

In regard to the nature and extent of the daily religious exercises of the School and the special religious instruction given to pupils, the Council of Public Instruction for Upper Canada makes the following Regulations and Recommendations:—

1. The public religious exercises of each school shall be a matter of mutual voluntary arrangement between the teacher and the parent or guardian of each pupil, as to whether he shall hear such pupil recite from the Scriptures, or Catechism, or other summary of religious doctrine and duty of the persuasion of such parent or guardian. Such recitations, however, are not to interfere with the regular exercises of the school.

2. But the principles of religion and morality should be inculcated upon all the pupils of the school. What the Commissioners of National Education in Ireland state as existing in schools under their charge, should characterize the instruction given in each school in Upper Canada. The Commissioners state that "in the National Schools the importance of religion is constantly

impressed upon the minds of children, through the works calculated to promote good principles and fill the heart with love for religion, but which are so compiled as not to clash with the doctrines of any particular class of Christians." In each school the teacher should exert his best endeavours, by both example and precept, to impress upon the minds of all children and youth committed to his care and instruction, the principles of piety, justice, and a sacred regard to truth, love to their country, humanity and universal benevolence, sobriety, industry, frugality, chastity, moderation and temperance, and those other virtues which are the ornament of society, and on which a free constitution of government is founded; and it is the duty of each teacher to endeavour to lead his pupils, as their age and capacities will admit, into a clear understanding of the tendency of the above mentioned virtues, in order to preserve and perfect the blessings of law and liberty, as well as to promote their future happiness, and also to point out to them the evil tendency of the opposite vices.

* * * * *

16) INSPECTOR'S REPORT FOR DURHAM COUNTY, 1875[3]

COUNTY OF DURHAM. Inspector's Report

John J. Tilley, Esq.—Good work has been done in our Schools during the year. The programme is, with slight exceptions, carefully observed, and regularity and system in the classification of pupils and in work done, are the results. All the Schools were kept open the whole year, and only one special Certificate, for six months, was granted. It affords me much pleasure to be able to say that arithmetic is taught in a very intelligent manner. Teachers do not think of confining their work to a text-book, but are developing independent thought and self-reliance. The examination questions for admission to High Schools are eagerly sought after by teachers, and in fixing a certain standard for their pupils they exercise considerable influence upon our Public Schools. Grammar and composition in the lower classes are invariably taught together by blackboard exercises—text-books being seldom used below the fourth class. Pupils are thus taught by direct application the practical use of what they learn. I am satisfied with the work done in these subjects. The results in spelling are also quite satisfactory. All classes from the Second Reader upwards are taught by dictation. Junior classes are also required to write a portion of their reading lessons each day, by which the spelling is much improved, and a freedom in writing acquired. All our teachers give much attention to the definitions of words. Reading is well taught in a few Schools, fairly in some, and poorly in many. Too many teachers have not learned that *hearing* reading is not *teaching* it, and that to have good reading something more is necessary besides pronouncing an occasional word and saying "next."

A report that does not complain of irregular attendance can scarcely be considered orthodox. I fear many teachers do not realize how much the regularity or irregularity of attendance lies within their own control. I usually find that the best teachers complain the least of this wide-spread evil. To teach those pupils that are sent, or may come to school, may fulfil the letter of the law; but the teacher whose interest in the welfare of his pupils is not strong enough to cause him, if need be, to go out through his section and do a little missionary work, is not fulfilling the spirit. The attendance is very much regulated by the influence the teacher exerts both in and out of school. When I visit a School taught by an energetic teacher, with a thorough system of marking and reporting to parents, I usually find the irregularity much reduced. Heretofore the clause relating to compulsory attendance has had little effect; but the supplementary report issued by the Department this year, which requires trustees to give the names of all children between seven and twelve years of age that have not attended four months in the year, has brought the matter very forcibly under the notice of trustees; and from my intercourse with many, I have no doubt this subject will receive more attention next year than it has ever received before.

The year has witnessed the usual influx of inexperienced Third-class teachers, who greatly outnumber all others. While the lowest grade of certificate is as easily obtained as it is at present, large numbers of young persons will obtain it, not through any particular effort on their part or desire to teach, but through their ordinary work in High Schools, or Superior Public Schools, having been induced to attend the examination in many cases for the credit of the School. When licensed, they are ambitious to teach, but experience proves that at least two out of three will not be found teaching after their three years of probation have expired. The consequence is that many of our Schools are but experimenting rooms for an almost perpetual apprenticeship. I believe the time has come when every person licensed to take charge of a School should be able to teach, to some extent, all the subjects in the programme. The reason why so many Third-class teachers fail to enter the Second class, and so many Schools are consequently obliged to change teachers, is, that having received no insight into the extra subjects for Second-class Certificates, being removed from assistance, and thinking the difficulties greater than they really are, they believe themselves unable to pass over the gulf. If no more Third-class Certificates were granted, and a lower grade made in the Second class, for which, say one-third of the marks shall be obtained, it would, in my opinion, be a great step in advance. To prevent any undue scarcity of teachers, the Third-class Certificates now in existence could be made valid for some definite time.

Competitive examinations were held in five townships during the year, and, considering that these were our first, the attendance was good and the results satisfactory. Prizes of the value of nearly $400 were distributed. I believe these examinations have done a great deal of good in infusing new life into teachers and pupils, and by developing a healthy spirit of emulation. I look for increased interest in those to be held in 1876. I think it would be well if something corresponding to the competitive examinations that have been held in a few counties were established on some uniform basis for the Province—an examination in connection with our Public Schools that shall bear some relation to the "intermediate" for High Schools. A uniform programme for all schools has undoubtedly done much to regulate the work, but bringing the schools into direct competition with one another by uniform written competitive examinations, would be a mighty lever to *raise* the work.

Our teachers' associations are in a flourishing condition, and a professional library in connection with the one for East Durham was established last June. Many of our teachers are working hard, striving to take a higher stand in their profession, and at the last examination we were enabled to grant ten Second-class Certificates—double the number ever given before at one time. Yet nearly three times as many were given in the Third class. 112 teachers were employed during the year, of whom 29 had attended the Normal School ....

School Accommodation.—Nearly all the old School-houses of former years have been replaced by new ones since the introduction of the law of 1871. There remain but seven structures that should give place to others without delay. Three sections at least will build next year, and two will provide accommodation for an assistant teacher. Six rooms were re-seated with improved desks on iron stands, nineteen play-grounds were enlarged and fenced, and ten were fenced. There remain twelve to be fenced, and eleven to be enlarged. Before forwarding cheques for municipal grants, I wrote to every section that had not complied with the law, and have received assurance in writing in all cases, except four, that the grounds will be enlarged and fenced in the spring. I think, therefore, it may safely be concluded that before the end of another year every section in the County will have complied with the regulations relating to play-grounds. For providing fencing and supplying play-grounds, $2,500 were expended during the year ....

There are 101 School-houses in the county, Brick 58; Stone 1; Concrete 1; Frame 39; Log 2.

Libraries.—But little was done during the year in supplying libraries. There are 39 in the County, divided as follows:

Darlington, 3,228 volumes; Clarke, 9,848 volumes; Hope, 8,408 volumes; Cartwright, 3,234 volumes; Manvers, 6,285 volumes; Cavan, 6,361 volumes; South Monaghan 4,250 volumes.

School Requirements.—All our Schools are furnished with blackboards and maps. Globes are found in 65 Schools, tablet object lessons in 80, and 35 report apparatus used, though in many cases I know the supply is quite limited.

* * * * *

17) TORONTO, INSTRUCTIONS FOR TEACHERS, 1869[4]

1. The appointment and remuneration of teachers are determined by the Board of Trustees, and teachers are prohibited from receiving payment from, or on account of, any pupils attending the City Schools.
2. Teachers after probation will be engaged by the year, but all engagements will be terminable on one month's notice in writing, to be considered as dating from the meeting of the Board at which such notice is given; except in the case of a principal teacher, who shall give three months' notice of his or her intention to leave the service of the Board, and shall remain in its service for that period unless specially released by the Board from his or her engagement. The Board reserves to itself the power to dismiss any teacher at any time for misconduct on giving him or her one month's notice.
3. It will be the duty of every teacher to observe and enforce the regulations established by the Trustees, a printed copy of which shall be permanently suspended in every class-room, and so far as they refer to pupils, read to the whole school on the first Monday in every month.
4. All teachers are required to conform to the directions of the Superintendent. The head masters will take priority of rank in the several schools, and all subordinate teachers are to give effect to the instructions of the principals of the departments in which they serve.
5. Every teacher is required, both by precept and example, to instruct the pupils in good manners, and to pay strict attention to their morals, habits, and cleanliness of person.
6. The principal of each department shall make such arrangements as will secure the attendance of one teacher in the play-ground, to overlook the pupils during the intermissions of study; and to be in charge during the dinner-hour.
7. The teachers shall be in the schools at all seasons of the year sufficiently early to have their rooms duly prepared for the scholars before the hour appointed for beginning the exercises; viz., fifteen minutes before nine o'clock in the morning, and five minutes before one o'clock in the afternoon. It shall be their duty to give vigilant attention to the ventilation and temperature of their rooms. In the Fall of the year no fires shall be lighted in the several schools unless with the approval of the Local Superintendent, and no fires shall be continued in the Spring longer than he shall approve. Each teacher shall endeavour to prevent the temperature raised by stoves or

furnaces in his or her room front exceeding 65°F. Every principal female teacher, assistant teacher, and caretaker, shall be under the immediate direction of the head master in all matters which affect the heating and ventilation of the several schoolrooms, and the head master shall in all such matters be amenable to the Local Superintendent and to the Board.

8. The teachers are required to take special care of their respective classrooms. The head master will be held responsible for the preservation of the school-houses, furniture, apparatus, yards, and appurtenances, and for maintaining them in clean, neat, and proper condition; and, when anything is out of order, requiring repair or restoration, it is to be promptly reported to the Secretary of the Board. No dog shall be kept on the premises of any of the Schools, by any teacher, caretaker, or other person.

9. A register shall be kept by the principal teacher in each department, in which shall be recorded the names, ages, dates of admission of the pupils, and the places of residence of their parents or guardians. The daily attendance of each pupil shall be registered by his or her teacher, and a monthly return, or abstract front the daily registers shall be made to the Superintendent, in a printed form provided for that purpose.

10. The principal teachers in each department shall examine the pupils under the care of the other teachers, in order to evaluate their promotion from a lower to a higher Division, and otherwise superintend the exercises of the subordinate Divisions, as far as may be considered the proper discharge of their own more immediate duties.

11. The teachers are required to practise such discipline in the schools as would be exercised by a kind and judicious parent; and shall avoid corporal punishment in all cases where good order can be preserved by milder measures. The teacher will be held responsible for the due exercise of his or her discretionary power.

12. For violent or pointed opposition to the teacher's authority, a principal teacher may suspend a child from attendance at school, immediately informing the parent of the measure, and reporting the case to the Superintendent for his instructions.

13. When the disobedience of any pupil becomes habitual and hopeless of reformation, and his example injurious to the school, it shall be the duty of the principal teacher to report the case to the Superintendent, who may suspend and ultimately expel the pupil from the schools, such act being subject to an appeal to the Board of Trustees; but any child thus expelled, who shall, in the presence of the school, ask forgiveness for his or her fault, and shall promise amendment, may, with the sanction of the Superintendent, be reinstated in the privileges of the school.

14. When any teacher is compelled by sickness or other cause, to be absent from school, the principal of the department shall make temporary provision for

the care of the classes, recording the case, and promptly reporting it to the Superintendent; and the appointment of a substitute shall devolve upon the Superintendent; and one-half of the substitute's remuneration shall be deducted from the salary of the teachers, by the authority of the Board.

15. No teachers shall award medals, or other prizes, to the pupils under their charge.

16. No subscription or contribution for any purpose whatever shall be introduced into any school.

17. No addresses shall be presented by the pupils to any teacher, or other school-officers or authorities, and no uses other than those connected with the regular exercises of the schools, shall be made ....

18. Teachers are expected to refrain from all public, political, and ecclesiastical controversy, and to remember, that the public schools are intended for the children of all, without regard to the party principles of any, in matters religious or political.

19. The daily exercises of each school shall accord with the general programme of studies adopted by the Board, and a printed time table denoting them shall be permanently suspended in every class-room.

20. The books used and the studies pursued in all the schools shall be such and such only as may be authorised by the board, or as, under special circumstances, may be temporarily sanctioned by the Superintendent.

*   *   *   *   *

18) A MONITORIAL SCHOOL, 1821[5]

INTRODUCTION

... [S]everal educated citizens of the City of Quebec were very much aware of the total lack of education in the poorest class and felt that this was one of the causes of insubordination and disturbances which seem to have increased for quite some time. They thus called a meeting of the citizens of Quebec to consider what means could be used for providing the advantages of a Christian education to the poor Catholic children of the City, who in effect were the only ones who lack instruction. This would be until such a time as the Legislature should pass a bill on this subject.

Many people, both Clergy and Laymen, attended the meeting and unanimously passed several resolutions. These were to try and provide for the children of this class a knowledge of the true God, to fill their young hearts with the need of all men to love Him and serve Him, and to give them an elementary education, that is to say: to teach them to read, write and do arithmetic.

A committee of 21 members was chosen to study this worthwhile work and a subscription was started to cover expenses.

ELEMENTARY EDUCATION COURSE

A little later this committee made a Report on the rules which they considered necessary for the government of schools and the instruction that would be given them. It is a summary of these rules and the teaching methods, modelled on those of Lancaster, Bell and others, which form the subject of this little work. It was thought important to have it printed in the hope of giving some uniformity to the elementary education courses and thus to help students when they are admitted to the seminaries to pursue higher studies.

The success of the Free School in Quebec and the progress that the children have made there are the best recommendations one can make to the public for adopting the teaching methods which are fully outlined in this little volume.

It has this special advantage that one man of ordinary education, with a little intelligence and application and using the adopted method, can run, on his own, a school of several hundred pupils with less difficulty than with fifty pupils under the old method. Besides, the progress of the pupils is much more rapid, as experience has already shown here, and the expenses are considerably less.

In addition, this work was undertaken under the scrutiny of devout Churchmen and learned lay people and has earned their approval.

All these advantages lead one to believe that it will be favourably received by the public and generally adopted in the elementary schools of this province ...

Classes

20) 1. The children who are learning their A, B, C, will be on the benches nearest the Master.
2. Those who are beginning to spell words of one syllable, next.
3. After them, those who are spelling words of two syllables.
4. Then those who are spelling words of three syllables and more.
5. Next those who are reading whole words, sentences and lessons.
6. Finally those who are learning the rules of arithmetic.

Publications

21) In order to avoid the expense of buying A, B, C,s and other books, there will be several boards with the alphabet printed in big letters; on others, words of one syllable; then some with two syllables and others of three, four, five and six syllables; some boards will have whole words; others phrases and sentences, and others whole lessons, figures, arithmetic tables and rules.

22) These boards will be put up in full view of the pupils of each respective class to be read, re-read and written by each class without moving them around ...

Writing

24) In order to dispense with the purchase of paper, ink and pens for the pupils,

shelves will be made in front of the first benches, with a rim to keep in the white sand and the base painted black. The beginners will write, with their fingers or with wooden pointers, the letters, words and figures which will be shown them. Slates will be provided for those who are more advanced.

Monitors—Teaching Methods—Moving Up and Down in the Class
25) The Master will name and place at the head of the class a Monitor, whose duty will be to see to the good behaviour of those on this bench, to point out the letters on the board to be named by each of them ...

Distinctions
26) The Monitors will have marks of distinction such as Monitor First Class, Second Class, Third Class, Fourth Class, etc.
27) The first in each Class will also have a mark of distinction, such as the First of the First Class Monitors, Second Class, Third and Fourth, etc ...

THE BASIS OF MUTUAL TEACHING

The adoption of the method of mutual teaching by the most civilized people in Europe is a certain proof of its superiority over the ancient methods of teaching; not only is this method preferred at the present time in the elementary schools, but they are still trying to introduce it in the colleges and academies for teaching more advanced studies.

Its superiority is not therefore a problem; but one mustn't be so blind as to think that as soon as this method is used there will be instant success. It has, like every system, its principles; and if these are not well understood, or if they are not properly utilised, only a moderate benefit can be drawn from them.

The main point in the method of mutual teaching is to keep the pupils constantly alert, to never let them be idle, without however keeping them at long and difficult lessons. For that it is necessary to put before their eyes something that continually focuses their attention ....

The Master must insist that they arrive the first in the classroom to put up the letters, word or lessons which each class must read from the large boards; they must also be the last to leave so that they can put back all the letters, words or lessons in their place, also all the other boards and the slates; then they must make their reports to the Master on absences, behaviour and the progress of the pupils in their respective classes, so that he himself can make the general report which must be ready to present to the members of the Society when required, so that the latter can decide on rewards or punishments for the pupils with a full knowledge of the background of each case.

The Master must never forget to make each class go over what has been shown them in the course of the week. This should be every Saturday morning. Then he should question the pupils on grammar, according to the standard of each class, and to make them learn the answers by heart.

He should begin with the class of children who are learning the alphabet. While they are doing their exercises out loud, the other classes must be kept busy doing their work in silence, either writing or doing sums until their turn comes to do their exercises out loud.

With these fundamentals established and carefully carried out, we must go on to the following exercises and commands:

Words of Command

On entering the classroom, the pupils, wearing their hats, must take their places where they were the last time they were there. When they have done that the Master says in a loud voice ATTENTION! at which the pupils all together at the same time let their arms fall to their side. Then the Master says HATS OFF! Immediately the pupils must put up their hands to their hats or bonnets and let the hats fall back on their shoulders where they will remain throughout the school day, hanging on a cord around their necks. Then the Master calls out KNEEL! and at this command all the pupils must kneel down. At the words CROSS YOURSELVES! each one makes the sign of the cross and at FOLD YOUR HANDS! they all will put their hands together in front of them and keep them there throughout the prayer, without leaning back against the benches. When the prayer is over the Master says STAND UP! whereupon all the pupils will stand up and sit down on the benches behind them at the word SIT! and here they will remain while awaiting the order that each Assistant Monitor, at the top of the bench, will give them. Each Assistant Monitor must give out to the pupils on his bench the lesson that they have to study.

1st Class

GET READY! The Monitor of the First Class, standing on his stool near the large board, calls out to them GET READY! At this order the children must stand up and hold their boards and pencils at chest level, with the board in the left hand and the pencil, between the thumb and first two fingers of the right hand.

LOOK! Soon after the Monitor points with his long stick at the letter A, which is hanging on the large board where there must not be more than three or four letters, and he says to them: "Look closely at this letter, it is called A. It is formed by a line sloping to the right, another to the left and cut across the middle by a horizontal line. To write it begin by making a line to the right and then to the left. At the bottom of each of these lines there is a small straight line. After that put the line across the middle." (The Monitor must show with his stick how the letter is made and how it must be written.)

WHAT IS THE NAME OF THIS LETTER? After this introduction the Monitor turns to the first pupil on the bench and asks him "What is the name of the letter?", while pointing out the letter A on the large board.

If the pupil doesn't remember it, he keeps passing on to another until he finds one who names the letter correctly. The one who names it takes the place of the first pupil who couldn't name it; he also gets his mark of distinction and the first one goes down and takes the place of the one who corrected him. The Monitor continues to have the letter named by all the pupils in the class and moves around the ones who make mistakes.

When this letter has been named by the whole class he passes on to the second letter, B. He points out that it is formed by a straight line with two curves on its right; he shows them with his stick how it must be written and proceeds as above for the letter A. He does the same for the letter C and so on for all the other letters of the alphabet, on succeeding days.

POINT! EXAMINE! When this is done by the whole class, the Monitor begins again by pointing out the letter A and without naming it or describing it, he orders the class to point to it on their cards, and at the word POINT!, each pupil must look for it on his board and hold his pencil above it until the Assistant from each bench has examined (by passing behind the bench and looking over the right shoulder of each pupil) and seen that it was correctly pointed out. At the word EXAMINE! he will point out to those who were wrong the letter which they should have pointed to.

WHAT IS THIS LETTER CALLED? When the Assistants have returned to their places with their pointers upright to show that the examination is completed, the Monitor questions whichever pupil he thinks he should, asking them (while pointing out the letter on the big boards) "What is this letter called?" If he replies correctly, he questions another pupil on another letter, which he also makes him point out on his board, and so on. He chooses letters from the right and the left until all the pupils in the class have been carefully examined on all the three or four letters hanging on the large board, at the same time taking care to move down to those who are wrong, or who have hesitated, and moving up those who have replied correctly and quickly.

SLATES. When the Monitor thinks that the pupils are familiar with all the letters shown on the large board, he orders the Assistants to distribute the slates. This they must do at the word SLATES! They go and get them from the place where they have been put away and give one to each pupil on his bench, along with a pencil which each pupil will hang around his neck on a string.

TO THE DESK! GET READY! When this is done and the Assistants have returned to their places with their pointers in the upright position, the Monitor orders the children on the first bench, who have not been given slates, to come up to the desk by calling out TO THE DESK! Immediately, the pupils from this bench come forward together to the desk and rest their left arms on the small shelf in front and bring their right hands onto the upper shelf where the sand is, with their pencils held firm between their thumbs and first two fingers. At the words GET READY! those who have slates hold them in their left hands, their pencils in their right hands between their thumbs and first two fingers. When this is done, the Assistant Monitors go up and down the rows to see if the pupils are holding their slates and pencils properly. Then having seen by the upright pointers that all is ready, the Monitor says WRITE the letter A like this. Then he shows them with his pointer where to begin and finish the letter.

EXAMINE! When it seems that this letter has been written by all the pupils, the Assistant Monitors go up and down the rows to examine and correct on the order EXAMINE!

CLEAN YOUR SLATES! When they have returned to their places and having given the signal, the Monitor calls out "Clean your slates!" At which the pupils must put their right hands to their mouths and take some saliva with which they clean off the letter written on their slates. The Assistant from the first bench smooths out the letters which were written in the sand. The Monitor carries on in the same manner having them write all the other letters hanging on the large board.

BEGIN AGAIN! When the monitor thinks that the pupils have written and know sufficiently well the letters on the large board, he orders the whole class to write them again in silence, saying "Begin again!"

It is on this second test of writing that the Mark of Distinction of First in the First Writing Class must be given.

As soon as the Master and the Monitor of this class are satisfied that all the capital letters of the Roman Alphabet are thoroughly familiar to the pupils, in the same manner as outlined above they will proceed to show them, and trace and make them write on the sand and on their slates the letters printed on the other side of the Roman Alphabet (that is, the small letters). When these have been duly taught, repeated and written, they will show them a third alphabet of large and small italics. Finally, fifth and sixth alphabets made up of large and small letters in writing. These alphabets will be shown to them in the same way as the first ones and they will have to write them for longer so that they can form a good hand before they go up to a higher class where they will make constant use of writing.

1.2.3.4.5.6.7.8.9.0. It must not be forgotten to show them, before they pass on to another class the names and the shapes of the numbers 1,2,3,4,5,6,7,8,9,0, and to have them add them in every way, asking them: how much is one and two; to which each pupil should reply, it is 3; and 3 and 3 are 6, and so on, taking all the figures and adding them in every direction. Every Saturday morning without fail, and sometimes during the week when all the exercises are finished early, the Master will ask the students of the First Class the following questions, to which they must give the answers given below, until they know them all perfectly.

Q. What do you call the figures shown on the large board?

A. They are called letters.

Q. How are letters formed?

A. They are all formed from three lines: straight, slanting or curved. Some letters are formed by only one of these lines, others by two, and in still others we see all three used as in the letter R.

Q. How are the letters divided?

A. They are divided into VOWELS and CONSONANTS, or VOICES and ARTICULATIONS.

Q. How many vowels are there?

A. Generally speaking, there are five.

Q. What are they?

A. A, e, i, o, u, and also one can include y.

Q. Why are they called vowels or voices?

A. Because by themselves they form one voice or sound.

Q. How may consonants or articulations are there?

A. There are nineteen.

Q. Name them.

A. B, c, d, f, g, h, j, k, l, m, n, p, q, r, s, t, v, x, and z.

Q. Why are they called consonants or articulations?

A. Because they only can form a sound with the help of vowels or voices.

Q. Are there not also double letters?

A. Yes there are some amongst both the vowels and the consonants.

Q. What are they?

A. Those from amongst the vowels are *ae, eu, eau, ieu, oe, oi, ou*; and amongst the consonants there are *ch, ft, ff, ph, sl, ss, st, w.*

Q. What are letters used for?

A. To form words.

As soon as the oral exercises of the First Class are finished and the order to begin again has been given to the pupils and they are writing in silence, the Second Class, made up of those who are beginning to spell words of two letters and more, must start ....

To complete the course of Elementary Education contained in this volume, consisting of READING, WRITING and ARITHMETIC, will take three years. They will have had to learn the spelling of 2897 words included in the different tables, and the 151 replies to the questions on grammar; the principal parts of verbs and their conjugations; also their prayers and the Longer and Shorter Catechism.

* * * * *

1 "Preface to the Murray Reader," Lindley Murray, *The English Reader, or Pieces in Prose and Verse* (Toronto, 1830), 3-4.

2 "Morality in the Schools," in *Annual Report of the Normal, Model, Grammar and Common Schools in Upper Canada for the Year 1853*, Appendix One, Regulations, pp. 170-171.

3 "County of Durham Inspector's Report," *Appendices to the Annual Report of the Normal, Model, High and Public Schools, in Ontario, for the year 1875* (1877), pp. 31-2.

4 "General Instruction to Teachers," *11th Annual Report of the local Superintendent of the Public Schools of the City of Toronto*, 1869, pp. 92-5.

5 Joseph-François Perrault, ed., *Cours d' éducation élémentaire à l'usage de l' Ecole gratuite, établie dans la Cité de Québec en 1821* (Quebec, 1822), pp. 1 passim. Translated by Janna Best. Quoted in Alison Prentice and Susan Houston, eds. *Family, School & Society in Nineteenth-Century Canada* (Toronto: Oxford University Press, 1975), 46-53.

Chapter Five:
Rural School Teachers

On the morning of 14 November 1928, in an isolated logging camp on Vancouver Island, two men knocked on the school teacher's door. Getting no response, they let themselves in. Twenty-year-old Mabel Jones lay dead on the floor with a bullet in her chest. Beside her lay a .22 rifle. Jones' suicide note read, "there are a few people who would like to see me out of the way, so I am trying to please them. I know this is a coward's way of doing things, but what they said about me almost broke my heart. They are not true. Forgive me, please. Say it was an accident." Apparently, three parents of the school's twenty-two children had complained that Jones left the school's flag continually flying, allowed children to march into school in a careless manner, lacked discipline, and did not disabuse pupils for wasting their scribblers. The Inquest declared her temporarily insane, but noted that Jones' "mental state was the result of unjustifiable, unfeeling and underhanded criticisms of her work on the part of two members of the school board," and recommended that ways be found to protect teachers in small, isolated school districts from "the gossip of irresponsible and petty citizens."[44]

Teaching in rural areas of Canada could be extremely trying. In addition to teaching classes, marking, disciplining, keeping the fireplace going, beautifying the school grounds, maintaining detailed records, inspecting the pupils' health, and carrying out janitorial duties, teachers were expected to be ideal role models and community leaders.

Most rural teachers were young, single women. In rural British Columbia in 1925, for example, 80% of the teachers were women. Their average age and teaching experience was 23.6 and 3.1 years respectively. Although many teachers suffered from loneliness, isolation, lack of freedom, and the attitudes of unfriendly trustees and parents, teaching paid more than domestic service or factory work. It also offered a chance for adventure away from home, and to some women it was a divine calling.

In the following article, Robert Patterson employs interviews to reconstruct the thoughts, feelings, and behaviour of rural school teachers on the Prairies from 1914 to 1939. Other useful secondary sources include: Jon Calam, *Alex Lord's British Columbia: Recollections of a Rural School Inspector, 1915–36* (Vancouver, 1991); Dianne M. Hallman, "'A Thing of the Past:' Teaching in One-Room Schools in Rural Nova Scotia, 1936–1941," *Historical Studies in Education*, 4, 1 (1992); Phillip McCann, *Schooling in a Fishing Society: Education and Economic Conditions in Newfoundland and Labrador, 1836–1986* (St. John's, 1994); Penelope Stephenson, "'Mrs. Gibson looks as if she was ready for the end of term': The Professional Trials and Tribulations of Rural Teachers in British Columbia's Okanagan Valley in the 1920s," in Jean Barman et al., eds., *Children, Teachers and Schools in the History of British Columbia* (Calgary, 1995); and Paul J. Stortz and J. Donald Wilson, "Education on the Frontier: Schools, Teachers and Community Influence in North-Central British Columbia," *Histoire sociale/Social History* 26, (November/novembre 1993), 265–90.

∗   ∗   ∗   ∗   ∗

Voices from the Past: The Personal and Professional Struggle of Rural School Teachers[45]

Under the heading, "The Schoolmarm" the editors of the February, 1930 *ATA Magazine* paid tribute to the female rural schoolteacher by highlighting on the magazine's cover the following words from Walt Mason, their "own Canadian rhymster,"

> The teacher in the country school, expounding lesson, sum and rule, and teaching children how to rise to heights where lasting honor lies, deserves a fat and handsome wage, for she's a triumph of this age.
>
> No better work than hers is done beneath the good old shining sun; she builds the future of the state; she guides the youths who will be great; she gives the childish spirit wings, and points the way to noble things.
>
> And we, who do all things so well, and of our "institooshuns" yell, reward the teacher with a roll that brings a shudder to her soul. We have our coin done up in crates, and gladly hand it to the skates who fuss around in politics and fool us with their time-worn tricks.
>
> In Blankville one common jay will loaf a week, and draw more pay than some tired teacher, toiling near, will ever see in half a year. If I were running this old land, I'd have a lot of statesmen canned; politicians and folks like those, would have to work for board and clothes; I'd put the lid on scores of snaps, and pour into the teachers' laps the wealth that now away is sinned, for words and wiggle-jaws and wind.[1]

Despite the existence of such praise, bestowed sometimes begrudgingly by their contemporaries and often more lavishly by later nostalgic commentators, these teachers—their thoughts, feelings, behaviour and challenges—remain relatively unknown contributors to prairie social life and growth. In part this has resulted from the judgment that the lives of teachers and activities in school are not significant enough to warrant attention. These individuals, mainly women, engaged in a low-status and low-profile occupation, are a part of a larger group who, because of lesser visibility due to role, occupation or status, have not received, until recent years, the attention of historians.[2] Their lives may not be epic, yet the student of history cannot overlook the fact that each life is a tiny capillary, a vein or artery contributing to the strong heartbeat of the collective experience. The unique, "lived" experience is a vital part of our history which we need to acknowledge, uncover and understand. Vera Lysenko recognized the importance of such a history when through the eyes of a teacher in her novel *Westerly Wild* the following observation was made:

> "I sometimes think the prairie provinces were built up by the labours of pioneer teachers," Julie would think on such a morning. As she recalled all those hopeful young Normal School graduates going out to teach in the bush country of Manitoba or the Dust Bowl of Saskatchewan, some of them mere slips of girls stranded alone in bachelor shacks in communities of alien people, she wondered that so many had survived at all, and had stuck it out, alongside the people, through droughts, frosts, hail and snowstorms. "Nobody has written their story, really," she thought. "Not the way it was."[3]

Such a story is difficult to tell because of the innumerable participants and conditions, but if it is to be told as it really was, the personal experiences of the participants must be utilized.

The subject of this chapter, the concerns of a novice, often female, rural schoolteacher, has been selected so as to provide insight into the personal trials and struggles of rural schoolteachers in western Canada and, also, to add to our understanding of a continuing, important professional issue. The transition from student to teacher or of shifting from the realm of teacher preparation to professional responsibility may be both dramatic and traumatic. Contemporary scholars, studying the phenomenon of profession-entry, refer to it as "reality shock." While the label and the interest may be relatively new, the experience is not. Just as conditions in our modern schools and the characteristics of beginning teachers cause some to forfeit their idealism, alter their behaviour, attitude and personality or even leave the profession, so, too, in our pioneer era did the reality of the prairie classroom and the qualities of teachers precipitate similar personal adjustments. Veenman has observed that "little is known about the cognitive and affective processes that characterize the transition into teaching."[4] This is as true, if not more so, for teachers beginning their careers fifty to seventy-five years ago as it is for their counterparts in our day. What follows is an attempt to reveal some of the reflections of pioneer prairie schoolteachers on what they encountered as young, inexperienced mentors in the period 1914 to 1939 on the Canadian Prairies.

The story of their solitary persistence in the face of adversity, helps us to appreciate why the establishment of a teachers' organization was so essential to teacher well-being and the improvement of schooling. Help was needed in order to change conditions which demanded far too much from individuals trying to provide schooling in rural western Canada and which were too entrenched for isolated individuals to change on a permanent basis.

The source material for this chapter, primarily accounts of retired schoolteachers acquired through questionnaires and interviews at the close of their careers, is problematic. Intervening years have dimmed, distorted or destroyed significant information. Even where memory is intact, privacy and personal discretion have limited the disclosures which have been made public. Therefore, in some instances the reader must fill in the blanks with conjecture and inference; these teachers, in describing their experiences, do not always state how they were affected by them. Nevertheless, the attempt to gain an empathetic appreciation of their experiences, even in the face of such limitations, remains important in enriching our knowledge of the past.

An effort could be made to derive from the hundreds of questionnaire responses and interview transcriptions a variety of historical topics including the ethnic and socio-economic origins of western Canadian teachers, their reasons for choosing teaching as a career, the nature of their teacher preparation programs, their employment opportunities, instructional problems, working conditions and community and professional help. As interesting as these observations might be, they are not the substance of this chapter. Teaching conditions, experiences, and responsibilities are highlighted, and the reader is invited to seek an understanding of how individual teachers reacted and managed their situations.

In the main, prairie schoolteachers in the period between the two world wars were female and of rural origin. Although women were numerically dominant in the profession, outnumbering men three to one, their ability and professional worth were undervalued, generally, in comparison to their male peers. Normal school officials noted declines in male recruitment, commenting that such trends did not "promise well for material from which to recruit our force of instructors, inspectors and supervisors."[5] Few, if any, seemed sensitive to the demeaning message being conveyed to the female teacher candidates. It was obvious men were preferred for leadership roles and often for classroom responsibility. Some women, like Nellie W., were not prepared to accept such biased selection procedures without a fight. Recalling her experience with the normal school principal who attempted to screen her out of the teacher preparation program on such irrelevant criteria as size and appearance, she notes how her resistance helped overcome the evident prejudice of his decision. The principal, Dr. Coffin, called her into his office at the end of the first week and informed her there were too many normal school students. She was among the group being asked to drop out of the program. The reasons given for her inclusion were that she was only seeking a second-class certificate, she couldn't pay her fees or purchase books, and she looked too young to discipline the children. The principal also wanted fewer female students in order to avoid combining men and women students in one class. Her account of the incident, as follows, reveals her willingness to stand up for her rights:

"What I said, I can't recall exactly, but I do remember that I told him:
1. My mother had died when I was a baby and I had helped with the family cooking and washing ever since. (No hired help in our farm home.)
2. I always stood first in all my classes and had won the Governor-General's Medal on my High School entrance.
3. I had helped the country teacher with all the little grades in my spare time.
4. We had driven four miles to school (3 little girls) and had taken the neighbour children, too—weather, no matter.
5. In High School we delivered 3—100 pound cans of milk each morning before we went to classes.
6. I had always dreamed of being a teacher, and would probably become the best one of the four hundred applicants. (I came 3rd.)

He grinned at my 5-foot 1 inch height and 110 pounds of self-confidence and said, "I believe you have the stuff from which a teacher is made. I have changed my mind. You may stay."[6]

Although the ranks of the teaching profession would have been virtually empty without female teachers, these young women learned, subtly and not so subtly, that their value to society in the role of teacher was not great. In some communities, their value was depreciated because the residents attached little importance to schooling. In other cases, they learned that their worth was measured by their eligibility for marriage or by their lower financial demands in salary and living accommodation. Whatever the source and nature of the indignity experienced through such messages directed at these young women, they largely went unchallenged and were accepted as conditions of the time.

There were those, albeit a limited number, who were critical of the unfair treatment of women and who were willing to pay a price for challenging bastions of male dominance. Edith M. tells of her decision, while attending the Calgary Normal School, to nominate and campaign for a female student as president of their student organization. This was a first. Heretofore, women candidates had not been allowed. Her action, confronting such a traditional practice, undoubtedly came at great personal cost, due to the worry, fear and conflict associated with the undertaking. As campaign manager, she led the parade through the men's common room, an area absolutely out-of-bounds to women. The principal, understandably, was shocked. Immediately, he summoned the candidate and the campaign manager to his office to censure their behaviour. The intimidation tactic did not daunt these upstarts. Aware that expulsion might result, the campaign manager accepted responsibility for organizing the parade and years later acknowledged that "he thought he could scare me to death, but I didn't back down."[7] As a result of the determination of these forceful, courageous young women, the administration was faced with difficult decisions. The principal who had agreed to the candidacy, in part on the belief that a woman could not win an election, eventually had to accept the first female student president in his school.

Confrontations precipitated by women students or by women teachers to assert their rights were not commonplace, and the differential treatment afforded males and females worked to the disadvantage of women throughout the period. Not until membership in professional organizations for teachers became law in the late 1930s was the inequity addressed and, then, rather slowly.

The disadvantages associated with being young and female as either a normal school student or a teacher in an isolated rural community were not limited to differential status or unequal opportunity. Novelists dealing with prairie life in the 1920s and 1930s commonly present the schoolteacher as a young female more interested in marriage than in professional responsibility. Typical is the picture presented by Arthur Storey in *Prairie Harvest*:

> Miss Mill was far from being an inspiration to the children. Like most of the young women who came to teach at Melness during and after the war, she had no real interest in the boys and girls or in education. Her teaching license she regarded merely as an admission ticket to a community in which there might be an eligible male. When she found one she married and left the school. Had she not found one within the year, she would have moved on to another school to continue her quest. So it was with Miss Crabb and Miss McIntosh and others who followed in quick succession.[8]

Even in the normal schools, the instructors reinforced this view of the women students by joking about preparing teachers who would become wives of farmers. Self-esteem as a professional, as a teacher with much to offer a community through its young people, must have been difficult to build when so many shared the view that women entered teaching to find a marriage partner.

Prospective suitors in a community unabashedly evidenced their interest in the teacher, contributing to the belief that marriage, rather than teaching, was the preferred object of her existence. According to a male teacher, observing the attention shown the new teachers in the district adjacent to his, "it was the custom that when the young teacher arrived all the eligible young men, as soon as was convenient, sometimes within the first day or two, would turn up at the school and introduce themselves."[9] Credibility is afforded this observation by an amusing anecdote told by Mary G. One day her students informed her that the inspector's car was approaching the school. When the driver knocked on the school door and was admitted by the teacher, he agreed to have her proceed with her teaching until recess when they would talk. The intervening twenty minutes of "The Ugly Duckling" passed quickly and then, at recess, the teacher discovered that the inspector "was an insurance salesman who had seen me at the last country dance and he had come to ask me for a date."[10]

There were other ways in which the rights of women teachers were denied or violated by the male members of society. Some men used positions of trust to take advantage of these teachers. Evidently, one normal school physical training instructor, enamoured with one of his class members, attempted to use another unwilling classmate to promote jealous feelings. He singled out an injured female student for his highly personal attention in the presence of the whole class. Considerable embarrassment, hurt and indignation resulted from the student's unwilling participation in this charade. She noted that:

Our physical training teacher had a "crush" on one of the girls in our class. By misfortune I had injured my right wrist. My wrist had been wrapped (with surgical tape and tongue depressors for splints) to prevent the cartilage from popping out. Two days later out P.T. instructor called me out of line and examined my wrist, while the class was instructed to circle the gym. Each time his student friend came by he teased her by "lovingly" stroking my hand, or embracing me, expressing his regrets at my suffering. Each time I tried to withdraw my injured wrist he held me closer just to see his friend's face turn red.[11]

Her position of vulnerability did not deter Florence M. from taking appropriate action. "I reported this to the principal, because he had hurt my wrist as well as my feeling of propriety."[12] Her concluding observation, "we lost our P.T. instructor,"[13] indicates that senior officials in the school were not prepared to tolerate such conduct.

Gaining a position of responsibility as a teacher did not free women from the demeaning and inappropriate behaviour of some men in the school district. Bessie M. remembers that at her boarding house, one shared periodically by threshing or railroad crews, the men (sometimes under the influence of liquor) caused considerable concern because it was difficult to "get them to keep their hands off."[14] School board officials occasionally manifested similar behaviour. Teachers were expected to attend the dances and parties of the community. Some were told by their hiring authorities "where to stay and which boy friends were acceptable."[15] One teacher reports how she "had to watch the chairman of the school board because he would get quite liquored up and he would start out to dance with the schoolteacher."[16] All night she was forced to be on guard in order to stay unavailable and out of reach until the dance concluded. She was a fair match for her drunken employer as she observed, "I never did dance with him."[17]

Some of the eligible bachelors were not above trading favours for the attention of the schoolmarm. Billie, the forty-two-year-old unmarried son of the landlady, offered the boarders a ride to school on his stoneboat in the cold weather. He informed Mairi B., during her ride, that the previous teacher had put her arms around him in order to be secure during the bumpy ride. Unlike her predecessor, Mairi ignored the invitation, observing that "never again was I offered a ride to school."[18]

Several observations emerge from these examples about what it meant to be a female teacher in prairie Canada after World War I. Many were confronted with conflicting signals about their place and responsibility in the community. People expected competence and virtue in their teachers. Yet, at the same time, these qualities were undermined or compromised. By failing to build the teacher's professional worth and contribution, by refusing to endorse the equal rights of women and men teachers and by minimizing the abilities of the large female membership, society ensured that large numbers of teachers would see the role as little more than a stepping stone to marriage or some other occupation.

Winning acceptance and respect in a community was difficult not only because one was young, inexperienced, female and single, but because teachers, whether male or female, frequently were viewed as outsiders in the community. Differences in ethnic or socio-economic background were used in some instances as excuses for treating the teacher as an intruder. In other cases the values represented by the teacher made parents and community members uncomfortable. Obvious differences in perspective and standard heightened the awareness of family or community practices and values which were not congruent with those of the teacher. It was risky, therefore, for teachers to seek living and employment conditions which further set them apart from others in the school district. To argue for better accommodation or remuneration, in the eyes of many, was a way teachers had of conveying that they were somehow superior to the rest of the community.

Teachers were required to endure considerable hardship and isolation in their teaching situations in order to maintain employment. This necessitated not only abiding physical deprivation or inconvenience, but also considerable emotional strength. While many were from rural homes, in the main, teachers were not familiar with the situations they encountered and endured. Living accommodations varied remarkably in standard. The query of one teacher aptly captures the challenge faced by those not raised on the farm—"Can you imagine a city girl being faced with green trees for kindling wood, coal buried under snow, janitorial duties or wrestling with a potbelly stove?"[19] In retrospect she could say little more than, "Ah well, I lived through it."[20]

In their living quarters, teachers were routinely plagued by mice, bed bugs, lice, the cold, the damp, poor food, primitiveness, lack of privacy, hostile neighbours and loneliness. Jean D. observed about her residence:

> The physical conditions during the first year were primitive. The main part of the house was made of logs which were swarming with bed bugs. My room was a lean-to made of lumber. In order to keep the bugs from invading my privacy, everything moveable in my room was taken outside and washed with coal-oil; this was a weekly occurrence. As my bedding-mattress, pillows and quilts were stuffed with raw wool from the local sheep (a smell I have always hated) I did not smell exactly like Chanel No. 5.[21]

Another teacher slept with the mother and child in one bedroom while a male boarder slept with the husband in the other bedroom. In her second boarding place Lenore S. found the temperature occasionally dropped below zero in her room during the night.[22] There were districts where no one wanted the teacher as a boarder. In one such area a family was willing to provide room and board in their mud house. The roof was thatched with straw and the walls were made of mud and straw. The house was one long building, first the kitchen and living room, then the bedroom for mother, father and three children, next the teacher's bedroom, and on the other side of her room was the barn attached to the house.[23] Some were fortunate to have the privacy of a teacherage, but like the boarding house, the quality of these varied considerably. Water stored in barrels froze and spilled over the floor.[24] Some living quarters were little more than a lean-to built on the school. One teacherage had a felt roof that absorbed water and sagged with the weight of water from melting snow. Poking a hole in the felt alleviated the threat of the roof collapsing, but it created the problem of running water.[25] Not only were these facilities primitive; they were also "lonely and scary."[26] That teachers endured such stressful conditions is a strong testimonial to their qualities of character.

Social conditions faced by some teachers added greatly to the demands of their assignment. Margaret G. acknowledged that in one home she had to abide "much quarreling and lying and violence."[27] The threat of a mentally unstable landlady hung over the head of Bessie M. When finally the landlady poured red ink on her clothes, she decided it was time to move.[28] Personal sacrifices of teachers were only part of their ordeal. The struggles of children facing abuse, malnutrition or deprivation affected the outlook of their teachers. Teacher Alfred H. was so offended by the conditions experienced by his students during the Depression that he decided to enter politics under the Social Credit banner in an effort to alleviate their pain.[29] The sense of futility or frustration experienced by teachers who faced the suffering of their students is captured by Vera Lysenko as she had her teacher Julie think out loud about one of her students:

> What is a teacher to do, when she sees a promising pupil like Katie slipping away from her, because her environment is too much for her to handle? What are those few moments I can give her each day? With fifty-five pupils, I have about six minutes daily with each. That's hardly enough to counteract the effects of a lifetime of abuse.[30]

Having to face children daily who were hungry and cold was a serious concern of teachers. "There were families who were really poor ... they didn't have anything really. I felt sorry for the children. I know the children were hungry."[31] Some little ones were inadequately clothed for the weather conditions they faced in winter. When a serious storm developed one day in Eva's school, sensing the children's lack of proper apparel she recalls, "I remember taking our school curtains and tearing them in strips and wrapping the children's limbs."[32] Not all teachers dealt successfully with life-threatening situations, particularly those associated with winter storms. Children like those recalled by Hector T. died in a blizzard, getting lost between the outhouse and the school.[33] Teachers willingly shared their beds, their food, their shelter in order to protect their students.

While there was much to do to keep busy as a beginning teacher facing large classes and multi-grades, and while there were trying physical conditions to endure, even more oppressive were hours of fear and loneliness with which rural teachers contended, not always successfully.[34] Some of the isolation and loneliness was overcome through association with families in the school district. Others longed for such an opportunity. "I was never taken anywhere with the farm family. They would spend Sunday with friends leaving me at home. Once I asked to go to town fifteen miles away. They didn't have room."[35] Young Bessie M. felt a similar loneliness, her unhappiness compounded by her unsuitable accommodation. She wished her parents would come get her and take her home. Yet she knew "it wasn't possible because my parents were poor and they couldn't do it. They didn't even have a car. They never came to see me in the three years that I was there which was only about fifty-five miles from my home. They never came to see me once in those three years that I was there."[36]

Beginning teachers armed with their normal school education and their Grade XI or XII schooling experienced endless challenges in their one-room classrooms. Whatever their struggles in their personal lives due to prevailing views about women or teaching and due to conditions of hardship and loneliness, the situation within the classroom was even more demanding. Foremost in importance was the concern of orchestrating instruction for twenty to thirty youngsters, even fifty to sixty at times, in numerous grades, sometimes including high school. The numbers of students, separate preparations and courses of instruction were enough of a professional challenge to the beginner to demand seemingly endless hours of work. "Handling grades one through nine was very, very difficult for me. I used to work until twelve o'clock at night preparing lessons and I would get up at five o'clock in the morning preparing lessons .... Many of the exercises that we did, I had to write on the board. So I would get up in the morning and fill the boards with exercises for these students and do the same thing after school and sometimes I would have to spend my noon hour putting questions on the board for the students to do."[37]

Survival and success as a teacher required more than hard work and management skills. Teachers were tested in a variety of ways. Forer, writing about a rural schoolteacher, noted that Miss Langois

> had survived that stench of urine poured into the school stove; she had laughed off rumours of an illicit affair with a student, she had conquered the midwinter cold of broken windows and stolen fuel-oil, and she had extinguished one serious attempt to burn down the schoolhouse. She had lived with nights of catcalls and peeping boys; she had confiscated real pistols, dynamite caps, kitchen knives, and obscene drawings.[38]

Some of the escapades were nothing more than harmless pranks. Ivan N. recalls coming to school one morning and discovering a bunch of chickens mysteriously locked in the school.[39] Hyacinthe B. had to contend with dead mice in her desk[40] and Moline W. with a freshly butchered pig's tail.[41] The contest for control between students and teachers was not always won by the teacher. Rifle shells exploding in the stove were enough to cause Miss Langois' predecessor to seek employment elsewhere. Some of the student pranksters engaged in dangerous sport on occasion. The school building was a favourite target. Ivan N. tells of his experience with an arson attempt on the schoolhouse.

> I don't know why it happened but some boys set the school on fire. They got up into the attic somehow and there was no doubt at all that the fire was set because there were rags and kerosene. Fortunately, a young man who lived in the neighbourhood was coming home rather late at night and saw this school on fire. I suppose the boys who set the fire didn't like school or didn't like me.[42]

Discipline was a concern of many teachers. One inspector readily acknowledged he "believed in hiring big people as teachers"[43] as one way of ensuring teacher dominance in the classroom. The older, bigger boys were not always willing to submit to the direction of their teachers. Davis K. tells of his gaining the upper hand over an unruly boy by physical means. When the boy defied him, Davis K. "just hauled off and gave him a slap on the side of his face and kicked his feet from under him."[44] He then stretched him over a register under a window and strapped him. There was no room for a teacher who could not keep order.

Similarly, there was no place for a teacher who could not deal with a wide variety of unpredictable crises and responsibilities. While practicing with the children for the Christmas concert, Mable M. was frightened by the behaviour of a student experiencing an epileptic seizure, something she had never seen let alone treated before.[45] She recalled a short talk on the subject given at normal school which enabled her to help the lad. Medical expertise was required of teachers for a variety of reasons. In normal school Florence M. was taught not to leave a dislocated finger or toe unattended or it would swell. When one of her students presented his dislocated toe to her for treatment, she remembered the instruction to reset it. Not knowing whether it was broken or dislocated, she experienced considerable relief when her pulling resulted in the toe being restored to its proper fit.[46] The absence of qualified medical personnel in rural areas meant that rural residents ran the risk of poor or non-existent treatment or long-distance travel under adverse conditions to see a doctor. Gertrude N., while boarding with an elderly gentleman and his daughter, had to care for the old man when he had a stroke. Even though they were over one hundred miles from a major city, the teacher decided to drive the girl and her father to the city, in a Model T truck. She knew that if she did not venture out, risky as the long drive was for two young women, the elderly man would die.[47]

Just as teachers faced social isolation and loneliness they also encountered professional isolation and neglect. There was no readily-available source of professional help for the teacher of the rural one-room school. The inspector was often the sole professional contact for the fledgling teacher. Unfortunately, their services often left much to be desired. They seldom visited one school more than once a year, nor stayed long enough during their visit to offer much constructive assistance. According to Cloe D. not one ever said, "Can I help you?"[48] When they were asked for assistance by those brave or needy enough to make the request, their responses were not always helpful. One teacher noted, "When the new Course of Study arrived, I wrote to my inspector and said, 'Why don't you come out and give me some instructions. I haven't a clue how to do this and I can't afford to go to summer school.'"[49] He wrote right back to say, "Neither have I. But do it anyway for this year, and next year I will get you a grant to go to summer school."[50] Olive M.'s first school was like that of many of her fellow rural prairie schoolteachers.

There were fifty-one children to grade seven. The people, I soon discovered, were all Eastern European—Ukrainian, Russian, Romanian and Galician. It was a badly built school. Light could be seen under the windows. The desks were the double seat variety and there were not enough of them. The little ones had to sit three in a desk .... Worst of all, there was a shortage of textbooks and no library at all.

Language was the real and worst problem .... It had never dawned on me that there were places in Alberta where English was not spoken. From grade three up English was spoken, but the beginners were my Waterloo. I did not know how to handle the situation. Now I know, I failed at it.[51]

Where was her professional help? Sadly she acknowledges, "The inspector did not come at all. I felt these schools should have been given special attention, that we should have had more assistance, supplies and backing. Nobody seemed to care."[52]

Changes in the curriculum, especially changes as pronounced as the Enterprise introduced in Alberta and Saskatchewan in 1936 and 1939 respectively, heightened teachers' awareness of their professional isolation and the inadequacies of their preparation and their support system. One teacher recalls that the enterprise system was introduced in her third year of teaching. "The inspector was firm in his opinion that the enterprise system must be taught, but did not give much idea as to what and how."[53] Many practicing teachers openly admitted, as did Nettie S., that when the new curriculum was introduced, "I wasn't prepared at all."[54] According to her "no one could tell you what to do, inspectors least of all."[55] She went so far as to ask the deputy minister, Dr. G.F. McNally, what to do. When she expressed her lack of understanding, he observed, "To tell you the truth Nettie, I don't know much about it either."[56]

It is not surprising that one Alberta inspector, W.R. Hay, commented that he had "found the quality of instruction given by teachers in the rural schools rather mediocre."[57] Prior to World War II little had been done to alter significantly the conditions of teaching in rural, western Canada. The personal accounts and recollections of the teachers of the period suggest that the rural school experience, the beginning assignment for nearly all normal school graduates, was physically, emotionally, and professionally demanding, so much so that many of these young people lived lives of quiet, lonely, desperation as they tried to provide a limited level of educational service to their students. Their willingness to endure these conditions at considerable personal discomfort and sacrifice has led to the establishment of a professional support system which enables modern beginning teachers to function at much higher levels of professional competence and personal fulfilment.

NOTES

1 Walt Mason, "The Schoolmarm," *The ATA Magazine* (Feb. 1930): cover.
2 In Canada this growing interest in teaching as a focus of historical research is reflected in such publications as Elizabeth Graham, "Schoolmarms and Early Teaching in Ontario," in *Women at Work* (Toronto: Canadian Women's Educational Press, 1974), Alison Prentice, "The Feminization of Teaching," in S.M. Trofimenkoff and A. Prentice, eds., *The Neglected Majority: Essays in Canadian Women's History* (Toronto, McClelland and Stewart Ltd., 1977), John Charyk, *The Little White Schoolhouse* (Saskatoon, Prairie Books, 1968), *Those Bittersweet Schooldays* (Saskatoon Prairie Books, 1977), *Syrup Pails and Gopher Tails* (Saskatoon Prairie Books, 1983) and Robert S. Patterson, "History of Teacher Education in Alberta," in D.C. Jones, N.M. Sheehan, R.M. Stamp, eds., *Shaping the Schools of the Canadian West*, (Calgary: Detselig Enterprises Ltd., 1979).
3 Vera Lysenko, *Westerly Wild* (Toronto: Ryerson Press, 1956), p. 173.
4 Simon Veenman, "Perceived Problems of Beginning Teachers," *Review of Educational Research* (Summer, 1984): 168.
5 Alberta Government, Department of Education, *Annual Report of the Department of Education* (Edmonton: King's Printer, 1917), p. 20.
6 Project Yesteryear Questionnaire No. 47, R.S. Patterson file, University of Alberta, p. 1, hereafter PYQ.
7 Interview No. 24, R.S. Patterson file, University of Alberta, p. 4, hereafter Interview.
8 Arthur Storey, *Prairie Harvest* (Toronto: Ryerson Press, 1959), p. 104.
9 Interview No. 32, p. 19.
10 PYQ No. 661, p. 5.
11 Normal School Questionnaire No. 78, R.S. Patterson file, University of Alberta, p. 3, hereafter NSQ.
12 Ibid.
13 Ibid.
14 Interview No. 45, p. 10.
15 PYQ No. 225, p. 4.
16 Interview No. 41, p. 9.
17 Ibid.
18 NSQ No. 95, p. 6.
19 PYQ No. 268b., p. 3.
20 Ibid.
21 PYQ No. 487, p. 3.
22 Interview No. 25, p. 7.
23 Interview No. 45, p. 3.
24 Interview No. 8, p. 7.

25 Ibid.

26 PYQ No. 151, p. 3.

27 PYQ No. 661, p. 3.

28 Interview No. 45, p. 10.

29 Interview No. 1, p. 2.

30 Lysenko, *Westerly Wild*, pp. 124-125.

31 Interview No. 25, p. 9.

32 Interview No. 26, p. 10.

33 Interview No. 8, p. 1.

34 PYQ No. 151, p. 3.

35 PYQ No. 197e, p. 3.

36 Interview No. 25, p. 8.

37 Interview No. 21, p. 21.

38 Mort Forer, *The Humback* (Toronto: McClelland & Stuart, 1969), p. 186.

39 Interview No. 29, p. 9.

40 Interview No. 27, p. 12.

41 Interview No. 34, p. 4.

42 Interview No. 29, p. 26.

43 Interview No. 33, p. 9.

44 Ibid.

45 NSQ No. 95, p. 6.

46 NSQ No. 78, p. 5.

47 Interview No. 50, p. 13.

48 PYQ No. 124C, p. 13.

49 Ibid., p. 15.

50 Ibid.

51 NSQ No. 2844, p. 4.

52 Ibid., p. 6.

53 PYQ No. 625, p. 5.

54 PYQ No. 5, p. 5.

55 Ibid.

56 Ibid.

57 Alberta Government, Department of Education, *Annual Report of the Department of Education*, (Edmonton: King's Printer, 1931), pp. 51-52.

*   *   *   *   *

Documents for Chapter Five

Robert Patterson conducted interviews to gain an understanding of why individuals decided to teach in the Prairies, what problems they encountered, and how they attempted to solve them. The following documents examine similar themes from different perspectives. Document 21, for example, is Mary E. Bisson's autobiographical account of teaching in Quebec's rural Protestant schools in the first half of the twentieth century. To what extent does each of these documents support Patterson's findings? What can be learned about gendered ideas from Documents 19 and 20? Following the Second World War, the Canadian Education Association surveyed Canadian teachers regarding salaries, and working and living conditions. Document 22 explores rural teachers' living conditions and these teachers' attitudes towards parents, school boards, and the community. Compare these survey results to the conditions discussed by Robert Patterson. The final document is an advertisement in the small Maritime newspaper *Messenger and Visitor*. What information about teaching and schools can be gleaned from this advertisement?

19) LETTERS TO THE WOMEN'S PAGES, 1907[1]

Dear Prim Rose:

Here comes another school teacher from Manitoba and Saskatchewan.

I was seventeen when I first left home, and went bravely off, some two hundred and fifty miles to my first school, and now, six years later, I wish to say in favour of the Western people, that in every place I have been, I have met with great kindness and consideration, and always managed to have a thoroughly good time. I think it is often a teacher's own fault if the people are not nice to her.

I wonder how many of my fellow teachers have experienced the awful loneliness that came over me one spring day when I stood, a forlorn creature, beside my boxes at a wayside flag station and watched the train (my last friend) rapidly diminishing in the distance. There was one other passenger besides myself, whom I envied as I saw him meet his friends and drive off, but no one came for poor me.

Finally when the feeling of desolation was becoming very strong, I saw a great lumber wagon, with a double box and spring seat on it approaching. The big farm horses were plunging through water and half-melted April snow, urged onward by a red-whiskered little man perched aloft on the aforesaid spring seat. It was a mercy I was prepared for emergencies, or else when he drew up beside me, and invited me to ascend, I might have looked rather aghast.

"This," I thought, "is rural life with a vengeance," as we went bumpety, bumpety, bump! over the hard icy roads. Since then I have ridden many times in a lumber wagon, often minus even a spring seat. (One of the best times I ever had was a ride ten miles to a picnic, with a merry party of young people, and on that occasion all the "spring" we got was from a straight, smooth board.)

How well I remember the first dinner I had in the district, bacon, fried eggs, and mashed potatoes! How I enjoyed it! And then after the dinner, the drive to my boarding place. The people were away except the three young children who were "keeping house" till papa and mamma came home from town. I sat down, not very cheerfully, I must confess, beside the kitchen stove, on which a big pot of horse feed was boiling. Then I began to conjure up an idea of what my landlady would be like. I had just decided she would be about 45, a big coarse, red-faced untidy Irish woman, with a tongue as long as your arm, when the oldest boy cried out, "Here they come!" The sound of wheels was heard, and the next moment came the freshest, sweetest young matron of twenty-five or thereabouts, you ever saw. She was Irish, with the most beautiful complexion, and eyes and hair, but above all, she had that purely Irish friendliness, so good to a homesick girl. I can't help remarking, before I pass on, what a bright, cheery light that little woman shed through that home and she is only one of the many admirable and noble country women I have met.

The next day was Sunday, and upon my asking about church, I was told service was held in the school house. Methodist one Sunday and Baptist the next. I thought I would much rather stay at home, but of course, that wouldn't do. Some who have passed through the same experience, can imagine the ordeal of that first Sunday, far worse that the first school day. Every one seemed, by the amount of gazing (I will not say staring) directed towards me, to be intensely interested in the new "schoolmarm." It made me feel rather uncomfortable, and I thought, "What dreadful people!" but before the summer was over, I learned to know and understand them better. Some of those same people are my fast friends to this day.

Then followed the first week of teaching. I remember how I calculated each day, what fraction of the whole term I had put in. Every day also meant long walks to the post office so many times to be met with disappointment: I was consumed with homesickness, and I recollect now how longingly I used to gaze after the train as it whizzed past my little school every morning.

The second week brought the first home letter. After that everything seemed all right. Every day I grew more interested in my work, and in the people. In the autumn it was with real regret that I said good-bye to my many friends.

Since then, I have had various experiences, some pleasant, some otherwise, I have walked two miles to school in the winter over unbroken road, have waded through water so deep as to come in over the tops of my long rubber boots, have had salmon sandwiches for two weeks straight for my school luncheon, have wrestled mightily with the dreadful insects, have had to light my own fires occasionally when the thermometer registered 40 deg[rees] below and last, but not least, have had the misfortune to be almost plagued to death by some of the Western bachelors!

But if I walked two miles in the winter, I have also had the pleasure of the early walk in the summer, with the dew sparkling on the grass and wild roses shedding perfume on every side; I have known what it is to have a long, delightful gallop over the prairie; have spent merry Saturdays nutting and berrypicking; have had delicious strawberries and ice cream instead of salmon. Also I have met some bachelors who were not plagues.

Wishing all other teachers and readers of the Prim Rose column, all sorts of luck, and hoping to hear from a few of them.

Imogen [Manitoba]

* * * * *

20) RULES FOR P.E.I. TEACHERS, 1879[2]

1. Teachers each day will fill lamps and clean chimneys before starting work.
2. Each teacher will bring a bucket of coal and a scuttle of coal for the day's sessions.
3. Mark your pens carefully. You may whittle nibs to the individual taste of the children.
4. Men teachers may take one evening a week for courting purposes or two evenings to attend church regularly.
5. After ten hours of school, you may spend the remaining time reading the Bible or other good books.
6. Women who marry or engage in unseemingly conduct will be dismissed.
7. Each teacher should lay aside, from each pay a goodly sum for his benefit during their declining years so that they will not become a burden to society.
8. Any teacher who smokes, uses liquor in any form, frequents pool or public halls, or gets shaved in a barber shop, will give good reason to suspect his worth, intention, integrity and honesty.

* * * * *

21) TEACHING IN QUEBEC'S PROTESTANT SCHOOLS[3]

Fifty years of teaching. What memories they evoke! Late in August 1913 I received a letter from the Secretary-Treasurer of the School Board in Peninsula on the Gaspé Coast, asking me if I would consent to teach in their Number Two Rural School for the coming term. I was then seventeen years of age and the thought of being asked to accept a teaching position made me very happy. The salary offered was one hundred seventy-five dollars for a ten-month term, which seemed to me at that time a fabulous sum. Since cost of board and lodging was only six dollars per month, I felt that I would soon be rich.

Early in September I travelled down the coast by train to the village of Gaspé. My feelings were mixed. I was excited at the prospect, but I had many feelings of uncertainty. Would I be successful? Would I be able to discipline big boys perhaps almost as old as I? Would I be homesick?

Finally the train puffed into Gaspé Station. I had reached the point of no return. I was met at the Station by the Chairman of the School Board who took me across the bay in his little boat. He had left his horse on the Peninsula side, so we drove the last two miles to his house. It had taken me approximately nine hours to make the journey, as compared with three or four hours needed to travel that same trip today. I shall never forget the kindness of the Chairman and his wife who made me feel comfortable that night in their pleasant home. Their warm welcome did much to dispel my fears.

The next morning was an exciting one because I was to be taken to the home where I would board, and I would also get my first glimpse of my new school.

The school was the usual one-room rural school of those days; but this one was bright and pleasant, set on a hill, surrounded by fir trees and overlooking the sparkling waters of Gaspé Bay. A small table served as the teacher's desk. The children's benches were homemade to accommodate three or four children each; a wooden chalkboard, painted black, was at the back of the room; and the inevitable wood-burning stove occupied the middle of the room.

The first school day arrived and although I reached school early that morning, the pupils were earlier. They had come to greet "the new teacher." They little knew how I was trembling inwardly.

School routine was soon established with emphasis on the Three R's. To have a scribbler and a lead pencil was indeed a luxury. Slates were the order of the day. Each child had a damp cloth to clean his slate when both sides were filled. The ink bottles were made of brown crockery, and sat on the desks of the older pupils. One bottle would contain about six months' supply of ink. The occasional accident was inevitable.

The drinking water from a nearby well was kept in a galvanized pail with a tin cover. One tin cup served the fourteen thirsty children.

In winter we faced other problems. Sometimes the wood refused to burn, so that the classroom was often uncomfortably chilly until about ten o'clock. Since matches were expensive, great care had to be taken that we didn't use too many at one time. By the end of May I had become an excellent stoker. Darkness came early in the afternoon and there was no illumination of any kind. Janitors were unheard of in those days, therefore monitors were appointed to haul wood and water, and to clean the room. If a monitor "forgot" his duties, I swept and dusted before leaving school and carried the wood from the porch to the classroom early next morning.

Life at my boarding house was pleasant but uneventful. Lessons were prepared and homework corrected by the light of an oil lamp. Mail arrived three times a week. How eagerly I listened for the courier to pass with his old horse going cloppety-clop.

For entertainment on Saturday evenings we visited the neighbours' homes where we had gay sing-songs and played parlour games. Sundays were devoted to morning and evening church service and a quiet walk or afternoon rest.

For months thus passed and finally the magic words "Going Home for Christmas" became a reality. In order to go home, it was necessary to drive by horse and sleigh across ice for many miles to reach Gaspé Station. The journey to my little village station seemed endless, but at last I arrived to be greeted joyfully by my father. To this day I can still remember sitting cosily beside him, warmed by buffalo robes as he drove his prize mare merrily homeward to the music of sleigh bells.

Aftr teaching on a permit for three years at the Peninsula School, I was convinced that I wanted to make this my career, and so I entered a teacher training class at Macdonald College. I little realized, when I graduated, that I would give my life to such a noble work.

* * * * *

22) RURAL TEACHERS' GRIEVANCES, 1949[4]

1) **Four-fifths of the teachers reporting in this survey make no mention of restrictions but the other one-fifth list 344 specific instances as given in the Table below.**

RESTRICTIONS PLACED UPON PERSONAL FREEDOM OF THE RURAL TEACHER

	Teachers' home	Community
Use of liquor	47	55
Use of tobacco	36	37
Choice of companions	15	25
Attendance required at church or Sunday School	18	19
Playing cards	10	10
Dancing	6	11
Listening to radio	17	—
Dating	7	8
Going away week-ends	5	4
Playing musical instruments	6	3
Use of general family rooms	5	—

2) Recreational facilities for rural teachers.

Number of Replies: 335

45.37% complain that recreational facilities are poor,
35.52% report they are fair only,
16.42% claim recreational facilities are good,
2.69% find such facilities excellent.

In replies to a question regarding the kinds of recreation in which they participate, these rural teachers gave the following (listed here in order of frequency mentioned):

Reading, dancing, movies, skating, softball and baseball, playing cards, hiking, music, radio, hockey, bowling, skiing, church and related activities, visiting neighbours and friends, community parties, fishing and hunting, handicrafts, swimming, motoring, and twenty other kinds each of which was mentioned not more than five times.

Some of those reporting indicate that as individuals they may seek out and buy some recreation in the form of dancing, movies, or skating in the nearest town or village, but the great majority find little opportunity to associate with others of their own age in any form of entertainment or recreation.

Out of 335 replies—

56 mention baseball and softball,
20 play hockey,
17 engage in curling,
25 mention community parties.

"Do you enjoy living in your community?"
84.69% answered YES

"Do you feel welcome in your community?"
91.17% answered YES

3) Teachers' observations regarding school boards

73.33 percent report that the School Board shows an interest in the improvement of the school and strives to provide the teacher with modern equipment. It may be presumed from answers received that about one-quarter of the rural school board members show no special interest in improving the school beyond the performance of their routine duties as trustees.

Occasionally we hear of interference by trustees in the internal administration of the school. This survey shows only 4.14 percent of the trustees accused of such interference.

4) Rural teachers' ratings of relations with parents and pupils are as follows:

	Good %	Fair %	Poor %
With parents	79.13	19.71	1.16
With pupils	92.22	7.78	....

5) Paramount needs in the school community as reported by 435 rural teachers:

	Number of Times Mentioned
Improvement of playground and playing facilities	258
More schoolroom supplies and equipment	207
Better sanitary arrangements	183
Health unit for periodic examination of children	179
More teacher assistance	164
(by supervisors and special visiting teachers for certain subjects such as music, art, manual training, home economics, etc.)	
Circulating library	145
Building repairs or additions	145
Formation of an active Home and School or	133
Parent Teacher association	
Better living quarters for the teacher	78
Consolidation of schools	69
Larger unit of administration	60

Among other needs mentioned (frequency under 20) were: Better water supply, Electricity, Better caretaking arrangements, More audio-visual aids, Some organized community recreation for the children.

* * * * *

23) TEACHERS' TROUBLES[5]

Teachers' Troubles

How Teachers May Prevent the Breakdown of the Nervous System which often Threatens.

The worry and work, the strain and anxiety of a teacher's life are such as to tell severely on the nervous system. Time and again teachers have had to give up good positions on account of run down health and shattered nerves. To such we confidently recommend Milburn's Heart and Nerve Pills, and in doing so we are supported by the testimony of Mrs. Reilly, Colborne Street, Chatham, Ont., who made the following statement:—"Milburn's Heart and Nerve Pills are, beyond question, the best remedy for nervousness and all exhausted conditions of the system I know of. My daughter, as a result of over study and close application to her duties as school teacher, became much run down and debilitated and was very nervous. Two months ago she began taking Milburn's Heart and Nerve Pills. They acted quickly and effectually in her case, making her strong and building up her entire system." Milburn's Heart and Nerve Pills cure Palpitation, Nervousness, Sleeplessness, Anaemia, Female Troubles, After Effects of Grippe, Debility or any condition arising from Disordered Nerves, Weak Heart or Watery Blood. Price 50c. a box.

* * * * *

1   Letters to the Women's pages of the *Family Herald and Weekly Star*, [Montreal], 17 April 1907, as quoted in *Historical Studies in Education*, 9, 1 (1997), 89-91.
2   Courtesy Mary Juanita Rossiter, P.E.I.
3   Mary E. Bisson, "Half a Century in Quebec Protestant Schools," *The Educational Record of the Province of Quebec*, 80, 1 (January-March, 1964), 11-12.
4   "Recommendations Concerning the Status of the Teaching Profession," *Canadian Education*, 5, 1 (December, 1949), 100-102, 107-108.
5   "Teachers' Troubles," advertisement in the *Messenger and Visitor* (28 February 1900).

Chapter Six:
Gender and Domestic Science

The leading advocate for the teaching of domestic science in Ontario schools was Adelaide Hoodless. In 1889, Adelaide Hoodless' 18-month-old son died as a result of drinking a glass of contaminated milk. Adelaide felt responsible and determined that the knowledge needed to prevent such a tragedy should be available to all women. "Apart from my family duties," she later wrote, "the education of mothers has been my life work."

At this time, the importance of cleanliness was not well understood. Flies swarmed in the kitchen, horse-drawn wagons delivered milk in open cans, and uncovered wells and sewers contributed to the spread of disease. In addition, with the growth of urbanization and industrialization, there was a growing concern that mothers who spent long hours as clerks, maids, secretaries, and factory labourers did not have the time to impart needed domestic skills to their daughters—resulting in broken marriages and sick and stunted children.

Hoodless was then 32 years old. As the wife of a wealthy Hamilton manufacturer, her life consisted of charity work and entertaining in her large home surrounded by four acres of lawns and gardens. She decided that schools should teach young women how to prepare food, look after children, and be cleanly. Hoodless defined domestic science as "the application of scientific principles to the management of a Home …. It teaches the value of pure air, proper food, systematic management; economy of time, labour, and money; higher ideals of home life, and its relation to the State; more respect for domestic occupations; the prevention of disease; civic and domestic sanitation; care of children; home nursing, and what to do in emergencies; in short, a direct education for women as home-makers."

Adelaide Hoodless faced intense opposition. Many people, both men and women, argued that women were born with the knowledge of how to be good homemakers. Since it was as natural as breathing or walking, there was no need to teach domestic science. Adelaide spent the next few years explaining her ideas to anyone who would listen. Her son later recalled, "She was ridiculed in the press as one of those despised 'new women.' The most frequent piece of advice people gave her was to stay at home and take care of her family."

When the male trustees on the Hamilton school board rejected her ideas, she turned to the YMCA for help. Hoodless became the national president of the YWCA in 1894, and it established cooking classes. The previous year, Hoodless helped to establish the National Council of Women, which also sought to have Domestic Science classes included in the public school system.

Hoodless again tackled Hamilton Board of Education. Even though the

YWCA promised to pay the domestic science teacher's salary, the board again refused to add classes in cooking and sewing to the public school's curriculum.

In an age when most women avoided controversy, Hoodless took the initiative. She gave more than 60 speeches to school boards and teachers' groups throughout the province. In 1903, Hoodless persuaded tobacco millionaire Sir William Macdonald to create the Macdonald Institute in Guelph to train Canadian women in the teaching of domestic science. At the request of the Ontario Minister of Education, she wrote a domestic science text book. This "little red book" contained calorie charts, information about proper nutrition, and chemical analysis of various foods. Finally, in 1904, the Hamilton board of education established cooking and sewing classes. When Adelaide Hoodless died in 1910, thirty-nine Ontario schools had domestic science courses.

In the following article, Barbara Riley uses the struggle to establish domestic science classes in British Columbia as a vehicle to examine contemporary gendered ideas and the perceived role of education. Other useful secondary sources include: Robert M. Stamp, "The New Education Movement—Those 'Yankee Frills,'" in R.M. Stamp, *The Schools of Ontario, 1876-1976* (Toronto, 1982); Neil Sutherland, *Children in English-Canadian Society: Framing the Twentieth Century Consensus* (Toronto, 1978); Marta Danylewycz, "Domestic Science Education in Ontario, 1900-1940," in Ruby Heap, Alison Prentice, eds., *Gender and Education in Ontario: An Historical Reader* (Toronto, 1991); and Katherine Arnup, *Education for Motherhood: Advice for Mothers in Twentieth-Century Canada* (Toronto, 1994).

* * * * *

Six Saucepans to One: Domestic Science vs The Home in British Columbia, 1900-1939[46]

" ... very many young women of the present day fail to recognize homemaking as an art, and ... regard it only in the light of drudgery of housework. This we believe to be largely the result of a lack of scientific knowledge on the subject, and for the remedy of which we look largely to the study of the subject in a scientific manner by our girls in the public schools."

So wrote the Corresponding Secretary of the Local Council of Women to the editor of the Victoria *Daily Colonist* in March 1903. That same year the Victoria School Board accepted the Council's offer to equip a kitchen in Central School for the teaching of domestic science. The board fulfilled its side of the bargain by hiring a teacher, Winnifred McKeand. In September, the

Daily Colonist interviewed McKeand, who explained that her course would teach the theory and practice of household management along scientific lines. Educational theory stressed the development of the whole child by training the mind, eye, and hand; this theory, applied to household management, taught the "household arts" through a combination of scientific explanation and practical work.[47] In February, after the *Daily Colonist* visited McKeand's classroom, it noted the emphasis placed on cleanliness, exactness, and order as the students learned about the chemical properties of wheat and made muffins.[48] Later in the school year, McKeand lectured on domestic science to the Local Council of Women, explaining that as there was not enough time in the home for teaching, the school had to train young girls in woman's "noblest" occupation, that of homemaker.[49]

Winnifred McKeand, graduate of the Boston School of Cookery and the Montreal School of Cookery, had taught domestic science classes at two schools in Nova Scotia. Her approach to the teaching of domestic science incorporated the most up-to-date social and educational theories supporting its inclusion in the school curriculum:

a) the school had a duty to develop the child's habits and character so as to produce a responsible and useful citizen;

b) girls needed formal training, which the home was not able to provide, to prepare them for their future careers as homemakers, or, in some cases, servants;

c) education in the household arts would teach girls to apply scientific principles to the management of the home;

d) domestic science classes would provide a practical education to train the hand and the heart as well as the head.

These ideas fuelled the struggle to establish domestic science as an accredited subject in the public school system of British Columbia, as in the rest of English Canada. Behind the ideas lay strong convictions about the role of young girls and women in the home, the role of the home in society, and the role of the educational system in strengthening both.

The period 1900-1930 encompasses two key points in the development of domestic science in British Columbia. Although needlework had been introduced as an optional subject for girls in Victoria schools in 1895, the first formal classes in domestic science in British Columbia began with the hiring of Winnifred McKeand in 1903. This was made possible through the initiative of local women in persuading their school board to establish the subject. Local initiative remained the essential factor in the spread of domestic science classes over the next decades.[50] In 1926, the province appointed its first Director of Home Economics. In this year, British Columbia had fifty-five home economics teachers supervising 11,455 girls, or twenty-three percent of all girls enrolled in primary and secondary schools across the province.[51] The appointment of a full-time, professionally trained home economist as director served notice that the province, or at least the department, recognized the need to provide a standardized approach to domestic science in teacher training, in classroom theory and practice, and in the relationship of domestic science to the school curriculum and to the provincial educational system.

While the struggle to prepare British Columbia's girls to take their places as homemakers was underway in classrooms across the province, these same girls continued to be trained as girls had always been—at home, by their mothers. This was confirmed through interviews with thirty-six women who had spent most of their childhood in British Columbia and who had taken domestic science in the province's elementary schools between 1910 and 1930. The majority had been raised and had attended school in an urban locale, usually Victoria or Vancouver; their backgrounds were Anglo-Saxon and mostly middle-class.[52] The interviews shed light on established household practice and the real conditions of domestic labour in British Columbia homes during the first decades of the twentieth century.

Frances' family came to Victoria from Ireland in 1911 when she was nine years old. She could not remember a time when she was not helping her mother with the housework required to keep a family with nine children. She and her sisters washed the dishes, made the beds, scrubbed the linoleum floors on their hands and knees, and peeled vegetables. When Frances was high school age, she quit school to stay home. She became the full-time family cook so that her mother could do the laundry, ironing, and cleaning. The family could not afford to hire help. Kathleen was born in 1909. By the time she was six years old she was washing dishes and setting the table; when she was older she vacuumed, made beds, and cleaned windows. Hired help assisted with cleaning, kitchen work, and other household chores. Her mother preserved "quarts and quarts" of fruit and vegetables from the garden, salted green beans, and canned salmon and other fish. Lauretta, born in 1916, was busy in the kitchen when she was six years old. As her mother was often ill, she made most of the family's meals. Every Saturday she made five pies for the week; every Monday morning she phoned in the grocery order for delivery. She spent the summer putting up preserves. The laundry was done commercially as the family had no hired help.[53]

At home, as in the school system, although there was individual variation from one household to the next, patterns are discernible. These patterns reveal that the girls who grew up and learned how to keep house in British Columbia during the 1910s and 1920s were the generation of change. They bridged the transition from older, traditional forms of learning-watching and imitating their mothers, to the new, state-imposed structure of the classroom. The content of learning was also different. In place of family customs in diet, menus, and methods, the girls were introduced to new foods and recipes whose selection was justified on scientific grounds and whose preparation was taught according to standardized procedures. Finally, many girls may have first been introduced to new consumer goods—the carriers of new technologies—and new patterns of consumption through domestic science classes. This transition in domestic work in British Columbia will be considered by using the teaching of domestic science in primary schools as a counterpoint to the work of women in the home during the period of 1900-1930. The study will focus primarily upon food preparation in examining the tension between school and home with respect to theory, practice, and material conditions.

The impetus for teaching domestic science to British Columbia's girls had its beginnings in ideas about Canadian society and education which were gaining acceptance and influential adherents in the first decades of the twentieth century.[54] One of these was the concept of the school as an agent for forming children to be mature and productive adults, and thereby improving Canadian society. The school had not only a role to play in shaping the young, but also a responsibility to produce "practical men and women, who would make themselves useful to society and their country."[55] What came to be called "technical education" in British Columbia developed in response to this obligation. The Department of Education's *Annual Report* of 1919-20 cited the recommendation of an earlier study that "the experiences of the school should tend more directly towards the inculcation and conservation of a love of productive, constructive, and conserving labour."[56] In this respect, for example, another *Annual Report* described Vancouver's high school technical course, established during 1916-17, as one which from either an academic or vocational point of view prepared a boy or girl for life as a citizen and a worker.[57]

Contemporary beliefs held that industrialization had seriously dislocated Canadian society and that with the disintegration of traditional institutions, such as the home, the school had to take an active role in shaping those who would shape the social order.[58] An essential part of the moulding of future citizens was to train them for their work, which necessitated a broad range of vocational courses. In its 1918-19 *Annual Report*, the Department of Education recognized that "a Dominion-wide system of industrial training is necessary to the economic prosperity and supremacy of Canada."[59]

Far from being excluded from these educational reforms, girls played a central role in the new order—the most crucial one, according to the rhetoric of the day—because of their unique responsibility for the home: "our first and greatest social institution.[60] An impassioned article in the Vancouver *Daily Province* argued for the teaching of domestic science because "the home instinct which is endangered must be nurtured, the love for home must be cultivated."[61] Supporters of domestic science declared that by helping to restore the home to its proper place of dignity and importance domestic science would not only make family life happier, but would also produce greater cohesion and harmony in the Empire.[62]

The Department of Education's *Annual Reports* included regular pleas by the Organizer of Technical Education for the expansion of domestic science classes in the province. A particularly eloquent appeal appeared in the memorandum which the Educational Committee of the Local Council of Women in Victoria presented to the Putnam-Weir survey of British Columbia's schools:

> We believe that the home is the natural and rightful domain of women, and therefore that home economics, the science of the home, is preeminently the proper and logical study for womankind; we believe that as women are largely the spenders of money, national thrift would dictate that they be taught to spend wisely; that as the keepers of the health of the nation we believe they should be taught the principles of hygiene and dietetics; we believe that in the different branches of this subject there is ample scope for the varying abilities of the most brilliant minds of the sex; we believe that much undesirable and unnecessary competition between the sexes will be avoided, and many other social problems solved when the dignity of homemaking is adequately recognized and home economics given its rightful place in a national and international scheme of education. Finally, let us never forget that upon the physical stamina, the mental and moral fibre of the mother-to-be, depends the character of the life, yea, the very life of tomorrow.[63]

The training of future servants had been part of the initial impetus to establish home economics on the part of the National Council of Women and was one of the anticipated results from domestic science classes:

> The recognition of the scientific importance of this subject will do much to raise the status of the hitherto "looked down upon" domestic help and make it worthwhile for our efficient and educated girls to take up housework as a sphere of employment that does not carry with it the stigma of degradation. In thus raising domestic work to the dignity of a scientific study we not only educate the housekeepers and homemakers of the future, but provide a stimulus to the production of a class of helpers sadly needed in British Columbia.[64]

This objective was acknowledged in Putnam and Weir's report in 1925:

> Home economics for girls is not on the school programme merely or mainly to train them to be housemaids or cooks or seamstresses or laundresses, but because while doing these things, in some degree, it

also gives the girl a sane attitude toward life by requiring her to solve life problems and deal with real projects.[65]

Occasional references to the existence of servants appeared in the department's approved programs of studies under such sub-sections as "Paid help in the home," "When no servant [is] possible," "Dinner served without a maid, dinner with a maid."[66] Over time, concern for occupational training through domestic science courses focused on work opportunities outside the home. In its recommendations on home economics to Putnam and Weir, the Provincial Parent-Teacher Association requested the establishment of technical and vocational schools for girls throughout the province since many girls who did not attend high school had "abilities along purely vocational lines, such as cookery, home decoration, commercial art, dressmaking, etc., for which there is at present little or no training."[67] Employment based on domestic science training also opened up "many interesting and lucrative careers" for women as dieticians in hospitals and sanitariums, as managers of cafeterias, tea rooms, hotel dining rooms, and university halls, in nutrition clinics, laboratories and factories, and as financial counsellors in banks.[68]

The major thrust of the argument for domestic science, however, focused on the future role of girls as homemakers. In order to undertake the weighty duties of homemakers to their families and to the nation, it was essential that girls were properly trained in all aspects of domestic responsibility. Such training had traditionally been given in the home, but now the home was no longer capable of fulfilling this obligation and so society, in the form of the school, had to come to the support of the home.[69] Of all the arguments for and against the establishment of domestic science in British Columbia schools, the issue of home training probably provoked the most heat. Opponents of domestic science charged that the school denigrated the mother's role in educating the daughter and undermined her authority at home. The corollary of this was that domestic science classes were an unnecessary expense. Supporters of domestic science responded that mothers had no time to teach at home, that because of this school girls had no time to be taught at home, that girls entered marriage from working careers rather than from their mothers' homes and hence had no preparation beyond what the school could provide, and that trained teachers could explain the theory of domestic science as well as demonstrate the practice; further, some mothers did not have good home practice, were impatient, and did not know how to teach.[70] A darker side of the need for domestic science is revealed in references to the "inexcusable ignorance of housewives," "untrained and unorganized women," and the "thriftlessness of the poor."[71] The needs were clear. Whatever her home environment, the British Columbia girl should have:

systematic and well-directed instruction and practice in those activities—cooking, sewing, washing clothes, ironing, mending, darning,
sweeping, making beds, scrubbing, simple nursing, judging and testing textiles, marketing, budgeting—which are fundamental to homemaking and therefore fundamental in building up and preserving a
healthy nation.[72]

The educational method whereby these goals would be achieved was based
on the application of scientific principles to the management of the home.
Scientific management gained prominence in North America in the late nineteenth and early twentieth centuries, and from its initial application to industry and corporations it soon spread to social institutions such as the school and
the home. The scientific approach predicated that all processes could be broken down to their component parts and measured as to efficiency, and that the
knowledge gained could be used to promote more efficient productivity. In a
1916 address, educator Alice Ravenhill defined efficiency as the effort to
accomplish certain definite ends without loss of substance or motion. She went
on to demonstrate the principle with respect to the prolificness of unfit families and the limitation, slow growth, and final elimination of alert, intellectual,
and generally valuable families. "In the discouragement of the one and the
encouragement of the other she saw the best inductive conclusion of the logic
of efficiency."[73] This somewhat ruthless example was in keeping with the public policy of the day, which sought to solve social problems through the reorganization of society along more efficient lines.[74] Ravenhill later identified the
sciences which had a bearing on the daily routine of home life as biology (diet
and cooking), chemistry (cleaning products and processes), physics (light, heating, ventilation, fuel), bacteriology (preservation of food and resistance to
germs), physiology (clothing, sleep, exercise), as well as psychology, child study,
hygiene and sanitation, sociology, education, music, and decorative art.[75]

"Scientific" and "efficient" were the watchwords in the domestic science
classroom. The Department of Education reported in 1915-16 that while teachers used various methods to teach the subject, they all practiced those which
were "more or less scientific in character and discarded those of a purely empirical nature" Even with the later emphasis on practical methods, teachers still
paid "due attention to the theoretical and scientific side of the subject."[76]

In 1913, the Department of Education issued its first domestic science
text, the *Girls' Home Manual*, as a three-year course outline in the subject. After
acknowledging its debt to the recent scientific status of homemaking, the
Manual stated its objective:

On investigation, it was found that only a small percentage of house-
keepers possess any library bearing on their work with the exception of
an occasional cook-book and manufacturers' sample cook-books.

This Manual was prepared in the hope that girls, not only at school, but in after life also, may find it helpful in making them more efficient in the noble art of "home-making."

The *Manual* advised that the kitchen should be the first room furnished "since the health of the inmates of a home depends upon the efficiency of the work done there," and emphasized the necessity of proper kitchen tools, the lack of which affected the housewife's strength and the efficiency of the work. In the thirty-four chapters devoted to "Cookery," the *Manual* discussed the source, composition, nutrient value, digestibility, preservation, storage, and cooking of foods, invalid cookery, how to set and clear a table and serve the meal, proper table etiquette (the knife should never be put into the mouth), how to wash up after the meal and dispose of garbage, a list of "first-class" kitchen equipment, house plans and furniture, and directions for making a cookery uniform. Throughout, the directions stress quality, simplicity, and convenience.[77]

What did the scientific approach mean in the classroom? Thirteen-year-old Olive Dean, a student at Sir Walter Moberly school in Vancouver, wrote down the aims of the household science course in her notebook for September 1922:

1. to make household management an interesting lifework
2. to make each day's duties an instructive lesson
3. to make of housekeeping a modem science
4. to develop business methods
5. to preserve health and prevent disease
6. to reach the highest development possible
7. to raise the ideal.

According to the notebook, Olive learned personal cleanliness in handling food, the importance of a clean, screened, and ventilated kitchen, the need to have pure water for drinking and soft water for laundering, how to wash dishes and saucepans and clean the woodwork, sink, and stove, the principles of combustion, foods and their digestion, how to keep milk and meat properly, how to sort and prepare the laundry, and how to boil, wash, starch, dry, dampen, iron, and fold clothes. The notebook had recipes for cocoa, oatmeal porridge, stewed beef, and suet dumplings. Directions for measuring ingredients reminded her to be accurate in order to ensure success.[78] At Vancouver's Lord Nelson School in 1917, Lois Kinley carried out experiments which demonstrated the properties of yeast and gluten and the effects of boiling, lukewarm, and cold water and of the combining of different flours and grains. She drew a diagram of a cross-section of a grain of wheat and took down recipes for brown bread, gingerbread, plain cake, and baking powder biscuits. Each lesson on a particular food or process was followed by appropriate recipes. A lengthy section on preserving described both canning and drying methods and concluded with a canning chart for various fruits and vegetables.

Reporters and other visitors to domestic science classrooms commented on the attention to order, cleanliness, and good equipment found there. One noted that the instructor gave her pupils:

> a thorough training in systematic methods, the work of her classes being performed with almost military promptness and precision, each dish in each girl's cupboard being in its exact place, and even the knives, forks and spoons being ranged like a row of little soldiers.[79]

The *Daily Colonist* praised the emphasis on cleanliness (noting white pinafores and caps on the girls and white paint on shelves and cupboards) which guaranteed that "the virtues of fresh air, pure water and sunlight and the dangers of unswept floors and uncleaned sinks will be understood." The girls were taught to make exact calculations in measurements, to work quickly and deftly, and to recognize that "housekeeping is a business that requires not only skill and resourcefulness, but ability and knowledge." To this end they learned practical lessons in chemistry, biology, personal hygiene, geography, and market values. Their equipment was the best and thus a "lesson in true economy."[80] The domestic science classroom at Nelson was a model of up-to-date equipment with aluminum cooking utensils, stationary washtubs, drying rooms, electric irons, a large, built-in refrigerator, and twenty-four electrical discs on which all the individual cooking was done. Nelson was only "the third school on the continent of North America equipped with electrical utensils."[81]

Inherent in the scientific approach to domestic science was standardization. There was a correct way to dress oneself and wash one's hands to prepare food, can peaches, make apple sauce, roast a chicken, bake a cake, and select and purchase food for the family; there was proper equipment to use and a proper way of keeping it clean and in good working order; and there were proven methods for combatting the germs and diseases which lurked in improperly stored food and unsanitary, unplanned kitchens. Teachers were responsible for enforcing appropriate standards. According to the Organizer of Technical Education:

> care should ... be taken to develop habits in domestic-science centres which are above reproach, and no girls should be found cooking without aprons and caps nor sewing without thimbles.[82]

Olive Dean's notes were accurate; domestic science did indeed aim to "raise the ideal" of housekeeping by making it a modern science based on business methods.

Whatever the appeal of the scientific approach for educators and social reformers, however, it did not immediately win the hearts and minds of British

Columbia parents and taxpayers, at least not in its application to the teaching of domestic science in the public schools of the province. There was of course much public and private grumbling about the teaching of domestic science itself. Some of the arguments have been referred to above. Throughout the period under study, proponents waged a continuing public relations campaign on behalf of domestic science in order to maintain the classes established and to promote the spread of the new subject across the province.[83] This struggle is echoed in the Department of Education's *Annual Reports*, where the customary optimism was tempered by the acknowledgement that public acceptance of the new subject was not wholehearted. Separating out criticism of the method (scientific) from criticism of the subject (domestic science) is difficult since the two were often not separate in the minds of opponents. Nevertheless, in the department's response to public indifference or hostility to domestic science, one can read the problems created by what may have been a too narrow application of the scientific method and model of efficiency.

Teachers and school administrators employed various strategies in fighting for domestic science: improvement of educational methods, service to the community, and the demonstration that domestic science had practical value. The first strategy, improving the teaching of the subject, dealt with two different perspectives on the position of domestic science in the school curriculum: that of educational theory and that of provincial fact. A full discussion of the new educational theory behind the introduction of domestic science (and other related subjects such as manual training) is beyond the scope and purpose of this paper. In brief, the original intent was to use these subjects as a means of developing an integrated education which trained the child's hands, heart, and head.[84] This aim was never realized. The important point for the present discussion, however, is that school administrators believed that the solution to the better teaching and the greater public acceptance of domestic science lay in its closer ties to the traditional subjects on the curriculum. They were convinced of the need to train teachers who could "correlate the theoretical lessons of the class-room with those practical lessons given in the domestic-science centres," and that the best results were found with the "closest co-ordination between the hand-work [domestic science, manual training, etc.] and the classroom studies."[85] The department stated that:

> the complete success of the work depends in a great measure on the way the contents of these courses, which are inseparable from home-life, are linked up with kindred class-room studies.
>
> The educational authorities have always maintained that manual-training and domestic-science centres must be an integral part of the school system, and that the activities in the workshops and cookery centres must emphasize the book lessons of the class-rooms, making

them more realistic and thus firmly fixing them in the minds of the pupils.[86]

The acceptance of the theory meant confronting the reality of domestic science's position in the province's school system. Teachers did not prepare the three-year course outline necessary to ensure a "pedagogically sound" series of lessons; they did not check their students' notebooks, their courses of study were "frequently scrappy and poorly graded"; lack of recipe books meant class time taken in copying from the board; school principals did not ensure the correlation of domestic science and other subjects.[87] The most damning criticism is implicit in some of the recommendations by Putnam and Weir that certain classes of municipalities be required to teach home economics, that regular reports on student progress be made to parents, that home economics be a high school entrance course equal with other subjects, and that the Normal School provide adequate training in home economics for student teachers.[88] Given the implied deficiencies, it is hardly surprising that many members of the public did not take the subject seriously.

The declared objective of domestic science was to enable girls to be competent and knowledgeable homemakers. It is ironic, then, that much of the criticism seemed to be directed against the subject precisely because it was not practical. As early as 1911-12, the school inspector for Vancouver reported that "a constant effort is being made to make the work in this department [home economics] as practical and intimately related to the home conditions as school equipment and teaching of large classes will permit." Later reports commented that there was still a tendency to teach too much theory during the first year. Administrators urged that "great care must be taken not to let the domestic science lessons evolve into talks. 'Learn by doing' should be the motto."[89] One of the most effective responses to criticism evidently lay in "home practice," an approach which recognized the value of linking school lessons to the actual work of the home. This approach took a number of forms. Students learned to cook in family quantities rather than the individual quantities originally taught; change was gradual, however, because family quantities required new and larger equipment (with a concomitant increase in costs) and a "market for the products" (presumably to offset charges of waste and extravagance). Students were also encouraged to practice at home what they had learned in class and in some cases were graded by their mothers. In 1927 the department published *Recipes for Home Economics Classes* to be sold to pupils for 25 cents. Recipes were adapted with an eye to economy and were reliable for use in feeding a family of six. Jessie McLenaghen, the first Director of Home Economics for British Columbia, hoped that:

this book will not only save time in the class-room for more valuable work, but that it will also be a means of stimulating greater effort in home practise. By its very entrance into the home it should help to secure the interest and co-operation of the parents—something absolutely vital to the success of any home-economics programme.[90]

The foregoing has described the ideas which lay behind domestic science in the British Columbia school system and some of the practices which developed from these ideas. Problems encountered in achieving these objectives, and ways in which the school system responded to the problems at the classroom level, have also been explored. The reactions, sympathetic or otherwise, of various individuals and groups in the province have been touched upon to suggest the impact which domestic science had at various points in British Columbia society. The picture is incomplete, however, without evidence of the impact which the teaching of domestic science had on its intended target: the girl in the classroom. Analyzing the effect of the classroom experience can indicate how domestic science measured up to its educational and social goals and the nature and extent of its influence on the new generation. More importantly for the purposes of this paper, domestic science can serve as a mechanism to help analyze change and continuity in women's work, as revealed by the students who, as the province's future homemakers, had been the subject of so much concern. The comparison between home routine and school instruction illustrates a period of transition in British Columbia kitchens, combining elements of continuity and change as mothers and daughters moved closer to the role of consumers.

Almost all the women interviewed learned to cook and to perform other housekeeping duties at home, usually beginning well before they were old enough to attend domestic science classes at school. In most cases this was a gradual and informal process. The child started by peeling vegetables, setting the table, and washing or drying dishes, then learned more complex skills so that by age twelve or thirteen some could prepare a complete dinner. The learning process combined observation and practice; the girl watched her mother, then tried the same tasks herself, often with her mother's active encouragement and direct instruction. Only in a very few families did the daughter not learn to cook at home. This was usually because the mother either disliked cooking herself or disliked teaching her children. In the majority of families not only was cooking directly encouraged but the child's participation in this and in other domestic chores was expected, tacitly or by direct order.[91] In certain cases, the daughter could have very heavy responsibilities in the home, especially when the mother was ill or when the family could not afford to hire help. There was little discussion between mother and daughter about any larger objectives for the household apprenticeship. Interviewees recalled that no direct connection was openly made between their childhood responsibilities and their future as wives and mothers; the connection and the future were simply assumed.

Interestingly, in almost one-third of the families, the mother did work in addition to her normal family responsibilities: ten took in boarders or relatives; four helped in their husbands' businesses; others sewed piece-work for a tailor, sold milk, eggs or bread, or worked as a salaried clerk or housekeeper; three eventually helped to raise grandchildren when their widowed or divorced daughters went out to work. A similar proportion of the daughters worked for pay full-time or part-time during their adult lives. Of these, two worked in their husbands' businesses; three were divorced and one widowed; one's husband was disabled; three never married; and four worked for other reasons. Some also took in relatives at various times. Domestic science courses offered no advice on how to deal with the circumstances of women who undertook additional responsibilities such as working for pay. For that matter, neither did the students' mothers. Neither school nor home consciously recognized the reality of the lives of many women during the decades under study.

One of the main objectives of domestic science advocates was to raise the level of housekeeping practice in the province by training homemakers to be more knowledgeable and scientific. Nutrition was an important part of the curriculum; students were taught what foods were best and why, and how to prepare them and why. Were British Columbia households in desperate need of dietary guidance? Most interviewees characterized their mother's cooking as good, plain food, with more heavy dishes than contemporary Canadians are accustomed to and a greater monotony of diet. Breakfast was usually porridge, sometimes corn flakes, toast, milk, or tea, occasionally stewed fruit, seldom juice; eggs and bacon were more likely to be a Sunday treat. The noon meal, if lunch, was often eggs or soup and sandwiches; dinner (noon or night) usually meant meat, potatoes, vegetable, and dessert—either pudding or pie. Many were able to describe the progression of the Sunday roast through various reincarnations right down to shepherd's pie on Thursday night, with the week finishing on macaroni and cheese. On the other hand, most families had a great variety of fruit and vegetables available, thanks to the climate. Of thirty-six families, twenty-seven had a vegetable garden and sixteen had fruit trees or fruit bushes. Virtually all put up preserves: bottled fruit, jams, jellies, relishes, pickles, salmon, salted fish, and vegetables.[92] Salads, which were infrequent items on the family menu, disappeared completely in the winter.

Some mothers' nutritional concerns were unusual. One considered cucumbers and bananas indigestible; others maintained that eating crusts produced curly hair, carrots were good for the eyes and fish for the brain, and that the white lining of oranges brought on epilepsy. On the other hand, this folk wisdom was not out of step with prevailing medical opinion. After the father of one interviewee became sick in the great influenza epidemic of 1918, the attending doctor told his wife not to let the children eat bananas. Domestic science classes did increase some pupils' knowledge of nutrition: the value of vegetable water, food values, proteins, carbohydrates, and the best way to prepare foods. The classes also introduced students to new foods and new ways of preparing food. This was not always a positive experience. One interviewee remembered suffering indigestion from a Waldorf salad which never was made at home because the family could not afford to buy celery or nuts. Neither could she understand what all the white sauce was for. She has never used it before or since. One girl, though she had cooked at home, learned to cook in many different ways in class and another learned to cook well using the class recipes. One of the other students found her domestic science textbook so useful that she gave it to her daughter to use when the latter married.

However, it was method, not content, which demonstrated the most significant differences between school and home. Data from the interviews indicate that many of the mothers cooked "out of their own heads." This approach had been passed from one generation to the other. The most usual cookbook consisted of hand-written recipes collected from or exchanged with family and friends; over a third of the mothers had such a collection. A distant second place was shared by Mrs. Beeton and a Five Roses Flour cookbook.[93] Even those women who had cookbooks, however, seldom used them. What did it mean to cook "out of one's head"? First, there was no standardization: ingredients and amounts varied from one time to the next, as probably did the result—at least until the process became almost automatic. Measurements were not precise as individual judgement determined the relative proportions used. As a result, the cook could give full rein to her creative talents or to her ability to make do; on the other hand, the success of the final product could not be guaranteed. Also, the recipe could only really be learned from another person by observation and by repeated attempts to achieve the desired result.[94] Further, the "pool" of recipes available was restricted to what people knew through experience.

Many girls were first introduced to measuring cups and spoons in their domestic science classes. One learned that a wooden spoon was the correct utensil to use in mixing ingredients. She also learned there was a right and wrong way to make cocoa although her family had been making it at home for some years without knowing that. Girls were taught to sew and wear a proper "uniform" in the kitchen, consisting of white cap and full apron with a potholder and a towel hanging on the left-hand side of the apron. They also copied out many recipes which teachers encouraged them to try at home; in a few cases the students were marked on their home cooking. Standardized methods, recipes, and practices were taught to the younger generation with some success as these girls eventually used the recipes and measuring cups and spoons in their own homes. Was there an impact on the older generation as well? The evidence suggests a very limited one. Two mothers and one grandmother learned some of the new recipes; another girl's mother who bought measuring cups and spoons declared that she had better results by cooking with uniform amounts. Most mothers did not change their established methods of food preparation. Yet this did not mean that they opposed domestic science lessons for their daughters. Most seemed to have approved of the classes and many encouraged their daughters to try recipes at home—not surprising since these same mothers had been teaching their daughters to cook for some years.

A few interviewees, and their mothers, considered the classes a waste of time and money, impractical and unnecessary:

> It's very hard to change the habits of a lifetime. And the things that I would learn in school—what had that got to do with our way of life? ... If they had, say, taken a bunch of leftovers and mixed something out of that, why that would have been more to the point.[95]

Complaints focused on the introduction of strange recipes or unusual foods, the expense of supplying the food, the use of numerous and unnecessary utensils, or the belief that girls could learn everything necessary in their own homes. The recipes and methods used in class did seem to require the use of a greater amount of equipment than was usual at home. Mothers complained about the number of pots and bowls dirtied. Even the students who enjoyed domestic science admitted that they really learned to cook at home, not school, and complained about the finicky "dibs and dabs" of food which they were allowed to prepare in class. One woman recalled using half an egg to make custard, another a recipe calling for half a strip of bacon.

One of the justifications for teaching domestic science in the school was that girls entered marriage from a working career, not from a mother's home, and therefore had no preparation for scientific homemaking. The interviews suggest that this was true for many of those who went into middle-class occupations such as teaching and nursing; most boarded with families, lived in resident-type accommodation, or rented with others and hired a housekeeper who cooked. A very few young women shared an apartment with a friend or relative or stayed at home until they married. However, even though housekeeping experience was not part of the lives of many women who worked prior to marriage, it was clear that most had served an apprenticeship for complex household tasks as young girls.

One of the criticisms directed towards the teaching of domestic science was that it encouraged extravagance in equipping the classroom itself and in making girls dissatisfied with the equipment in their homes. Putnam and Weir acknowledged these complaints but considered them to be exaggerated:

> There is a type of man, even among good citizens in rural communities, who will spend any amount of money for modern labour-saving

devices about the farm and in the barn and stables, but who begrudges his wife and daughters anything except the most primitive necessities for kitchen or laundry. It is notorious that all over Canada—there are of course thousands of exceptions—women, in farm houses, have less labour-saving machinery than their husbands who work in the fields. And it might not be a really serious matter if sometimes school instruction in home economics created in a girl a discontent with the primitive furnishings of her mother's kitchen. Real economy has reference to the wise use of money and not to saving it for the mere sake of saving.[96]

The evidence suggests that classrooms were usually very well equipped. Departmental directions in 1912 for domestic science centres reflected the desire to teach efficiency:

> The building itself and the equipment of a Domestic Science Centre should be of such a nature that from it lessons may be learned as to the best way to furnish and arrange a home kitchen. The newest and most up-to-date inventions should be installed.[97]

The Nelson domestic science centre boasted twenty-four individual electrical disc stoves, a large built-in refrigerator, aluminum cooking utensils, steel range, drying rooms, and electric irons. A plan for furnishing domestic science centres in Burnaby included the following: table tops of thoroughly seasoned spruce, 1 and ⅛ inches thick, electric stove (described as three-heat, six-inch disc stoves), a six-hole, Canadian-made range connected to a 30-gallon hot water boiler, a sink with enamel drainboard and splasher, and aluminumware equipment. The department's Supervisor of Technical Education noted that the aluminumware was more expensive than the equivalent enamelware and the three-heat, six-inch stove more expensive than the single-heat, four-inch model, but that in both cases the more expensive choice would give better satisfaction and wear.[98]

Certainly some of the equipment used in domestic science classes would have been new to the students. In most classes the teacher demonstrated on a wood and coal range while the students used gas rings or electrical discs. Many of the girls would have been familiar with the gas rings as these were often used in homes to supplement the wood and coal range; however, electrical stoves were an unusual feature. Aluminumware and enamel drainboards were not standard equipment in kitchens at the time. One of the interviewees recalled that her mother had purchased the first set of aluminum cooking ware sold in Victoria. Manufactured by Wear-Ever, it consisted of triangular pieces which formed a circle when stored together and included a fry pan, steamer, large pot, and detachable handle. A woman who had studied home economics at the

University of Alberta during the mid-1920s recalled that the aluminum fry pan was all the rage.[99] Several interviewees had wooden drainboards that had to be vigorously scrubbed to be kept clean. Flatirons, not electric irons, were the standard in most homes at this time.

There is some evidence that in spite of its endorsation of up-to-date equipment,' the Department of Education was sensitive to charges of extravagance. It is also apparent that the new, improved equipment was not always reliable. In approving the electrical contract for wiring in the Armstrong domestic science centre, the Supervisor of Technical Education commented that the cost of installing electrical stoves was such that the department might have to eliminate them in the future: "the oil stove is just as satisfactory and less than half the cost."[100] In advising the Prince Rupert School Board on establishing a domestic science centre, the Supervisor stated that the substitution of oil for electric stoves would lower costs and that oil stoves were being used successfully in various parts of the province.[101] Economical methods of equipping home economics classrooms were described in an inspector's report listing the materials which could be used by manual training teachers and students to make supply cupboards and fireless cookers.[102] The domestic science teacher from Coal Creek reported that she had encouraged her students to make their cookery uniform (apron, cap, sleeves) from flour sacks.[103]

One tantalizing question raised in connection with classroom furnishings is the influence of commercial suppliers upon home economics teachers and students. Manufacturers were alert to the promotional potential offered by the establishment of domestic science centres. For example, the Singer Sewing Company supplied a complimentary sewing machine to the provincial summer school for home economics teachers and also sent someone to demonstrate the attachments.[104] The McClary Manufacturing Company complained to the Supervisor of Technical Education that American-made "Monarch" and "Majestic" ranges had been specified for domestic science centres under construction in the Okanagan.[105] The Hotpoint Electric Heating Company, based in California and with offices in Vancouver and Toronto, sent a representative to call on the Supervisor of Technical Education in Victoria, invited him to visit the Vancouver showroom to see the samples on display, and forwarded a brochure and price list of its products. The Supervisor was offered a twenty percent reduction, less five percent for cash within thirty days, on the Standard Bake Oven, "El Bako." The company had already installed cooking equipment in schools in Windsor and Collingwood, Ontario, and at the University of New Mexico in Albuquerque.[106] Suppliers offered discounts on equipment, as, for example, on a minimum order of forty electrical disc stoves from Canadian Westinghouse and on the purchase of a "Perfection" oil stove specifically from the Imperial Oil Company in Vancouver.[107] Others donated items or supplies, as did Ridgeway's Tea of Vancouver, whose donation was apparently to be accompanied by promotional material.[108] Some indication of commercial interest appeared in the pages of *School Days*, a monthly magazine published in Vancouver for pupils in grades five, six, seven, and eight during the period 1919-27. The heaviest advertisers among firms selling products related to home economics were BC Electric, Squirrel Peanut Butter, Fraser Valley Dairies, Empress Jams, and Pacific Milk.[109] In her 1928-29 report, the recently appointed Director of Home Economics for British Columbia approved co-operation with commercial firms:

> This year has seen a greater attempt on the part of the teachers to utilize the facilities available in the local stores. In February, David Spencer's Limited, Vancouver, made provision for a competition in homefurnishing which did much to broaden the ideas of the public as to the general conception of the scope of home economics. The prize for the most practical and most artistically furnished bedroom for a high school girl was divided between Kitsilano High School, Vancouver, and North Vancouver High School. Fashion parades for the purpose of acquainting the girls with the prevailing styles for spring were provided by the Hudson's Bay Company. Commercial concerns, when approached, have been most willing to co-operate.[110]

Although it is difficult to gauge the impact on young students of new goods and new technologies, and their manufacturers and their promoters, the domestic science classroom did provide an initial introduction to some household products.

Home economics classes in elementary school introduced thousands of British Columbia girls to exact measurements, white sauce, electric stoves, and the importance of food nutrients. Some students found the classes helpful; some considered them a waste of time; most decided that they had learned more practical food preparation methods at home. Yet as adults all used the standardized methods, the authoritative cookbooks, and the new technological devices first introduced in the classroom. All eventually cooked, with no hired help, in standardized kitchens equipped with built-in cupboards, stoves, new fuels, and electric refrigerators. Domestic science instruction was not the only factor in this transformation, nor could it have been the most important. During 1900-1930, the period under study, seventy-five percent or more of the province's school girls did not attend home economics classes. These were also the years when an alliance of advertisers, manufacturers, and mass circulation media were establishing the mechanisms necessary to induce women to consume.[111] The future homemakers who did attend domestic science classes, however, caught a glimpse of new ways of working in the kitchen, defined and reinforced by the principles of scientific management and women's unique responsibility to nurture the individual and the nation.

Note

The research for this paper was sponsored by the National Museum of Man with the collaborations of the British Columbia Provincial Museum and the Provincial Archives of British Columbia. My thanks to Daniel T. Gallacher and James Wardrop of the Modern History Division, BCPM, Allen Specht of the Sound and Moving Image Archives, PABC, Barbara Latham of Camosun College, and particularly to the student researchers Marian Brown, Lesley Duthie, Star Rosenthal, Kathy Chopik, and Lynn Bueckert, Christine Godfrey, Kathryn Thomson, and Catherine Hagen. I am especially indebted to the British Columbia women who shared their recollections with us.

* * * * *

Documents for Chapter Six

The writings of European philosophers Johann Pestalozzi and Friedrich Froebel, and Americans G. Stanley Hall and John Dewey initiated a "New Education Movement" in Canada at the end of the nineteenth century and into the twentieth century. This child-centred pedagogy emphasized learning by doing rather than by rote memorization, and the importance of play and physical activity in the learning process. Initiatives based on the "New Education" included kindergartens, domestic science, social studies (especially civics and moral education), manual and vocational education, nature studies, and physical training. The first document, by J.E. Wetherell, principal of Strathroy Collegiate, Ontario, argues the merits of the "New Education" movement. To what extent did the teaching of domestic science, as discussed by Barbara Riley, justify Wetherell's claims?

Initially, the authorities discouraged females from becoming teachers. However, since women were willing to accept less pay than men for equal work, females soon came to dominate the teaching ranks, especially in the lower grades where their perceived nurturing qualities and moral superiority were considered important. The rapid growth in the number of female teachers and the differentiation in salaries are illustrated in Documents 25 and 26. Use the first document to evaluate the impact of location on salaries. What conclusions does Document 26 suggest, and why? Use the final document to examine provincial attitudes, as well as the opinions of teachers compared to those of principals, towards co-educational instruction.

24) EDUCATIONAL REFORM[1]

The motto of the "Old Education" is "Knowledge is power." And so it is. But the experience of centuries has proven that knowledge is not the greatest power.

The omniscient man is not always the omnipotent man. In the realm of mind the scholar is often distanced by his inferior in knowledge. The motto of the "New Education" is, "Activity and growth are power." A good saying it is, too, but not entirely novel. Its essence was one of the apothegms of Comenius, the distinguished educational reformer of the seventeenth century, "We learn to do by doing." The "Old Education" stored the mind with knowledge, useful and useless, and only incidentally trained the mind. The "New Education" puts training in the first place and makes the acquisition of knowledge incidental.

The "Old Education" was devoted to the study of books. Too often the text-books were used as an end rather than as a means. "How far have you been in Sangster's Arithmetic?" and "How far have you learned in Bullion's Grammar?" were common queries of the school-master in the old days, and these queries betrayed the educational aims of the questioner. Quantity was everything; growth was little or nothing. The "New Education" is devoted more to things than to books. Text-books are used, but only as repositories of knowledge to be consulted as occasion requires—that is, they are used not as an end but as a means of acquisition and improvement.

The "Old Education" was fond of *memoriter* recitation. In fact, "learning the lesson" was the be-all and the end-all of the schoolroom. How many a woe-begone victim has felt the weight of some martinet's wrath because of ignominious failure in reciting some precious morsel like this: "A Relative Pronoun, or, more properly, a conjunctive pronoun, is one which, in addition to being a substitute for the name of a person or thing, connects its clause with the antecedent, which it is introduced to describe or modify!" To repeat words correctly was everything; to understand them was of secondary importance. In all branches of study definitions had to be carefully memorized as a basis for future work. The "New Education" reverses all this. What Coleridge calls "parrotry" is reduced to a very comfortable minimum. Definitions have their place, but if they are memorized it is at the final rather than at the initial stage in the pursuit of a study or topic. Original human thought takes the place of imitative jargon. Intelligible facts displace unintelligible rules and definitions.

The "Old Education" was eminently subjective, dealing largely in abstractions. The "New Education" employs objective methods, preferring the presentation of truth in the concrete.

The "Old Education" began its work with the unseen and the unfamiliar, and dangerously taxed the weak reflective faculties. The "New Education" begins with the seen and the common and gradually develops the reflective faculties by reference to knowledge already obtained by the strong and active perceptive faculties of the child. The former system initiated the tyro in geography by forcing him to commit to memory the names of the countries and the capitals of Europe; the latter leads him on a happy jaunt over his immediate environment. The former asks the little head to carry the names of all the bones in the skeleton of a rhinoceros; the latter shows to fascinated investigators the anatomy of a leaf. The former taught our infant lips to lisp the dimensions of ancient Babylon, and the name of Jupiter's grandmother; the latter opens dull ears to the melody of birds, and unfilms dull eyes to behold the glory of the heavens. The wail of Carlyle will find an echo in many hearts; "For many years," says he, "it has been one of my most constant regrets that no schoolmaster of mine had a knowledge of natural history so far at least as to have taught me the grasses that grow by the wayside, and the little winged and wingless neighbours that are continually meeting me with a salutation which I cannot answer, as things are. Why did not somebody teach me the constellations too, and make me at home in the starry heavens which are always overhead, and which I do not half know to this day?"

The old system of tuition was marked by mechanical routine; the new boasts of almost complete absence of machinery, of infinite variety of programme, of multiplicity and attractiveness of devices. On the one hand joyless thraldom and lifeless monotony; on the other continual novelty and an exhilarating sense of freedom.

In the old order of things each subject in the curriculum was regarded as a distinct entity, and was entirely isolated. The order of things requires that the subjects should be so co-ordinated and studied together, that each as far as possible may be the ally of some other. Thus geography is the handmaid of history. Thus reading, writing, spelling and composition go hand in hand as far as possible. The spelling-book is discarded as a useless educational tool; and English composition, which had its fortnightly terrors in the past, has become the most seductive of school occupations and is practised every day in the year.

In the old days among teachers there was common a most pernicious though benevolent vice, the vice of talking too much—called by someone the "didactic disease". The teacher was prone to tell everything, to explain everything, leaving the pupil little to do but everything to learn. The new method— if I may call it new—a method practised so persistently and successfully by Dr. Arnold—is, that the pupil should do the maximum of original work and that the teacher should give him the minimum of assistance; in other words, the pupil must think and show results, the teacher must study to hold his own tongue as much as possible.

The "Old Education" was not only faulty, it was also one-sided. Certain faculties of the mind were exercised, while the body and the heart were neglected. One of the ruling principles of the "New Education" is, "Harmoniously develop the whole being, the mental, the moral, the physical."

The "Old Education" carried the military idea into the schools and taught by squads, and companies, and battalions; and the "boding tremblers" were apparently under good discipline, but it was the discipline of subjection and fear, not the discipline of freedom and love. The "New Education" carries the method of the Great Teacher into the schools and pays much attention to individuals. The former system attended to the aggregation and almost neglected the unit. The latter studies the peculiarities of each child and adapts its teachings to his past experiences and his existing attitude: and thus the dull pupil receives, as he should, more attention than the brilliant pupil.

The "Old Education" made much of examinations. The passing of examinations was the goal in all grades of schools. The preparation for examinations was the constant and debasing toil. The examinations, like the text-books, instead of being kept in their proper place as a useful means for a desirable end, usurped the exalted place of the end itself. The "New Education" puts written tests in their proper and secondary place. Examinations and promotions are not continually before the pupil's mind; and when written examinations are held, their old use is abandoned. The questions are such as test not so much the pupil's knowledge as his power of doing.

* * * * *

25) TEACHER'S SALARIES IN ONTARIO, 1867-1902[2]

1   Highest salary paid.
2   Average salary, male teacher, province.
3   Average salary, female teacher, province.
4   Average salary male teacher, counties, etc.
5   Average salary female teacher, counties, etc.
6   Average salary male teacher, cities.
7   Average salary, female teacher, cities.
8   Average salary, male teacher, towns.
9   Average salary, female teacher, towns.

YEAR	1	2	3	4	5	6	7	8	9
1867	1,350	346	226	261	189	532	243	464	240
1872	1,000	360	228	305	213	628	245	507	216
1877	1,100	398	264	379	251	735	307	583	269
1882	1,100	415	269	385	248	742	331	576	273
1887	1,450	425	292	398	271	832	382	619	289
1892	1,500	421	297	383	269	894	402	648	298
1897	1,500	391	294	347	254	892	425	621	306
1902	1,600	436	313	372	271	935	479	667	317

*   *   *   *   *

26) WINNIPEG TEACHERS BY GENDER, 1944-47[3]

Distribution of Winnipeg Teachers, Male and Female, 1944-47

	1944			1945			1946			1947		
	M	F	%F	M	F	%F	M	F	%F	M	F	%F
Elementary												
Principals and supervisors	5	26	84	6	25	80	7	25	78	8	24	75
Teachers	0	430	100	2	451	99	8	478	98	12	48	27
Junior High												
Principals and supervisors	21	2	8	24	2	7	22	1	4	22	1	4
Teachers, academic	61	116	65	64	160	71	81	145	64	81	138	63
Teachers, Ind. Arts & H.Ec	24	15	38	28	21	43	28	17	28	29	18	38
Senior High												
Principals	5	0	0	5	0	0	10	0	0	10	0	0
Teachers, academic	76	64	46	81	70	46	88	75	46	90	74	45
Teachers, Ind. Arts & H.Ec.	12	12	50	12	11	48	13	12	48	13	11	46
Others	3	12		2	28		2	29		6	28	
TOTAL	207	727	78	224	768	77	259	782	75	271	776	74

*   *   *   *   *

27) ATTITUDES TOWARDS MIXED GENDER EDUCATION, 1968[4]

Many of the problems confronting elementary and secondary schools stem from the fact that their input student populations are heterogeneous. Students vary with respect to social background, ability, physical and emotional maturity, and a host of other characteristics. Such variation complicates curriculum planning as well as the process of teaching itself.

The present paper presents the views of Canadian secondary school principals, teachers and counsellors regarding various organizational ways of coping with students' differences in two crucial areas—ability and sex [the data on ability is reprinted in Chapter 13].

The data utilized derive from a national survey of public secondary schools carried out in the fall and spring of 1965-66. The sample was designed as a stratified probability sample, and included academic, composite, vocational and technical, and academic and commercial schools ....

[It] is based on the results of the "Career Decisions of Canadian Youth" project, a study of the educational and occupational plans of a national sample of Canadian high school students conducted by the Federal Department of Manpower in cooperation with the Provincial Departments of Education. Roughly 150,000 students from 360 schools were surveyed, as well as teachers, counsellors and principals from these schools.

TABLE 4

PERCENTAGE AGREEING TO THE FOLLOWING STATEMENTS

CAN	NFL	P.E.I.	N.S	N.B	QUE	ONT	MAN	SASK	ALTA	B.C.
Principals:										
It is as important for girls to have a high school education as it is for boys.										
93	93	100	93	89	97	96	82	82	91	96
Boys and girls should follow the same high school curriculum										
52	40	37	90	48	49	80	41	35	50	43
Teachers and Counsellors:										
Education as important for girls as boys										
93	85	93	96	89	93	93	92	97	97	93
Boys and girls should follow same curriculum										
57	40	64	67	52	52	65	65	52	63	50

TABLE 7

ATTITUDES OF PRINCIPALS, TEACHERS AND COUNSELLORS TOWARD CO-EDUCATION (%)

	CAN	NFL	P.E.I.	N.S	N.B	QUE	ONT	MAN	SASK	ALTA	B.C.	Under 35	50+

Do you think that high school boys and girls should be educated in:

Principals:

Co-educational classes

CAN	NFL	P.E.I.	N.S	N.B	QUE	ONT	MAN	SASK	ALTA	B.C.	Under 35	50+
57	63	87	69	76	30	99	70	70	72	99	52	57

Separate classes, but in co-ed schools

24	20	10	31	24	41	1.2	18	6.3	18	-	34	21

Separate schools, but in co-ed campuses

3.1	3	-	-	7	-	9	-	-	-	5	-	-

Completely separate educational environment

11	4	-	-	-	16	-	3	18	10	-	5	17

Teachers and Counsellors:

Co-educational classes

65	71	88	75	78	40	83	79	81	77	71	65	65

Separate classes but in co-ed schools

20	13	10	14	16	32	10	16	10	15	20	20	19

Separate schools, but in co-ed campuses

5	2	2	2	2	12	2-	1	1	2	3	6	5

Completely separate educational environment

5	5	0	2	2	10	2	2	3	2	3	4	7

* * * * *

1 J.E. Wetherell, "Conservatism and Reform in Educational Methods," *Proceedings* (Ontario Teachers' Association, 1886), pp. 85-88.

2 "Teachers' Salaries in Ontario, 1867-1904," *Report of the Minister of Education, Province of Ontario for the year 1905*, p. XVII.

3 Mary Kinnear, "'Mostly for the Male Members': Teaching in Winnipeg, 1933-1966," *Historical Studies in Education*, 6, 1 (Spring, 1994), p. 5.

4 Stephen Richer, Raymond Breton, "School Organization and Student Differences: Some Views of Canadian Educators," *Canadian Education and Research Digest* (March, 1968), Tables 4, 7, pp. 23, 29, 34. Percentages have been rounded to the nearest whole number.

Chapter Seven:
The Goals of Physical Education

In Nova Scotia, prior to about 1880, physical education was not taught in the schools. If a school had a playground, it was to provide students with a diversion from the monotony of the classroom, not to promote fitness.[112] Nova Scotian educators took it for granted that young people were physically fit. Children helped with the livestock, split wood for kindling, planted and harvested crops, and walked considerable distances to and from school.

Beginning in the mid-1880s, callisthenics (also termed physical training or physical culture) began to appear in many of the province's schools. In the next decade, the Normal School in Truro appointed a callisthenics instructor (who also taught drawing); the Halifax school board hired Sergeant-Major Bailey to give teachers lessons in callisthenics; and it also approved funds to purchase dumbbells and wands.

The growing interest in physical education was part of the "New Education Movement" that emphasized the importance of play and physical activity in the learning process. Exercise would promote "a healthy mind in a healthy body." It would take the drudgery out of learning the three R's, while inculcating good manners and behaviour. Interest in physical exercise was also related to the growing urbanization and industrialization of the province which had created sanitation and health problems, and was making students, in the words of many school inspectors, "soft."

At the turn of the century, military drill and the cadet corps began to replace callisthenics. Military drill was introduced to the Normal School in Truro in 1911 and soon all male students were required to enrol in the Truro Cadet Corps. Seven years later, Nova Scotia signed an agreement with the federal Department of Militia in which the Militia provided instructors for the Normal School, supplied arms, ammunition and drill books for the cadets, and granted from $50 to $100 to teachers who received an A Certificate in military training. In return, the province allotted school time for cadets, approved the *British Syllabus of Exercise* as a teachers' guide, and required a B Certificate in military training for first and second class teachers' licenses.

These changes reflected the rise of imperialism, as European nations competed for colonies in Africa, Asia, and South America. This struggle for markets, raw materials, and national glory intensified existing international conflicts. For Canada, imperialism meant drawing closer to Britain and its empire. Canadian troops, for example, were sent to help Great Britain defeat the Boers in South Africa. In 1899, Nova Scotia set aside an entire school day for Empire Day (23 May, the day before Victoria Day), to be devoted "wholly to the inculcation of patriotic sentiment." Military drill would create the ideal Canadian male—a person who was strong, loyal, moral, obedient, patriotic, and fit.

As the following article by Morris Mott indicates, physical education had slightly different origins and goals in Manitoba. Also consult Helen Lenskyj, "Training for 'True Womanhood': Physical Education for Girls in Ontario Schools, 1890-1920," *Historical Studies in Education*, 1, 2 (Fall, 1990).

* * * * *

Confronting "Modern" Problems Through Play: The Beginning of Physical Education in Manitoba's Public Schools, 1900-1915[113]

At present, the physical education program in Manitoba's public schools has two purposes. One is to "foster the development" of "habits" and "leisure-time activities" which can be practised and enjoyed "throughout life." The second is to "contribute to ... present levels of health and fitness."[1] In Manitoba as in other provinces, the first objective was really only identified, or at least articulated, after World War II. Its presence reflects the assumption, held by educators and others for nearly forty years now, that youngsters need to be prepared for the vast amounts of "free" time they can expect to have as adults, and in particular must be exposed to constructive, or at least harmless, leisure activities. The second objective was not so recently introduced in Manitoba. In fact, it was dissatisfaction with "present levels of health and fitness" among school-aged boys and girls that led to the establishment of physical education in the province.

This took place between about 1900 and 1915, when hundreds of individuals involved in education in Manitoba, and thousands of members of the general public, rather suddenly became aware that too many of the children around them were physically unhealthy. They assumed that this state of affairs would inevitably cause—perhaps it already reflected—mental and moral weaknesses. They realized, as public school Inspector Charles K. Newcombe put it, that the education system paid "scant attention ... to the needs of the physical organism," and concluded that it was "defective" for that reason.[2] As a result, far more than previously, teachers attempted to educate their pupils physically. In doing so they tried to utilize what was often referred to as the "play instinct," hoping to bring it, to use the words of Inspector E.E. Best, "under control as an educative force."[3]

Historical developments never occur "out of the blue," of course, and prior to the turn of the century certain Manitoban educators had taken some interest in the physical development and activities of students. From the 1870s on, many of them had certainly become familiar with the athleticist ideals emanating from the British public schools, and in particular with Thomas Hughes' articulation of those ideals in his extremely popular novel *Tom Brown's Schooldays*. This had been true especially of several teachers and administrators at Winnipeg's three private Protestant denominational colleges, St. John's (Anglican), Manitoba (Presbyterian), and Wesley (Methodist), where a real attempt to put the ideals into practice had occurred. The college newspapers had constantly reminded students of the importance of activities on the playing field and in the gymnasium; reasonably impressive facilities for games and formal exercises had been provided; leagues and teams for a number of sports had been set up.[4] In the publicly supported schools too, the physical well-being of pupils had not been completely ignored, although less emphasis had been placed upon it, primarily because these pupils were normally younger than those at denominational colleges and were seldom if ever housed in residence. Still, several teachers had encouraged participation in "manly" games. One who did so was Nellie Mooney, later Nellie McClung, the famous woman's suffrage leader. She had accepted her first position at a rural school near Manitou in 1889, and had tried to get her students to play football at recess and noon hour, largely because she had read *Tom Brown's Schooldays* and believed that through games like football youngsters acquired valuable qualities and learned important lessons.[5] Moreover, in the city of Winnipeg, from the 1880s forward a few teachers had conducted classes in "military drill," and beginning in 1895 the Winnipeg school board had hired a Major T.S. Billman to visit specific schools, evidently about once every two weeks, to run students through calisthenics and military exercises.[6] In the late nineteenth century, then, "physical education" had not been completely unknown.

After 1900, however, there was much, much more of it, and individuals involved in education were conscious of its purposes and importance to a degree they had never been before. These facts are made clear by several developments. In 1902, for the first time, some prospective teachers—in this case all who wanted to earn "second class" permanent certificates—were required to learn how to conduct "physical training" classes.[7] In 1903 the Department of Education published new plans and specifications for rural schools, in which trustees were told that "sufficient room should ... be left at the rear of the building for a good large play ground, and nothing should be done to diminish this all-important breathing space."[8] In Winnipeg's schools, after about 1904 the amount of attention given to formal drill increased dramatically.[9] In 1905 the Brandon school board, and shortly thereafter for a short time the Portage la Prairie board, followed Winnipeg's lead and hired special physical training instructors to conduct classes in schools in those cities.[10] Beginning around 1909 the annual field day, in which children from various schools in a district competed against one another in track and field events, in ball games, and in "parade" or competitive drill, became an institution, especially in rural centres.[11] In 1911 Manitoban authorities made arrangements to receive money from the Strathcona Trust, set up two years earlier by Sir F.W. Borden, minister of militia and defence, and Lord Strathcona, long known to Manitobans as Donald A. Smith of the Hudson's Bay Company and the Canadian Pacific Railway syndicate. This fund was designed to stimulate physical and military training in public schools, and it succeeded in doing so in Manitoba as in other provinces.[12] From 1911 on, a textbook containing an outline of appropriate physical exercises was made available to all teachers, and they were told that they must use it daily; every new teacher was now required to receive instruction at normal school on how to conduct "physical training"; teachers previously certified were now encouraged to take special summer courses offered so they could "upgrade" themselves; and, in schools where the teacher was not qualified to instruct in physical education, members of the militia often came to conduct classes.[13]

All these eventualities revealed a new commitment to physical education. Even more notable is that large numbers of teachers acted on the recommendations they received time and time again to the effect that they should get out on the playground at recess, at noon hour and after school, to organize and supervise games and other activities for their pupils.[14] Only one indication that they followed these exhortations is that dozens of new sports teams and leagues were formed between 1900 and 1915 for inter-school and intramural competition. In Winnipeg, for example, in 1900 and 1901 respectively, a Schools Football (Soccer) League and a Schools Lacrosse League were set up by teachers and principals; by 1914 each of them arranged games for perhaps one thousand boys of eleven to sixteen years of age.[15] In Neepawa in 1914 a six-team schools lacrosse league existed, and by then school teams or leagues had been formed, especially for football (soccer), lacrosse and hockey, in a number of centres around the province.[16] Not all teachers became enthusiastic supporters of games and sports, of course. However, their willingness to organize these activities reveals that many if not most of them agreed with Inspector Best's opinion that knowing "the how and why of the playground" was more important than they had assumed.[17]

There were several reasons why Manitoban educators and the general public became aware of the value of physical education, and anxious to incorporate it into the curriculum in the early twentieth century. One was that they were generally in favour of the notion, becoming more and more widely held throughout the western world, that schools should offer more than primarily academic training to normal children. They were adjusting to the ideas associated with "new education," and in this period they began to provide "special" education for the handicapped or others with particular needs, and to offer "manual training," "vocational training" and "domestic science" as well as "physical training." In short, physical education emerged in part because, as Keith Wilson has noted, "the aims and scope" of education were being broadened.[18]

Its implementation and the emphasis it received, however, owed more to Manitobans' new appreciation of the importance of play. By the first decade of the twentieth century many of them were familiar with opinions associated with G. Stanley Hall, Joseph Lee, J.J. Kelso and other child psychologists and child savers. Educators and others in the province seemed convinced that, as Dominick Cavallo has written in reference to turn-of-the-century American play organizers, "children's play was too important to be left to children."[19] Unorganized, unsupervised play was too often "aimless racing and yelling" that encouraged bullying and a wide variety of undesirable forms of behaviour.[20] Play activities should be structured and watched over by a responsible adult, though not to the extent that the youngsters' spontaneity was completely eliminated or their fun ruined. If activities were organized and supervised properly, especially by someone familiar with the capabilities of young people at various "stages" of growth, then children at play would unconsciously learn very important lessons at the age when they were best able to learn them, indeed when they had to learn them if they were to develop normally.[21] Moreover, when a teacher was the responsible adult in charge, there was an added benefit: he or she would really get to know each of the students, and be better prepared to deal with individual personalities in the classroom.[22]

By far the most important reason for the new emphasis on physical education, however, was that after 1900 Manitobans suddenly realized they were confronted with many of the problems associated with "modern civilization." These problems had been already spotted and to some extent dealt with, partly by broadening school curricula and harnessing play, in other parts of the English-speaking world. This was why Manitobans were able quickly to advance solutions to modern difficulties once they recognized them.

The modern problem that received the most attention was declining health. In Manitoba in the early twentieth century, as in other parts of the English-speaking world in the nineteenth, technological innovations, industrialization and rapid population growth all represented, on balance, "progress." But there were some bothersome developments associated with it. For one thing, the physical demands of virtually every occupation diminished.[23] For another, the growing population became more and more concentrated in urban centres. Manitoba's population grew 117 percent between 1901 and 1916, from 255,211 to 553,860, but during the same period the number of people living in communities of 1,000 or more grew from 70,436 to 241,014, or 242 percent.[24] Winnipeg's population grew from 42,340 to 163,000, or 285 percent, and in Winnipeg as in other large "modern" cities the health problems were both widespread and visible. The many poorly-heated, poorly-ventilated, overcrowded houses, with inadequate water supply and with very inferior facilities for waste disposal created appalling infant mortality and death-by-disease rates.[25] No wonder the *Western School Journal*, a periodical published for and by Manitoba educators, evidently took seriously a New York medical doctor who wrote that it had been "authoritatively reported that a family in the city dies out in three generations unless crossed by country blood."[26]

The problem of deteriorating physical health would not have seemed so significant had not Manitobans assumed that it would inevitably lead to mental and moral degeneration. In fact sometimes they seemed to argue that physical regression *revealed* moral decay that had already reached an advanced stage, thus echoing the opinion of Charles Kingsley, the famous English "Muscular Christian" clergyman and novelist, who once said that "souls secrete their bodies, as snails do shells."[27] Most Manitobans would not have gone quite that far. They assumed, however, that the healthy body was in some way associated with and accompanied by the healthy mind and the healthy soul.[28] It therefore seemed of a pattern to them that, at the same time as the overall physical health of the population seemed to be falling, the rates of juvenile delinquency, prostitution and violent crime seemed to be rising. Also increasing, in This Age of the Great Barbecue, was the appeal of those false gods, Mammon and Pleasure. In fact, it was the depraved and ultimately unwise desire for money and excitement that made it so difficult to keep young men and women on the farm or in the small village; despite all the evidence that showed how wicked and unhealthy life in the big city was, young people kept moving there.[29] The absence of fitness went hand-in-hand with irrational, immoral behaviour.

Therefore, educators who arranged for periods of formal exercises and supervised games and sports believed they would thereby foster the development of strong, efficient bodies, but they also assumed they would evoke much more than that. They would elicit a particularly commendable sort of calm courage because many of the ball games and other activities rewarded determination and physical bravery while penalizing recklessness and fierceness. Educators might contribute to sexual purity because at least in males, according to pre-Freudian assumptions, strength and vitality and especially endurance (which team games like hockey and lacrosse tested to a greater extent then than they do now) could not be present if semen were wasted.[30] Teachers would inculcate discipline, which was viewed by many as synonymous with "control of the body by the will," and which was regarded as the main benefit to be derived from periods of formal calisthenics and drill. They would help children learn how to win and lose in the proper spirit, so that they would become neither falsely proud in victory nor enraged and disgusted in defeat, but instead reflective and therefore capable of learning something from what they had done rightly or wrongly. Teachers would create respect for rules, laws and legitimate authority. They would surely nourish an awareness that success depended upon perseverance, planning and skill. They would instill a sense of loyalty to the group, the essence of patriotism. They would help develop skills and attributes needed to cooperate effectively with others, thereby providing useful training for citizenship. They would stimulate wholesome amusements among rural young people, making it less likely that youths would head for the city in search of good times. Teachers would help form alert minds capable of making decisions rapidly and accurately. By organizing and supervising the right exercises, games and sports for children at the appropriate stages in their lives, educators would, to adopt the word they so often used themselves, develop "character."[31]

Not the least important point educators and others considered when they advocated physical education was that, as D.S. Woods (a prominent teacher who later became the first dean of the Faculty of Education at the University of Manitoba) put it in 1913, play "leads to the heart of the foreign child as readily as [to that of] the British-born."[32] Between the turn of the century and the beginning of World War I the number of Manitobans of "foreign" origin expanded much more rapidly than did the population as a whole. As already mentioned, between 1901 and 1916 the population of the province more than doubled to over half a million people. However, during the same fifteen years the number of Jews in the province jumped from about 2,000 to nearly 16,500, and the total number of Austrians, Bukovinians, Galicians, Hungarians, Ruthenians, Poles, Russians and Ukrainians rose from just under 25,000 to over 100,000.[33] More than a few members of the host British-Protestant culture group felt that allowing central and eastern Europeans into the West in such large numbers was a mistake. One who did so was the Methodist clergyman Rev. Wellington Bridgman, who believed these "foreigners" were "criminally inclined" by nature and should be left "at home" so there would be more room for "sturdy, trustworthy" immigrants of British stock.[34] Most British-Protestants were not exclusionists like Bridgman. Nevertheless, they assumed that immigrants from continental Europe were products of backward civilizations—some of them "a thousand years behind" the British-Canadian one, according to the agrarian leader G.F. Chipman—and they believed that no more serious modern problem confronted the majority of Manitobans than how to assimilate the newcomers.[35] Among the important agencies for Canadianizing at least the children of immigrants were, as Woods' comment would suggest, structured play activities, especially games, and still more especially team ball games.

Though they did not spell out the point, educators and other Manitobans of the early twentieth century were aware that games are designed activities, structured so as to reward, and therefore evoke, certain perceptions and forms of behaviour. They demanded a shared awareness and appreciation of different roles, rules, customs and actions.[36] When "foreign" youngsters played a "Canadian" game with a number of "Canadian" children they were, for the time being at least, obligated to think and act like Canadians. It was all but unanimously assumed that the perceptions, values and attributes acquired in games were transferable to, and valuable in, "real-life" situations. This is why immigrant youngsters who attended schools such as W.J. Sisler's Strathcona School in Winnipeg's North End, or who lived in the Presbyterian Boys' Home in Teulon and attended the local public high school, were virtually forced to play soccer and baseball.[37] By entering into these "Canadian" games they were compelled, at least for the duration of the contest but probably for longer, to see the world in a "Canadian" way, and to appreciate "Canadian" skills and qualities.[38]

That the establishment of physical education was motivated by the perceived necessity to respond to modern problems is revealed in particular in the encouragement given to girls to engage in formal exercises and games. In the very late Victorian and the Edwardian eras in Manitoba as in the rest of the English-speaking world, many people of "British" origin, or of what was imprecisely referred to as the "Anglo-Saxon" race, became troubled by perceived racial degeneration. A low birth rate and the evident negative consequences of living in large urban centres seemed to suggest that the British peoples might not have the physical, mental and moral qualities needed to carry out their mission to civilize the world. Suddenly, bringing forth healthier babies became a priority. Therefore the health of prospective mothers became of immense concern.[39]

Their health would benefit, so educators now believed, if they participated in exercises and games which called for grace, co-ordination and judgement but which were at least vigorous enough that deep breaths were required and a sweat appeared. Assumptions carried forward from the nineteenth century still dictated that females should not engage in activities in which significant degrees of strength or endurance were demanded, or in which there was body contact, or in which a highly competitive personality was rewarded. It was still accepted too that special care had to be taken to make sure that, when performing exercises or participating in a game, young ladies were not placed in embarrassing positions, and that they did not over-exert themselves and harm their reproductive capacities.[40] But by the early twentieth century the time was past when, as happened in 1883, a Winnipeg clergyman could seriously suggest that one of the eventual consequences of allowing boys and girls to play together was prostitution! The time was also past when, as happened through the early 1890s, school girls tested themselves in "silence" matches, the objective of which was to keep quiet for as long as possible; and no longer, for games requiring vigour, did girls choose boys to compete for them by "proxy."[41]

Females now took part in many of the track and field events, especially the standing long jump, the shorter dashes, and the softball or volleyball throwing-for-distance competitions.[42] They now took part in formal drill. Sometimes they did so in segregated classes, especially in large schools like those in Winnipeg, for which a separate girls' physical training instructor was hired in 1912. More often they did so with the boys, in which case they performed most of the exercises the young males did, but were expected to emphasize grace rather than power.[43] They now played baseball, hockey and the relatively new game of basketball which was, among them, for the time being primarily a summer outdoor sport. When playing these and other ball games they still wore remarkably inefficient clothing that made it all but impossible for them to run "too" hard for "too" long. In basketball there were even special girls' rules observed which made it still more unlikely that they would overtax their bodies; these rules might require six-a-side rather than five, or confine individual players to certain parts of the court.[44] Nevertheless, the young ladies were now far more active, in a wider variety of sports, than they had been a generation earlier and they were praised for being so. In 1913 a writer in the *Winnipeg Telegram*, probably a male, said that the old fears about the negative consequences of vigorous exercises for women had been simply unfounded. "There can be no doubt," he said, that when "reasonably conducted" they were "just as excellent for girls as for boys."[45]

Among young males or young females, then, play could be employed to inculcate attributes that seemed required and generally lacking in the modern age. The school was not the only institution through which this could be done, of course. In fact, educators as well as other influential people made sure that it was not.

Among the other institutions now utilized as never before to develop character through play were the churches. In the early twentieth century the major Protestant denominations as well as other churches began to facilitate and arrange exercise classes, team ball games, tennis, swimming, skating, and track and field, especially for teenagers. The Christian churches in Minnedosa formed an Inter-church Amateur Athletic Association in 1910.[46] In other towns similar organizations were established during the pre-war years, and in Winnipeg by 1914 churches sponsored so many teams, leagues and events that it was all but impossible to keep track of them all.[47] In Winnipeg and, to a lesser extent, in Brandon, the municipal governments provided funds to sponsor recreation. In these two cities organized, supervised playgrounds emerged between 1908 and 1913. Through the co-operation of school boards, these were normally set up on school grounds during the summer vacation months, and they were viewed as indispensable in the formation of character. In Winnipeg, besides the playgrounds, publicly funded, supervised skating rinks and swimming pools were inaugurated, to mention only those public facilities established primarily for minors.[48] In Brandon and Winnipeg there were also very active local branches of the Y.M.C.A. Their officers, like officers of branches throughout the world, were now more committed than ever to developing the "whole" man, and in particular to instilling the best qualities of a Hercules, as well as of a Socrates and a Jesus. These officers set up impressive new facilities in both cities which were especially suited for indoor exercise classes and sports; thus they became more capable of meeting their goal than they had been previously.[49]

Another institution which used play activities to develop character was the Boy Scouts. Troops were formed in a number of centres in the half-dozen years after 1909. Their leaders employed track and field, basketball, baseball, hockey, soccer and lacrosse "to make of boys honorable, truthful, upright, punctual, honest, neat and tidy men of good morals."[50] In Winnipeg, for "neglected" young fellows such as newsboys, shoe-shine boys and others who learned about life "on the street" rather than in respectable homes, churches and schools, there were still further organizations founded such as the Winnipeg Boys' Club, through which concerned adults attempted to make working lads into "clean, strong, healthy, upright" Canadians, largely by arranging recreational activities for them.[51] The schools were not the only places where play was marshalled to meet modern problems. However, they were the places where this seemed capable of being done most effectively if only because, despite the absence of compulsory attendance laws, so many children spent so much time in them.[52]

It was in the early twentieth century, then, that Manitoban educators and Manitobans in general began to appreciate the importance of physical education. Play activities, they realized, could be deployed to instill a wide variety of praiseworthy attributes called for by modern conditions. Their efforts to utilize play met with some problems, of course. For example, those among them who especially appreciated precision and discipline tried to emphasize military drill. They discovered that among the general public there was a good deal of opposition to the encouragement of militarism. This meant that they could not insist on the use of "guns," which were for the most part broom handles anyway, and they usually agreed to compromise by having pupils do calisthenics in "military fashion," which is to say on command and in unison.[53] Another problem was that the children themselves often found the formal exercises boring. They approached games and sports much more enthusiastically; in the interwar years in Manitoba as elsewhere, these latter activities would receive more emphasis in "phys. ed." partly for that reason.[54]

The difficulties of using play effectively were especially acute in rural one-room schools which, even as late as 1914, were attended by between one-third and one-half of Manitoba's school children.[55] At recesses, at noon hours, and after school, teachers in these institutions often found it next to impossible to supervise recreational activities, because they had to use these times to prepare lessons, mark assignments, and help children who had been absent recently or who were simply a bit "slow" to catch up in their reading, writing and 'rithmetic.[56] Moreover, even if they had the time, one-room school teachers had neither the facilities nor the equipment to arrange activities in which children of both sexes and all ages could joyfully engage, and from which all could benefit.

One-room schools, like all other schools in the province, were built and maintained at the expense of local taxpayers. Almost never did they possess a gymnasium or auditorium of the kind the larger schools were acquiring. In one-room schools, at least in winter, formal exercises had to be done in unused space in the basement if there was one, or in rows between the desks. The playground around the building was likely to be large, but often unsuited for some of the recommended activities because the outdoor toilets, the well, or the school barn might be in the way, or because the ground was not level, or was muddy, or was covered with trees or gopher holes.[57] The rural pupils rarely brought the lightweight, spiked athletic shoes, the tube skates, the colourful uniforms, or the recently manufactured bats, balls, gloves and sticks which, in the early twentieth century, were making such sports as track and field, soccer, baseball, lacrosse and hockey much more kinaesthetically and aesthetically satisfying. They normally played with their regular, slippery leather-soled boots, their everyday, cumbersome pants, sweaters and coats, their homemade, unreliable, inefficient balls, mitts and sticks, and their skate blades that snapped onto, or screwed into normal shoes, and which had an infuriating tendency to fall off. Of course, the lack of equipment and facilities could also represent obstacles to the utilization of play in the cities and large towns. But in urban centres greater tax revenues were available for each school, and frequently individuals or men's sports clubs donated equipment, so that the problems did not exist to the same degree.[58]

The first systematic efforts to capitalize on the power of play may not have been as successful as desired. Still, a great deal was accomplished in physical education in the first decade and a half of the twentieth century. In these years most Manitoban educators became aware of the subject's importance and, to adopt Neil Sutherland's words, they were able to "draw the plans for and rough in many of the dimensions of" this new part of the curriculum.[59]

NOTES

1 *K-12 Physical Education Curriculum Guide* (Winnipeg: Government of Manitoba, 1981), p. 3.

2 *Manitoba Department of Education Annual Report,* 1906, p. 54.

3 *Department of Education Annual Report,* 1910, p. 54. See also Geo. J. Fisher, M.D., "Physical Training in the Public Schools," *Western School Journal,* II (Jan. 1907): 3; D.S. Woods, "Playground Activities," *Western School Journal,* VIII (Apt. 1913): 135.

4 See Morris Kenneth Mott, "Manly Sports and Manitobans, Settlement Days to World War One" (Ph.D. thesis, Queen's University, 1980), pp. 115-117.

5 Nellie L. McClung, *Clearing in the West, My Own Story* (Toronto: Thomas Allen Ltd., 1935), p. 272.

6 J.B. Wallis, "Military Drill in the Winnipeg Schools: An Historical Sketch," *Western School Journal*, I (Nov. 1906): 7-8; *Annual Report of the School Trustees of Protestant School District of Winnipeg No. 1*, 1888, p. 14; *Annual Report of the Trustees of the Winnipeg Public School District No. 1*, 1894, pp. 10-11.

7 David Alexander Downie, "A History of Physical Education in the Public Schools of Manitoba" (M.Ed. thesis, University of Manitoba, 1961), pp. 63-64.

8 S.A. Bedford, *Plans and Specifications for Rural Schools, Approved by the Advisory Board. Suggestions for the Planning and Decoration of School Grounds* (Winnipeg: Government of Manitoba, 1903), p. 21. Thanks to Mr. R.R. Rostecki for this reference.

9 Richard Collier Green, "The History of School Cadets in the City of Winnipeg" (M. Ed. thesis, University of Manitoba, 1950), pp. 32-34, 37-39; *Manitoba Free Press,* hereafter *MFP,* July 4, 1908, sports section, p. 4.

10 *Department* of *Education Annual Report,* 1905, in Manitoba: *Sessional Papers*, no. 7, 1906, p. 385; *Annual Report*, 1906, in Manitoba: *Sessional Papers*, no. 6, 1907, p. 353; *Annual Report*, 191 1, p. 40; *Annual Report*, 1912-13, p. 50.

11 *MFP*, Oct. 14, 1913, p. 6; *Minnedosa Tribune,* June 6, 1912, p. 2, June 5, 1913, p. 2, May 28, 1914, p. 2, June 11, 1914, p. 2; *Brandon Sun*, Oct. 27, 1910, part 1, pp. 2, 6; *Souris Plaindealer*, Sept. 29, 1910, p. 1; *Killarney Guide*, June 15, 1911, p. 1; *Dauphin Press*, Oct. 19, 1911, p. 7; Boissevain History Committee, *Beckoning Hills Revisited. Ours is a Goodly Heritage, Morton-Boissevain, 1881-1981* (Boissevain: Boissevain History Committee, 1981), p. 152; Lundar and District Historical Society, *Wagons to Wings, History of Lundar and Districts, 1872-1980* (Lundar: Lundar and District Historical Society, 1980?), pp. 40, 48.

12 See James L. Gear, "Factors Influencing the Development of Government Sponsored Physical Fitness Programmes in Canada from 1850 to 1972," *Canadian Journal of History of Sport and Physical Education,* IV (Dec. 1973): 11-14; Lorne W. Sawula, "Notes on the Strathcona Trust," *Canadian Journal of History of Sport and Physical Education*, V (May 1974): 56-61; L. Donald Morrow, "Selected Topics in the History of Physical Education in Ontario: From Dr. Egerton Ryerson to the Strathcona Trust 1844-1939" (Ph.D. thesis, University of Alberta, 1975), chapter 4; L. Goodwin, "A History of Physical Education in Alberta," in *Proceedings of the First Canadian Symposium on the History of Sport and Physical Education, University* of *Alberta May 13-16, 1970* (Ottawa: Government of Canada, 1970), pp. 381-382; Robert F. Osborne, "Origins of Physical Education in British Columbia," in *Proceedings, First*

Canadian Symposium, pp. 367-371; John MacDiarmid, "The Strathcona Trust—Its Influence on Physical Education," in *Proceedings, First Canadian Symposium*, pp. 397-409.

13 Downie, "Physical Education in Manitoba," pp. 66, 75; N.A., "New System of Physical Drill," *Western School Journal*, VI (Oct. 1911): 300-301; J.S. Duncan, "The Cadet Instructor's Course," *Western School Journal*, VI (Oct. 1911): 278-280; *Department of Education Annual Report*, 1911, in Manitoba, *Sessional Papers*, no. 12, 1913, p. 617.

14 N.A, "Physical Culture," *Educational Journal of Western Canada*, II (Dec. 1902): 571; Catherine M. Condon, "The Teacher as a Director of Play," *Western School Journal*, I (Dec. 1906): 19-20; H.R. Hadcock, "The Need of Physical Training," *Western School Journal*, II (Feb. 1907): 37-38; Woods, "Playground Activities," pp. 135-138; *Department of Education Annual Report*, 1911, pp. 98-99, 114-115; *Annual Report*, 1912-13, p. 83; *Annual Report*, 1915, pp. 96, 99, 111.

15 *MFP*, Sept. 20, 1900, p. 5, Apr. 13, 1901, p. 5, Apr. 16, 1901, p. 5, July 11, 1908, sports section, p. 3, Oct. 10, 1913, p. 7, Apr. 4, 1914, p. 8; *Annual Report of the School Trustees of the School District of Winnipeg No. 1*, 1907, pp. 18-19.

16 *Neepawa Press*, May 29, 1914, p. 1; *Brandon Times*, Nov. 6, 1902, p. 9, Nov. 2, 1905, p. 6; *Boissevain Recorder*, Jan. 22, 1914, p. 4.

17 *Department of Education Annual Report*, 1911, in Manitoba: *Sessional Papers*, no. 12, 1913, pp. 655, 657.

18 Keith Wilson, "The Development of Education in Manitoba" (Ph.D. thesis, Michigan State University, 1967), chapter 6, especially pp. 300-308.

19 Dominick Cavallo, *Muscles and Morals: Organized Playgrounds and Urban Reform, 1880-1920* (Philadelphia: University of Pennsylvania Press, 1981), p. 25.

20 N.A., "Value of Games for Children," *Western School Journal*, IV (June 1909): 203; Condon, "The Teacher as a Director of Play," pp. 19-20; Woods, "Playground Activities," p. 136; *MFP* May 22, 1909, sports section p. 3.

21 *Winnipeg Saturday Post*, June 14, 1913, p. 5; H.R. Hadcock, "Winnipeg Playgrounds, 1910," *Western School Journal*, V (Sept. 1910): 228; Emma G. Olmstead, "Play in Relation to Age and Sex," reprint from *Primary Education*, in *Western School Journal*, IV (Feb. 1909): 65-66; Major Joseph McLaren, "Physical Training with Special Application to Rural Schools," *Western School Journal*, IX (May 1914): 103; n.a., "Play," *Western School Journal*, VII (Jan. 1913): 33.

22 Condon, "The Teacher as a Director of Play," pp. 19-20; Woods, "Playground Activities," p. 136; n.a., "Physical Culture," p. 571; W.G. Pearce, "The Effect of the General Conduct on the Pupils of the

Teacher's Presence on the Playground," *Western School Journal*, XII (May 1917): 208-209; H. Lambert Williams, "The Teacher on the Playground," *Western School Journal*, XII (May 1917): 209-210.

23 *MFP*, Nov. 7, 1908, sports section, p. 1.

24 *The Census of Canada*, 1931, vol. II, p. 87; *The Census of the Prairie Provinces*, 1916, p. 2; Alan Artibise, *Winnipeg An Illustrated History* (Toronto: James Lorimer and Company, 1977), p. 200.

25 Some information on this is contained in Alan Artibise, *Winnipeg: a social history of urban growth 1874-1914* (Montreal: McGill-Queen's University Press, 1975), chapter 13.

26 Fisher, "Physical Training in the Public Schools," p. 3.

27 Robert Bernard Martin, *The Dust of Combat, A Life of Charles Kingsley* (London: Faber and Faber Ltd., 1959), p. 235; *MFP*, Nov. 7, 1908, sports section, p. 1; A.E. Garland, M.D., "Why the City Man Needs Gymnasium Exercise," *Western Sportsman*, II (Dec. 1906): 318.

28 W.G. Cates, "The Relationship of Athletics to College Life," *Western Sportsman*, II (Oct. 1906): 283-284; J.M. McCutcheon, "The Relation of Physical Education to Moral Development," *Western School Journal*, XV (Sept. 1920): 291, McLaren, "Physical Training," p. 97; "Play," p. 32; *MFP*, Feb. 17, 1908, p. 5, Sept. 25, 1909, sports section, p. 1. On the mind, body, soul relationship, there is very interesting material in Bruce Haley, *The Healthy Body and Victorian Culture* (Cambridge, Mass.: Harvard University Press, 1978), chapters 1 and 2, in Donald J. Mrozek, *Sport and American Mentality, 1880-1910* (Knoxville: University of Tennessee Press, 1983), chapters 2 and 7, and in James C. Whorton, *Crusaders for Fitness: The History of American Health Reformers* (Princeton, N.J.: Princeton University Press, 1982), chapter 9.

29 *Brandon Times*, May 11, 1905, p. 1; n.a., "City Life Problems," *Grain Growers' Guide*, Apr. 8, 1914, p. 5; J.S. Woodsworth, "Some City Problems, III—The Solidarity of Modern Society," *Grain Growers' Guide*, May 6, 1914, p. 7; Nellie L. McClung, "Why Boys and Girls Leave the Farm," *The Nor'-West Farmer*, Sept. 5, 1913, p. 1106. On this theme in the entire Western Canadian context, see David C. Jones, "'There is Some Power About the Land'—The Western Agrarian Press and Country Life Ideology," *Journal of Canadian Studies*, XVII (Autumn 1982): 96-108.

30 See Bryan Strong, "Ideas of the Early Sex Education Movement in America," *History of Education Quarterly*, XII (Summer 1972): 129-132; Michael Bliss, "'Pure Books on Avoided Subjects': Pre-Freudian Sexual Ideas in Canada," in Michiel Horn and Ronald Sabourin, eds., *Studies in Canadian Social History* (Toronto: McClelland and Stewart Ltd., 1974), pp. 334-339; *MFP*, June 8, 1875, p. 3.

31 *MFP*, Feb. 15, 1904, p. 7, Nov. 14, 1908, sports section, p. 1, Nov. 21,

1908, sports section, p. 1, Aug. 31, 1911, p. 7; *Annual Report of the Trustees of the School District of Winnipeg No. 1*, 1900, pp. 18, 35; *Department of Education Annual Report*, 1910 p. 54; *Annual Report*, 1914, in Manitoba: *Sessional Papers*, no. 3, 1915, p. 313; "Toba 03-04," p. 12, Manitoba College File, MG 10 B23, Public Archives of Manitoba; H.R. Hadcock, "Athletics and Sport in the West," *Western Sportsman*, II (Oct, 1906): 281-282; Professor Joliffe, "On Sport," *Vox Wesleyana*, XII (Nov. 1908): 25-26; "Value of Athletics," reprint from *Medical Record in Western School Journal*, I (June 1906): 19; n.a., "It is Character that Counts," *Western School Journal*, III (Mar. 1908): 98-99; "Playgrounds" *Western School Journal*, IV (June 1909): 209-210; Dr. Mary Crawford, "Physical Training in Public Schools," *Western School Journal*, VII (May 1912): 176-178; n.a., "Play," pp. 32-33; Woods, "Playground Activities," p. 136; McLaren, "Physical Training," pp. 96-103; *Neepawa Press*, Mar. 27, 1914, p. 1.

32 Woods, "Playground Activities," p. 137.

34 *Census of the Prairie Provinces*, 1916, p. 142; *Census of Canada*, 1931, vol. 1, pp. 717-718.

34 Rev. W. Bridgman, "The Immigrant Problem As It Affects Canadian Methodism," *Vox Wesleyana*, XII (Nov. 1907): 63-66. Bridgman had more scathing remarks to make about the "foreigners" in his *Breaking Prairie Sod*, published in 1918. See Mott, "The Foreign Peril: Nativism in Winnipeg, 1916-1923" (M.A. thesis, University of Manitoba, 1970), pp. 11-13.

35 G.F. Chipman, "Winnipeg: The Melting Pot," *Canadian Magazine*, XXXIII (1909): 413; *Neepawa Register*, June 27, 1912, p. 4; J.S. Woodsworth, *Strangers Within Our Gates or Coming Canadians* (Toronto: Methodist Mission Rooms, 1909), especially chapters 9-11.

36 W.J. Sisler, *Peaceful Invasion* (Winnipeg: W.J. Sisler, 1944), chapter 5, especially p. 47; *MFP*, May 22, 1909, sports section, p. 3, Aug. 31, 1909, p. 7. On this theme in general, see Cavallo, *Muscles and Morals*, pp. 43-46, 96-106.

37 Sisler, *Peaceful Invasion*, pp. 35-40; Peter Humeniuk, *Hardships and Progress of Ukrainian Pioneers. Memoirs from Stuartburn Colony and other Points* (Steinbach, Man.: Peter Humeniuk, 1977), p. 123; Orest T. Martynowich, "Village Radicals and Peasant Immigrants: The Social Roots of Factionalism among Ukrainian Immigrants in Canada, 1896-1918" (M.A. thesis, University of Manitoba, 1978), pp. 184-190.

38 Soccer and baseball were not peculiarly Canadian games, of course. However, they and the other team ball games had evolved among, and were most popular among, the English-speaking peoples of the world with whom British Manitobans identified.

39 MFP, Nov. 7, 1908, sports section, p. 1; "Diary of a Trip to Europe, July and August 1910," entry for July 31, Sisler Papers, Box 5, file 56, MG 14 C28, Public Archives of Manitoba; "Athletics," *Vox Wesleyana*, XII (Mar. 1908): 107; Geoffrey Harphan, "Time Running Out: The Edwardian Sense of Cultural Degeneration," *Clio*, V (Spring 1976); 283-286; Stephanie Lee Twin, "Jock and Jill: Aspects of Women's Sports History in America, 1870-1940" (Ph.D. thesis, Rutgers University, 1978), pp. 115-127; Anna Davin, "Imperialism and Motherhood," *History Workshop Journal*, V (Spring 1978); 9-22; Heather Rielly, "Attitudes to Women and Sport in Eastern Ontario, 1867-1885," in *Proceedings, 5ᵗʰ Canadian Symposium on the History of Sport and Physical Education, University of Toronto, August 26-29, 1982* (Toronto: University of Toronto School of Physical and Health Education, 1982), p. 385.

40 *MFP*, July 11, 1899, p. 3; McLaren, "Physical Training," 99; n.a., "Ladies Column," *Northwestern Sportsman*, I (Apr. 8, 1896): 10; *Dauphin Press*, Oct. 28, 1909, p. 6; H.R. Hadcock, "Physical Training," *Western School Journal*, II (Apr. 1907): 116; Mrozek, *Sport and American Mentality*, chapter 5; Patricia A. Vertinsky, "The Effect of Changing Attitudes Toward Sexual Morality Upon the Promotion of Physical Education for Women in Nineteenth Century America," *Canadian Journal of History of Sport and Physical Education*, VII (Dec. 1976): 26-38; Helen Lenskyj, "Moral Physiology in Physical Education and Sport for Girls in Ontario," *Proceeding, 5ᵗʰ Canadian Symposium*, pp. 140-148; Isobel E. Disney, "College Athletics for Women," *Vox Wesleyana*, VI (July 1902): 153.

41 *Winnipeg Times*, Apr. 9, 1883, p. 8; n.a., "Sports," *St. John's College Magazine*, IV (Apr. 1888): 189; MFP, Oct. 30, 1893, p. 5.

42 *MFP*, Aug 31, 1909, p. 7, Oct. 14, 1913, p. 6; *Minnedosa Tribune*, June 5, 1913, p. 2, May 28, 1914, p.2.

43 Sisler, Peaceful Invasion, p. 61; Annual Report of the Winnipeg School Board, 1912, pp. 18-19; Hadcock, "Physical Training," p. 116; Crawford, "Physical Training in Public Schools," p. 177.

44 *MFP*, Oct. 10, 1902, p. 5, Nov. 4, 1905, p. 5, Oct. 14, 1913, p. 6; *Brandon Times*, Feb. 6, 1908, p. 9; *Brandon Sun*, Feb. 20, 1908, p. 5; Women's Institutes of Arrow River and Miniota, *Bridging the Years, 1879-1967*, (Arrow River: Women's Institutes of Arrow River and Miniota, 1970), pp. 94, 201; Beulah History Committee, *Minnewashta Memories, 1879-1970* (Beulah: Beulah Women's Institute, 1970), pp. 98-99; *History of Blanshard Municipality, 1884-1959* (n.p.; Blanshard Municipality, n.d.) 151; Darlingford Historical Book Committee, *The Darlingford Saga, 1870-1970* (Darlingford: Darlingford Historical Book Committee, 1970), p. 366; Marian W. Abra, ed., *A View of the Birdtail: A History of the Municipality of Birtle, the Town of Birtie and the Villages of Foxwarren and Scolsgirth, 1878-*

1974, (Birtle: History Committee of Birtle Municipality, 1974) pp. 205-206; Anne M. Collier, *A Rear View Mirror, A History of Austin and Surrounding Districts* (Austin: Anne M. Collier, 1967), p. 130; Binscarth History Committee, *Binscarth Memories* (Binscarth: Binscarth History Committee, 1984), p. 62; Reta Shore, ed., *Ten Dollars and a Dream: Parkhill-Cheval:* (n.p. Parkhill-Cheval Community Club, 1977?) p. 363. Many of the local histories contain photographs illustrating athletic attire for girls.

45 *Winnipeg Telegram,* Apr. 12, 1913, section 3, p. 2. See also, *Grandview Exponent,* May 29, 1903, p. 5; *Dauphin Press,* Oct. 28, 1909, p. 6; Disney, "College Athletics for Women," p. 153.

46 *Minnedosa Tribune,* Dec. 8, 1910, p. 2.

47 D.C. Coleman, "The Church and Wild Olive," *Western Sportsman,* II (Sept. 1906): 246-247; *Dauphin Press,* Feb. 4, 1915, p. 1; *Souris Plaindealer,* Apr. 1, 1914, p. 1; *Brandon Sun,* Aug. 19, 1909, part 2, p. 3, Jan. 8, 1914, part 2, p. 1; *North West Review,* July 16, 1910, p. 9; *MFP,* Dec. 17, 1910, p. 33, Apr. 25, 1914, pp. 19-20.

48 Mott, "Manly Sports," pp. 204-206; *MFP,* Nov. 14, 1908, sports section, p. 1, Nov. 21, 1908, sports section, p. 1, Apr. 6, 1909, p. 6; *Brandon Sun* Feb. 20, 1913, part 1, p. 1.

49 Murray G. Ross, *The Y.M.C.A. in Canada. The Chronicle of a Century* (Toronto: The Ryerson Press, 1951), pp. 169, 186-192; *MFP,* Jan. 18, 1901, pp. 6-7, June 12, 1909, sports section, pp. 1-2, Feb. 14, 1914, sports section, pp. 1, 4; *Brandon Times,* Apr. 11, 1907, p. 7; *Brandon Sun,* June 22, 1957, section A, p. 9.

50 Col. C.W. Rowley, "Greetings from the Boy Scouts," *Western School Journal,* XI (May 1916): 185. See also, *Hartney Star,* June 29, 1911, p. 1; *Minnedosa Tribune,* Aug. 8, 1912, p. 3; *Gladstone Age,* Feb. 19, 1914, p. 1; *Dauphin Press,* Feb. 20, 1913, p. 1, May 7, 1914, p. 4.

51 "Fifth Annual Report of the Winnipeg Boys' Club," 1909, p. 8, Winnipeg Boys Club Collection, MG 10 B15, Public Archives of Manitoba; *MFP,* Jan. 18, 1908, p. 6, Sept. 27, 1909, p. 6, Feb. 13, 1914, p. 7, Apr. 17, 1914, p. 7.

52 J.W. Bengough, "A Practical Suggestion," *Educational Journal of Western Canada,* I (Nov. 1899): 197.

53 J.B. Wallis, "The Advantages of Military Drill," *Western School Journal,* I (Nov. 1906): 11-12; *MFP,* June 24, 1905, p. 7, July 4, 1908, sports section, p. 4; Frank Belton, "Military Drill in Ungraded Schools," *Educational Journal of Western Canada,* II (June-July 1900): 439-440; McLaren, "Physical Training," p. 99; n.a., "Physical Culture," *Western School Journal,* VIII (Jan. 1913): 34; J.W. Chafe, *An Apple for the Teacher: A Centennial History of the Winnipeg School Division* (Winnipeg: Winnipeg School Division No. 1, 1967), pp. 79-80; Sisler, *Peaceful*

Invasion, pp. 61-62; *Winnipeg Free Press,* May 7, 1974, section C, p. 2; Green, "School Cadets in Winnipeg," pp. 33-37.

54 Hadcock, "Physical Training," p. 117; n.a., "How To Make Men," *Educational Journal of Western Canada* I (Mar. 1899); 27; Morrow, "Physical Education in Ontario," pp. 235-236, 255, 257-258; Helen Margaret Eckert, "The Development of Organized Recreation and Physical Education in Alberta" (M.Ed. thesis, University of Alberta 1953), pp. 123-126; Downie, "Physical Education in Manitoba," pp. 56-57.

55 N.A., "The Convention," *Western School Journal,* IX (May 1914): 82.

56 Department of Education *Annual Report,* 1911, p. 40, *Annual Report* 1913-14, p. 131; McLaren, "Physical Training," p. 100.

57 Some excellent photographs of one-room schools, and sometimes the landscapes around them, can be found in Emmy Preston, ed., *Pioneers of Grandview and District* (Grandview: Pioneer Book Committee, 1976), pp. 14-17; Grosse Isle Women's Institute, *The Grosse Isle Story* (Grosse Isle: Grosse Isle Women's Institute, 1977?), pp. 90-91; Douglas History Book Club, *Echoes of a Century: Douglas Manitoba Centennial, 1882-1982* (n.p. Douglas History Book Club, 1982), pp. 49-63; Deloraine History Book Committee, *Deloraine Scans a Century. A History of Deloraine and District, 1880-1980* (Deloraine: Deloraine History Book Committee, 1980), pp. 123-147; Ivan J. Saunders, *A Survey of Manitoba School Architecture to 1930* (Ottawa: Parks Canada Research Bulletin, 1984), especially pp. 18-25.

58 Some information on, and pictures of, equipment in rural and urban schools can be found in *MFP,* July 8, 1908; Kenneth Osborne, *Daniel McIntyre Collegiate Institute: A History* (Winnipeg: Collegiate Institute Alumni, 1973?), p. 17; Sisler, *Peaceful Invasion,* pp. 36-40, 49; Connie Davidson, ed., *Gnawing at the Past* (Lyleton: Lyleton Women's Institute, 1969), p. 26; Domain Women's Institute, *Down Memory Lane: A History of the Domain Community, 1876-1967* (Domain: Domain Women's Institute, 1967?), p. 183. Some instructive photographs can also be seen in PAM, Still Images Section, W.J. Sisler Collection, Foote Collection, Oak Lake—Schools Collection, and in Western Canada Pictorial Index, University of Winnipeg, indexed under "Schools—Lifestyle—Parks."

59 Neil Sutherland, *Children in English Canadian Society: Framing the Twentieth Century Consensus* (Toronto: University of Toronto Press, 1976), p. 241.

* * * * *

Documents for Chapter Seven

The first document may be analyzed from many different perspectives—the most obvious of which is to compare the state of physical education from province to province, and between Catholic and Protestant schools. In which provinces were conditions the worst, and, more importantly, why? The two tables may also be examined for what is quantified. What factors did the investigators consider important in the delivery of physical education? What criteria are not examined? During the 1960s, the growing interest in leisure activities shifted the emphasis in physical education from callisthenics to general fitness and lifelong sports. Compare Morris Mott's article to Document 29. How had both the motivations and the justifications for teaching physical education changed? What is the current state of physical education in the schools?

28) PHYSICAL EDUCATION CONDITIONS, 1945[1]

TABLE XVII
**Percent of Elementary Schools with Certain Conditions
Affecting the Teaching of Physical Education**

CONDITION	B.C.	Alta	Sask.	Man.	Ont.	Que. (P) *	Que. (C) *	N.B.	N.S.	P.E.I.
1 Teacher has special departmental certificate ... (not Strathcona A or B)	15.8	6.3	8.8	14.8	12.7	9.4	3.3	0.7	2.9	0.0
2 Adequate indoor accommodation	18.3	5.8	5.9	9.2	8.4	12.1	2.8	5.5	8.4	0.4
3 Adequate playgrounds	69.9	73.3	70.8	86.9	68.6	73.2	45.4	37.9	31.3	20.1
4 Equipment for a comprehensive program is ...										
(i) adequate	25.0	5.9	7.7	6.7	7.1	14.7	3.3	2.2	0.7	1.0
(ii) inadequate	52.4	86.9	90.2	87.1	90.5	84.7	77.2	96.7	79.8	87.6
(iii) no data given	22.6	7.2	2.1	6.2	2.4	0.6	19.5	1.1	19.5	11.4
5 Source of music is available, used regularly	47.7	37.1	19.3	41.4	56.4	27.4	13.2	4.8	50.0	6.5
6 Cases of continuous excuse from classes in Physical Education are decided by ...										
(i) school medical officer	19.6	11.0	2.4	8.0	7.4	15.9	4.0	3.8	4.8	0.0
(ii) family doctor	9.3	14.3	6.9	1.7	12.9	2.1	1.7	1.4	1.1	0.6
(iii) school inspector	0.1	1.4	0.2	0.0	0.2	0.0	0.0	0.0	0.0	0.0
(iv) teacher	19.6	36.0	17.8	19.9	19.9	16.8	1.1	33.5	3.4	11.9
(v) parent	2.3	3.5	5.0	0.4	5.1	11.5	1.8	0.6	1.1	12.2
7 Records of progress of students are kept	31.9	8.0	5.4	6.5	5.7	15.9	0.2	1.9	8.9	0.0
8 Participation in organized sports days	53.5	67.6	68.3	46.3	20.5	26.7	3.0	1.1	17.7	4.2
9 Allotted time given to Physical Education	80.9	42.0	35.1	28.2	†	43.5	17.9	28.7	11.8	12.8

*(P) Protestant Schools, (C) Catholic Schools. † No data available.

TABLE XVIII

Percent of Elementary School Inspectorates with Certain Conditions Affecting the Teaching of Physical Education

CONDITION	B.C.	Alta	Sask.	Man.	Ont.	Que. (P) *	Que. (C) *	N.B.	N.S.
1 Grading in Physical Education is comparable with that in academic subjects ...									
	37.0	19.2	18.8	15.8	†	20.0	14.7	0.0	8.3
2 Sports days are held periodically									
	96.3	100.0	93.8	78.9	72.1	40.0	32. 4	35.3	66.7
3 Students receive a medical examination before participation in athletic competitions ...									
	25.9	9.6	6.3	21.1	†	30.0	4.4	5.9	8.3
4 Incomplete Physical Education program due to ...									
(i) lack of accommodation	33.3	65.4	72.9	78.9	†	40.0	64.7	52.9	50.0
(ii) lack of equipment	22.2	48.1	77.1	78.9	†	40.0	55.9	35.3	41.7
(iii) lack of trained personnel	18.5	57.7	79.2	78.9	†	50.0	72.1	64.7	58.3
(iv) lack of time	7.4	0.0	2.1	10.5	†	0.0	2.9	11.8	8.3
(v) lack of interest	0.0	0.0	8.3	5.3	†	0.0	10.3	11.8	0.0
5 Present methods of teaching are ...									
(i) satisfactory	26.7	11.5	4.2	0.0	9.0	0.0	22.1	11.8	0.0
(ii) partially satisfactory	50.0	59.6	43.8	68.4	50.8	30.0	33.8	35.3	16.7
(iii) unsatisfactory	23.3	26.9	41.7	15.8	35.2	50.0	30.9	52.9	58.3
(iv) no data available	0.0	2.0	10.3	15.8	5.0	20.0	13.2	0.0	25.0

*(P) Protestant Schools, (C) Catholic Schools. † No data available.

* * * * *

29) PHYSICAL FITNESS IN CANADIAN SCHOOLS, 1976[2]

The present low level of cardiorespiratory endurance in our adult population has prompted the Canadian government to spend considerable sums of money in an attempt to raise this physiological value .... A recent survey using correlation techniques suggests that a saving of some $13,000,000 per year in heath care costs could occur in Ontario if all people over 35 years had average cardiorespiratory endurance. Nutrition Canada has indicated that our major nutritional problem is obesity. It and cardiorespiratory endurance are intimately linked; a person who is obese is unlikely to have a high cardiorespiratory endurance value. In this paper I wish to present results from our laboratory and other relevant material on possibly the most important period of decline in cardiorespiratory endurance and increase in obesity—the school-age years.

Recent reviews indicate that the amount of time provided for physical education in Canada is less than most other industrialized nations. In Table 1a the number of periods per week and the total time allotted is presented. The minimal amount of time provided in Canada is a consequence of several factors. The main one is the capital cost of providing adequate indoor facilities, especially for the numerous elementary schools with class sizes of 30-35 students. Large student enrolments are such that even the most careful time-tabling often permits just two 30-minute classes per week in a gymnasium.

It is possible that the time-tabling itself may influence some teachers and principals as to the amount of time necessary for sound physical education programs. When climatic conditions are such that the teacher and children can go outside, often the time taken is still two periods per week, while the class should be outside taking part in *daily* physical education. It seems that classroom teachers believe that the two periods per week are sufficient and that the decision has been made (that is, two periods per week) with some degree of empirical evidence. At present children require at least five periods of approximately 40 minutes each of physical education per week in order to meet the objectives of most provincial physical education guidelines. These guidelines emphasize areas such as acquisition of physical skills, physical fitness, enjoyment of activity and development in other areas such as socialization and leadership.

TABLE (1a)
Amount of Time Provided for Physical Education
(Minutes per week)

	SASKATOON	ONTARIO	JAPAN	DENMARK	W. GERMANY	E. GERMANY
Kindergarten To grade 6	60	60	135	150	135	180
Grade 7-9	90	160	150	150	135	180
Grade 10-12	90	160	150	150	135	180

TABLE (1b)
Percentage of Time Spent on Physical Education
and Academic Education in Ontario and Saskatoon
in Elementary and Junior High School

	PHYSICAL EDUCATION	ACADEMIC EDUCATION
Elementary	3	97 (6% for art, vocational training)
Jr. high school	8 (in Saskatoon the time is 4%)	92

Earlier studies by Ekblom suggest that activity when children are still growing appears to be more contributory to fitness than if activity is pursued before or after the period of their optimum growth. Heart volume, vital capacity and maximal oxygen uptake were more fully developed in children who are active than in the control children. Ekblom's program involved two 50-minute periods of continuous activity per week, composed of sprint, distance and interval training as well as cross-country running, soccer and ice hockey. This training was in addition to two regular 45-minute periods of ball games per week.

When one compares this program to what is at present offered in Canada, a considerable gap exists. In Canadian elementary schools the average amount of time is two 30-minute periods per week, kindergarten to grade 6, ages five to eleven. This falls well short of the time provided, for example, by Japan, Sweden, East and West Germany (three to four 45-minute periods per week). In the Ontario junior high school program (12-14 years) the allotted time is four 40-minute periods per week. This would seem most desirable provided the program is planned. In the years beyond grade 10 the program is often optional. An impression is that students who enjoy physical education or whose parents realize its value will select it and those who do not are often those who would benefit by it.

When one takes into account what occurs in many current programs offered by physical education teachers and others, the amount of activity is found to be minimal; that is, even in the small amount of time provided in our programs, maximum use of it is not made ....

Goldbloom has suggested if an increase in daily calorie expenditure (one hour of school time each day in vigorous organized physical activity) did take place as a part of the school program, this could alter our children's lifestyle and bring about an ultimate reduction in the incidence and severity of obesity and could benefit the health of the entire population.

In the gymnasium the total amount of activity is even less than during an organized hockey practice, for conditions are not as optimal as on the ice rink, that is, one teacher per 20 players on the ice rink, as compared to one teacher per 36 students in the gymnasium, and often with students who are not as highly motivated as a competitive team. In a basketball period the actual amount of whole body movement is found to be approximately 11 minutes out of a 45-minute period, while in wrestling it drops to some five minutes. The pulse rate is observed to get above 150 beats per minute for only one to two minutes during these periods. It becomes evident that if movement, vigorous movement, is considered to be an important part of physical education and the teacher has only some 40 minutes per day which includes a time for change of clothes (leaving 30 minutes), then planning must take place for sufficient movement to occur.

With this small amount of activity in a regular physical education program it is not surprising that a decline in a child's cardiorespiratory endurance or his or her ability to do work or play occurs as he or she progresses through the school year. Despite four periods per week of physical education in a junior high school studied by our group, the physical work capacity of the school children declined over a four-month period, November to February; that is, not only was there insufficient activity to maintain the child's cardiorespiratory endurance during this four month period, it actually decreased. This is likely the only subject area in which a decrease in capacity occurs as the child goes through the school years. The lack of activity is evident in the increase in skinfold thickness in both boys and girls during the winter months. This is more apparent when one designs a program to offset this lack of vigorous activity.

During the same period, November to February, 500 students in an experimental school took part in six minutes per day of vigorous activity, such that the heart rate reached the minimal level for a training effect, 150 beats per minute. The activities selected by the teachers were skipping, running over obstacles, hopping and dance, all to music. The teachers taught the student to take a ten-second pulse immediately at the end of exercise in order to establish if the activity was sufficiently intense to give a training effect. If not, then the youngster was encouraged to be more vigorous. The level of activity was not so uncomfortable that the student could not talk; there were signs of perspiration and slight breathlessness.

In the experimental school the cardiorespiratory endurance improved in the children, whereas in the control school it generally decreased as the child went through school. Six minutes of daily exercise with the exercise heart rate at least at 150 beats per minute during the exercise period were sufficient to effect a significant increase in cardiorespiratory endurance.

When one examines the Ontario curriculum of physical education, *The Formative Years*, it is evident that an appreciation of activity exists. The general aim states that the school program should develop creativity and competence in physical fitness through physical activity. Two of the specific aims are directly related to physical fitness: "Develop an understanding of movement and a love of vigorous activity" and "Develop an appropriate degree of balance, strength, speed, position and economy of effort of physical actions."

The phrase "love of vigorous activity" is most apt. Studies of adults have not found evidence to suggest that maximal effort has any more prophylactic effect on heart disease than moderate activity. Often the experience of maximal effort, especially in the unprepared, can result in a repugnance for activity in general. Both adults and children can readily establish whether the activity is moderate in nature.

Our own best guideline is that the child or adult should be able to talk. One example may assist in clarifying this technique. A 60-year-old male was swimming the butterfly stroke, an exhaustive skill for an unconditioned individual.

As he touched the end the instructor asked the swimmer a question: he was able to respond directly without signs of breathlessness. The exercise was within his capacity. The second technique was the use of pulse rate as described above. The pulse rate in this individual was 20 beats in the ten second at the end of exercise; this is equivalent to a heart rate of 120 beats per minute and is well within the pulse range for training effect, 110-114 beats per minute, 60 years of age. Teachers can ensure that students who are involved in large muscle activities such as cross-country running, cycling, tobogganing are well within their capacity by observing whether they can talk briefly to each other during the activities and what level the pulse has reached.

The cardiorespiratory endurance, though decreasing in Canadian children up to the age of 10-11, is similar to the levels of children of the same age from different countries. However, there is an apparent weakness in strength in our females and some of our males. Several females in a recent survey aged 13-14, were not able to pull their own body weight off the floor (chin-up), yet these girls were representatives of the province of Ontario in competitive swimming. As a minimal level of strength I believe the child should be able to carry his own weight, in this case one should be able to lift oneself off the floor and be capable of climbing five to ten feet. On several occasions we have observed females in extreme difficulty after having fallen while skiing, and, because of insufficient strength, were unable to get to their feet. This is most frustrating for adolescents, especially when one begins an activity for the first time. These students may be more sensitive to failure and it is possible that the child will not attempt the experience again. It is important that the school program develop a minimum level of strength so that the student will be able to take up an activity and not be influenced by a lack of muscular strength.

Up to the age of 10 to 11 we would recommend spending nine minutes a day in fitness activities. This means planning. The child should involve himself in large muscle activities for four minutes, and upper body strength activities for five minutes. Some of the large muscle activities could be in the form of tag games, dancing, soccer drills, European hand-ball and skating if sufficient ice time is available. The main feature of these activities is that the legs are used to offset gravity. Upper body strength activities could be such items as hand-over-hand travelling along a horizontal ladder, rope climbing or gymnastic activities.

After age 11 cardiorespiratory endurance in our students begins to decline at a faster rate than other countries. We would recommend that nine minutes of a 50-minute physical education period be spent on physical fitness and, during this nine minutes, six minutes be spent on large muscle activity so that the students' pulse rate was in the training zone. Cycling, skating, jogging, skipping, water-polo, rugger, dancing, are some of the activities that could be pursued as well as skill activities, with or without equipment, that might involve themselves within games: for example, jumping up for a volley ball, dribbling with a field hockey stick or soccer ball, dribbling with a basket ball. The final three minutes would be spent on upper body activities to increase or maintain upper body strength.

Work by Saltin has shown that activity can be intermittent or continuous for a training effect on the cardiorespiratory system. Our studies were successful with three minutes of continuous activity, followed by light callisthenics and then a second three-minute period of large muscle activity.

It would be most agreeable if sufficient time were available for children to obtain an adequate level of cardiorespiratory fitness and muscular strength through games. While tag games and games such as soccer are most suitable for younger children, older boys and girls may enjoy playing soccer, field hockey, rugger, ice hockey, basketball and water polo as well as participating in individual sports such as cycling, cross-country skiing, down hill skiing over moguls (bumps), and figure skating.

In the junior high and public schools a large emphasis should be placed on skill development, especially in one or two carry-over individual activities, such as badminton, swimming and skating. Team sports such as basketball, rugger, field hockey, soccer should not be de-emphasized, but should be continued and promoted. A positive attitude toward activity, the desire for physical exercise, and love of vigorous activity can come through vigorous games, especially team games where social and emotional factors often over-shadow the exercise benefits. A teacher-coach can make a student aware of his personal fitness level achieved at team games and this way provide a model for him to attempt to maintain later on in life. With a moderate degree of fitness, an adult can keep his options open for physical activity.

In the past year there has been a large increase in movement education in our elementary schools. This activity is not usually vigorous enough to improve cardiorespiratory endurance, nor without planning can it maintain or increase a child's strength. Movement education is important and should continue, but in addition, during the physical education period, nine minutes, as suggested, should be set aside for a planned program that will increase the child's physical fitness.

Although there are many other areas involved in physical fitness, such as flexibility and balance, agility, power, we have emphasized cardiorespiratory endurance and upper body strength for three reasons: first, the prophylactic value of increased endurance in reducing one of the risk factors for coronary heart disease and improving the recovery from that disease; second, the decrease in obesity that can occur with increased physical activity; and third, an improved capacity for play and work. The development of upper body strength is promoted so that the child can enjoy the many pursuits that require this element, as well as for certain safety implications, especially those associated with water.

The use of pulse rate by the teacher can, as an index of exercise intensity, be a most helpful technique for deciding which activities should be emphasized in a physical education program. A standard for upper body development would be that the child should develop sufficient strength to support and lift his or her own body weight.

The teaching methods used to promote physical fitness are varied. Three successful programs we have observed involve individual programming in two and traditional task teaching in the third.

With planning it is possible in 40 to 50 minutes of daily physical education to teach skills, experience and enjoyment through participation in physical activity, and inhibit processes that are linked with our sedentary lifestyle which decrease cardiorespiratory endurance and increase obesity in the school-age years.

* * * * *

1 *A Health Survey of Canadian Schools, 1945-1946,* Report No. 1 of The National Committee for School Health Research (Toronto, 1947), pp. 58-60.
2 Robert C. Goode, "The Physical Fitness of Our School Children," *Education Canada* (Winter, 1976), pp. 26-31. Footnotes have been deleted.

Chapter Eight:
High School Culture Between the Wars

In 1900, only those individuals who intended to be teachers or enrol in university attended high school. Thus, for example, only five percent of school-aged children in Ontario, and one percent in New Brunswick, advanced to high school. The period after the First World War witnessed a massive growth in the number of students continuing on and through high school. In 1923, thirty-four percent of all 15 to 17 year-old teenagers in English Canada attended high school. These numbers increased during the years of high unemployment in the 1930s.

This unprecedented growth resulted from a combination of factors. Increasing the compulsory school age and making secondary education free naturally helped.[114] So too did labour laws that forbid employment of minors in factories and mines. The affluence of the 1920s led to lower birth rates and to higher expectations by parents for their offspring—which required better education. *Maclean's Magazine*, for example, reported in 1925 that "Each day in High School adds $25 to a man's life's earnings."

The practice of streaming students into commercial, technical, and collegiate high schools began in the 1920s. This gave birth to the guidance movement to help students select the most appropriate secondary school. Since many students failed the entrance examination to high school, junior high schools emerged to prepare students for the next level. In the 1930s, the new vocational guidance movement emphasized job placement and the composite high school emerged to combine the technical and commercial streams.

"Inventing the Extracurriculum" by Cynthia Comacchio draws upon student yearbooks and other youth-generated sources to examine school-controlled extracurricular activities in Ontario high schools between the two world wars. In a familiar refrain to today's complaints, adults worried that a plethora of commercial amusements were weakening the moral fibre of the country's young people. One solution to this "youth problem" was to keep children in school longer. Extracurricular activities such as athletics, music and drama clubs, and school dances were intended to convince youth to stay longer in high school and to promote proper citizenship. The high school, claims Comacchio, played a critical role in influencing the lives of young people in the interwar years.

Other useful works dealing with this period: R.D. Gidney and W.P.J. Millar, *Inventing Secondary Education: The Rise of the High School in Nineteenth-*

Century Ontario (Toronto, 1990); Robert M. Stamp, "Canadian High School in the 1920's and 1930's: The Social Challenge to the Academic Tradition," Historical Papers (1978); and George S. Tomkins, *A Common Countenance: Stability and Change in the Canadian Curriculum* (Toronto, 1986).

∗   ∗   ∗   ∗   ∗

Inventing the Extracurriculum: High School Culture in Interwar Ontario[115]

In many ways, the history of adolescence is a chronicle of the anxieties and pre-occupations of adults. By the end of the First World War, Canadians were becoming increasingly uneasy about a so-called youth problem which was attributed to a litany of related causes: the disruptive impact of the war, particularly on families; the "hectic" qualities of modern life; and, most important, the waning influence of such traditional sources of sociocultural reproduction as family, church, school, community, and workplace. To worried observers, it also appeared that popular culture, more and more a youth culture, posed a special challenge to the existing order of things, including personal morality and the historic relations of authority derived from class, gender, "race," and age. Eager to be "modern," young people seemed dangerously close to rejecting all that was held to exemplify a young, ambitious nation, especially industry and self-discipline. As an Ontario high school inspector remarked in 1920, there was a "pretty general complaint among teachers" that, since the close of the war, their adolescent students had been "unsettled by the general spirit of unrest that is prevalent throughout the province." It was agreed that "the allurements of the automobile and the movies and the craze for dancing" had "seriously interfered" with their attention to their studies. The situation in some high schools had evidently deteriorated to the point that several principals had "protested publicly," feeling compelled to warn parents that "the moral fibre of the young is being weakened and their success in life endangered by their pursuit of pleasure."[1]

The invaluable "raw material" of a modern industrial democracy, adolescents represented the nation's potential in the wake of a war that had killed or maimed 60,000 Canadian men, a resource of leaders, fathers, workers, and soldiers that a sparsely populated country feared it could never replenish. In view of such concerns, the young came to constitute a "youth problem" that contributed significantly to the myriad "social problems" of the time which were demanding the attention of all right-minded Canadians.[2]

While the physical attributes of biological puberty manifest little change historically, its cultural traits are clearly subject to ongoing revision. Early-twentieth-century theories and practices respecting adolescence were part of a larger process that was placing childhood socialization in the hands of experts in pedagogy, medicine, and psychology, increasingly active participants in the modern family. Influenced by the seminal work of American psychologist G. Stanley Hall (1904), which shaped perceptions of adolescence for much of the century, the emergent body of experts helped to devise policies and programs— intended to contain and regulate—which were premised on institutionalized age segregation and subordination.[3] In their hands, adolescence was construed not so much as a passage to adult status and responsibility as a condition of physical and mental anarchy, fraught with nervous disorders and all their imagined ill-effects for both individual and society. Even if the desire for excitement was explained biologically as a "natural" youthful inclination, its possibly unnatural repercussions called for close supervision of all outlets for adolescent urges—especially those involving the commercial amusements which typified modernity, the cinema and dance hall representing the foremost choices of the young. Adult vigilance was required to protect and nurture adolescents safely through the maelstrom, although this would have to be carried out cautiously, in that the young were "sensitive" and resented any hint of "interference" from the adults in their lives.[4] A balanced and regulated regimen of school, work, and play was the ultimate aim. As Hall himself remonstrated, "we are progressively forgetting that for the complete apprenticeship to life, youth needs repose, leisure, art, legends, romance, idealization, and in a word, humanism, if it is to enter the kingdom of man well-equipped for man's highest work in the world."[5]

Although images of adolescence as a "dangerous time" characterized discussions of the "youth problem" during the interwar years, they were generally matched by more hopeful theories hinging on the power of education. The "adventurous instinct" intrinsic to adolescence was proclaimed to be the same spirit "that grips the heart and soul in passionate devotion to the national ideal," the motive force so evident at Vimy Ridge, the Canadian wartime experience that came to memorialize that ideal. Wholesome recreation organized by "capable and inspiring leaders" and, above all, "constructive education in citizenship and the ideals of national and individual life" would see it channelled properly.[6] A prime objective of the period's broad-ranging campaign for social order, consequently, was to coax young Canadians away from the troubling new commercial amusements and into adult-sanctioned and supervised "educational" venues offering the sort of "character training" that was seen as the only viable solution to the pressing youth problem. And the most obvious starting point for the organization of youthful free time was the high school, increasingly central to the adolescent experience. If adolescents were being "made or marred, for the most part before they are sixteen years of age," they remained nonetheless susceptible to the positive influences of the school. The high school's purpose went far beyond training productive and efficient workers; equally important was its role in imparting "the training which is to produce the future character." Through the school, community spirit could be fostered "as it could never be through church, home or press," for the school would "fit [the young person] for future service and citizenship."[7]

If secondary schooling was a nineteenth-century invention, the high school's historical moment, manifested in "the second great transformation" of Canadian education, arrived in the years immediately following the First World War.[8] Still largely unexplored in this context of educational expansion is the function of the extracurriculum. As high schools began to serve a wider community in the 1920s and 1930s, their socializing functions changed as much as their population and curriculum. This article considers the development of school-based, out-of-class socialization for adolescents through an adult-supervised extracurriculum, in relation to public concerns about youth and citizenship in a modern Ontario determined to lead the nation to a prosperous, productive future. Borrowing from theories about the key role of educational institutions in the transmission of cultural capital, I argue that the extracurriculum taking distinctive shape in Ontario high schools during the interwar years was critical to the shaping of a modern adolescence. It reflected and projected the new social meanings ascribed to adolescence, and consequently to the high school as the key formative influence in the lives of young Canadians. A sampling of high school yearbooks suggests the degree to which the extracurriculum imparted convention and conformity. However much—or little—they reflect majority experience, these publications self-consciously promoted ideas, behaviour, and values representing the official institutional culture—as they could not help but do, seeing as they were not unmediated expressions of adolescent views. Despite their obvious limitations in disclosing the voices of youth, these student-generated sources reveal the measures that the young were meant to use to motivate themselves and to assess their "progress" as they matured.

*　*　*　*　*

The historiography of Canadian secondary education has highlighted such vital developmental issues as the expansion of public schooling in the closing quarter of the nineteenth century, the growing importance of credentials in a modernizing society, and the design of a curriculum to meet public notions about adolescence as a preparatory phase for adult labour. It has been demonstrated that wider access to secondary schooling, along with new demands for occupational training, culminated in the introduction of class- and gender-delimited technical subjects, commercial studies, and domestic science. The outcome was not simply more relevant or practical education, however, but the reinforcement of gender, "race," and class inequalities which "deferred to the principle of mass schooling while maintaining rigid curricular distinctions in terms of status and cultural capital."[9] The growth of the high school was integral to the formation of a new middle class, itself part of a process of nation-building premised on anglo-conformity. In the late nineteenth century, the high school still functioned primarily as the privileged enclave of the academically oriented middle class, a preparation for university or further professional training. By the start of the Second World War, it was a nearly universal experience for Canadian adolescents, the vast majority of whom were heading into the working world. During this transition, the entire meaning of the high school experience underwent fundamental change.[10]

In regard to the expansion of secondary education, Ontario, the most populous and industrialized province, took the lead. The Industrial Education Act of 1911 provided provincial funding for technical education for adolescents beyond the school-leaving age of fourteen years.[11] In 1919 the Conservative government of Howard Ferguson passed the Adolescent School Attendance Act, implemented in 1921, which fixed the age of school-leaving at sixteen years. The population of Ontario's high schools quadrupled during the 1920s and 1930s, growing 325 per cent in the twenty years between 1918 and 1938.[12] Every annual report of the province's Department of Education through the interwar years comments on the rising crest of enrolment across the province, including the rural areas serviced only by "continuation" schools. For the province's three high school inspectors, the growing numbers were the outcome not only of legislation: "undoubtedly the greatest cause," in their view, was a new public appreciation of the importance of education, as well as "a general desire among parents to have their children share in its benefits." As Robert Stamp has effectively argued, however, the reasons probably had as much—or more—to do with the structural changes intensified by war and their concomitant sociocultural adaptations. Modern technology demanded more schooling at the same time that it provided fewer job opportunities for untrained adolescents, while the rise of a consumer economy also heightened youthful expectations for "something better" than the material conditions of life that their parents had known.[13]

As noteworthy as the numbers was the growing proportion of working-class adolescents now spending more time in the classroom than in the shop or factory. Although class patterns in attendance persisted well past the Second World War, secondary schooling was becoming an option for more young members of working-class families. The modern high school was idealistically proclaimed "the school of the common people," where "the rich and the poor, the high and the low, the Protestant and the Roman Catholic, mingle together and work together in the spirit of amity and equality, regardless of distinctions of class or creed." In the northern resource town of Timmins, the new high school opened in September 1923 was filled to capacity a year later; already plans were being made to enlarge it to accommodate new students, "many of them with foreign names but with loyal Canadian hearts."[14] In the industrial city of Hamilton, despite the strain on working-class family economies when the wages of teenaged children were forfeited, the high school population doubled in public academic schools and exploded (from 206 in 1921 to over 1,400 in 1930) in the new technical schools. A similar process was at work in the expansion of London's secondary schools.[15] With the extension of secondary schooling, working-class youth were more likely than ever before to experience an adolescence closer to that enjoyed by their middle-class peers. For many young Canadians, modern adolescence was a newly configured stage of life, characterized by schooling and guided social and cultural activities rather than full-time wage labour, a historic modification in the very structures of adolescence.[16]

Class formation and gender identity are transmitted, and their associated values consolidated, as much through home and school as in community and workplace. They also depend on the acquisition of cultural capital as well as its material forms. In the settings of family and classroom, young people learn what is expected of them, both in their day-to-day behaviour and in terms of how they will make their way as adults, expectations shaped by socioeconomic and familial position as well as by contemporary ideals about what constitutes "success" and full membership in adult society. These expectations are further developed through the kind of schooling that they receive and, more to the point, through their experiences, individual and collective, in the wider institutional culture of the school. In his influential study of sociocultural reproduction through schooling, sociologist Pierre Bourdieu argues forcefully that the school functions "in the manner of a huge classificatory machine which inscribes changes within the purview of the structure," thereby helping "to make and to impose the legitimate exclusions and inclusions which form the basis of the social order." What his empirical research has shown is an altogether unsurprising "very close statistical relationship" between achievement and "ascription," the latter referring to social origins and birth. Thus, cloaked with the rhetoric of equality and merit, schools perpetuate and legitimize social hierarchies. The extracurriculum, an increasingly integral part of the "pedagogic action" pertaining to modern secondary education, plays a vital role in this selection process.[17] On one level, much like the expanded high school itself, the extracurriculum contributed to the "containment" of problem youth by providing "safe" alternatives to "dangerous" commercial, or otherwise unsupervised, leisure activities. More important, however, the newly structured extracurriculum reinforced lessons about citizenship that equated loyalty to the school with national pride and performance, lessons that helped to preserve and reproduce the class, gender, and "racial" identities of a "Canadian" middle class intent on stabilizing itself amidst jarring sociocultural change.

By the 1920s, then, there was, for the first time, a significant age cohort which would make its way collectively through high school. This demographic watershed provided the basis for an institutionalized, teacher-supervised peer-group culture which largely replaced the less formal traditional framework of student clubs and teams by the 1930s.[18] With the attainment of sufficient numbers to support a complex network of peer-group societies, the cultural system of the modern high school took more definite form in such mixed-sex activities as student government, clubs, journalism, and the newly important (though not new) expressions of identity signified by traditional school colours, school songs and cheers, and gender-segregated athletic teams.[19]

Keeping young people in school longer, however, was seen as only a partial solution to the "youth problem," which initially was construed as the problem of an urban subculture of working-class adolescents, primarily, but not exclusively, boys. It was hoped that the new commercial and technical streams would mitigate boredom and its attendant evils while preparing the boys to become all-round productive adults in both work and play.[20] But the extracurriculum also featured strongly in the making of ideal male citizens. In Ontario, "a noticeable feature" of the high school student body was that girls outnumbered boys in the majority of schools. It was surmised that "through personal desire or for family reasons, the boys are impatient to be free to be out in the world, earning their own living." In all likelihood, the economic opportunities that continued to favour young men over young women were the primary reason for this disparity. The new attendance legislation and the revised course of study were important approaches to the problem, but it was also argued that "larger playgrounds" and "a more general encouragement" of games, sports, and other school-related, non-academic pastimes would be a strong incentive to boys to attend and to remain longer at school. "All work and no play" could not appeal to "the average boy," but "the chance of getting a place on the school's baseball, hockey or basketball team, or taking part in the school's literary society, dramatic or debating club," educators contended, would give him "an entirely different view of the high school."[21] Girls also participated actively in all these activities, but the leadership positions usually went to boys, particularly where student government and student publications were concerned. When girls did aspire to leadership positions, their ambitions were considered— by their peers—to be so unusual as to merit comment. At Kitchener Collegiate Institute, the first-ever female student council president was elected in 1931; the student newspaper editorialized that "undoubtedly a girl would have emerged victorious earlier had she succeeded in securing the votes of her own sex," among whom, in the view of this male commentator, "competition seems to be more vital ... evidently they hesitate to concede victory to their own sex."[22]

This expanding roster of organized activities legitimized the peer group as a socializing agency, giving it a crucial role in the process of cultural transmission. It was believed that students benefited by learning from each other in this setting, though in fact they were mostly learning from their adult supervisors. What they learned were progressive middle-class goals encompassing both competition *and* teamwork, commitment to the community *and* individual leadership, as well as a type of personal success increasingly denoted as "popularity." Through the medium of adult-organized social, recreational, non-academic activities, young Canadians were exposed to ideals of adult behaviour that would help them define their own goals while supplying some of the requisite training for adult social success—at least as this was defined in middle-class circles.[23] Faculty were quick to correlate successful extracurricular programs with "exceptional capacity in achievement" and, significantly, with "the charm manifested in the personalities of the leaders," a feature of school culture thought to be "quite striking."[24]

For high school students, social participation and modern citizenship were encapsulated in the concept of "school spirit," the very premise of the extracurriculum. During the interwar years, "school spirit" became the rallying call and symbolic expression of Ontario's high school culture. Although representing "the fun and comradeship of school-days," the larger purposes of school spirit were noted by students themselves. School spirit instilled loyalty, cooperation, and fairness. During a time when Stanley Hall's theories about adolescent angst held sway, school spirit was held to "invariably cheer those pupils who are prone to pitch their tents on the north side of life," their "morbid outlook" conquered by "such enthusiasm, loyalty and friendliness." Special measures were taken during regular school hours in order to foster this spirit, and these measures were then reinforced in publications, student government, clubs, and teams. At Ottawa Collegiate, as in many other high schools, an "assembly" was held each morning in the auditorium. Before the regular opening exercises, consisting of prayer, anthem singing, and announcements, the students engaged in a sing-song "under the baton of a competent conductor and to the accompaniment of the school orchestra," an exercise kept up for about ten minutes and constituting "a happy ushering in of the school day."[25] The auditorium was increasingly the "central feature" of the modern high school, home to these daily assemblies which did so much to nurture "a healthy school spirit, to train the pupils in public speaking, in self control, in orderly habits, in consideration for others and in respect for authority."[26] Moreover, school spirit could not be contained by school walls; as one young yearbook editor proclaimed, it gave "vivacity" to the entire community and prepared students "for the greater field of activity than our school environment, the field where mistakes are not so kindly overlooked—life."[27]

As high schools integrated gymnasiums and assembly halls into their functioning physical space, and strove to provide organized recreational programs under trained leadership, the trend was lauded as one of the "more progressive signs in modern education." A new understanding of adolescent education as preparation for a healthy, wholesome, balanced adulthood, in its every sense, meant a new emphasis on the balancing of intellectual achievement with the development of social and citizenship skills. High school was to be valued as much for the cultural experience that it provided through peer-group activity as for its learning experiences. In fact, social activities would enhance both scholarship and mental and physical health by replenishing the energy expended in book study. As one high school principal pointed out, "it should not be forgotten that our young people are also preparing for future leisure ... and the mind well stored with interesting knowledge ... does not have to go abroad for entertainment. The entertainment of such a student is self-contained."[28]

Self-containment was also the implicit purpose of the extracurriculum. The larger strategic response to the "youth problem," which revolved around keeping adolescents out of danger once they headed home after all their school-related activities, saw much promotion of carefully directed youth clubs in close association with churches and schools. "Group work" advocates—social workers and educators foremost among them—argued that "the group system contributes much to the team play necessary to democracy and unselfish cooperative living." It also took advantage of the youthful "gang instinct" that would otherwise lead to anti-social, even criminal, activity. In properly supervised clubs, the peer group would be put to useful effect: "In common activity with his compeers, [the young person learns] the responsibilities of social living which no adult can teach him."[29] Student government, which "not only encourages students to take a greater interest in their school" but also "provides excellent training for their future lives," became an important new component of the high school experience in Ontario by 1930. In Toronto's Northern Vocational High School, the student council was responsible for the management of social and athletic events, the morning assembly, and minor discipline problems such as smoking, bad language, and "unbecoming conduct" in the school's halls and washrooms. London South Collegiate Institute inaugurated its School Council in 1931; it was believed to "serve as a medium for encouraging student responsibility" as well as "regulating and supervising all student activities and organizations." School governments were not only mechanisms for self-policing, they were also meant to teach adolescents an appropriate code of conduct within an ethical context that could effectively utilize "peer pressure" to ensure conformity.[30]

High school athletics became increasingly institutionalized during these years, coming to represent, as never before, both the motive force of school spirit and its ultimate measure. Since "life itself is based on fair play, the knowledge of how to win and how to lose," it was obvious that "nothing in the world will develop a better, more noble character than sport."[31] In this manner, sports became instruments of socialization for the children of immigrants, promoting a "Canadianism" based on the physical discipline, fair play, and teamwork that were perceived to be lacking in other cultures. Even while "styles of play" changed historically, it was argued, the "gold standard" would ever be "the desirable citizen of the future." If the school and its playing fields were made "the centre and servant of a satisfying community life," youth would easily find an attractive alternative to the streets, the dance and billiard halls, and taverns, with their countless unhealthy and immoral pursuits in the name of fun. "Well-conducted" physical exercises, gymnastics, and games were means not only of keeping the body fit but also of "training the characteristics essential to a virile manhood and womanhood." School boards were duly empowered by law to set aside annual funds "for the encouragement of athletics and to defray the expenses of school games."[32]

Records indicate that, by 1920, almost every high school had an athletic association. The 1928 Fort William High School yearbook declared that "athletic societies play a big part in school life. They have the most to do with extracurriculars."[33] "Inter-form" and inter-scholastic matches provided opportunities for healthy competition and camaraderie, even romance, all under the watchful eye of adult teachers and coaches. Operating at once as activity, spectacle, and ultimate manifestation of "school spirit," the modern sports regime also offered up a new set of adolescent heroes, and in a manner explicitly gender-defined. The muscular Christianity of the Victorian age, with its correlation of moral integrity with manly strength and endurance, was being eclipsed by an emphasis on physique as the measure of both manliness and the newly coined "sex appeal" that the period's advertisers sold alongside new consumer products. At London South Collegiate, a school serving the middle-class and affluent families near the city core, the benefits to (male) adult life were once again emphasized in the promotion of school sports: "This development of the body, so important to the player, will always stand in good stead in after life. No employer wants a man working for him who is on the sick list frequently. He will employ the man who is on the job in good physical condition."[34]

While never named explicitly in student publications, "sex appeal"—obliquely referred to as "it"—was certainly important to young people. The common scenario at matches was an all-boy game with a mixed audience featuring the newly organized and feminized extracurricular activity of cheerleading, which was becoming both a sport in itself and an emblem of feminine social success. The school's "reputation" was considered to be upheld not by victory alone but by the intensity of its members' support. In fact, the "rooters" themselves were part of the competition, school spirit being judged in regard to cheering, horn-blowing, "snake-walks," and, of course, the size of the crowd.[35] Annual "field days," even in small towns, could draw as many as 300 spectators. The Guelph Collegiate yearbook, in 1926, reported that "everyone seems to be taking more interest in sports than hitherto, and many were eager to help in any way, even if they could not play the games themselves," with "the girls in particular showing more than their usual interest."[36]

In fact, the 1920s appear to have constituted a new peak for girls' sports in Ontario high schools, with extracurricular opportunities expanding and intramural leagues growing rapidly. Basketball, invented in 1891 by Ontario native

James Naismith, was especially popular, as noted in the Renfrew Collegiate year-book for 1922: "Every year basketball becomes more and more the real game among the collegiate girls and is played not only by the favoured few on the regular team but by nearly every girl in the school." At one infamous game between Guelph Collegiate and Galt Collegiate girls, as recalled by a male spectator, one of the players felt her bloomers slipping, at which point "in the extremity, all the other girls of both teams formed a circle around her while repairs were made— we men all seated or standing around the hall, a few hundred of us, quite fascinated by this unforeseen development."[37] But girls' athletic clubs often served up more than sports activities, with yearbook references indicating that recitations, songs, and dancing demonstrations were common components of meetings. In Toronto, in the late 1920s, Jarvis, Harbord, and Parkdale collegiates all chose to discontinue their girls' athletic associations in favour of the new Hi-Y clubs, which were school-based but organized and supervised by the Young Women's Christian Association. The new clubs still featured sports but also included drama and arts in their programs, in an effort to broaden their appeal and bring into the safety of the group the young women who were not athletically inclined.[38] Thus, sports prowess for both boys and girls, and personal connection to high school sports heroes for girls, provided an entry into the hierarchy of "popularity" within the age group—just as their absence could as readily spell social failure for some. All this physical energy and enthusiasm was exactly the sort of "pep" that 1920s popular culture applauded.

High schools also began to formalize their "identity markers," the colours, cheers, crests, mottoes, and songs that had traditionally signified exclusive private school membership. At Arnprior High School, A.H.D. Ross, appointed principal in 1919, made one of his first projects the "casting about for a suitable motto and crest" for the school. Upon consulting with his staff (but not students), it was decided that the motto should consist of "three or four simple Latin words which would be understood even by those who have only an elementary knowledge of that ancient language." After due consideration of 120 mottoes, "the choice fell upon *Hodie non cras*, which means 'today, not tomorrow,' and constantly holds before us the idea of making the best possible use of present opportunities." The crest, it was decided, "should be as elegant and chaste as possible," the chosen one featuring an hour glass to signify time, a "lamp of knowledge," and an open book. Finally, the principal, noting that "the outstanding characteristics of college and school yells which have stood the test of time are the frequent repetition of the name of the institution, the introduction of some startling foreign word or phrase, and the reiteration of an unalterable determination to overcome all opposition and finally achieve victory," composed the following school cheer: "Arnprior High School!! Rah, rah, rah!! On the field and in the class—*hodie non cras*!! Our colours are the red and white for which we'll fight with all our might!! Arnprior High School!! Rah, rah

rah!!"[39] At Guelph Collegiate, the rallying cry was a simple and—it was hoped—infectious "Chee Hee! Chee haw! Chee haw! Haw! Haw! Collegiate, Collegiate, Rah! Rah! Rah!"[40] Similar mottoes, crests, and cheers were devised across the province, reflecting both the new importance ascribed to the "school spirit" that they signified and the involvement of principals and staff in their creation. At times, students were actively encouraged to participate: at the Fergus High School, the school motto, *Per ardua ad astra* (Strive for the Stars), was the direct result of a student contest held in 1930.[41] Kitchener Collegiate, on the other hand, found its faculty-motivated campaign to replace the old school song ("O Fair Ontario") with a new student composition sadly "unconsummated" after several years, a failure that caused much lament among student leaders about the embarrassing lack of school spirit behind it.[42] In many ways, school spirit was an adult project, actively manufactured and disseminated through the relationship between faculty and a recognized student elite. Recognizing this, some students complained about the "feeble" character of student government. Its promised management of student affairs on behalf of students was "practically a dead issue," the reality being that the student council was "overrun by staff supervision."[43]

Perhaps most important, in their obvious appeal to the young and in their increasing frequency, were the "socials," commonly involving dancing, that modern high schools incorporated into their extracurricular activities, allowing young men and women opportunities to meet and get to know each other—a primary, if not the primary, purpose of adolescent socializing. As "dating" became the modern custom, often in peer-group settings away from the home and the adult chaperone that signified old-fashioned courtship but also kept "danger" at bay, these school-supervised activities appeared a wise alternative to the public spaces where "spooning" might otherwise take place. Capitalizing on the "modern dance rage," school dances were especially important.[44] These were memorable events for many of their participants, as one man recalled: "They were great occasions. Much competition amongst the boys to invite the popular girls, the girls dressing in 'formals,' and the boys in their best suit, their 'Sunday' or 'Church' suit."[45] At Guelph Collegiate, "tea dances" were held between four and six in the afternoon in the school auditorium, and given "splendid" support by the lower-form students for whom they were specifically intended, with music often provided by school bands. Although the Depression limited the number of dances held under school auspices for lack of funds, the school's 1933 yearbook described the end-of-term festivities in a manner that suggests anything but austerity: the auditorium was decorated with streamers "stretching from the skylight to the balcony, and multicoloured balloons awning over the heads of the dancers; green Collegiate crests stood out in sharp relief upon each pillar; a background in futuristic design brought into prominence the orchestral stand at the front." Jean's Night-Hawks provided "all that could be desired in the way of dance rhythm." The varied program included a lucky balloon dance and a "Paul Jones" as well as what the yearbook described as "an extraordinary rose-dance," in which young men tossed rosebuds over the balcony and then danced with the young women who caught their particular rose, combining romance with competition and probably no small amount of disappointment for the less nimble. There was little sign of Depression restraint in Kitchener, either, where the high school's Christmas dance in 1937 saw "young ladies and escorts" entering the gymnasium through a "snow-laden cottage."[46]

Even if such events were intended to be healthy substitutes for declining familial and community supervision of mixed-sex socializing, some critics wondered at the schools' place in encouraging these activities, with their propensity for "extremes." Toronto's Board of Education, echoed by other boards in the province, considered that more attention was being paid to such "frills" as dancing and swimming than to "really necessary studies."[47] Along these lines, the Ottawa Collegiate "scandal" of 1927 struck such nervous chords among parents, teachers, and other worried adults that a provincial royal commission was established to investigate the allegations of immorality levelled against the school. The scandal was precipitated by the Ottawa *Evening Citizen's* front-page coverage of a Presbyterian minister's statement, under the sensationalist headline, "Charges unspeakable conditions at O.C.I. dances."[48] In fact, the minister declared that he was not singling out one school: his statement was meant as a "blanket condemnation" of the entire co-educational high school system in the province of Ontario. As he saw it, modern high schools were the dangerous playgrounds of "children with the freedom and license of adults but lacking the experience and balance." They were made all the more dangerous because of the mixing of the sexes and the employment of young female teachers. His only supporting evidence, however, consisted of stories that parents had told him about "petting parties" and "drinking parties" in connection with school events, though not actually on school premises. A woman with a daughter and two sons attending the school testified that she never permitted them to go to any school dances, because of the "rumours" about "looseness of morality" involving "hip flasks and hasty marriages."[49]

For the other side, a Collegiate student, having never missed a dance in the previous four years, maintained that he had seen "nothing he would classify as objectionable." The principal himself insisted that "insubordination did not exist as a general thing," and that boys and girls were kept strictly segregated in both playground and classroom arrangements. The commission concluded that there was "no reason to believe [that] any of the conditions [the minister] alleged as rendering it unsafe for parents to send children to Ottawa Collegiate Institute exist at all."[50] Whatever adolescents were up to off the premises, official extracurricular activities were evidently above reproach. Yet one of the Ottawa commissioners "could not help" advising parental accompaniment for youth attending dances, especially girls, because "modern conditions are such that they have to be met in some such way." Despite the evidence, or its lack in this case, the unease of adults concerning "modern conditions" made for a generational suspicion that was itself an emergent modern cultural trait.

The Depression would have curiously mixed effects on the culture of the modern high school, in that financial straits confronted by school boards put a halt to some important extracurricular activities—student publications were among the first to be axed, as the community businesses that underwrote their costs through advertising often withdrew support—while reinforcing a common perception of the critical role of such programs in the lives of young people who now had even fewer alternatives for wholesome socializing. The crisis bore down especially hard on the young. Among youth between the ages of fourteen and twenty, even the unreliable statistics of the period indicate an unemployment rate far surpassing that of any other age category.[51] The minister of education consistently reported a "considerable increase" in "congestion" and "serious overcrowding" in high schools throughout the province because of "enforced economics" on the part of municipalities and, more specifically, because more young people were staying in school or returning because of unemployment.[52] Many were embarrassed and ashamed as their deteriorating family circumstances compelled them to attend in ever-shabbier attire at a moment in their lives when appearance counted for so much.[53] Other young people, less fortunate or perhaps less patient than these, took to the streets and to the rails, collectively embodying the archetypal "lost generation," having attained the threshold of adulthood in this time of international crisis.

In the midst of raging, and largely futile, debates over state responsibility for the suffering masses, the only palliative offered to youth, besides postponing the date of unemployment through extended schooling, was "to ensure to the young people participation in some definite activity." After some years of seeming progress in organizing them into purposeful clubs and pastimes, there were worrisome indications that adolescents left to their own devices were turning to less positive outlets than those preferred for them by adults. As funding for both school and community recreational programs dried up, the "gang" appeared to be "again developing into a contaminating source of infection."[54] By the late 1930s, the flourishing of various anti-democratic movements around the world made the young appear even more threatening to the social order, since these movements had "recognized and exploited the potential power for social change which youth possesses." Social workers emphasized the equal importance of vocational training and recreational opportunities, especially sports and games. Any recreational activity based on "a broad social view" would represent a step towards reintegration of alienated youth into the social mainstream.[55] Organized recreation was a form of "social education" that would demonstrate to the young "the idea of democracy involving unselfishness, his or her own worth, conventions with respect to sex, the worth of religion as a workable philosophy of life." Consequently, it was both "economical and safe to conserve a source of future good citizenship."[56] The "citizenship" arguments that justified the school's centrality in the adolescent world were reinforced by the crisis atmosphere of the Great Depression: "Now, more than ever before, [the young person] is a social being, a citizen of the world, he must develop a social consciousness ... it is to make good citizens that the modern school must bend its energies."[57]

The Depression, some maintained, was delivering a necessary lesson to modern youth by teaching them the benefits of active participation and weaning them away from "the easier way of paying to be amused."[58] Recognizing the importance of keeping up morale under these historic circumstances, teachers were reportedly devoting much time to non-academic activities, with music given high priority. "Glee clubs," which featured chorus singing, often dominated by girls, were thought to be especially motivational, but the important point was the "advantage found in working together for a common end." The extracurriculum was also becoming even more organized and formalized with the creation, in "three or four sections of the province," of "leagues" to ensure "high standards of efficiency" in extracurricular activities, to foster "a fine sense of honour in interschool competitions," and to maintain, "as in athletics, a proper balance between the physical and the intellectual."[59] Yet, despite these efforts on the part of teachers and administrators, students themselves noted the overall "seriousness" of tone, the dampening of "school spirit," wrought by the Depression: "In fact, depression seems rampant in the school, as much in esprit de corps as in anything else." Participation in extracurricular activities dropped decidedly across the province. At Guelph Collegiate, a drama club production of Julius Caesar was "sadly handicapped" by students who either did not appear at practices or withdrew the day before the play's opening. There was evidently difficulty in getting members of the school sports teams, especially the senior teams, out to practice.[60]

By the outbreak of the Second World War in 1939, compulsory school attendance to age sixteen had made high school a much more common adolescent occupation. It was not, however, a universal or uniform experience for those outside the Canadian-born middle class. The modern high school reinforced class, ethnic, and gender distinctions in significant ways, not only through particular types of schooling but also by making more apparent the contrasts between high school culture and the outside lives of less-favoured students. The peer society at the basis of the extracurriculum contributed to the construction of a behavioural code and disciplined, usually by exclusion, those who did not conform to recognized group standards. This allowed for a rigidly defined status hierarchy of "in and out," good and bad, increasingly expressed in the political terminology of "popular and unpopular." Those who did not, or could not, fit in, had three choices: reconstruct a group identity among others like themselves, suffer alone, or leave. Clearly, young people did not simply "take" whatever form of social activity that adults deemed was good for them. They were quite capable of subverting attempts to "train" them by setting up alternate, "secret" societies or by participating in existing clubs only to the degree, and in the measure, that they chose to, as well as by simply refusing any involvement.

Even in public high schools exhibiting an unprecedented class, ethnic, and gender mix, and even with a new roster of academic and social opportunities, many young people could not measure up against the cultural capital inherited by their better-established peers.[61] Those from affluent families continued to enjoy certain advantages in shaping the clubs and their activities, and, in turn, derived special class-specific benefits through their participation. In effect, high school clubs became small-scale youthful replicas of the various organizations dear to the heart of white middle-class adults, mimicking their internal organization, platforms, regulations, fund-raising, promotion, and activities. The customary gendered hierarchies were upheld: boys dominated student and associational governments as presidents and vice-presidents and headed newspapers and yearbooks as editors-in-chief. Girls often filled secretarial or assistant or otherwise auxiliary positions.[62] It also appears that, in high school as in other institutional cultures, the axiom that "nothing succeeds like success" held true: the same student, usually male, often occupied several official extracurricular positions. At one high school, the 1928 valedictorian was also president of the Hi-Y Club, treasurer of the student council, secretary-treasurer of the badminton club, advertising manager of the school newspaper, manager of the basketball team, sergeant in the cadet corp, and, "in spite of all this," the student newspaper marvelled, "he has some time for sports."[63]

The socioeconomic transformations of the early twentieth century opened up new worlds to youth, prompting a reconfiguration of adolescence in ways that made it significantly different from the experience of previous generations. Adolescents came to identify, and to be identified, more with school and leisure than with paid labour. But even a stronger generational identification did not obliterate hierarchies within that generation, as suggested by the culture of the modern high school, newly institutionalized in the peer societies of the extracurriculum, with its status cliques and exclusionary divides. Before public schooling, restricted admission ensured the reproduction of existing social relations. In the twentieth-century educational system, and especially in the modern high school, the schools themselves replicated the differentiating structures of the larger society.[64]

The extracurriculum is fundamental to the concept of the high school as a "container" for unruly youth. In co-opting the less objectionable aspects of an increasingly commercialized youth culture by the 1920s, high schools attempted to supply safe alternatives under trained adult leadership. The expanding extracurriculum consequently also expanded the labour of teachers as well as the potential influence of extrafamilial adults on the lives, and lifestyles, of young people. Reporting on the importance of vocational guidance to high school students, the minister of education contended that "it is the duty of every teacher to give direction to those under his care—he probably knows his pupils better than the parents do."[65] The kin- and class-based, often work-based, cultures of working-class and immigrant youth were opened wider to middle-class example. If generational tensions were exacerbated by the culture clash inherent in the relationship between "old world" immigrant parents and their "Canadian" adolescent children, they could be made all the worse when the latter opted for the teacher's "modern" guidance over that of "old-fashioned" parents and other adult kin.[66]

An even more likely short-term outcome was a solidifying sense of difference among young people whose social success was measured in terms of "joining," "fitting in," and becoming "one of the gang." In many ways, those who could not or would not conform appeared all the more as "outsiders." Living in Toronto's working-class Cabbagetown neighbourhood, the young protagonist of Hugh Garner's autobiographical Depression-era novel attended the "Tech" in the hope that "somehow the school would release him from his shabby district and even shabbier home, and make him a belonging part of its friendliness and comradeship and happier life." He found, instead, that socioeconomic divisions "were of fine complexity but nevertheless clearly marked," given away by such things as after-school jobs and shabby clothes that prevented young people from participating in extracurricular socializing. The fictional hero, in common with many of his real historical counterparts, remained "an outsider from the cliques revolving around athletics, the school magazine, the auditorium stage, the possession of a Model T Ford."[67]

Its proponents argued that organized, school-supervised social activity allowed for a wider, more diversified participation across the customary social boundaries, opening doors to young people who might not otherwise have had access to clubs, sports, and wholesome cultural and intellectual activities. In reality, the extracurriculum, like the curriculum itself, continued to favour those economically better positioned to begin with, boys over girls, and white Anglo-Celtic Canadians over all others. Social "tracking," in effect, crossed the boundary from curriculum to extracurriculum.[68] Reinforced by growing attendance, the apparently universal nature of the high-school experience allowed an illusion of youth cohesion and reassuring uniformity at a time when a sense of national objectives and national identity were of tremendous importance. But it was exactly that—an illusion, just like the historical brand of "national identity" that it mirrored.

NOTES

I would like to acknowledge the Social Sciences and Humanities Research Council, whose funding for my ongoing research into the sociocultural history of English-Canadian adolescents during the first half of the twentieth century is much appreciated, and also the Research Office, Wilfrid Laurier University, for its heartening support. Thanks are also owing to Erica Morant, who, as unpaid but dedicated archivist/librarian at Guelph Collegiate and Vocational Institute, did much to encourage my work on this topic; likewise to Susan Bellingham, archivist for the Dana Porter Rare Books Room and Archives, University of Waterloo; and Inge Sanmiya, who took time to find material on London high schools in the Weldon Library, University of Western Ontario, despite her own research agenda. This paper is for my daughter, Stefanie, GCVI, class of 2001.

1 Ontario, Department of Education, *Annual Report of the Inspectors of High Schools*, 1920, 49; also ibid., 1922, 45-6. The latter also notes the increase in juvenile delinquency since the war and comments on the "great need for moral training."

2 Contemporary commentaries include, for example, T.R. Robinson, "Youth and the Virtues," *Social Welfare* (October 1928): 9; H. Dobson, "Youth: Scapegrace or Scapegoat," *Social Welfare* (July 1929): 228; Editorial, "Hygiene of Recreation," *Canadian Practitioner* (June 1924): 309. On similar European developments regarding "modern youth," see K. Alaimo, "Shaping Adolescence in the Popular Milieu: Social Policy, Reformers, and French Youth, 1870-1920," *Journal of Family History* 17, 4 (1992): 420; W.S. Haine, "The Development of Leisure and the Transformation of Working-Class Adolescence in France," *Journal of Family History* 17, 4 (1992): 451. I explore these anxieties more fully in C.R. Comacchio, "Dancing to Perdition: Adolescence and Leisure in Interwar English Canada," *Journal of Canadian Studies* 32, 3 (fall 1997): 5-27. Although used occasionally in the media during the interwar years, the term "teenager" does not seem to have come into popular usage until the 1950s; on post-Second World War developments, see M.L. Adams, *The Trouble with Normal: Postwar Youth and the Making of Heterosexuality* (Toronto: University of Toronto Press, 1997).

3 Alaimo, "Shaping Adolescence," 419-21.

4 D.N. McLachlan, "The Spiritual and Ethical Development of the Child," *Social Welfare* (December 1929): 68.

5 G. Stanley Hall, *Adolescence: Its Psychology and Its Relation to Physiology, Anthropology, Sociology, Sex, Crime, Religion and Education*, vol. 1 (New York: D. Appleton, 1904), xvi-xvii.

6 Ibid., 4.

7 Ontario, Department of Education, *Report of the Inspectors of High Schools,* 1919, 32-3; ibid., 1922: 45-6; R. Udea, *Avenues to Adulthood: The Origins of the High School and Social Mobility in an American Suburb* (Cambridge, U.K.: Cambridge University Press, 1987), 141.

8 On "the second great transformation" in American schools, see C. Goldink and L.F. Katz, "Human Capital and Social Capital: The Rise of Secondary Schooling in America, 1910-40," *Journal of Interdisciplinary History* 29, 4 (spring 1999): 685-6.

9 I.F. Goodson and I.R. Dowbiggin, "Vocational Education and School Reform: The Case of the London Technical School, 1900-1930," *History of Education Review* 20, 1 (1991): 55. On vocational education, see also N.S. Jackson and J.S. Gaskell, "White Collar Vocationalism: The Rise of Commercial Education in Ontario and British Columbia, 1870-1920," in R. Heap and A. Prentice, eds., *Gender and Education in Ontario: An Historical Reader* (Toronto: Canadian Scholars Press, 1991), 165-94. T.A. Dunn, "Teaching the Meaning of Work: Vocational Education in British Columbia, 1900-29," in D.C. Jones, N.M. Sheehan, and R.M. Stamp, eds., *Shaping the Schools of the Canadian West* (Calgary: Detselig, 1979), 237-53. Classic works on the development of Canadian education include J.D. Wilson, R. Stamp, and L-P. Audet, eds., *Canadian Education: A History* (Scarborough, Ont.: Prentice-Hall, 1970); R. Stamp, *The Schools of Ontario, 1876—1976* (Toronto: University of Toronto Press, 1982); A. Prentice and S. Houston, eds., *Family, School and Society in Nineteenth-Century Canada* (Toronto: University of Toronto Press, 1975); N. Sutherland, *Children in English Canadian Society* (Toronto: University of Toronto Press, 1976; repr., Waterloo: Wilfrid Laurier University Press, 2000); R.D. Gidney and W.P.J. Millar, *Inventing Secondary Education: The Rise of the High School in Nineteenth-Century Ontario* (Toronto: University of Toronto Press, 1990). For an overview of recent writings, see P. Axelrod, "Historical Writing and Canadian Education from the 1970s to the 1990s," *History of Education Quarterly* 36, 1 (spring 1996): 20-38.

10 P. Axelrod, *The Promise of Schooling: Education in Canada* (Toronto: University of Toronto Press, 1997), 68. See also J. Modell and J. Trent Alexander, "High School in Transition: Community, School, and Peer Group in Abilene, Kansas, 1939," *History of Education Quarterly* 37, 1 (spring 1997): 1-2. P. Axelrod, *The Making of a Middle Class* (Montreal and Kingston: McGill-Queen's University Press, 1995), discusses the class, gender, and ethnic basis of the university population during the 1930s.

11 Ontario, *Statutes of the Province of Ontario,* 1911, An Act Respecting Education for Industrial Purposes. The federal government would follow suit in 1919 with its Technical Education Act; see Ontario, Department of Education, *Report of the Division of Industrial and Technical Education,* 1919,

13; Technical Education Act, *Statutes of the Dominion of Canada* 9-10, George V, c.73, 7 July 1919.

12 Ontario, Department of Education, *Report of the Minister of Education,* 1919, 15; W.F. Dyde, *Public Secondary Education in Canada* (New York: Columbia University Press, 1929), 41; J.M. McCutcheon, *Public Education in Ontario* (Toronto: Best, 1941), 171; F. Johnson, *A Brief History of Canadian Education* (Toronto: McGraw-Hill, 1968), 142-3. See also Robert Stamp, "Canadian High Schools in the 1920s and 1930s," Canadian Historical Association, *Historical Papers,* 1978, 79-84; Sutherland, *Children in English Canadian Society,* 164.

13 Ontario, Department of Education, *Report of the Inspectors of High Schools,* 1922, 34. Stamp, "Canadian High Schools," 78-9; he develops this further in *High Schools of Ontario.* I discuss the rise of consumer society and its impact on the family in *The Infinite Bonds of Family: Domesticity in Canada, 1850-1940* (Toronto: University of Toronto Press, 1999), 75-81.

14 Ontario, Department of Education, *Report of the Inspectors of High Schools,* 1920, 56, which notes that the yearly expansion of high schools is the "outstanding feature" of the system. The minister reported in 1923 that attendance had reached a "point never reached before" during the 1922 school year: enrolment was 60,395 an increase of 41.9 per cent during the two years under the Adolescent Attendance Act; see *Report of the Minister of Education,* 1923, iii. In 1929 there were 63 collegiate institutes and 142 high schools in the province; of the collegiates, only 7 of 63 had retained their original buildings, and of the high schools, more than half were in new buildings or expanded and modernized structures; see ibid., 1929, 38.

15 C. Heron, "The High School and the Household Economy in Working-Class Hamilton, 1890-1940," *Historical Studies in Education* 7, 2 (fall 1995): 242, 246; see also the oral histories in J. Synge, "The Transition from School to Work: Growing up Working Class in Early 20th Century Hamilton, Ontario," in K. Ishwaran, ed., Childhood and Adolescence in Canada (Toronto: McGraw-Hill Ryerson, 1979), 249-69. On London, see Goodson and Dowbiggin, "Vocational Education and School Reform."

16 Similar trends were at work in Australia: see C. Campbell, "Family Strategy, Secondary Schooling and Making Adolescents: The Indian Summer of the Old Middle Class, 1945-60," *History of Education Review* 22, 2 (1993): 19, 38.

17 P. Bourdieu, "Reproduction in Education," *Society and Culture,* 2nd ed. (London: Sage, 1990), ix-xi, 102, 158. Similar themes are explored for Australia by Campbell, "Family Strategy"; for the United States, see Goldin and Katz, "Human Capital and Social Capital."

18 Ueda, *Avenues to Adulthood,* 119.

19 Gutowski, "Student Initiative and the Origins of the High School Extracurriculum," 83-100.

20 *Statutes of the Dominion of Canada,* 9-10 George V, c.73, 7 July 1919. The Royal Commission on Industrial Training and Technical Education was appointed in 1908 and reported in 1911; see also Sutherland, *Children in English Canadian Society,* especially chapters 12 and 13; see also R. Stamp, "Those Yankee Frills: The New Education in Ontario," in M. Piva, ed., *History of Ontario: Selected Readings* (Toronto: McClelland and Stewart, 1985).

21 *Report of the Inspectors of High Schools,* 1920, 49-50.

22 Editorial, Kitchener Collegiate Institute, *The Grumbler,* 1931, 18. KCI (formerly Berlin Collegiate) was the only public high school in Waterloo County during these years; it had an estimated 2,000 students by the outbreak of the Second World War. *The Grumbler* began publication in 1907 as "a few mimeographed sheets" produced bi-weekly by the Literary Society. By 1931, it had become a hybrid newspaper/annual, published three times a year, with as many as 300 students involved; see ibid., "Principal's Message," 1938. By 1938, there was also discussion of making it a monthly venture: "Shall We Change *The Grumbler?*" 1938, 4.

23 Ueda, *Avenues to Adulthood,* 150.

24 "Principal's Message," *The Grumbler,* 1937, 2.

25 *Report of the Inspectors of High Schools,* 1919, 39; the report notes similar events taking place at other Ontario schools.

26 *Report of the Minister of Education,* 1929, 14.

27 "School Spirit," Guelph Collegiate and Vocational Institute, *Acta Nostra,* vol. l, 1926, 90. This was the first edition of the yearbook of Guelph Collegiate and Vocational Institute. In 1879 the Guelph Grammar School became the Guelph High School, then the Collegiate Institute in 1886, when a gymnasium was added. A new school Building was erected in 1923, with technical-education facilities. By the 1920s, it was the largest high school in Wellington District and served a combined rural/urban population of about 10,000; see G. Shutt, *The High Schools of Guelph* (Toronto, 1961). The particularly rich and well-kept archives of GCVI have permitted me to use the school as a case study for my larger project on adolescence.

28 "Principal's Message," *Acta Nostra,* vol.l, 1926, 11.

29 M.W. Beckleman, "The Group Worker in the Modern Scene," *Canadian Welfare Summary* (July 1938): 64.

30 "The Advantages of Student Government," *The Grumbler,* 1924, 5. KCI was evidently one of the first Ontario high schools to establish a student council, consisting of an elected executive and representatives for each year under a teacher "advisory committee." This was accomplished in 1922, though the editorial cited argues that "in the future it will be a recognized organization" throughout Canada. C.E. Phillips, *The Development of Education in Canada* (Toronto: W. Gage, 1957), 534, describes student

government as "accepted practice" in secondary schools across Canada by the 1930s.

31 D.G. Bell, "Teaching Young Canada to Play," *Macleans,* 15 July 1926, 19.
32 Editorial, *Child Welfare News,* May 1927, 31; Rev. E. Thomas, "The Church of God and the Homes of His People," *Social Welfare,* November 1920, 48; *Report of the Minister of Education,* 1929, 14; on funding, see, for example, Ontario High Schools Act, *Revised Statutes of Ontario,* c.360, 1937.
33 Quoted in H. Gurney, *Girls' Sports: A Century of Progress in Ontario High Schools* (Don Mills, Ont.: Ontario Federation of School Athletic Associations, 1979), 24.
34 "Athletics," *The Oracle,* 1932: 81. London's Technical and Commercial High School likewise strongly promoted "physical culture" and a variety of intramural and provincial sports competitions; see J.J. Talman Regional Collection, Weldon Library, University of Western Ontario, London, Ontario, Pamphlet Collection, "School Activities," London Technical and Commercial High School, 1932-3 [promotional pamphlet], 3.
35 "Athletics," *The Grumbler,* 1937, 85. KCI was proclaimed "second to none" for its enthusiasm, in terms both of participation and of audience support for its teams.
36 "School Sports," *Acta Nostra,* vol.l, 1926, 31-2; vol.3, 1929, 15.
37 Renfrew Collegiate, *Yearbook,* 1922, 12; Guelph Public Library Archives, Shutt Family Papers, item 7-1, letter to G. Shutt, undated [1960s], signed "A Happy Reader," from a former GCVI student who attended during the 1920s; on sports, see also Axelrod, *The Promise of Schooling,* 116.
38 The earliest on record is the Girls Athletic Club at Jarvis Collegiate in 1897. Jarvis was also the first to affiliate with the YWCA in 1924, naming its new club ROAD to reflect the new emphasis on reading, outdoors, athletics, and dramatics; Oakwood Collegiate maintained the two as separate clubs. See Gurney, *Girls Sports,* 24-6.
39 A.H.D. Ross, *A Short History of the Arnprior High School* (Ottawa: Popham, 1922), 53.
40 "The School Spirit," *Acta Nostra,* vol.l, 1926, 91.
41 Fergus High School, *Vox Scholae,* vol.l, 1930, 3.
42 *The Grumbler,* 1928, 21.
43 Ibid., 1931, 8.
44 *Acta Nostra,* vol.2, 1927, 47-8.
45 Shutt Family Collection, item 7-l; letter to G. Shutt, unsigned, undated [references to 1920s], 2.
46 *Acta Nostra,* vol.8, 1933. The yearbook ceased publication with this issue, as advertising revenues from local businesses dwindled; it resumed publication only in 1942; *The Grumbler,* 1938, 77.
47 Editorial, "Avoid Extremes," Toronto *Star,* 13 January 1921.

48 Archives of Ontario, RG 18-88, box 1, B-72, Royal Commission: Ottawa Collegiate Institute Inquiry, 6 January 1927, Evidence, 2, 11-15. The commission is given full coverage in Stamp, "Canadian High Schools in the 1920s and 1930s," 72-7.

49 Ibid., 22, 29.

50 Ibid., 72.

51 J. Struthers, *No Fault of Their Own: Unemployment and the Canadian Welfare State, 1914-1941* (Toronto: University of Toronto Press, 1983), 100, 132-5; R. Pierson, "Gender and the Unemployment Insurance Debates in Canada," *Labour/Le Travail* 25 (spring 1990): 82-4.

52 *Report of the High School Inspectors*, 1932, 15; also *Report of the Minister of Education*, 1934, 3; ibid., 1939, viii. By 1939, there were 198 high schools in Ontario, including 58 collegiate institutes; there were also 217 continuation schools. Enrolment in the former was 53,400, with 9,654 in the latter.

53 See the letters to R.B. Bennett in M. Bliss and L. Grayson, eds., *The Wretched of Canada* (Toronto: University of Toronto Press, 1971); see also the memories collected by B. Broadfoot, ed., *Ten Lost Years* (Toronto: Doubleday, 1973), and W. Johnson, "Keeping Children in School: The Response of the Montreal Catholic School Commission to the Depression of the 1930s," Canadian Historical Association, *Historical Papers*, 1985, 197.

54 F.T. Sharpe, "Stopping before Starting," *Child Welfare News*, January 1934, 43-4. The classic contemporary survey is K.H. Rogers, *Street Gangs in Toronto: A Study of the Forgotten Boy* (Toronto: Ryerson Press, 1945).

55 M. McLeachy, "The Effect upon Young People of the Economic Depression and Unemployment," *Child and Family Welfare*, November 1935, 15; E. Muncaster, "Strengthening Family Ties through Recreation," *Child and Family Welfare* (November 1933): 47; see also Canadian Council on Child and Family Welfare, Division on Leisure Time and Educative Activities, "Relief Is Not Enough: The Idle Time of Compulsorily Idle Canadians," *Bulletin No. 1* (25 September 1933): 1-4; "Will Canada Have a Youth Movement?" *The Canadian Doctor*, January 1939, 7-18.

56 S. Brent, "Reinforcing Family Strengths by the Provision of Leisure Time Activities," *Child and Family Welfare*, September 1931, 53; W.R. Cook, "Getting Down to Brass Tacks in Community Planning for Leisure Time," *Child and Family Welfare*, March 1938, 10-11.

57 Department of Education, *Report on Vocational Guidance*, 1931, 4.

58 W. Bowie, "The Character of a Nation," *Social Welfare*, July 1931, 199.

59 *Report of the High School Inspectors*, 1932, 17; ibid., 1934, 3.

60 Editorial, *Acta Nostra*, vol.8, 1933, 11; Gurney, *Girls Sports*, notes that sports competitions and such groups as the Hi-Y seem to have "faded" by the mid-1930s.

61 On "secret societies," see W. Graebner, "Outlawing Teenage Populism: The Campaign against Secret Societies in the American High School, 1900-1960," *Journal of American History* 74 (September 1987): 412-15; Ueda, *Avenues to Adulthood,* 119-20.

62 Ueda, *Avenues to Adulthood,* 121.

63 Goderich Collegiate Institute, *The Challenger,* June 1940, 4.

64 Modell and Alexander, "High School in Transition," 23.

65 *Report of the Minister of Education,* 1931, 4.

66 Certainly this view of the immigrant family seemed to prevail among the period's social workers; see H. Atkinson, "Boys in Trouble," *Child and Family Welfare* 7, 6 (March 1932): 2. P. Fass, *Outside In: Minorities and the Transformation of American Education* (New York: Oxford University Press, 1989), 108, found that, in practice, ethnic patterns in students' extracurricular choices within the newly diverse high schools of New York City during the 1930s revealed "a deeply divided social universe."

67 H. Garner, *Cabbagetown* (Richmond Hill, Ont.: Penguin, 1971), 12-13. Although written after the Depression, this is a semi-autobiographical story set in Toronto's notorious working-class district. According to the author (who grew up there), Cabbagetown was "a sociological phenomenon, the largest Anglo-Saxon slum in North America." See author's preface, i.

68 Ueda, *Avenues to Adulthood,* 119-20; Modell and Alexander, "High School in Transition," 12-18.

* * * * *

Documents for Chapter Eight

To what extent did the schools follow the ideas of the "New Education Movement?" New courses (see Document 31) and textbooks are signs of change, but the most telling indication of what educators thought was important was how the students were tested. Was thinking or memorization more important? What types of knowledge, subject matter, and skills were pupils expected to learn, and thus what pedagogy was most likely to be employed? Documents 30 and 33 provide answers to these questions for the period from 1881 to 1946. To be admitted into high school at the end of the 19th century, grade 8 students sat province-wide examinations. Only a small percentage of students attended grade 8 at this time; and an even smaller percentage wrote the high school exams— with a failure rate of about thirty percent. Document 33 was reprinted for Grade 13 students preparing for the Ontario Provincial examinations. The final document, which details examination practices in various provinces in the first third of the twentieth century, reveals the extent to which the ideas of the "New Education Movement" held sway in education circles.

30) TORONTO PUBLIC SCHOOLS EXAMINATIONS, 1881

HISTORY
FIRST DIVISION.

1. Name some principal event in the reign of William the Conqueror, John, Edward II., Henry V., Henry VIII., Mary Elizabeth.
2. Give the names, in order, of the Stuart Kings, and the date of the Stuart Period.
3. From A.D. 1629 to 1640, Charles I held no Parliament. Why?
4. State the principal cause that led to the Civil War of 1642.
5. What battle closed the Civil War, and what followed?
6. What events of English History mark the period of the Commonwealth?
7. What is the nature of the Test Act, and the Habeas Corpus Act?
8. How long did the French govern Canada?
9. What do you know of General Brock? Lord Monck?

SECOND DIVISION

1. What principal events are the following names connected with: William Tyndall, John Wycliffe, and Martin Luther?
2. Who founded the order of the Jesuits?
3. For what were the Waldensians noted? Also the Huguenots?
4. When did Spain lose the Straits of Gibraltar?
5. In the reign of Elizabeth, Queen of England, what event transpired affecting the power of Spain?
6. Give a brief account of the life of Napoleon Bonaparte.

THIRD DIVISION

1. Name the first principal nation that occupied a place in Europe. What nation succeeded and surpassed it in greatness?
2. In the wars between Greece and Persia what three principal battles were fought? Name the Grecian commander in these battles.
3. What caused the Peloponesian war? How long did it last?
4. Tell what you know of Alexander the Great.
5. Who were called Patricians and who Plebians of the Roman Empire?
6. How long did the first Punic War last? Who was Hannibal?
7. Give a general statement of the extent of the Roman Empire at the birth of Christ.
8. Three great changes marked the reign of Constantine: name them.

* * * * *

31) ENROLMENT IN HIGH SCHOOL COURSES
BY PROVINCE, 1927

SUBJECTS	N.S.	N.B.	ONT.	SASK.	ALBT.	B.C.	TOTAL
English	11,662	3,511	76,703	6,352	7,760	13,481	119,469
History	5,920	3,474	21,854[1]	6,160[2]	7,232[2]	12,014	56,654
Geography	5,123	3,474	32,103	3,229	1,304	1,269	43,028
Arithmetic and Mensuration	9,011	2,586	33,493	4,301	2,083	10,904	112,378
Algebra	11,279	3,394	44,797	5,761	6,104	11,515	82,850
Geometry	5,894	3,340	31,588	5,521	5,447	10,956	62,746
Trigonometry	430	114	3,941	786	681	289	6,241
French	9,092	3,317	58,752	5,023	4,663	9,842	90,689
Spanish	-	-	254	-	-	-	254
German	462	-	1,960	376	23	33	2,854
Latin	5,528	2,540	48,422	3,701	2,134	6,000	68,325
Greek	57	70	335	177	-	14	653
Italian	-	-	4	-	-	-	4
Zoology	-	-	10,762	463	-	-	11,225
Botany	1,984	3,256	13,108	463	-	549	19,779
Chemistry	2,103	1,327	14,501	2,526	1,615	5,024	271,096
Physics	5,391	1,300	20,331	2,098	2,600	3,308	35,037
Bookkeeping	-	1,510	12,106	585	611	1,936	16,798
Stenography	-	-	10,119	617	742	2,044	14,402
Typewriting	-	-	11,317	644	777	2,111	14.849
Business Law, etc	-	-	2,702	-	-	702	3,404
Art	4,681	917	14,899	1,307	1,782	5,199	28,785
Physical Culture	-	-	77,891	4,309	3,009	4,710	89,919
Agriculture	501	-	4,753	1,522	1,046	562	8,384
Manual Training	-	-	7,565	1,134	41	-	8,740
Household Science	-	-	4,346	1,244	26	3,325	8,941
Elementary Science	-	-	-	3,007	3,098	-	6,105
Music	-	-	-	1,045	96	183	1,324
Military Drill	-	-	-	1,630	1,170	-	2,800
Physiology	-	1,380	-	3,837	-	501	5,718
Practical Mathematics	1,791	-	-	-	-	-	1,791
Total Number of Pupils	11,170	3,511	80,383	6,127	1,209	13,853	125,853

1. Canadian History.
2. Approximate.

* * * * *

32) A SURVEY OF EXAMINATIONS, 1938[1]

The Problem of Examinations in the British Commonwealth of Nations and theUnited States of America

CHAPTER ONE
EXAMINATIONS IN CANADA
(See also YEAR BOOK, 1937, pages 170-85 and 294-307)

Introduction
NEW programmes of studies have been introduced in all provinces of Canada with the exception of Quebec and New Brunswick (revision 1937-8) within the last five years, and the emphasis on examinations has been removed. The methods of instruction have been changed because of new philosophies of education and new objectives for the different schools of the systems. The present study includes a resume of past practices, some indication of the trends and a little prophecy. Certain features of the examination system in the different provinces have been described. These were selected for various reasons: (1) It is very difficult to make comparisons because of the variety of practices in the different provinces. (2) So many influences, political, social and economic, have shaped the systems that educational procedure in one province might not be accepted in another province. (3) A description of examination methods in Canada could best be given in terms of regulations and examination results, but that is available in Reports of Ministers of Education for the provinces. To present some of the special problems and difficulties, some of the things educationists are saying and doing about these in their own provinces would perhaps be more useful and comprehensive ....

Present Tendencies
The past tense has been used in the preceding part with some restraint because some of the evils attributed to examinations still exist. What are the tendencies? The elementary school course of seven or eight years is being reorganised and a primary course of six years and an intermediate course to overlap the secondary school course is being introduced. This change has been made already in six provinces. The new programmes of studies are planned to direct the attention of the teacher to the individual child, his interests, his capacities, his growth. Instead of providing teachers with detailed courses in the different subjects of the curriculum, suggestions are given that he may direct the pupil's activities in relation to the immediate environment. This preludes any possibility of uniform examinations. It also reduces knowledge from dominance in the school and provides situations for use of knowledge, development of skills, attitudes and appreciation ....

The responsibility for promotion and grading of pupils in both the elementary and the high schools is gradually being given by the Departments of Education to the teachers. Throughout Canada, with the exception of Quebec, internal examinations have taken the place of departmental examinations in all but the last two years of the secondary school. Each of the nine provinces still conducts external examinations for normal college entrance, university matriculation and school leaving, in various combinations, but the tendency is towards accepting the principal's recommendations in cases of brighter pupils from all schools or the recommendations from accredited schools.

New-type examinations, oral examinations in languages, and practical tests in science and manual work are used little in the normal entrance or matriculation examinations. The essay type of examinations persists. A survey revealed that, with the exception of English composition and art, the great majority of these papers placed emphasis on knowledge of facts and principles and problems in the application of principles. There were few questions that demanded original or creative thinking.

Greater use in the schools is being made of a variety of indices in determining a pupil's advancement. Some of these are: class work during the year, laboratory and practical work, teachers' estimate of success, new-type tests, and occasionally personal factors, such as industry, power of concentration and creative ability ....

I. BRITISH COLUMBIA
Accredited High Schools and Graduation Diploma

A survey of the school system of British Columbia was made by two commissioners in 1925, and their report contained a chapter on the examination system. The writers called attention to ten defects which are the familiar arguments against external examinations. They are reported here for purposes of contrast. (1) The examinations are unreliable. (2) The cost is not warranted. (3) Teachers lacking in culture and weak in inspirational power in the classroom are frequently successful in preparing pupils for examinations. (4) School life is made miserable for pupils who fail or are likely to fail. (5) The primary concern of each teacher in a large high school is to have a pupil "pass" in his subject, so the aim of education is not effected. (6) Examinations are based on the traditional formal disciplinary doctrine. (7) Scientific standards of measurement are not used. (8) Examination subjects in Grade VIII are emphasised to the neglect of non-examination subjects. (9) The high school entrance examinations show a wide variation in difficulty from year to year. (10) The examinations exert a retarding influence on many pupils.

In 1927, many changes were made in the courses of study: a junior high school programme was introduced; new objectives were outlined that removed much of the former emphasis on external examinations. There was further revision in 1932. In 1936, a new programme of studies for Grades I to VI was prepared. Three bulletins of more than 200 pages each, dealing with the work of the first six grades, were issued, making it clear that the development of the pupil, rather than the passing of examinations, is the end in view. In presenting the course in each subject, the purpose of the subject and its relation to boy and girl development are clearly stated. When the focus of attention changes from subject-matter to the child, the testing of quantity and quality of subject-matter to assess educational advancement disappears. This has largely been accomplished to the end of Grade IX.

Adoption of System of High School Accrediting

A serious difficulty that has been obvious for some time is the articulation between university (i.e. the University of British Columbia) and senior high school. In 1930, a committee of high school teachers was set up to study the question of high school accrediting. A report on the advantages of and objections to the existing system of university admission (matriculation examination) was sent to each high school principal. A referendum on the accrediting system demonstrated that an imposing majority of teachers favoured its inauguration. A complete report with recommendations was presented for the consideration of the Minister of Education. At the 1937 Convention of Teachers the Minister announced that a system of high school accrediting would come into effect concurrently with the new programme of studies for the upper grades of the secondary schools.

Aside from the purely technical objections in the report to the Minister, certain indicting evidence against the matriculation examination was given. "The matriculation has been for so long the only certificate of success in high school studies that many parents, employees and others insist upon high school students securing matriculation diplomas, irrespective of ability, tastes, probable future occupation and individual differences in general. Thousands of students are thus diverted from courses that might be of much greater value to them."

The correlation between the relative ranking of students at the matriculation examination and the ranking of the same students in the third year of their university studies was found to be positive, but not high.

As the recommendations of the teachers' committee will be the basis of a provincial system of accredited high schools, they are pertinent to this study. For some years there have been accredited schools in Nova Scotia, and the method is likely to be adopted in some form in other provinces. In British Columbia, the personnel of the accrediting Board is to be: The Superintendent of Education, two high school principals, two members of the Faculty of the University, three representatives of the Department of Education, *pro tempore* the Director of Education or Inspector in the area. An accredited high school is one whose records are to be taken at their face value when the University or other body is determining which or how many students shall be deemed qualified to apply for admission. Certain rules and standards governing the accrediting of the schools are being prepared. A simple objective type of examination is to be provided to meet the needs of applicants for university admission who have not been trained and graded in accredited schools, or whose standing in these schools has not met the required standard ...

II. THE PROVINCE OF ALBERTA
Grade VI Attainment

A new programme of studies has been introduced, and in it the word "Grade," which formerly included a year's accomplishment in several subjects, has lost some of its meaning, and in rural areas where pupils are grouped in divisions, has disappeared entirely from the school vocabulary. An average pupil is expected to proceed annually from year to year without examination barriers until the end of his ninth year at school (Grade IX). It might be interesting, however, to note what standard of attainment in different subjects is expected of Grade VI pupils, remembering, of course, that these are suggested for the guidance of the teacher, but are not compulsory attainments for pupils' promotions.

Reading—The pupil should have the ability to read aloud in correct thought groups, with a pleasing voice, clear enunciation and natural expression, any selection of suitable character and difficulty. Tests suggested for use are comprehension tests based on readers and a junior vocabulary test prepared by the Department of Psychology, University of Alberta.

Literature—Familiarity with six books; participation in twelve choral selections; ability to reproduce the narrative of twelve stories; recitation of two hundred lines of poetry; reading with reasonable intelligence and sympathy twelve selections.

Writing—Ayres Scale, Quality 57; Speed 63 letters per minute.

Arithmetic—Addition, subtraction, multiplication and division, simple fractions, business forms, units of measure, two-step problems.

Selective Examinations

The Department of Education now conducts a Grade IX Examination, one which all pupils who have completed the programme of Grades VII, VIII and IX, and desire promotion to the high school, are required to write. The pupils' status and achievement are graded by a High School Entrance Examination Board according to certain standards of quality, and on this basis pupils are directed to appropriate courses of the high school programme.

The examination comprises four question papers: one on English, one on mathematics, one on social studies, and one on general science and health education. There are no Departmental examinations on optional subjects, standing being granted on the recommendation of the teacher to pupils who complete the course in any of these subjects. A pupil must have full standing in three optional subjects for promotion to the high school.

A Grade IX candidate's standing on the Departmental examination is reckoned by averaging his achievement on the four question papers mentioned above. A reasonable minimum, decided by the High School Entrance Examination Board, is required on each paper.

The following schedule governs promotions. If the average achievement of the candidate on the four papers is change to 60 per cent, or over, the pupil is promoted and is free to take any course or subject of the high school programme. If the average achievement is between 45 per cent and 60 per cent, the pupil is promoted under recommendation. He may, in the first year of the high school programme, proceed to courses in the optional subjects (type-writing, music, dramatics, oral French, general shop, household economics, junior business), and also to courses in not more than three of the following subjects: mathematics, languages, English, social studies, science. If the pupil's average is between 30 per cent and 45 per cent, he may, where facilities permit, be allowed to take certain optional subjects in the high school. If his average is under 30 per cent, he fails and must repeat the Grade IX course ....

Students may be recommended for credit by the teacher or principal in the following high school subjects: Latin I, French I, German I, literature 2 and composition 2. These recommendations are to be based on the work of the student as indicated by term tests and general classroom work, a pass mark of 50 per cent. being required in each unit. The unit system of promotion obtains in order to assist teachers in arriving at a basis for recommendation; question papers in these units are prepared by the Department of Education and forwarded to the teachers or principals who apply for them. Their use is not compulsory, and the answer papers are not forwarded to the Department of Education for marking. The teachers or principals are expected to provide the Department of Education with a confidential report on each candidate under the following headings: length of time preparing for examination, regularity of attendance, ability, attitude towards work, physical fitness, relative standing in class ....

III. THE PROVINCE OF SASKATCHEWAN
Regulations for Admission to High School

The Minister of Education, speaking before the Trustees' Association, summed up the Saskatchewan system of examinations as follows: "In the lower grades I-VII, promotions are made by the teachers without formal examinations. Grade VIII examinations (for entrance to high school) were abolished in 1931, with certain reservations. The promotions from Grades IX and X are made under two systems: (a) on the basis of examinations; (b) on the basis of the year's work without examinations. Of 38,912 students in Grades VIII-X in June of 1936, there were 5,522 promoted on their year's work without examination. The Department, by regulation, provided that certain students in the larger schools in June 1935 might be promoted from Grade XI without examination. The examination system may be properly criticised, and yet it is conceded by the critics that it would be impossible to delete the examinations entirely from our system."

The elementary school in Saskatchewan comprises Grades I-VIII and the high school Grades IX, X, XI and XII. The regulations for admission to high school are briefly as follows: Pupils may be promoted to Grade IX on the recommendation of the elementary school principal—(1) if there is a high school in the same building; (2) if there is a high school in the same school district; (3) if the pupil attends a school in a town or city where there is employed a superintendent of schools. In spite of this limited provision for disposing of an examination barrier between the elementary and the secondary school, the objectives of the elementary school course as advocated by the Department of Education do not include success of pupils at a final examination. The following is quoted from the authorised booklet, *Public School Curriculum and Teachers' Guide*: "To pass an examination, to be promoted to the next grade, to win a prize, to absorb information, or even to acquire desirable skills or to form desirable habits cannot be considered as objectives. The final objectives of public school education are stated briefly as follows: (a) Health activities (to include happiness and mental well-being); (b) social activities; (c) spare-time activities."

Considerable study has been made of tests and measurements to be used in schools, and the College of Education has devised and advocated the use of certain objective achievement tests, character tests, standardised intelligence tests. Special mention should be made of the twenty-four standardised tests in the fundamental operations of arithmetic. The time standards for the tests suitable for different grades are given in the curriculum booklet.

Much has been written recently in Canada on the subject of standards of attainment. A pupil is required to do a promotion assignment, even in a skill subject and given credit for a 50 per cent achievement. He is given high praise if he obtains 75 per cent of the maximum marks awarded. It is refreshing to read the directions of the Department of Education in Saskatchewan to their teachers. Students require 100 per cent accuracy in the 200 addition combinations in Grade III. Standard of achievement in spelling is 100 per cent accuracy. In writing, achievement is required according to the norms of the Ayres Scale.

Annual departmental examinations, based upon the course prescribed for Grades XI and XII, are conducted. According to the size and equipment of high schools attended, certain pupils are granted standing on the work of the Grade XI course on the principal's recommendation. Admission to the

University is based upon success at the matriculation examination taken upon the completion of the work of Grade XII. Students who have Grade XII standing with an average mark of less than 60 per cent in the required subjects are required, if entering arts, engineering or household science, to take a preliminary year of work before entering upon the regular course.

IV. THE PROVINCE OF MANITOBA
Examinations criticised by a Committee

In Manitoba a Committee was appointed to revise the Programme of Studies for Grades VII-XI. They prepared a Report in 1927 which has had considerable effect, not only upon the courses of study, but upon the education of adolescent children in that Province. The observations on the examination system in the Province are valuable for this present study because they indicate the practice at the time and certain improvements which have since been incorporated in the system. The following quotation is from the report:

> It is admitted that preparing young persons for examinations has a very considerable educational value. The process makes for industry, for the development of memory and of some forms of reasoning power, and even at its worst for a certain skill in expression. But the emphasis is placed upon the accumulation of fact lore, upon word for word reproduction of dictated notes, upon surface indications rather than thought values. Worst of all, it paralyses the initiative of the teacher and intelligent adaptation of school work to community needs and life.
>
> Music is of great educational worth, but the high school staff must not spend time upon it else the children will fail in algebra. Skill in oral expression is of great value in community life, but it pays no dividends in written examinations. Physical needs are too often neglected. The community life of the school, which should be our best training for citizenship, is suffering severely for this reason. Your Committee believes that the high schools are prevented by arbitrary examination requirements from rendering the service which they should perform. We are demanding that they grasp after the shadow and seem perturbed at their losing the substance.
>
> The examination system has, of course, often been criticised. Probably no one recognises its limitations better than those who are constrained to depend upon its results in the admission or promotion of students. The answer to criticism has always been, "What are you going to put in its place?' Your Committee does not suggest the abolition of examinations. What it does assert is that the secondary school is examination ridden, and to an extent that considerably cripples its usefulness."

The average Grade XI student prepares, in the heat of the latter part of June, for eleven three-hour papers which follow frequently at the rate of two per day, a load far in excess of that borne by the university student two or three years his senior. The number of papers required is too great. The test is set chiefly to determine knowledge of fact lore, and knowledge of fact lore has little relation to the possession of power on the part of the student. One paper should be sufficient in each of the languages, one in mathematics and one in science. Properly set and carefully marked, these papers would give a truer indication than is gained at the present of the capacity of the individual undergoing the test. Such an examination, checked against the term record of the school, and supplemented by an intelligence test, would be of real value. The intelligence test is slowly making its way, and its worth is gradually being recognised.

V. THE PROVINCE OF ONTARIO
History of Examinations

The School Law of 1871, Section 38, provided that, "The County, City or Town, Inspector of Schools; the Chairman of the High School Board; and the Headmaster of the High School shall constitute a Board of Examiners for the admission of Pupils to the High School according to the Regulations and Programme of Examinations according to Law."

In the 1870's the Legislative grant to grammar schools (high schools) was apportioned on the enrolment in Latin classes. The result was that almost every pupil was forced to study Latin. It was, of course, a matriculation subject, so pupils entered high school from a competitive examination and began a matriculation course for entrance to the University. Much educational history has been made in Ontario since 1871, but the changes in the examination system have not kept pace with changes in the science or philosophy of education.

Dr. Egerton Ryerson was primarily responsible for the introduction of the competitive examination system in his native Province. From Ontario its influence spread to Western Canada. One writer has said, "The provincial examinations are the outgrowth of an educational system essentially Prussian, rather than British, in spirit. Each department of education exercises a highly centralised control over the schools under its jurisdiction. The attainment of definite and uniform provincial standards on uniform examination papers is the most convenient, if not the most scientific, method of rating the efficiency of the large number of schools that come under departmental supervision."

Permissive regulations in Ontario giving, first to the principals of city or town elementary schools and later to teachers of rural schools, permission to recommend pupils for entrance to high school were cautiously given, not because the Department of Education was unwilling, but because the teachers were hesitant about assuming the responsibility. There were many possibilities:

(1) members of school boards and other influential people might seek to persuade teachers to recommend unworthy candidates. If the child was unworthy in the teacher's estimation, the teacher might face dismissal. (2) Parents would demand examinations, so the burden of setting and examining papers would be shifted from the Department to the teacher. (3) In a recommendation system there would be many standards; under the examination system, one. Would the teacher's standard of achievement set for the pupils gradually lower with his or her waning enthusiasm in advancing years? With the great majority of teachers these were groundless fears. Others met the difficulties bravely as parents gradually learned that the formal entrance examination was unnecessary for about 60 per cent of the pupils.

As the elementary school course continues in Ontario until the end of Grade VIII (the change to a 6-3-3 plan is gradually being made and new courses of study for Grades I-VI and for Grade IX are now available for use, September 1937), and the pupil is now about 13 or 14 years of age, his entrance certificate is, in many cases, his graduation certificate from school in some rural areas. He has been prepared for entrance to high school, and he has to enter life work on the farm or in a trade instead. So an examination has to some extent controlled a child's training for life. This condition is being changed with the new course of study.

Changed Attitude towards Examinations

Gradually the concession made to elementary school teachers of Grade VIII pupils was extended to principals of high schools; first giving permission to grant lower school standing (a certificate issued at the end of the first two years in high school), and later middle school standing (at the end of four years of high school work).

Generally the plan has worked quite satisfactorily from the point of view of selection of pupils who are best fitted to do the next year's work in a subject. A pupil does the work of second-year mathematics and the teacher of the subject decides at the end of a year if he is able to do third-year mathematics. The chief defect in this unit-promotion is the lack of a cumulative opinion or co-ordinated estimate of the pupil's advancement towards an occupation or profession. In the larger high schools where vocational guidance committees have been formed, the defect is not so serious.

The committee of teachers responsible for the preparation of a new programme of studies for elementary schools (Grades I-VI) has objected to the use of external examinations in the following words: "If the curriculum is properly drawn, it should so fit the capacities and interests of children that they will find in the experiences and activities of the classroom a good and sufficient motive for learning, without the unwholesome pressure of a "promotion" examination. Anything in the nature of a final examination to measure the physical, intellectual and spiritual growth of children is not only unnecessary but is prejudicial to such growth." An unusual feature of the programme is that, although a 6-year elementary course has been planned, an average child may do the work in 5 ½ years, and a bright child in 5 years or 4 ½ years. No child will at any stage fail. He may have to advance more slowly than a brighter fellow-pupil, but he will make gradual progress rather than have his school career marred by recessions after progress.

VI. THE PROVINCE OF QUEBEC
The High School Leaving Examination

Of the two educational systems in Quebec, one is Roman Catholic and the other is Protestant. The chief differences in the systems, besides that of religious denomination, are language, administrative control and grading. These differences were described in *The Year Book of Education*, 1934.

In the high school of the Protestant system there are two courses, the academic and the general. Both courses lead to a High School Leaving Certificate. The academic course is followed by pupils intending to matriculate into the arts faculty of a university. The general course, besides qualifying for a High School Leaving Certificate, leads to entrance into the school for teachers (Macdonald College), and to certain faculties, other than the arts faculty of a university, provided the pupil takes the prescribed subjects and the number of subjects necessary in each case.

Survey and Questions for High School Leaving Examination
A brief survey of the question papers of the High School Leaving Examination, June 1937, follows. Only special features are discussed.

On the geometrical drawing paper there were 6 questions, with 5 marks for each of the first four questions and 15 marks for each of questions 5 and 6. All were practical questions, and precision, neatness and accuracy besides procedures were being tested.

The freehand drawing and perspective paper had an additional two questions on craft design. The choice in the general art paper was wide, the student being allowed to select from five phases of art for a test of skill and ability. The questions covered work in light and shade, water colour, lettering, poster designs, sketching, commercial advertising.

There was no oral examination in music, nor were there questions on musical appreciation on the written test. That, however, may be difficult to examine. There were twelve questions that tested knowledge of technical terms, harmony, musical composers, classical music and orchestra.

The English literature paper had a choice of six questions of the "describe" and "discuss" type. Eight books had been prescribed by the Department of

Education for study, and the questions indicated that an intensive, analytical study was expected. Two questions on the paper gave scope for literary criticism.

A note at the top of the English composition paper was as follows: "Three things will be considered—the arrangement of your material; the language in which it is expressed; the correctness of the grammar, spelling, punctuation." There were two questions; one asking for an essay of about four pages and one a friendly letter.

There had been an earlier oral examination in French, but all candidates were required to write the French grammar and composition papers. The questions written in French tested spelling, composition, vocabulary, grammar, idiomatic constructions and translation from English to French.

Questions requiring the "essay" type of answer were asked on the history paper. The students were required to attempt six questions of eight given on the paper. It was largely a test of knowledge of factual information with one question inviting criticism or the students' attitude toward a certain radical social change.

"Draw a diagram and explain" was a type of question repeated on the physics paper. The candidates were not asked to do experiments but to describe experiments that may have been done in class. This was true also of the chemistry paper, although there were questions on practical uses of chemicals, and questions on industrial chemistry.

The Intermediate algebra paper tested knowledge of square root, ratio, quadratic equations, geometric progression, permutations and combinations, logarithms. There was one problem relating algebra to arithmetic. Geometry and trigonometry were grouped on one paper, with six questions. Proving theorems that had been studied from the textbook was the only requirement in geometry.

There were two Latin papers comprising translations from the works of Cicero with questions on the grammar of the selections, translations from English to Latin, translations from Vergil's *Æneid*, and sight translation.

The household science paper included questions on sewing and cooking. There was evidence that the students had covered an extensive course, that everyday practical problems of the household had been dealt with and a wide sampling was made on the examination.

The extremists among examination critics would find many defects in the School Leaving Examination in Quebec. The questions of the different papers were surveyed above to present a picture of a type of examination that is still used in some form in other provinces, but is gradually disappearing or being changed. It is a natural associate of a prescribed course of study, and, although the examination could well be made more objective in Quebec, its purpose will change with the introduction of a new course of study that is being planned.

VII. THE PROVINCE OF NEW BRUNSWICK
The Examiner criticised

In New Brunswick there are two schools, the elementary and the high school. In the elementary school there are eight grades, in the high school there may be four. The Superintendent of Education has recommended that a 6-3-3 plan of organisation be adopted and committees have been appointed to prepare the new courses of study.

In line with the modern tendency to reduce the number of outside examinations, provision was made this year whereby students may be admitted to high school on the recommendation of the principal of the school and that of the school inspector. For those pupils of Grade VIII who are not recommended, a high school entrance examination is conducted by the Department of Education. In 1936, 866 pupils passed the examinations, and 698 were admitted conditionally. The Superintendent of Education made the following recommendations concerning examinations in his latest report. "In the lower grades promotion should be on the recommendation of the teacher by whom the pupils have been taught. The High School Leaving Examination should be abolished and the requirements for matriculation be reduced from nine to six subjects. Latin should be made optional and French compulsory. Students might be admitted to the University of New Brunswick and to the Normal School as they are now admitted to High School."

A strong factor in bringing the recommendation into practice is criticism of the external examination. The examination is frequently not consistent with the aims or purposes of the subject examined. One teacher in a recent article writes: "One of the strongest outside influences affecting the work of teacher and pupil is the examination set by an outside examiner. Teaching is done in the terms of the examination that is anticipated. Learning is influenced by the same factor. The order may well be reversed; it is for the examiner to anticipate the variety of teaching, and set a paper accordingly."

VIII. NOVA SCOTIA AND PRINCE EDWARD ISLAND
An Examining Board's Study of Marks

The high school examinations for the schools of Nova Scotia, Prince Edward Island, Newfoundland and for private schools are conducted by a Common Examining Board. Readers are selected by the Board to judge the answer papers. The Board has made an extensive study of types of questions best suited for selective purposes. For the 1936 examinations for Grades XI and XII the papers in certain subjects were planned with an objective part and an essay part that some comparison of the results might be made.

They found that the coefficient of correlation between marks on the objective part and marks on the essay part of the question paper in Grade IX chem-

istry was .65; in Grade XI physics .65; and in Grade XI French :74. The distribution of the marks in plotting these coefficients revealed that in Grade XI
French the candidates scored higher on the objective part; and in Grade XI
physics there was no definite tendency for the marks to be higher or lower on
either part. "The coefficients reveal a very satisfactory relationship between the
two parts of these examinations."

The median marks in the subjects of Grade XII for Nova Scotia in 1936
were as follows (reported by the Superintendent of Education). The bracketed
number indicates increase or decrease from the median mark in 1935: French
56.5 (- 4.8); history 50.5 (- 5.2); English (a) 45.3 (- 9.4); algebra 49.0 (+ 3.2);
economics 58.6 (+ 4.1); German 52.6 (+ 6.3); trigonometry 47.0 (- 4.9);
English (b) 57.2 (+ 2.5); geometry 50.4 (+ 1.4); physics 48.4 (+ 2.9); chemistry
49.5 (+ 1.0); botany 53.3 (+ 1.9) Latin (a) 47.0 (+ 3.9); Latin (b) 61.3 (+ 1.4).
The fluctuation of the median mark in a subject from year to year may be due
to various causes. It appeared in extreme form in Grade XI Spanish with a small
number of candidates, where the median mark was higher in 1936 by 24.0.

The Provincial High School Certificate of Grade XI requires an aggregate of
250 on English, history and any other three subjects at the provincial examinations for this certificate, the results of which have been discussed above. There
are two two-hour papers in English; two one and one-half hour papers in science; two one and one-half hour papers in mathematics; and one two-hour
paper in each of the other subjects. Provided that the prescribed English and
social studies courses are taken, students may take some or all of the remaining
subjects necessary for a full year's work from among the following: music, art,
crafts, commercial and agricultural subjects. For credit in these subjects the student must present a certificate from the institution in which the subject was
studied or pass an examination set by a special examining board in that subject.

The accredited schools from which the recommendation of principals on
pupils' success in different subjects are recognised by the Department of
Education must have employed three full-time university graduates on the
teaching staff. This is different from the method of accrediting adopted in
British Columbia. Under the accrediting system in Nova Scotia, the quarterly
and final examinations of these schools are reviewed by the Chief Inspector and
a definite plan of determining the students who will write the final local examination is determined. By this system all pupils still write a final examination,
but it is a local rather than external examination. In case of failure, at the local
examination, he must write the external examination also, for standing.

A few of the directions or hints as to the nature of the final examinations
in certain subjects may serve to show the emphasis in the subject and the type
of examination to be given. These are given in the *Journal of Education*, which
is the official publication for teachers. "The examination paper in composition
will require the writing of one or more full-length themes on selected subjects,

abstracting or précis work, outlining and exercises in sentence structure and functional grammar. The examination paper in literature will be designed to measure the student's appreciation and critical judgment of assigned selections and his knowledge of the important literary types—essays, one-act plays, short stories, lyric and narrative poems. The Latin paper will contain one compulsory question in sight reading. The examination in French will contain not more than one-third new type or objective questions on vocabulary forms and syntax. An examination in oral French may be substituted for one question on the provincial examination."

Many teachers have not accepted gratefully the responsibility of promoting pupils. Many still prefer the method of external examination. Perhaps they do not feel competent. This may be true, as not all teachers make efficient examiners. One inspector of schools in Nova Scotia found this situation and dealt with it as follows: "The examination by the teachers of the village and rural schools of their own Grade X pupils having proved to be almost a complete farce, at the unanimous request of the teachers themselves I planned and carried out a system of examination for Grade X pupils. As a result there was, of course, a sharp decline in the number of successful candidates. The results of my work have been so gratifying that I shall try to have Grade IX examined in the same way during the coming school year."

* * * * *

33) ONTARIO GRADE 13 PROVINCIAL EXAMINATIONS, 1946[2]

Upper School History, 1946
Note. *Five questions constitute a full paper.*

A

Note. *Three questions may be attempted from Part A and two from Part B, or two from Part A and three from Part B.*

1. Show the importance of the following in relation to the American Revolution:
   (a) the Stamp Act;
   (b) the influence of the West;
   (c) the Quebec Act of 1774.

2. (a) What were the principal political and economic causes of unrest in Canada before the outbreak of rebellion in 1837?
   (b) What remedies did Durham propose?

3. (a) In what respects did the constitution of Canada adopted in 1867 resemble that of Great Britain?
   (b) In what respects did it resemble and in what respect did it differ from that of the United States?
   (c) How do you explain the resemblances and differences mentioned in your answers to (a) and (b)?

4. Trace the advance of Canadian nationalism down to 1914 in connection with the following:
   (a) the growth of treaty-making powers;
   (b) foreign policy;
   (c) imperial defence.

B

Note. *Three questions may be attempted from Part B and two from Part A, or two from Part B and three from Part A.*

5. (a) What were the underlying causes of the Latin-American Revolutions?
   (b) Trace the course of these revolutions down to 1826.

6. (a) Describe the problems which confronted the Constitutional Convention at Philadelphia in 1787.
   (b) Explain the three important "compromises" of the American constitution.

7. Discuss the significance of each of the following in relation to the American Civil War:
   (a) The Missouri Compromise;
   (b) the issue of "states' rights;"
   (c) the Compromise of 1850.

8. Outline the international relations of the United States since 1860 with:
   (a) Spain;
   (b) Latin-America;
   (c) Canada.

* * * * *

1 A.E. Ault, "A Survey of Examinations," in Harley V. Usill, ed. *The Year Book of Education, 1938* (London: The University of London Institute of Education: Evans Brothers, 1939), pp.154-171.
2 *Upper School Examinations (Grade XIII) Modern History* (Belleville: The James Texts Limited, 1963), pp. 2-3.

Chapter Nine:
Native Education

The most disturbing aspect of Canada's educational system is how it treated minority groups. Throughout history, Canadian society has been racist and discriminatory. Examples are everywhere—the internment of Japanese Canadians in British Columbia during the Second World War; the destruction of Africville in Nova Scotia; the extermination of the Beothuk in Newfoundland; the rise of the Ku Klux Klan in Saskatchewan in the 1920s; restrictive immigration laws; the federal government's refusal to admit a ship carrying Jewish escapees from Nazi Germany; and segregated educational facilities for African Canadians.

African Americans who escaped to Canada via the underground railway in the mid-nineteenth century sought education for their children. School board after school board, however, either refused to allow African-American children to mingle with white children, or created vastly inferior separate schools. A school trustee in Amherstburg, Upper Canada, claimed that white citizens would rather "cut their children's heads off and throw them into the ditch," than have the two races study together. The separate school provided for blacks in Windsor, Upper Canada, lacked a blackboard and chairs, and the students' textbooks were in tatters. This building, for 45 black students, was 16 by 24 feet in dimension. Other communities also refused to allow their children to attend the same school as the blacks, or to go to the same church. When they crossed the invisible barrier, riots and sometimes murder resulted. Violence erupted in Nova Scotia when a black preacher baptized a white couple, in Ontario when a black man married a white woman, and in Victoria when blacks sat in the white section of a theatre.

As a result of such thinking, the Ontario and Nova Scotia governments authorized the establishment of separate schools. Once such schools were created, the courts usually refused black children admission to any other school, no matter how much closer or superior it was. In 1940, Lower Sackville, Nova Scotia, barred black children from attending the only public school in the area, and as late as 1960, there were seven black school districts and three additional all-black schools in the province. Ontario did not officially repeal racially segregated education until 1964.

The policy of segregated schooling arguable had its most significant impact on Canada's Aboriginal population. The first chapter examined aspects of aboriginal education in New France. The following article focuses on Native residential schools.

For minorities and education see: Jean Barman and Marie Battiste, *First*

Nations Education in Canada: The Circle Unfolds (Vancouver, 1995); Jean Barman, "Schooled for Inequality: The Education of British Columbia Aboriginal Children," in *Children, Teachers and Schools in the History of British Columbia*, eds. Jean Barman, Neil Sutherland, J. Donald Wilson, (Calgary, 1995); Robin Winks, "Negro School Segregation in Ontario and Nova Scotia," *Canadian Historical Review*, vol. 50, no. 2 (June, 1969); Rosa Bruno-Jofre, "Manitoba Schooling in the Canadian Context and the Building of a Polity: 1919-1971," *Canadian and International Education*, vol. 28, no. 2 (December 1999); Luigi G. Pennacchio, "Toronto's Public Schools and the Assimilation of Foreign Students, 1900-1920," *The Journal of Educational Thought*, vol. 20, no. 1 (April, 1986); Timothy J. Stanley, "White Supremacy and the Rhetoric of Educational Indoctrination: A Canadian Case Study," in J.A. Mangan, ed., *Making Imperial Mentalities: Socialisation and British Imperialism* (Manchester, 1990); J.R. Miller, *Shingwauk's Vision: A History of Native Residential Schools* (Toronto, 1996); and Bridglal Pachai, *Education in Nova Scotia: The African Nova Scotian Experience* (Truro, 1997).

$$* \quad * \quad * \quad * \quad *$$

Aboriginal Education in Canada: A Plea for Integration[116]

Indian residential schools were the product of the nineteenth-century federal policy of assimilation. (Furniss, 1995: 15)

Our object is to continue until there is not a single Indian in Canada that has not been absorbed into the body politic and there is no Indian question, and no Indian department, that is the whole object of the bill—statement in 1920 by Deputy Superintendent General Duncan Campbell Scott. (Haig-Brown, 1993: 31-32)

There were years of slavery as residential schools were supported by child labor; humiliation was the experience of every Indian child who attended one of these schools. (Grant, 1996: 17)

Those who ran the school tried to rob us of our collective identity by punishing us for speaking our language, calling us "savages" and "heathens." (Knockwood, 1994: 157)

The residential school was ... designed to separate Indian children from their families so they could be systematically fitted with the religious beliefs, social habits, and educational training that would turn them into "little brown white men." (Dyck, 1997: 14)

Badly built and ill-maintained, they were both the cause and the context of a dreadful crisis in sanitation and health. (Milloy, 1999: 75)

A special place must be reserved in perdition for those who abused residential school students sexually. (Miller, 2000: 423)

Many Native people remember with deep pain the experiences they suffered during their time at the ill-famed residential schools. As may be inferred from the above quotations, literature pertaining to the phenomenon of residential schools is growing rapidly documenting what historian John S. Milloy (1999) has called "a national crime." Personal stories related by former inmates of the system emphasize the inhumane conditions of these assimilation-oriented institutions, including child labor, personal humiliation, language loss, poor sanitation and health conditions, and sexual abuse.

The sad irony is that these tortured individuals were supposed to be inculcating the virtues of Christianity and European civilization. The reality was that this form of education dictated long absences from home. Some children never saw their parents for periods of time ranging from four to seven years, and in some cases even longer, depending on individual "success." Life in the residential school meant participating in an entirely different cultural milieu, replete with such alien features as corporal punishment, strict discipline, hard work, loneliness, and, worst of all, confinement. On the positive side (if there is one), residential schools *did* provide some training in EuroCanadian-centred language arts and today many Aboriginal leaders can trace their literary beginnings to the years they spent in residential schools. Assembly of First Nations' leaders, Phil Fontaine and Matthew Coon Come, for example, are both former students of residential schools. In interviews with former students in residential schools, Bull (1991: 40) identified at least a few positive memories.

Some Native students who enjoyed the vocational or industrial aspect of the curriculum were those employed in the "domestic" section. For example, one male in the bakery preferred this "practical aspect" and some females liked sewing .... On reflection, another "good" experience was that these Native students made friends with other children from other tribes and reserves. It was difficult to communicate initially in cases where Native languages were different, but once they had made the emotional bond between them, the students kept in connection all their lives.

The fact that some students had positive memories of some activities does not in any way justify the operations of residential schools, but it might offer at least a little consolation to those who in spite of the system benefitted from it. Cooper (1999: book jacket) stretches the parameters of belief when he suggests that "For some, like renowned Olympian and football star Jim Thorpe and physician Susan La Flesche, an Indian school education [in a residential school] led to success and prosperity." For the vast majority, however, life in residential schools offered isolating, alienating, and frightening experiences.

Today former residential school inmates still meet to reminisce and comfort one another. In some ways the bond they made with their fellow sufferers has served partially to alleviate the pain of the memory of the cruelties and hardships endured during their years of incarceration.

Origins of the System

The background to the formation of residential schools in Canada developed over many decades. The first schools for Indian children were operated by the Hudson's Bay Company which built them primarily for the children of their employees. Few Native children were actually enrolled. A second group operating schools for Aboriginal students were missionaries. By the 1630s the Jesuits had built a school for Huron children at Quebec City, established a mission, and encouraged the development of a series of agricultural villages. As earlier stated, Sister Marguerite Bourgeoys, who later founded the Order of Ursulines, arrived in New France in 1653 in response to a call from Governor Maisionneuve of Ville-Marie Montreal. Five years after her arrival Sister Bourgeoys opened a school for girls in a converted stable and eventually enrolled Native children as well. Although her primary targets were children of fur traders and explorers whose families lived in nearby settlements. (Chalmers, 1974).

In 1763 when New France fell and the English took over, Protestant denominations also became involved in Native education. The conclusion of the War of 1812, contributed to significant economic changes in the country and the fur trade was greatly affected. Now, instead of being viewed as allies, First Nations were seen as obstacles to the nation's progress. Increases in European immigration led to conflicts over land, and loss of hunting, trapping, and fishing grounds contributed to poverty among First Nations. Social humanitarian ideologies that arose during the 1800s drew attention to the Indians' plight stressing the need for basic literacy, and agricultural and industrial skills (Furniss, 1995: 19-21).

The spiritual and psychological conquest of the First Peoples of Canada via schooling produced many devastating results. Although the campaign to squelch the culture of First Nations was more militarily-deliberate in the United States, in many ways the Canadian crusade took on all the earmarks of a conquest of bloodshed. When the fur trade began to diminish the role of Indigenous peoples changed. No one had postulated what a post fur trade culture might be like nor laid plans for life following its aftermath. French imperialists were a bit of an exception in that they demonstrated an attitude which at least partially set the stage for the development of a new nation (the Métis) through planned racial amalgamation (Sealey and Lussier, 1975: 17).

The implications of the dwindling fur trade were far-reaching in consequence (Ray, 1974). The shift in economy affected all sectors of society, and hunting and gathering no longer had a place in the new world. Agriculture and industrial development replaced traditional forms of livelihood and urban dwellers became a phenomenon. Because the Aboriginal people found it difficult to gain any degree of satisfaction in any of these sectors, a place had to be found for them. Without too much analysis, the invaders concluded that the cultures of the First Nations should be transformed into European forms of civilization. The formula for initiating them into the new society featured residential schooling made up of an admixture of government funding and religious administration.

Pre-Confederation Practices

By the middle of the 19th century a number of church denominations in Canada were involved in Native education with the double-edged objective of spreading the Gospel and "culturally rehabilitating the Indian." The Catholic Church, represented by the Oblates, virtually dominated the early stages of the missionary education movement following their founding in the 1840s. A few years later Anglican and Methodist missionaries also entered the area.

The Oblates worked with the Grey Nuns and together they established mission posts across northern Alberta and preserved a French-Catholic presence in the west. The Grey Nuns moved to St. Albert in 1863, following Father Albert Lacombe, and built an orphanage, convent, and school there. Later on they added a hospital. The Grey Nuns were among the first educated non-Native women in Alberta and their legacy includes the founding of the General Hospital in Edmonton and the Holy Cross Hospital in Calgary.

Not everyone involved in the enterprise of making the Indian over shared the reductionist view that an assimilative recipe combining the message of the Christian religion with schooling would accomplish their complete acculturation. Some government bureaucrats saw the Indigenous People as unfortunate victims of the times and felt sorry for them. Incoming settlers perceived them as intruders, occupiers of lands more suitable for farming than nomadic hunting. Do-gooders pitied them as "strangers within their own country." In the final analysis, Indians were the "white man's burden" desperately in need of gaining a toehold on 20th century civilization; fortunately, their "salvation" was possible through His Majesty's Christian influence (Surtees, 1969).

When the success rate of the campaign to make farmers of Native youth via day schooling indicated "low returns," Roman Catholic priests turned their attention to the establishment of "seminaries" or boarding (residential) schools. Indian parents were naturally reluctant to part with their children for lengthy periods of time and the missionaries often had to bribe them into letting their children go. A special aspect of this program was to enroll some French children in Native schools as a means of encouraging Indian pupils to take on French cultural ways. Indian parents objected to this deliberate socialization plan wanting instead to teach their children their ancestral beliefs and culture. Still, the push to have residential schools for Indian children continued, and by the end of the 19th century every region of the nation had boarding schools for Indian children, financed by the government, with the church providing spiritual guidance and management. This move was promoted by Egerton Ryerson who in 1844 became the first superintendent of schools in English-speaking Canada. Ryerson promoted the idea that the First Nations could not accomplish civilization without a "religious feeling" and thus "the animating and controlling spirit of each residential school should be a religious one" (Brookes, 1991: 20). The Province of Canada endorsed Ryerson's plan, acknowledging "the superiority of the European culture and the need to raise them [Aboriginals] to the level of the whites" (Haig-Brown, 1993: 29).

One of the highlights of missionary work in the mid-19th century was the founding of a successful Aboriginal agricultural settlement at Credit River in southern Ontario by Methodist missionary Peter Jones. Jones (Sacred Feathers, or Kahkewaquonaby in Ojibway), was a young man of part Ojibway heritage who lived with his non-Native father until he was 21 years of age. At that point he became the Methodist Church's spokesman and helped attract Ojibway converts to serve as preachers, interpreters, and schoolteachers. It was through his efforts that the Methodist Church extended their mission westward from Ontario (Rogers, 1994: 125-126).

Jones convinced Indian leaders that building schools (day schools as well as residential schools), for Aboriginal children would assist the First Nations in adjusting to rapidly changing economic conditions. Band leaders readily bought into Jones' plan which was financed by government monies made available through the office of the Rev. Egerton Ryerson, Chief Superintendent of Common Schools for Upper Canada. At first Native leaders cooperated with the development of residential schools, however, they soon discovered that the educational objectives of those who ran these institutions were radically different from those desired by Indian leaders. Aboriginal parents thought the schools would teach their young skills necessary to enter the labor force of the industrial age. Instead the children were being primarily taught the Christian faith while being robbed of their language and cultural heritage. Indian resistance to missionary education peaked in 1863 so government officials pushed for legislation to enforce compulsory attendance. During this time a public system of education was being developed for non-Native Upper Canada, but Aboriginal children were educated in separate schools. When nonAboriginal settlers obtained government funds to build schools for their own children, Native children were not allowed to attend them. Sadly, the denominationally-run schools in the east later became the model for those developed in western Canada as well.

Post-Confederation Policy

Canadian Indian policy was actually rooted in British practices at the time when Great Britain was in control of this country. Prior to 1830 the British War Department handled Indian affairs, virtually ignoring their economic and social needs. Consequently, conditions in Native communities were deplorable. No longer needed for the fur trade, the First Nations found themselves fraught with disease and hunger, rapidly becoming a landless people. Their numbers were decreasing at an alarming rate and the British Colonial Office felt the "Indian problem" would soon be solved by the Indigenous people dying out. British ethnocentrism was the order of the day, and those who thought that something ought to be done for the Native people believed assimilation to be the best route. Thus in 1860 the Indian Department became part of the Crown Lands Department and shortly thereafter the position of Deputy Superintendent of Indian Affairs was created. Legislation entitled the Act for the Gradual Civilization of Indian Tribes in Canada was passed and responsibility for Indian affairs was transferred from military to civil authority (Grant, 1996: 57).

In 1867, when Canada officially became a country in her own right, the responsibility for educating Native youth (as well as all others), fell to the new government. True, the treaties signed shortly thereafter, specified the provision of schooling for Indian children, but the approach and mode was not specifically spelled out, that is, "Her Majesty agrees to maintain schools for instruction in such reserves" (Brookes, 1991: 168). An underlying governmental assumption was that the long-range forecast for Aboriginal survival was eventually cultural genocide, so why bother providing a first-class education? Since missionaries were already involved in the enterprise, why not merely finance the continuance of their schools until they were no longer required? Naturally, religious denominations were overjoyed with the arrangement and even competed with one another for students.

In 1868, in tune with legislation, the government authorized allocations of money "to schools frequented by Indians." At this point the government funded 57 schools, only two of which were residential (Milloy, 1999: 52). Then the number of residential schools skyrocketed. In 1894 the government was funding 45 residential schools, 11 of them in British Columbia. By 1923 there were 71 such schools, and at their peak in the 1930s there were as many as 80 of them in operation. Sixty-five of these schools were located west of Ontario. The Roman Catholic Church ran 44 schools, the Anglicans ran 21, the United Church of Canada ran 10, and the Presbyterians ran two. Other, less well-known denominations ran the remaining three schools.

Although educators and religious leaders perceived of permanent Indian settlements (reserves) as more conducive to effective assimilation-oriented education, reality dictated that the establishment of reserves would free up lands for settlement by incoming Europeans. The reserve arrangement was administratively convenient for governmental provision of services to Indians even though few industries were developed to sustain the Indian economy on reserves (Melling, 1967). Without a functional outlet for the skills attained through education a sense of hopelessness pervaded the Indian community, coupled with the realization that a "thorough" education implied a total lack of acknowledgement of traditional Indian culture. Despite these developments, the Indian people did not take quickly to attempted changes, neither did they acquiesce to dying out (Patterson, 1972).

One of the first tasks the new Canadian government set for itself was to arrange for the First Nations to sign treaties regarding Indian lands. With this out of the way the new nation hoped to determine her boundaries and get on with the business of governing the new territory. Ten major treaties were therefore signed with First Nations in western Canada. Treaty No. 1 was signed in Manitoba with the Peguis (Ojibway) First Nation in 1871, six more treaties were completed during the 1870s, and three more followed in the 1880s. In 1876 the federal government passed the Indian Act which formalized federal dealings with First Nations. The act also defined who was an Indian and gave government officials the authority to impose a form of elected local band governance on Indian reserves.

Treaty signing was basically a peaceful process even though many Indian leaders were not pleased with the terms presented. Some bargained for a better deal while others gave in for the sake of peace. The content of the treaties basically pertained to lands given up, the assignment of reserves, and the provision of tools, seed, farm animals and ammunition. It was agreed that the government would provide some form of schooling for Native youth, but its exact nature was not specified. As it turned out the schools were financed by government but operated by various religious organizations. The Canadian federal government authorized commissioner Nicholas Flood Davin, to initiate a report regarding industrial schools in the United States. These special schools had been established to teach Native American youth relevant trades. When Davin reported to the Canadian government he urged the development of a system of residential schools in Canada as a method of assimilating the First Nations. Davin recommended that Indian children be incarcerated in residential schools as soon as they were of school age. As he stated "if anything is to be done with the Indian, we must catch him very young" (Haig-Brown, 1993: 30).

Davin's objective for a system of Indian residential schools was twofold. First, he believed these schools would assist in depriving Aboriginal children of their simple Indian mythology by a "process of civilization." The underlying pedagogical principle on which he built this objective was that one should not take away without substituting something positive. Davin sincerely believed that the Aboriginal people would be appreciative of what they were being taught as a substitute for traditional ways. The second aspect of Davin's objective was that residential schools should be turned over to religious denominations in order to fulfil the need for teachers. He felt that though these teachers might be less qualified in terms of formal teacher training, because of their religious convictions they would work for less wages and thus save the government funds.

Prime Minister John A. Macdonald concurred with the Davin Report even though he believed that a secular foundation for public education was the best approach. When it came to the First Nations, however, he was of the opinion that the primary objective should be to help them become "civilized" men and women and this could best be achieved through religious instruction. Residential schools could function to achieve this goal in two ways; first, they would remove Aboriginal children from the negative influences of their parents, and second, church-trained teachers could teach the children Christian virtues (Miller, 1997: 103).

The Laurier Liberal government succeeded the Macdonald Tories and Clifford Sifton, Minister of the Interior, automatically became General Superintendent of Indian Affairs. This was the practice of the time. In 1936 the Indian Affairs Department was transferred from the Department of the Interior to the Department of Mines and Resources. In 1950 it was shifted to the Department of Citizenship and Immigration and then in 1966 the Department of Indian Affairs and Northern Development was established. In any event, Sifton carried on the tradition of funding Indian schools and letting church denominations run them. Unfortunately, he also transferred the office of Commissioner of Indian Affairs from Regina to Ottawa, leaving the management of residential schools entirely in the hands of local administrators.

Sifton first appointed Frank Pedley as Deputy Superintendent General, and Pedley was followed by Duncan Campbell Scott who held that office from 1913 to 1932. Scott was a true imperialist who believed that the British Empire was God's gift to mankind. It was his strong conviction that education would be the key by which to bring the First Nations into the 20th century. He entrusted this and other responsibilities to non-Native Indian agents whom he assigned to reserves and they were expected to obey his edicts. Although religious orders were in charge of schooling, they were expected to work hand in hand with the local Indian agent.

During both Macdonald and Laurier's reign, the campaign to make-over Indians became more pronounced. The arena of schooling was the obvious target, highlighted with the operation of a series of residential schools spread across the continent, aimed at turning Indian children into clones of European culture. The formal residential school period began in 1868 and ended in the 1980s. There is some disagreement among historians about exact closing dates since some residential schools were operated by local bands for a few years before their final closure.

A number of pre-20th century developments contributed to the ongoing problematic conditions of First Nations' education, primarily the signing of treaties and the development of the reserve system. The latter brought about permanent settlements for the Indian. With the demise of the buffalo by the mid-1880s, a radical shift in the Indian economy became a necessity. In the west, for example, it was expected that the buffalo economy would last until well into the 1890s but events moved too quickly. Even before the 20th century rang in, starvation and economic devastation were widespread among Plains Indians (Wuttunee, 1971; Dempsey, 1978).

Twentieth Century Developments

The first half of this century featured a fairly common pattern for Native education in Canada. Missionaries went about the work of "Christianizing, educating and civilizing," and generally trying to stir up enthusiasm for their cause among Indian parents and their children. Aboriginal parents were concerned about the loss of their culture through the assimilative efforts of federally-sponsored mission schools, and reacted strongly to what they perceived as a campaign to malign and denigrate their culture. They successfully sought to frustrate missionary efforts in the form of a high rate of absenteeism with the result that very few Aboriginal children graduated from elementary school.

The post-treaty era of 1921-1940 saw the perpetuation of the same assimilationist educational policy in Canadian Native education. Gradually government officials encouraged school administrators to continue to enroll Aboriginal children in their schools so that school enrollment figures rose from 3,000 in 1930 to 118,000 by 1940. Residential schools had a side benefit in that the arrangement made it easier to deal with health problems. For example, in 1936 when tuberculosis was virtually out of control, children in federal schools were targeted for health care while the rest of the Indian population could not be reached. Reports on Indian progress were mixed, ranging from outright condemnation to modest hope that the Aboriginals would valiantly bear the ordeal of contact with advanced European civilization. The next decade continued much in the same vein except that Indian people gradually began to organize and speak out against conditions regarding reserve education. Government reaction was to transfer administrative authority of Indian schools from religious organizations to the Federal Department of Indian Affairs and paralleled this action by phasing out residential schools.

Despite the best efforts of residential school educators, the two societal domains, Native and non-Native, continued to operate independently of one another. Aboriginal students who endured the system through the years to their time of leaving, in most cases still found it impossible to adjust to the outside social order. Moreover, they were often ill-equipped to deal with their own communities when they returned to them. In order to survive they formulated an artificial self when conditions required them to deal with both worlds simultaneously.

By the 1940s the handwriting was on the wall; the residential schools were not accomplishing what they were designed to do. In 1947 the shift in government policy was mandated in a paper entitled, "A plan to liquidate Canada's Indian problem in twenty-five years" (Pauls, 1984: 33). The scheme outlined a plan to transfer authority for the operation of Indian schools from federal to provincial governments, a stance which was later reiterated in the White Paper of 1969. Integration, rather than assimilation, was envisaged as the basis of the new policy except that it was to be one-way. First Nations students would interact with their non-Native peers who would influence Indian students with their dominant societal values. In the final analysis, Aboriginal children were still expected to absorb the values of European culture (Allison, 1983: 119). The "Indian problem" remained unresolved, and the economic gap between Aboriginal peoples and other Canadians had not been eliminated. Before another line of attack was devised, however, plans were made to turn over administration of residential schools directly into the hands of government bureaucrats instead of religious leaders.

The process of transferring administration of residential schools to secular control began in 1949. That year a Special Joint Committee of the Senate and the House of Commons recommended that wherever possible Indian children should be educated in integrated schools. The bottom line was that education following the traditional European format was still perceived as the vehicle by which the assimilation of First Nations could come about (Hawthorn, 1967). At most Aboriginal parents would be invited to sit on advisory boards, but not have an official voice in determining either educational policy-making or school procedure. Integration in this mode was to be the order of the day. By 1970, Indian opposition peaked, and the Indigenous people made it clear that they were serious about wanting to control the education of their children. This determination continues to this day. Successive, minor changes in government attitude have illustrated that such a format will indicate a significant directional change for Canada's First Nations. In the meantime, it will be difficult for Aboriginal People to offset the inertia of several centuries of attempted assimilationist thrusts forced at them by sometimes well-meaning pedagogues backed by government funds and policies.

The decline of residential schools began in the 1950s, basically at the time that the government began to increase its involvement in Native education (King, 1967: 87). Administrative control of the schools was taken away from religious bodies and assigned to civil servants. Simultaneously, in line with the North American Indian renaissance movement which motivated many First Nations to question government policies (Lincoln, 1985), Aboriginal parents began protesting school operations. It took more than a century of resistance to religious and cultural indoctrination before First Nations forcefully expressed that they were very unhappy with the arrangement. One of the primary arms of the cultural renaissance movement was to try to halt the assimilationist thrust of the school. Since then the campaign has increasingly been fortified by an ever intensifying spiritual and cultural resurgence of traditional ways. The magnitude of this movement is difficult for outsiders to comprehend or assess, but its future impact is unmistakable and easy to underestimate.

When the Native resistance movement first began its principal speakers were often Aboriginals who had been educated in residential schools and who knew first-hand what they were talking about. In 1970, following a successful experiment in local control on the Navajo Reservation at Rough Rock, Arizona, a group of protesting Aboriginal parents at St. Paul, Alberta, took charge of their own school. This event significantly changed the face of Native education in Canada.

Life in Residential Schools

To begin with, occupants living in a residential school of necessity had to cope within a highly structured form of institutional life. Church-employed staff constituted the power structure and the ideological ethos of the school. Since their identity was theologically-derived (European style), it was inevitable that their view was to be regarded as having a higher authority than that of parents or students. The status of religious leaders was different than that of hired teachers, since these leaders made the rules. Even then, there was often disagreement about how children should be treated and how schools should be run. As King has pointed out (1967: 58), many teachers who worked in residential schools were ill-qualified to do so. Often they had only recently immigrated to Canada, and did not fully understand Canada's history or value system. Even more importantly, they knew little or nothing about the First Nations' way of life. At best they were only minimally-educated and came from lower socio-economic backgrounds, but they were armed with a strong sense of mission. If their mission was frustrated in any sense, the natural outlet for personal aggression was to target the children. Teachers also discovered that personnel in the upper administrative echelons were virtually inflexible and unmovable.

In residential schools the relationship between students and adults was basically set in a fixed mode of power structure. Students were forced to see adults as controllers of their fate. Because the children often did not know what the precise rules dictated (and there were rules about everything), students appeared to be uncertain and easily directed. No doubt this kind of socialization pattern greatly affected the students' decision-making abilities in later life. Grant (1996: 89) argues that the intent of residential school education was never to fully educate Indian youngsters because if they were too well prepared they would become a threat to dominant society. Barman (1986) supports this observation and suggests that non-Native Canadians never wanted young Aboriginals to enter their socio-economic order, even at the bottom rung because they feared the Indigenous people might be successful. This implies that if Indian youth triumphed by surviving residential school, they would face additional road-blocks and discrimination ahead. The bottom line was that Indian children were imprisoned on the pretext of educating them, while in reality their potential to develop fully as members of either Native or non-Native society was squelched.

Daily Schedules

Daily activities in a residential school were quite crude and very public. Initially the huge brick buildings had sealed windows which often produced a foul smell or rank odor, and no doubt contributed towards the spread of diseases. Grant (1996: 123) cites one school in which 26 of the boys were bedwetters. When it was discovered that fresh air might be a solution to dormitory odors, the other extreme was practiced and the windows were left open at night. Thus the children often slept in what seemed like freezer compartments because of frigid air invading their rooms.

Bathing was done in groups, with the younger students bathing first. The water was often too hot when they started the ritual, but by the time the older students got their turn the water was cold and dirty. Calloway (1996: 14) notes that when the children arrived at residential school they were given new names to replace their traditional ones, stiff uniforms in place of their Native clothing, and haircuts. As if cutting the hair was not a sufficient form of insult to cultural adherents who revered long hair, students who ran away had their hair completely shorn. As one young female student put it:

> When I got back to school, because I ran away, they were going to give me punishment. So instead of strapping me, they said, "You got to kneel down on the floor, in front of everybody, and tell them you're sorry you ran away ...." Because I ran away, they said they were going to give me a real short haircut for my punishment. So my hair was cut really short, almost like a boy's. (Alice in Haig-Brown, 1993: 84)

Quality of food consumed was a common complaint with many former residents recalling long periods of time when they went hungry. Some students were driven to steal bread from the kitchen, but if they were caught their punishment was severe. Haig-Brown (1993: 99) indicates that sharing stolen food resulted in the development of a unique subculture. Stealing food was such a complex operation that it involved a number of participants, some to serve as look-out guards, others to engage in the act of stealing, and still others to distribute the goods.

In most schools, the staff ate better food than the children although there were exceptions. Food supplies were limited and portions were small. If the prospect of a second helping was feasible, students would wolf down their food as fast as possible in hopes of getting an additional helping. Later on parents were often aghast when they discovered the undisciplined eating habits of their offspring. Once downed, the food was seldom allowed to digest naturally for the condition of the children's bowels was another staff concern. Part of the daily routine was to administer a laxative to the children, many of whom really did not need it. Often the number of toilet pails provided was insufficient for the need. At times students would dare to use a nearby staff bathroom only to run the risk of being caught and severely punished.

On entering the residential school children were issued an annual supply of clothing and told they would get no additional items until the following year. If the youth outgrew certain items like shoes, or if the holes in them got too large, it was the students' problem. There were no additional issues. This policy seemed to apply to other areas as well, for example in the issuance of medical supplies. Many nuns and teachers were not trained in the area of health education, and they disdained the use of Aboriginal remedies, so they were ill-equipped to help when the children got sick. Unless hospital facilities were close by, children were treated in the school, a situation which often led to the spread of the illness. Extensive illnesses also led to death, although no one ever talked about this in the schools. Grant (1996: 133) reports that in 1928 in one school, 15 percent of the students died.

School Content

The curriculum of residential schools was primarily based on the four "R's"— readin', 'ritin' and 'rithmetic—plus large doses of religious instruction. Perley (1993: 123) notes that the latter was indubitably the most important of the four components. The range of subjects taught generally included reading, writing, grammar, composition, and art with specialized subjects such as farming and trades (blacksmithing) for boys. Girls were taught housekeeping, mending, knitting, and fancy work. Rote was a valued form of learning and students spent endless hours learning to feed-back the desired bits of knowledge. The flip-side of learning was to dismantle the children of any traditional Aboriginal ideas and concept they might be harboring in their minds. The use of Aboriginal languages was discouraged and students were severely punished if they were caught speaking their mother tongues. There were never any references made at any time to the history or cultures of First Nations. These were completely ignored. Music and songs taught reflected only the themes of English and French societies, and later on those of the new dominant society. Academic achievement was low, based partially on the fact that teachers had low expectations of students and many teachers were ill-prepared to teach. When students later transferred to provincial schools for high school training they were often ashamed of their poor records. Truly the basis of the system was inadequate, demeaning, and dehumanizing, as may be substantiated by the practice in some schools of referring to students only by their assigned numbers instead of using their names. Small wonder that less than three percent of those children attending residential schools ever graduated from high school.

The question often arises, "Why did Indigenous parents even consider enrolling their children in such a dreadful environment?" The answer is not singularly dimensional because the publicity about residential schools was not always straightforward. In Canada, for the most part, parents did not have a choice. Members of the Royal Canadian Mounted Police came to their homes and took the children away. There were some parents who sent their children to residential schools because they believed that the schools were the "only way to salvation," having been given such information by religious personnel. Other parents, who were having a difficult time supporting their families because of changing economic conditions grudgingly released their children with the hopes that they would have a better chance because of the promised enhanced skills they would learn in school. Ellis (1996: 779) suggests that some parents gave up their children in order to gain points with the local Indian agent; by coming on side with his recommendations they hoped to be more favorably done by in terms of gaining needed supplies.

Despite the grievous nature of happenings in the residential milieu a small number of former residential dwellers managed to hold onto a workable form of self-esteem and today they are able to communicate effectively about the current needs in First Nations' education. Perhaps they learned too well, what was being taught so that government and church leaders got more than they bargained for. These individuals are now able clearly to articulate in language which bureaucrats can understand how to compensate for the years of cruelty and neglect which First Nations in Canada have suffered at their hands.

Grant (1996) catalogues the negative results of the residential school phenomenon to include an inability to express feelings, apathy and unwillingness to work, values confusion and culture shock, anti-religious attitudes, and long-term negative impact on succeeding generations. Many former inmates, unable to rid themselves of the unhappy tendencies which they witnessed and experienced at the hands of the staff and teachers, by modelling simply passed them on to their children. Their behavior in parenting much resembled that of their own caregivers in residential schools.

When the residential schools began closing down, a number of them were modified to suit other purposes. Several of them were managed for a few years by committees and school boards established by First Nations themselves. In 1995, for example, six residential schools in Saskatchewan were operating under Native management. Several former residential schools that were not demolished were converted into cultural centres, adult learning centres, or private schools, but many were simply demolished. When the administration of these schools was transferred to Native control, the influence of Indian input was quickly evident. Gradually, First Nations' influence had won out over past EuroCanadian domination. For example, when the final closing exercises of several residential schools transpired in the 1980s (for example, Qu'Appelle Indian Residential School in Saskatchewan), Native dancing and social events took precedence over denominational activities (Gresko, 1986: 89).

The largest residential school on the prairies was located at Lebret, Saskatchewan, and enrolled 350 children. At community request it was demolished in 1999. As a local Aboriginal resident stated to the author, "It's not so much a matter of anticipated extensive expenses to keep the building going; the school has too many bad memories to remain standing."

The Aftermath

Researchers in Canada have identified three separate stages of Indian education prior to the First Nations' takeover of their schools (Haig-Brown, 1993). From about 1930 to 1945 religious denominations worked hand in hand with government in promoting education to keep Aboriginal children apart from dominant society in residential or day schools. The overarching atmosphere in these schools was paternalistic, protectionist, and isolationist. Then things changed, and from 1945 to 1960, partially due to protests from Aboriginal parents, government bureaucrats began to involve themselves increasingly in the operation of these schools (Littlebear, 1992). This was the second stage.

The third stage witnessed increased concern on the part of Indian parents who observed that the emphases of school curricula and program content were depriving their children of their cultural heritage and identity. They were devastated by the 94 percent drop-out rate of Indian students in Canada and bemoaned the lack of adequate role models. Their educational objectives for their children were sometimes phrased in this manner:

> Our aim is to effect a true sense of identity for ourselves by recognizing traditional values while simultaneously preparing ourselves to function effectively in the larger society. (Haig-Brown, 1993: 132)

When the residential school system was finally shut down, it did not signal an end to the ongoing struggle for cultural recognition and meaningful education for Native people. They still faced the perpetual challenge of not yielding to the subtle influence of assimilation. Assimilation takes on quite subversive forms. Even today, as the trend towards increasing involvement in local schooling on the part of First Nations continues, observers have to note with caution that it is a step on the right direction. However, those who are more optimistic believe that local governance of this institution will reinforce the needed components of cultural awareness and enhanced self-esteem, and lend political energy to the First Nations' campaign to reestablish themselves in the 21st century on this continent on their own terms.

Residential School Litigations

The residential school phenomenon will not go away. While only about 20 percent of First Nations children ever attended residential schools, many of them and/or their descendants are claiming sexual and/or physical abuse or cultural loss as a result of the experience. There are more than 6,000 cases before the courts, naming church denominations as well as government in their litigations. Anglican, Presbyterian, Roman Catholic, and United Churches now face significant costs which could bankrupt them if the Indian people are successful (Copley, 2002; Frank, 2000; Outerbridge, 2000; Wilson, 2000; Woodward, 2000).

So far the Anglican Church has been hit hardest by residential school litigations, shelling out as much as one hundred thousand dollars a month in legal fees. Their total costs to date for nine dioceses for this purpose have passed five million dollars, but observers suspect that only one percent of the winnings ever reaches the plaintiffs. One party found guilty is the Diocese of Cariboo in southeastern British Columbia which declared bankruptcy in 2001. The move affected 17 Anglican congregations in British Columbia's interior valley region (Copley, 2002: 31).

The resolution of residential school court cases is not always what it might appear to be. For example, on July 12, 2001, the Supreme Court of British Columbia authorized an award of half a million dollars to a group of six Aboriginal litigants for damages suffered because of their residential school experiences. Originally the group had asked for five million dollars, but when the bills were settled, it appeared doubtful that the litigants would receive any of the money. Their lawyers deducted 40 percent for their expenses, and when court costs were calculated, the prosecutors would "hardly see a dime of the awards" (*Calgary Herald*, April 14, 2001). The court ruled that in this case the United Church of Canada was 25 percent responsible for these crimes and the federal government was 75 percent responsible.

In an unexpected development, in December 2001, British Columbia Supreme Court Justice Bruce Cohen awarded an Aboriginal man identified only as EB the sum of $200,000 for sexual abuse he suffered as an eight-year old in the Christie Residential School on Meares Island. It was the highest award for such a case in the province's history. Christie Residential School was run by the Oblates and the offender, now deceased, had a previous murder conviction before he started working at the school as a baker. Central to the case was the claim that the church should have done a background check before hiring the man. Brian Savage of *The Alberta Native* News (January 2002: 7) quoted Chief Robert Joseph,

It's quite common to discover that the pedophiles who reigned throughout these schools moved from school to school. It's a clear pattern and there should have been a much more stringent background check of employees to make sure that young children were protected.

The encouraging results of this settlement could motivate many more. The number of cases before the courts could go as high as 15,000 or more since many as many as 90,000 children attended residential schools throughout the years that the system operated. The Oblates have appealed the decision of the British Columbia Supreme Court and are demanding that EB pay for their court costs.

Student Memories

In addition to laying claim to settlement funds for physical and sexual abuse, some Aboriginals are asking for damages pertaining to loss of language and culture (Hookimaw-Witt, 1998). The federal government seems reluctant to bargain in that area, choosing to define the issues in narrow terms. If interpreted on a wider scale, individual damages could go well beyond the parameters of residential school cases. However, court settlements, financial awards, and sometimes even personal counselling cannot eliminate the painful tragedy of young lives having been spoiled by preying perverts in the past. The following personal quotations give testimony to this sad fact.

> The "Graduates" of the "Ste. Anne's Residential School" era are now trying and often failing to come to grips with life as adults after being treated as children in an atmosphere of fear, loneliness and loathing. (Albany Chief in Milloy, 1999: 295).

> It will be difficult for many of us to talk about our experiences and how they affected our lives after we left the schools because of the simple fact that they bring back too many painful and unhappy memories. (Chief Bev Sellers in Furniss, 1995: 121)

> I was frustrated about how we were treated, humiliated, and degraded, so I drank and took drugs to numb the frustrations of how my life had turned out. (A. Collison in Hare and Barman, 2000: 342)

> I've lost a lot of friends. A quarter of them are dead, they couldn't stand it. They put me through seven years of hell for no reason—just because I was a Roman Catholic Indian. (Philip Michel in Grant, 1996: 247)
> But that is one of the things I want to stress; the lonely part of residential school life. The other things you can live through, like the food and the bad clothing and stuff like that. That's minor. But when it has to do with feel-

ings. That was something that I thought would never heal. I understand. I got through that a few years ago. (Dan Keshane in Miller, 1997: 342)

Hugs were something I never experienced in school. (Chief Phil Fontaine in Miller, 1997: 339)

Sometimes 1 get scared-scared for the children. Language takes my children away from me, that is why I am scared. They do not hear my words. When he throws his language away, that is when it starts. He makes fun of his father and mother, his grandfather and grandmother. (Alex Bonais in Ing, 1991: 81)

Despite these unfortunate experiences, the vitality and strength of the Aboriginal worldview is affirmed in the following testimony:
In retrospect there are times when I thank them [residential school teachers] ... because they put fight into me physically and mentally ... and having survived that, I think I can survive anything. (Charlie in Haig-Brown, 1993: 116)

The physical, mental, and spiritual strength inherent in this last quotation could be the spark by which to ignite a forest fire of a renewed Indigenous renaissance (Miller, 1987). Hopefully, non-Native Canadians will be sufficiently alert to heed it and work in tandem with Indigenous people to help them recover and build for the future.

REFERENCES

Allison, Derek (1983). "Fourth World Education in Canada and the Faltering Promise of Native Teacher Education," *Journal of Canadian Studies*, 24:2, 92-101

Barman, Jean (1986). Separate and Unequal: Indian and White Girls at All Hallow Schools, 1884-1920. *Indian Education in Canada, Vol. 1: The Legacy.* Jean Barman, Don McCaskill, Yvonne Hebert, eds. Vancouver: University of British Columbia Press, 110-131

Brookes, Sonia (1991). "The Persistence of Native Educational Policy in Canada." *The Cultural Maze: Complex Question on Native Destiny in Western Canada.* John W. Friesen, ed. Calgary: Detselig Enterprises, 163-180

Bull, Linda (1991). "Indian Residential Schooling: The Native Perspective," *Canadian Journal of Native Education*, 18: Supplement, 1-63

Calloway, Colin G. ed. (1996). Introduction. *Our Hearts Fell to the Ground: Plains Indian Views of How the West was Won.* New York: Bedford Books of St. Martin's Press, 1-20

Chalmers, John W. (1984). "Northland: The Founding of a Wilderness School System," *Canadian Journal of Native Education*, 12: 2, 2-45

Cooper, Michael L. (1999). *Indian Schooling: Teaching the White Man's Way*, New York: Clarion Books

Copley, John (2002). "Kamloops Church First to Close Over Lawsuits," *Alberta Native News*, 19:1, 31

Dempsey, Hugh A. (1991). "The Role of Native Cultures in Western History: *The Cultural Maze: Complex Question on Native Destiny in Western Canada*. John W. Friesen, ed. Calgary: Detselig Enterprises, 39-52

Dyck, Noel (1997). *Differing Vision: Administrating Indian Residential Schooling in Prince Albert, 1867-1995*. Halifax, Fernwood Publishing

Ellis, Clyde (1996). "Boarding School Life at the Kiowa-Comanche Agency," *The Historian*, 58:4, 777-784

Frank, Steven (2000). "Getting Angry over Native Rights," *Time*, 155:20, 16-23

Furniss, Elizabeth (1995). *Victims of Benevolence: The Dark Legacy of the Williams Lake Residential School*. Vancouver: Arsenal Pulp Press

Grant, Agnes (1996). *No End of Grief: Indian Residential Schools in Canada*. Winnipeg: Pemmican Publications

Haig-Brown, Celia (1993). *Resistance and Renewal: Surviving the Indian Residential School*. Vancouver: Tillacum Library

Hare, Jan and Barman, Jean (2000). "Aboriginal Education: Is There a Way Ahead? Vision of the Heart," *Canadian Aboriginal Issues*. Second Edition. David Long and Olive Patricia Dickason, eds. Toronto: Harcourt, 331-360

Hawthorn, H.B. (1996 and 1997). *Survey of Contemporary Indians of Canada*. Two Volumes, Ottawa: Indian Affairs Branch

Hookimaw-Witt, Jacqueline (1998). "Any Changes since Residential School?" *Canadian Journal of Native Education*, 22:2, 159-170

Ing, Rosalind (1991). "The Effects of Residential Schools on Native Child-Rearing Practices," *Canadian Journal of Native Education*. 18: Supplement, 65-118

King, A. Richard (1967). *The School at Mopass: A Problem of Identity*. New York: Holt, Rinehart & Winston

Knockwood, Isabelle (1994) *Out of the Depths: The Experience of Mi'kmaw Children at the Residential School at Shubenacadie, Nova Scotia*. Lockport NS: Roseway Publishing

Miller, J.R. (2000). *Skyscrapers Hide the Heavens: A History of Indian-White Relations in Canada*, 3rd Edition. Toronto: University of Toronto Press

Milloy, John (1999). *A National Crime: The Canadian Government and the Residential School System, 1879 to 1986*. Winnipeg: University of Manitoba Press

Outerbridge, Ian (2000). "Residential Schools: Finding a Way through the Debacle," *Fellowship Magazine*, 18:3, 4-7

Pauls, Syd (1984). "The Case of Band-controlled Schools," *Canadian Journal of Native Education*, 12:1, 31-37

Perley, David (1993). "Aboriginal Education in Canada as Internal Colonialism," *Canadian Journal of Native Education*, 20:1, 118-128

Ray, Arthur J. (1974). *Indians in the Fur Trade: Their Role as Trappers, Hunters, and Middlemen in the Lands Southwest of Hudson's Bay, 1660-1870*. Toronto: University of Toronto Press

Rogers, Edward S. (1994). "The Algonquian Farmers of Southern Ontario, 1830-1945," *Aboriginal Ontario: Historical Perspectives on the First Nations*. S. Rogers and Donald B. Smith, eds. Toronto: Dundurn Press, 122-166

Sealey, D. Bruce and Antoine Lussier (1975). *The Métis: Canada's Forgotten People*. Winnipeg: Manitoba Métis Federation Press

Surtees, R.J. (1969). "The Development of an Indian Reserve Policy in Canada," *Ontario Historical Society*. LXI, 897-899

Wilson, David (2000). "Residential Schools: History on Trial," *The United Church Observer*, 64:4, 28-31

Woodward, Joe (2000). "Caribou Bishop Cruickshank Speaks on the Need for Healing and Being Bankrupt," *Calgary Herald*, OS1O

Wuttenee, William (1971). *Ruffled Feathers: Indians in Canadian Society*. Calgary: Bell Books

*　*　*　*　*

Documents for Chapter Nine

The first document is a reprint of the educational demands of the Aboriginal Peoples of Ontario in 1971. In Document 35, John Taylor provides advice for non-Natives teaching on rural reserves. He offers concrete advice for non-Native teachers regarding how to adapt to the reserve environment and how to teach the Native children. Compare Native attitudes towards education as outlined in Document 34 with Taylor's ideas. Imagine that you are a Native elder on the local reserve school board that is preparing to hire a non-Native teacher. What questions would you ask of the applicants? Why do the Aboriginal Peoples consider Native history to be such an important subject?

34) NATIVE OPINIONS ON EDUCATION, 1971[1]

1. *Education*—Education is not the only key to a better tomorrow but it is a vital part of a total effort required to improve the lives of the native peoples. New schools, well equipped, well staffed, cannot alone combat lack of employment, poor housing, limited medical care, prejudice, lack of equality, a poor self-image—but must be a major part of a well co-ordinated and well-integrated attack on the ills facing the native peoples ... an attack which must be *with* and *not for* the people concerned.

2. An underlining factor missing from education is the *need for the native peoples to be recognized* as those who have a cultural identity, who belong to different nations (Cree, Ojibway, Six Nations, Delaware), who are alike and who are different—who have histories, who have a past, a present, and must have a future, who are not "just Indians." There is the need for the recognition of a history and a culture which belong to not just the native peoples, but belong to the people of this country—for this country, its history and its cultures began before 1492. Recognition for the cultural identity for each native person must be inherent in any educational program. This recognition must be evident in the classroom to help the child realize his own cultural identity, to grow in strength and security and security in his Indianness.

3. To be successful, education for native children must involve the parents of these children and those parents must have some responsibility for the education of their children. In some reserve communities, there are school committees, but the oldest have existed for only one generation of elementary school children—16 years. School committees not only do not exist on every reserve but lack powers of authority and responsibility. This must be changed. If bands are to have self-administration this must include education as well as roads, housing, welfare and water. The degree of success of children in schools reflects the degree of

involvement and the degree of responsibility of parents in the education of their children.

4. *The teachers* who work with Indian children should have the best of qualifications, should be ready and capable of change to meet the needs of the children relative to the child and his environment, must have knowledge and understanding of the community and of the people who are the community. Teachers should be oriented *before* they are sent into a native community. Any training given to teachers who are going into native communities must be such that it prepares them for these children .... It would be preferable if the teachers were of native descent but a good teacher will be accepted by children of any community if the teacher comes to help the child in his growth. Teachers going into native communities should be prepared to stay for two years if this is acceptable both to the teacher and the community. The people of the community should have involvement in the selection of the teachers who will be going into that community. The community must be prepared to welcome the teacher and to help her feel at home. Teachers often feel inadequate in a community where the culture is different. Because the teacher should understand the cultural differences, it is the responsibility of the community to help the teacher realize these differences.

5. *The curriculum* followed in any community includes the school, the programs, the texts, the courses, all that is needed and used to help a child to learn. The curriculum in a native community must be one of flexibility and relativity—it cannot be an urban non-native culture impressed on the child and his native culture.

The language of the classroom should be the language of the community. If the language of the community is a native language then the child should start school in his own language and at a later date (age 8 or 9) should begin in English. This will encourage the child and leave with him positive memories when he is a young adult whereby he will be strengthened in his cultural identity.

This means that the teacher should be fluent in the language of the community in which he will teach. There should be an opportunity in communities to encourage the learning to read and write in that native language, as well as the rediscovery by the young of their own language. This does not mean that English or French should not be taught but that English or French should not be taught at the expense of the native language of the children or of the community.

The printed matter in the classroom should be that which is relative and relevant to the people to this community. Books for the teaching of reading should be those which are meaningful to the children of an Indian community. The printed matter should include the use of both languages—the native and the English or French.

Items which should be included in the program include:

a) *Civics*—the governmental processes of the community chief, council, band, band clerk, superintendent, as well as the civics of the province and the nation. Other items such as the Indian Act, the Treaty and Treaties which directly or indirectly fit the community should be known and understood.
b) *The geography* of the local community and reserve should be a major item of study. The location of other native communities in the province and in Canada could form the basis of learning in which the child would learn to which nation the people of the communities belong. This would develop a link of knowledge and understanding of other groups, lands and nations.
c) *History* should include the story of the people, of that reserve, of that band, of that nation.
d) *The culture* should be taught in the school by the teacher and *with the co-operation and help of the people of the community*. This would include the native religions and art forms (dancing, chanting, drumming, crafts, painting, songs) and the value system of the people of that community.
e) *Human Relations* should be taught where by the child will learn of his and other native peoples, of white people, of the world beyond the native community.

6. *Schools for elementary children* should be at home in the native community. Small children should not be required to travel great distances to residential schools or to schools in an urban non-Indian community. *The secondary schools* in major centres should be prepared to receive the student coming more than should children be prepared to enter the high school. There should be involvement on the part of the secondary school staff with the housing and social accommodation of the student and not just with his academic role. There should be courses in Indian culture and language in secondary schools. Strong consideration should be given to the creation of a secondary school located in a native community to which native students may go and this secondary school would be equivalent to any secondary school in this province .... Serious thought should be given to the creation ... of a cultural *centre for native students* whereby they could attend and learn of their own culture by nation and by nations so that they could create a new expression based upon a knowledge and understanding of their inherited past. Urgent consideration must be given to providing educational opportunities to *young adults* who have dropped out of school and who wish to return; to *older adults* who want or need to upgrade their skills in reading, writing, mathematics, to the *old people* who wish to learn of the new and who wish to be of use in the teaching of the young. Those who return to education must be treated as adults and not as children.

7. The program called integration or joint school programs must be made into a program of bi-culturism at both the elementary and secondary schools where-

by the native student finds within the school that which says, "it is good to be an Indian;" which permits him to choose from both cultures; which permits him to choose the path along which he will develop as a person and as a student. This would include the teaching to non-native children of the culture of their native brothers and sisters ....

* * * * *

35) NON-NATIVE TEACHERS TEACHING IN NATIVE COMMUNITIES[2]

Presently in Canada hundreds, perhaps thousands, of non-Native teachers work on reserves. Each year, due to the high turnover of non-Native teachers, many more are hired and begin teaching in Native communities. Ninety per cent of Native children in this country will, at one time or another, be taught by a non-Native teacher, and many of these children will receive most of their education from non-Native teachers. The Native student's self-image, perception of Native/non-Native interaction, and chance of graduating will all be influenced by their non-Native teachers. The school itself will be affected; its atmosphere, vitality, and community support will be influenced by the non-Natives working there. The effect that the non-Native teacher has on a school and its students is obviously not beyond control. However, to direct that influence the educational authorities, school administrators, and teachers themselves must all be aware of the non-Native teacher's role in the school and community.

This chapter is based on my personal experiences while teaching at two band-operated schools in western Canada. During the first three years of my teaching, I gathered information not only from the two schools at which I taught but also from numerous other band-operated schools which I visited. In the course of these visits and several conferences and workshops, I verified my belief that my experiences were not isolated occurrences.

After a short period as a teacher, I realized that virtually no support or direction was available to new non-Native teachers on culturally appropriate teaching methods or materials. Furthermore, the school administration gave little thought to the role it wanted non-Native teachers to play in its school. It became readily apparent that the majority of teachers were unsure of their role both in and out of school. Non-Native teachers begin their job with little support or previous training, and the role they play is never directly discussed with the people for whom they work.

Teacher Motivation and Predisposition to Change

Non-Native teachers entering a reserve school should not simply begin teaching and let their role in the school be shaped by circumstance. The relationship they develop with students, other teachers, parents, and the community will greatly influence how they are perceived, and this will alter their effectiveness as teachers. Many, perhaps most, non-Native teachers accept teaching positions on reserves with the intention of completing a couple of years before landing the job they really want. Often non-Native teachers envision their time at a reserve school as an "interesting, learning experience." Non-Native teachers sometimes believe that if they can survive this experience, they can survive anything. They hope that these two or three years will equip them to gain employment in a community (usually a non-Native southern community) where they plan to settle permanently. This prelude to their career may also enable them to pay off a student loan or accumulate the down payment for a house. Still other non-Native teachers see teaching on a reserve as an adventure that they can relate to their children and grandchildren.

The above scenarios have one preconceived notion in common—the reserve school is a temporary station to achieve or begin to achieve personal goals. Of course, this is not as selfish as it sounds. As teachers fresh to the profession, these non-Native people may feel strongly committed to their pupils and will quite often invest a lot of themselves in their work. The difficulty does not lie in commitment but in the teachers' perception of their role as teachers.

It is fair to say that non-Native teachers generally perceive themselves as dedicated professionals. If I do my job well that is sufficient; I have satisfied my employer and myself and I have given the child good, caring instruction. A young single teacher began work in a band-run school on the prairies after completing a Master's degree. For three years this teacher gave excellent instruction to her students. She worked tirelessly, regularly working from six a.m. to six p.m. and half-days on Saturdays and Sundays. While she found the students difficult to teach, her dedication to their learning was questioned by none. This teacher lived in a teacherage right beside the school. She had no car and walked to school daily. Other than that she rarely left her apartment. She did not interact with the community and only visited one or two other non-Native teachers occasionally. She completely isolated herself from the community, even though it was very active socially.

The reason for her seclusion was risk avoidance. She once indicated that she did not feel safe going onto the reserve. She also stated that she did not want to do anything or be seen in places that the school board might regard as inappropriate. Perhaps she might have risked community involvement if this was to be her permanent community. However, this teacher, like so many others, simply saw reserve teaching as a prelude to her career in her chosen community. Risks can come in the form of friendships and ties. Why should she become part of a community she was probably going to leave forever?

This type of risk-taking became very real for me when I lost a close friend who lived on the reserve. He had died a tragic death from exposure and I remember thinking at his funeral how the other non-Native teacher, who chose to avoid risks, could not feel the pain I felt that day.

This particular teacher left the band school after three years. She returned home where a new car awaited her. My point is not to condemn the teacher—far from it, for she was an excellent teacher in many ways. My point is that her preconception of her role as a teacher at a band-run school limited what she could do while she was there. Interaction between non-Native teacher and community is important because it helps define how that community and its students perceive the teacher. Although few students express the thought openly, they are concerned about what their non-Native teacher thinks and feels about their reserve. They want their teacher to like and respect the community. Obvious isolation is interpreted by students as rejection of the community and, indirectly, of themselves. One student questioned this teacher's unwillingness to participate in the community and simply concluded that she did not like the place. A student needs to feel respected in order to give respect. Non-Native teachers will benefit by seeing the community in which they teach as their community; that is, the community in which they live. Participation in community daily life as well as major community events may cause the non-Native teacher to want to be part of reserve life and will, therefore, assist in establishing mutual respect between teacher and community.

However, if the initial involvement by the non-Native teacher is unpleasant, the teacher may withdraw and become negative. The reality is that the non-Native person may be met with hostility when attempting to enter the reserve's social milieu. On one occasion, a teacher went to a local bar whose clientele was largely Native. He became the focus of a Native customer's attention and abuse and was eventually attacked by him. He had to defend himself and leave the establishment.

Such incidents may lead non-Native teachers to view social interaction with the reserve as undesirable. Such stories often build up over the years and are passed down from year to year by non-Native staff members. These stories serve to deter socialization outside the circle of non-Native teachers. However, negative social experience does not have to result in avoidance of further community involvement. If it is understood that cross-cultural situations can and most likely will produce uncomfortable initial circumstances, the discomfort will not be as great. In this case the non-Native teacher will be more willing to attempt community participation a second time.

Most communities have several points of entry. The teacher needs to consider other, perhaps more suitable, avenues. Teachers' involvement will benefit their work and most likely their day-to-day lives. Each teacher is different and each should find a different way to participate in a community. The point is that the students and the community must know that you respect them and want to support them. In turn you may receive community support.

Culture Shock

For many non-Native teachers these simple suggestions are very hard to accept. The majority of non-Native teachers experience varying degrees of culture shock upon arriving at their jobs, and this shock may never leave them. Awareness of the concept of culture shock can make the adjustment easier. Culture shock is a state of mind. It occurs when a person is faced with an unfamiliar environment. The person no longer has the usual set of social stimuli to encourage appropriate behaviour. The result is often poor communication and strained relations.

One of my colleagues from eastern Canada was unhappy with life on the reserve. I asked her if she wanted to go home and her answer was "No, just anywhere else." This surprised and confused me. I told my friend from the community who was the Native Studies teacher, and he simply commented that it was culture shock. For this woman from eastern Canada, the reserve was frustratingly different from what she had experienced before. She had just left university and a very active life. As an outgoing and energetic person she was probably used to a great deal of socializing activity. She probably felt her social life had almost stopped and blamed this circumstance on the reserve. By saying 'anywhere else,' she expressed the perception that her discontent was not her fault. This is a very common reaction. To acknowledge that the fault might lie in her inability or unwillingness to adjust would have been difficult.

A similar example involved a non-Native couple who had been living on reserve for many years and continually found fault in the community around them. They would often verbalize their complaints to other non-Native teachers, expecting, and usually receiving, affirmation that certain things in the community were inadequate. These complaint sessions are what Berger and Luckman, in *The Social Construction of Reality*,[147] describe as "Legitimation or Universe-maintenance.' Legitimation is a process by which people justify their reality or their concepts of "the way things should be." Simply put, it is a method by which individuals convince themselves that their way is the right way. This process is necessary for people to protect their symbolic universe, which is a socially produced set of realities within which a group of people exist.

For five years this couple continued to plant flower beds around their house and find fault in others for not doing so. They simply could not accept that the particular community did not plant flower beds and that this was not a matter of right or wrong. Admission that the absence of flower beds was acceptable would threaten their reality, which had always included flower beds.

The male partner ran a student organization and was receiving very little parental support or involvement. Native parents generally hesitate, for obvious historical reasons, to become involved with schools. Adding to his difficulties was his failure to involve himself in the community and to get to know people and parents. Faced with minimal support from parents, the teacher was unable to refrain from passing judgment. He lashed out at the students in an assembly, asking, "What is wrong with your parents?" The result of his not understanding his role as a non-Native teacher and of not nurturing his position in the community was painfully clear. This teacher's expression of frustration offended Native staff members and struck a blow at the students' self-image. It is an established educational principle that developing a positive self-image in students is important. In a Native community it is even more so. Many of these students are struggling with their identity and that identity should be a positive one. Students have to contend with prejudice, stereotypes, and lower standards of living, which affect their self-image. A non-Native teacher can either affirm or help to offset many of these negative influences.

The role of a teacher is complex and multilayered. The role of a non-Native teacher in a Native community is even more complex given the unique situation on reserves. The reserve presents the non-Native teacher with a different culture and different sets of cultural values and behaviour. The non-Native teacher's role is also more complex because the Native student faces more complex difficulties. The Native student must deal with such challenges as lack of parental involvement, multiple social problems, an unstable teaching population, and a general lack of resources. Acceptance of and interest in the student's community and way of life should provide the non-Native teacher with a better understanding of the student's difficulties ....

The non-Native teachers wanted things to conform to their past experiences. They could not understand a different society and culture. This is a manifestation of culture shock. This is why they stuck together and did not enter their new community. To enter the community would be to accept it and to accept it would be to reject their own quite different pasts. Instead, the non-Native teacher simply tries to survive for two or three years in this "crazy place."

One non-Native teacher was speaking about a non-Native colleague who had been in the community two years longer than her and who was planning to leave. The first teacher said, "I don't blame her for wanting to leave, she must want to get on with her life. It must be hard for her being alone here. I would have gone crazy by now if my husband wasn't here. Well maybe not, because Pat and Sarah and Becky are here." This teacher regarded herself as isolated within the community. She also saw the other teacher as alone even though there were 1,000 people living around her. She felt her sanity was intact only because her husband and other non-Native teachers were there to support her or, as Berger and Luckman would say, to help her maintain her universe.[148]

To be successful, non-Native teachers entering Native communities must do so with an open mind, aware that life will be different and that different and new ways do not have to be threatening. With this acceptance, involvement in the life of the community becomes possible....

Student Views of the Non-Native Teacher's Role

As discussed earlier, it is important for students to see that the teacher accepts and takes part in their community. This is particularly true of the junior/senior high school student. Primary/elementary school students are not sufficiently aware of the world to gauge their teacher's acceptance of and involvement in their community. However, they are still affected by their teacher's feelings and beliefs about the community. Lack of acceptance by the non-Native teacher of the student's community will very likely impair the effectiveness of learning.

Part of the difficulty lies in incompatible perceptions of the teacher's role. Non-Native teachers often come from large communities to teach on a reserve and do not see community involvement as part of their role as teachers. This role they see as school-centred, so that involvement in activities outside the classroom is not an issue for them. For many non-Native teachers their personal experience as students would have included little or no social contact with their teachers. The Native student perceives the role of the teacher more holistically. On one occasion, I told a student of my plans to travel to the neighbouring province for the weekend. He surprised me by asking if he could come along. For him the request was not at all unusual and demonstrated his view of what my role as a teacher entailed. For non-Native teachers this request might seem aggressive and the idea of such a joint trip inappropriate.

If a non-Native teacher harbours negative or, at best, neutral feelings towards the community, it is difficult for the teacher to keep them from students. The students either consciously or subconsciously detect the teacher's unwillingness to participate in reserve life. Many non-Native teachers on reserves who dislike the communities they work with continue to work there for various reasons. The students are less likely to respond to this type of teacher. There is little basis for trust between teacher and student and therefore a weak basis for teaching. Students rarely explain the reasons for the lack of trust; instead they simply refuse to work with the teacher. The excuse given by the student may be something as simple as "she's/he's a jerk." Often students will not say more because they may simply not understand why they dislike the teacher ....

It is common for non-Native teachers to find one or more of their students reaching out and trying to establish friendships. In many cases the student's home or social life is such that he/she longs for friends, a "big brother or sister" to look to for advice and companionship. As explained earlier, any involvement in the community carries elements of risk, and someone may become jealous or upset at this friendship. However, a student who reaches out should never be denied. This is an opportunity to help a student and build a relationship in which the teacher as a friend can ask the student to achieve and excel. Obviously life is not always so simple and straightforward, but this is an effective approach which, while it may not ensure success, will enhance the chances of it.

Native Curriculum Content

The use of Native content in the curriculum is another way for non-Native teachers to develop a positive relationship with students. While it is fully recognized that Native content is not only desirable but also necessary for effective teaching and learning in reserve schools, this goal has not been fully achieved. Many non-Native teachers feel that time spent on Native content materials is time spent poorly because they are prevented from achieving their goals for the year and students are prevented from accumulating the required academic knowledge by year's end. Some non-Native teachers do include Native content but give it only a small amount of time in their anxiety to move on to the "important" material.

Part of the reason for excluding or glossing over Native content is because many non-Native teachers are uncomfortable with the material. They find it difficult to understand or relate to materials dealing with Native people and therefore avoid the discomfort. Also the non-Native teacher does not see the value in the material because it was never part of their own training. Once non-Native teachers recognize the worth of the material they will be more likely to take on the challenge of presenting it.

Native content is usually foreign to the non-Native teacher. First, teachers must locate and familiarize themselves with the material. Second, they must decide on an appropriate, effective way to present it. It is hard for the non-Native teacher to know what is appropriate and what is not. The real challenge, however, comes in presenting the material.

The non-Native teacher will receive varying levels of acceptance from students and parents. Quite often the students' immediate reaction to the presentation of Native material by non-Natives is discomfort and withdrawal. Their faces seem to say: "Why is this white person talking to us about Indians?" With time, some students relax and begin to participate but others continue to display displeasure. It is important to let students teach you what they know about the topic. Teachers may be more knowledgeable about a topic they have researched, but the student is dealing in life experiences and knows things that non-Native persons do not know. For example, I was discussing the high number of Native inmates in federal prisons with a class and presented several "textbook reasons" for this situation. One student told of a crime and the subsequent incarceration of a relative. The student was making his learning relevant to himself. Students must be allowed to discover their own levels of comfort in dealing with a topic which is essentially about themselves.

Many complications may arise in dealing with Native curriculum content, and these will vary from community to community. Non-Native teachers must be aware of the type of content appropriate to the community they are in. In one community school, discussion of anything to do with Native culture was known by everyone to be unacceptable. Pictures of eagles and teepees were considered appropriate but anything more was discouraged. Discussions of the sweat lodge or medicine wheel or sweet grass did not occur in that school. In fact the school was once closed down because of a confrontation between traditional and Christian people on the reserve. Today, Easter services are held in the gym and square dancing is encouraged in the cafeteria, but no drumming and sweet grass is allowed. Non-Native teachers may believe that more cultural teachings would benefit students but what they believe is irrelevant: their responsibility is to include Native content which is acceptable to the community. However, no community is homogeneous. Therefore, even appropriate Native content may still be met with resistance from some students and parents. Perhaps they wonder why more Native content is not being taught or why it is being taught at all. Providing satisfactory answers can be difficult ....

Conclusion

I was asked by the superintendent of a band-run school what I thought my role in his community was. I had been giving that exact question a lot of thought. It was then that I realized that he had been giving it a lot of thought as well. I knew that our concepts of my role would not be the same. In fact, other teachers, Native and non-Native, had ideas on where I fitted into the community. Administrators, parents, and students also had their own perception of what non-Native teachers were to the community and where they fitted in. Everyone's beliefs varied and everyone's reasons for those beliefs varied.

In the end, I had to decide what role I would play in that community. That decision was mine but it was not a decision taken in isolation. It is important that each non-Native teacher takes time to consider the role he or she will play in the Native community where he or she teaches. The multilayered dynamics require a great deal of ongoing consideration. Constant analysis and redefinition is required.

It is also essential that non-Native teachers are aware of the community and the culture where they teach and live. The more aware teachers are, the more effective they can be in their jobs. Increased awareness of community will lead to culturally appropriate teaching styles and materials.

Non-Native teachers should be responsible for educating themselves about the community, culturally appropriate content, and culturally appropriate teaching methods. However, more effective non-Native teaching on reserves could be more easily achieved through organized teacher education in cross-cultural teaching specific to Native people. Candidates would no doubt be difficult to obtain in large numbers. Part of the answer is training workshops for working non-Native teachers (and perhaps Native teachers) which aim at increasing their awareness of their roles and effective teaching styles.

One important area which has not been addressed is hiring. The people responsible for hiring need to give greater consideration to hiring people who are suitable for cross-cultural teaching. This is an important issue for each reserve school board. Most Native children will be taught by non-Native teachers. There have been many attempts to improve education for Canada's Native people. Yet little attention has been paid to improving training for the large non-Native teaching force which will continue to exist for a long time. When this issue is addressed by teacher education faculties, band school administrations, and by the teachers themselves the results should benefit Native students immensely.

*   *   *   *   *

1 "Education of the Native Peoples of Ontario," (Toronto: Union of Ontario Indians, 1971), pp. 4-7.
2 John Taylor, "Non-Native Teachers Teaching in Native Communities," in Marie Battiste, Jean Barman eds., *First Nations Education in Canada: The Circle Unfolds* (Vancouver: UBC Press, 1995), pp. 224-227, 238-241.
3 Peter L. Berger and Thomas Luckman, *The Social Construction of Reality* (New York: Doubleday 1966), 92.
4 *Ibid.*

Chapter Ten:
Growing Up: 1914–1960

Following a recent series of student strikes/boycotts in high schools from St. John's, Newfoundland, to northern Ontario, Ottawa's Board of Education Research Office surveyed students in 1970 to discover what their students wanted. Sixty-three percent of the 466 students responded to the opened-ended mail questionnaire. To the question "What was the best thing about the school you were in last year?" most students expressed satisfaction with their extra-curricular experiences in athletics, social events, clubs, and students' associations. To the question "What did you consider to be the most serious problem you and your fellow students encountered during the past year?" the most commonly mentioned topics were boredom with classes and the monotonous daily routine. The next most serious problems were the lack of communication between teachers and students and the arbitrary exercise of authority.[117]

In the following article, "Children in 'Formalist' Schools," a chapter from Neil Sutherland's ground-breaking book, *Growing Up: Childhood in English Canada from the Great War to the Age of Television*, the author used open-ended interviews with individuals born between 1919 and 1960 to recreate the sights, sounds, smells, discipline, teaching pedagogy, and daily routine of the typical Canadian classroom between 1920 and the 1960s. In keeping with Sutherland's child-orientated perspective, Document 37 surveys the opinions of Atlantic Canada's grade 8 students about school life in the mid-1990s. Document 36, "Youth Challenges the Educators," reveals the attitudes of young people between 15 and 24 years of age to questions about their school experiences. The Canadian Youth Commission, which conducted this survey, was established in 1943 to evaluate the problems youth would experience at the conclusion of the Second World War.

Other useful sources include: Neil Sutherland, "'The Triumph of "Formalism': Elementary School in Vancouver from the 1920s to the 1960s," *BC Studies*, nos. 69-70 (Spring-Summer, 1986); Rebecca Priegert Coulter, "Schooling, Work and Life: Reflections of the Young in the 1940s," in *Rethinking Vocationalism: Whose Work/Life Is It?*, Rebecca Priegert Coulter, Ivor F. Goodson, eds. (Toronto, 1993); Linda M. Ambrose, "Collecting Youth Opinion: The Research of the Canadian Youth Commission, 1943-1945," in *Dimensions of Childhood: Essays on the History of Children and Youth in Canada*, eds. Russell Smandych, Gordon Dodds, Alvin Esau (Winnipeg, 1991); a more recent national survey of youth may be found in Donald Posterski, Reginald Bibby, *Canada's Youth "Ready for Today": A Comprehensive Survey of 15-24 Years Olds* (Ottawa, 1988).

Children in "Formalist" Schools[118]

Of the three central elements in adult memories of childhood—family, friends, and school—those of school display the greatest amount of consistency from one person to the next. Whether as children they loved, hated, or were indifferent to school, they described in interviews and memoirs a structure and set of classroom scripts that, over the whole of these years, were characterized by a remarkable degree of similarity from school to school, from place to place, and from public to separate and parochial systems. That structure, in turn, was a product of a mode of thinking about schooling that its critics came to refer to as "formalism." Advocates of this theory believed that education consisted of training such 'faculties' of the mind as memory and reasoning because such training generalized itself. Studying algebra and formal grammar, for example, trained reasoning ability. Acquiring competence in these subjects also enabled one to apply reasoning to actual situations throughout life.

While formalist pedagogy assumed a much more elaborate form in large urban schools than it did in small rural ones, it characterized the latter as much as it did the former.[1] Although I refer to rural schools in what follows, I lay out formalist schooling as it elaborated itself in an urban elementary school that I have assembled out of the memories of those who attended such schools in Vancouver and other parts of Canada.[2] There I follow the pupils through their day, their week, and their school year, describing how their teachers taught and what they learned. Next, I explain how the school ensured its "peace, order, and good government." Finally, I show how schooling extended, reinforced, or countered notions of self-identity begun in family and extended in congregation and culture of childhood.

Most children starting school were initiated into its ways long before they arrived for their first day. Parents, brothers and sisters, playmates, and older children helped to craft in the preschool child expectations of a traditional sort of schooling. The characteristics of the teachers, the rituals of discipline, and the content of the curriculum were part of the lore of childhood. On a bright summer day, a brother, a sister, or an older playmate had taken the prospective beginner to the schoolyard. Together they had climbed the fire escape to peer into the shadowed classrooms; the neophyte heard exaggerated tales of "rubber nose," or "weasel mouth," or "Pussy Foot," or "Dynamite Dunsie," or "the strap," or "Mr Robb," who cast so all-pervasive an aura over the school of which he was the principal that in the minds of some pupils he and his school almost merged together as one being.

Some children were afraid to start school, and often remained frightened by it throughout the whole of their school careers. They knew about events which gave a grim touch of reality to apocryphal lore—of the boy from down the lane who was strapped for throwing a spitball, of a girl who had a rash brought on by fear of physical-education classes, of another child's stomach cramps before each weekly spelling test, of a sister's outburst of tears when a page of her exercise book had been ripped out by her teacher. They expected such things to happen to them, too. Those whose families moved occasionally or frequently had to go through the ritual of "starting to school" a number of times.

Most beginners were only partly taken in by ritual tales of "horrors" ahead. They recalled the carefree departures of friends and neighbours to school as recently as the previous June, and themselves set off in the same way; typically, most children were "very excited about school." Although some people have few memories of the early years of their schooling, few have forgotten the excitement of the very first day: "I could smell how clean my clothes were that day." Most departed for their first day with their mothers or an older sibling. ("The first day arrived and my mother escorted me to school that morning;" "My mother took me up there and that was all there was to it.") As she went with her sister to her first day in Bonavista, Newfoundland, Jessie Mifflen repeated "the first page of the Primer over and over ... for no respectable child ever started school without having learned all the letters of the alphabet and without knowing the first page of the Primer by heart."[3]

Other first-day memories are equally vivid but less pleasant. On his first day in a rural school in Ontario, Roy Bonisteel and the other Grade Ones were strapped, the teacher explaining, "This is to get you started out on the right foot."[4] "I remember wetting my pants on the first day of school," noted one woman. "I was very upset and went back home ... After lunch my mother took me back and my teacher was very kind to me and let me carry around the waste-basket to help her." Some children insisted that their mothers accompany them for the first few days and, very occasionally, the first few weeks. Some, even among those who were really keen to go to school, cried when their mothers left them on the first day.

However they came and whatever their expectations of how the school would be ordered, most beginners shared one very clear idea of what they would do in school. They were going to learn to read. Even after a half-century or more, many can recall stories, such as "Chicken Little," and even phrases and sentences such as "A" says "ah" like in apple'; "pretty pink ice cream from a pretty pink glass;" "Cut, cut, cut," said the King'; "I am a boy. My name is Jerry;" and "See Spot run," which were among the first that they decoded.[5] Older children also had a clear idea of the purpose of schooling. Susan Eng, born in Toronto in the early 1950s, said, "School was fascinating for me ... I knew precisely what I was there for. I was to learn and I did what I was told and I got very good marks."[6]

Despite problems posed by periods of rapid growth, many Canadian cities provided substantial buildings to house their pupils.[7] In Cedar Cottage and Kerrisdale, Lord Selkirk and Kerrisdale schools stood out as the most impressive buildings in their neighbourhoods. The front of each presented its best side to the community; the buildings were set back behind low fences which protected lawns and shrubs. At about 8:00 o'clock each morning, the janitor or a monitor raised the flag in front of the school. Schools had a boys' entrance and a girls' entrance, generally at ground level. Behind the school lay the main playing field. Since intensive use made grass impossible, this part of the playground was usually covered with packed earth, gravel, or even cinders, which meant that those who fell on the playing field often tore their skin or pitted their knees. Those who attended Kerrisdale fondly recall the small clump of trees in one corner of the school ground.

Most children arrived at school well before the bell. As they did so, they joined in the complex culture of childhood, described in chapter 10 [of Sutherland's book, *Growing Up*]. There they also met the first symbol of the school's authority. The "duty" teacher circulated from field to field, sometimes carrying the brass bell by its clapper. If she taught one of the primary grades, she might have a small chain of girls attached to each hand. Unless they were one of those privileged youngsters—generally girls—who had minor housekeeping or administrative tasks to perform before school, pupils were not admitted to the corridors or classrooms before the bell.

There was a ritual to entering school. At about five to nine, those schools equipped with bell towers or electric bells sounded a warning ring. In other schools a senior pupil or a teacher circulated through the corridors and on the grounds, ringing the brass hand bell. At the bell, monitors collected the meagre ration of sports equipment. (In the late 1920s, South Park School in Victoria provided its boys "one softball and bat, one basketball, one rugby ball, and one soccer ball.")[8] Children moved rapidly to the inside or outside assembly point for their classes. There they lined up in pairs—girls in front, boys behind, younger children holding hands with their partners. Since the front was a much-coveted position, girls who wanted it reserved it by placing coats, lunch bags, or other possessions there, or even lined up well ahead of the bell to ensure their prime positions. One girl would "race to school so I could be the first in line to enter." At the bell, boys raced up and tussled either for first position behind the girls or for the very last position in the lines. The principal, vice-principal, or the duty teacher appeared and stared—or roared—the children into silence. He or she then signalled the classes one by one to march into the school.

Once inside, classes passed more or less silently along the corridors, some of which had a traffic line painted down the middle. Teachers stood vigilantly by the doors of their rooms. After the children entered their rooms, they placed their coats and lunches in the right place—some classes had dark, high-ceilinged cloakrooms which were often the scene of semi-silent scuffling, shin-hacking, and the like—and then moved to their desks. Those with problems in hearing or seeing—more did then than now—sat at the very front of the room. In the 1920s, some teachers still arranged their pupils according to their academic rank in the class, a practice that had generally disappeared by the 1950s.

Children entered classrooms that were dark and gloomy by today's standards. On the left-hand side of the room were windows that could be opened and closed. In most schools, freshly washed black slate chalkboards—on which white chalk was used—covered two, or even three, of the other sides of the room. In the new schools of the 1950s, the brighter fluorescent lights were installed, and yellow chalk was employed on green chalkboards. The floors were oiled wood or, later, tan-coloured "battleship" linoleum. The former gave off the characteristic odour of raw linseed oil.

Much of the board space was already full. The morning's seat work covered much of it, sometimes concealed by a rolled-down map of the world, British Empire in red, or of a Canada surrounded by Neilson's chocolate bars. On a side panel, the teacher or some favoured pupils had gently tapped chalk brushes on onionskin stencils to etch out a ghostly scene appropriate to the season—autumn leaves, or Santa Claus, or valentines—and filled it in with coloured chalk. Another space displayed the list of classroom monitors whose tasks included cleaning blackboards and chalk brushes (*never* on the wall of the school), operating the pencil sharpener, filling ink-wells from copper containers or glass bottles with delicate glass stems, watering plants, and so on. Beneath the monitors' names came the "detention" list, which, first thing in the morning, held only the names of those who had collected more of these punishments than they had yet been able to serve. Other lists showed those receiving milk, those who had bought war savings stamps, and other unofficial records. On one panel, a timetable dictated the regular pattern of the events of the day and of the week.

Portraits hung above the front boards. Over the years public schools displayed King George V and Queen Mary, and then George VI and Queen Elizabeth, and then Queen Elizabeth II. From 1927 onward in Vancouver, children also gazed at a lifeless copy of Robert Harris's *Fathers of Confederation*, that the Canadian Club had presented to schools in celebration of the fiftieth anniversary of Confederation. In 1940 it was joined by a coloured picture of the Union Jack, beneath which appeared the words:

"One Life One Fleet
One Flag One Throne
Tennyson" [9]

For children whose classrooms had one, as did that of E.A. Harris, "the clock was the main focus of attention at the front. The pendulum swung back and forth behind its little glass door, and the minute hand slowly, sometimes ever so slowly, edged its way around the dial's circumference in a series of sixty spasmodic jerks."[10] Above other boards hung such scenes of British prowess as the capture of Quebec, the Battle of Trafalgar, and the signing of the Magna Carta, and model alphabets, health posters, or murals created by the pupils.

Roman Catholic schools had a different display. A crucifix occupied the centre position above the front blackboard. In place of the monarch there was a picture of Pope Benedict XV, Pius XI, or Pius XII. Instead of political or military scenes, pictures showed events in the lives of Jesus or one of the saints. Otherwise, the classrooms contained the maps, the plants, the displays of children's work, and the piles of text and exercise books that characterized other schools.

Pupil desks, by the 1920s commonly individual rather than double ones (although the latter persisted in some places right through the 1950s), were generally screwed onto wooden runners. A metal ink-well or glass ink bottle sat in a hole that had been bored into the top right-hand corner of the slightly sloping desk. A pencil trough crossed the top of it. Beneath lay a shelf for storing pencil boxes, crayons, textbooks, and exercise (copy) books. On the days when the windows could not be opened, the characteristic classroom odour was particularly strong: on the one hand, Plasticine, sour paste, pencil shavings, orange peels in the waste-baskets, chalk dust, oiled floors, and dustbane; on the other, stale bodies and sweaty feet, occasionally enriched by "sneakers" or "fluffs." Characteristic sounds complemented these smells: steam radiators clanked, "blakeyed" toes and heels clattered down the aisles, chalk screeched on the blackboard, and bells divided the day into its segments.

Teachers began the day by calling the roll and marking the class register, a process repeated in the afternoon. In public schools in British Columbia in the 1920s and 1930s, some teachers followed roll call with a scriptural reading or biblical story, and then a prayer. From 1944 onward, British Columbia public-school teachers read, without introduction or comment, a prescribed selection from the King James version of the Bible. After the reading, the teacher said, "Class stand," paused for quiet, and the children recited "The Lord's Prayer" in unison.[11] In Catholic schools children took part in more elaborate morning devotions, and went once a week as a class to Mass.

Other routines followed the religious exercises. Teachers conducted a daily health inspection; they looked for nits, clean hands, clean nails, clean faces, combed hair, and possession of a handkerchief. Once a week they collected the milk money and, during the war, quarters for war savings stamps. They gave iodine tablets to whose who had paid a dime for a year's supply.[12] Pupils who aspired to be nurses, one recalled, "would count out the tablets with a tongue depressor onto a tray and then carry them around the room, pushing out each kid's with the depressor." Monitors gave out new pen nibs to those who needed them, from which children had to suck the thin coating of wax before they would hold ink. As these routines came to an end, the children took out their texts and exercise books for the first lesson. Many called the latter "scribblers," a practice that annoyed some teachers because it suggested slovenly work.

Whether pupils attended school cheerfully or apprehensively or in a state of fear, curriculum, teaching methods, and the pattern of school discipline combined to press them into the formal mode of learning. Its system was based on teachers talking and pupils listening, a system that discouraged independent thought, a system that provided little opportunity to be creative, a system that blamed rather than praised, a system that made no direct or purposed effort to build a sense of self-worth. Even those who enjoyed it then now recall a system that put its rigour into the rote learning of times tables, of spelling words, of the "Lady of the Lake," of the capes and bays of Canada, of "the twelve adverbial modifiers (of place, of reason, of time ...)," and of the Kings and Queens. "I can still name and date every monarch from Elizabeth the First to George the Sixth," boasted one man. Such rigour began early. While talking to a social worker about the problems her son was having in the first grade, "Donald's" mother described "with what tension he arrived home, took a piece of paper from his pocket to show her the words he got wrong that morning, begging her to help him. He was also worried about getting stars."[13]

Teachers in both rural and urban schools taught groups of children rather than individual youngsters. Of the former, Frances Fleming recalled, "Every morning work for each class was set out on the blackboards. Miss Warburton would start with the beginners and work her way across the room, teaching, marking, assigning."[14] In urban schools, the very size of classes made other forms of teaching and learning virtually impossible. In classes that, in Vancouver, for example, averaged for most of these years about forty pupils, teachers could not get to know much about their charges as individuals. Classes of this size forced them to teach to the whole class, to let the good look after themselves, and to let the weakest fall by the wayside. Their responsibility for so many children also forced many teachers to take a stance in their classrooms that emphasized children's weakness and propensity to err, to capitalize on their vulnerability, and to keep an extremely wary look out for bad behaviour. They tested their pupils' memories and evaluated their work habits; they commented freely on these and other characteristics of their pupils. In the jargon of a later era, they unashamedly ran "teacher-centred" classrooms. "I didn't think a thought in the whole of school," recalls one person with an excellent school record; "I just regurgitated."

Small-group teaching found its most extensive articulation in the teaching of reading. In the 1920s, a few teachers still taught reading as it was done in the nineteeth century: in one cryptic recollection, "Well, you had to learn your ABCs to know what it is about. Then you found out that the words were not what they meant." Most primary teachers, however, divided their pupils into reading groups roughly based on ability. In the 1920s, these groups were usually labelled by letter or number: thus, groups "A," "B," and "C," or "1," "2," or "3." Later, it became fashionable to name groups in ways that concealed ability designations: thus, "Bluebirds," "Robins," "Tony's," or "Pauline's" groups. Such euphemisms did not fool the children; they soon grasped the reality behind them.

Whatever they were called, primary reading groups went, in turn, to the front of the room, where they sat on little chairs or on the floor in a semicircle in front of their teacher. After the teacher conducted a "phonics" drill, she introduced and drilled the new words. Then, in what was often the highlight of the day, the children each read a short segment of the day's story; "I enjoyed it when it was my turn to read," recalled one; another explained that the dull repetition didn't matter at all because "learning to read was such a fabulous thing." One man recalled 'sitting in front of a giant-sized book and the teacher using a pointer for each word of Dick and Jane." After the Second World War, new readers with detailed guidebooks brought ability grouping and related practices to reading in the upper grades as well.

While one reading group worked with the teacher, the others did seat work at their desks. (One page of an unlined scribbler, completed in 1933, shows, in its owner's printing, "the cat sits on the rug;" "the rug is by the fire;" "the fire is warm;" followed by a coloured drawing of a cat, a fire, and a rug.) Some classes had library corners or "interest centres" or sand tables to which the children who had finished their seat work could go. Others had a dress-up box or a store where children quietly practised using money made from cardboard circles or milk-bottle tops. Intermediate-grade teachers encouraged those who had finished their work to move onto other tasks or to read library books.

Although the tone varied from room to room, the methods of teaching the whole class were remarkably consistent from teacher to teacher and subject to subject. Teachers began each lesson by reviewing what they had taught in the previous one. In arithmetic, teachers conducted individual or group drills of the number facts, or the times tables: "Daily we had arithmetic first; always drill, drill, drill, flash cards, flash cards;" "What a proud thing it was" to come first in an arithmetic race. Children also chanted drills of spelling words, or times tables, or number facts, or capitals of the provinces.

When teachers decided that the class was ready for the next segment of the topic, they instructed the pupils to put down pens, pencils, and rulers; to place their hands on their desks or behind their backs; and to "sit up straight and face the front." With all pupils' eyes on the blackboard, teachers then demonstrated, sometimes through question-and-answer, the letters for handwriting, the syllables in and the pronunciation of the new spelling words, or took the pupils a further step in the language, arithmetic, or grammar sequence. Then, some pupils moved eagerly and more moved reluctantly to work examples on the blackboard. The rest of the class was instructed to watch for mistakes. Teachers moved along the board, releasing those who had the correct answer or taking those in error through the question again. A man remembered a girl sent to work at the board "almost as a punishment;" the "teacher wouldn't let her sit down and she peed her pants. It was quite devastating."

In reading, history, geography, and science lessons, pupils often read sequentially from textbooks. Teachers broke into the sequence to read themselves, to "thrust a question at wandering minds," or to explicate some point in the text. Some teachers followed a regular and predictable pattern, up one row and down the next. Others, to keep pupils alert, "called out our names at random and we would respond immediately." In Franklin Horner School in Long Branch, Ontario, in the early 1930s, "Miss Healey ruled Third Book with an iron hand ... When one child was reading, the rest of us were required to follow word for word against the terrible moment that Miss Healey would point her finger and demand to know what the next word was. It was the strap if we were lost."[15]

In some classes, children were allowed to volunteer to read. Those who read well read long bits, and those who read badly short ones. "I could read with 'expression'," reported one woman, "but sometimes would say the wrong word, and would be embarrassed." Some teachers passed over really poor readers altogether, or had them read later while the class did seat work. Most pupils found these sessions boring. Those who read well had long since read ahead and mastered the content. Those who did not worried about getting through their own portion.

Terrified by the thought of public performance on their part, some children never volunteered an answer to a question, and avoided any other oral participation as much as they could. "In grade school," wrote Lynn Fiddes, "I lived in terror—not imagined terror, but real, physical, terror—that someone would try to talk to me, or, worse, that a teacher would call on me. Neither happened very often. Like most shy children, I became adept at being invisible."[16] Kathryn Furlong recalled herself as "sitting quietly at the back of the class, very studiously not bringing attention to myself ... I found it safer to withdraw. I had learned how to melt into the class. It was too scary to stand out."[17]

Teachers occasionally varied their routine in science classes by performing experiments for their pupils. In a format that was "progressive" in form rather than content, they laid out on the board what they were doing step by step, tackling a "problem" through a precisely prescribed sequence that led from a "plan" through "apparatus and materials," "method," "observations," to a "conclusion," the last sometimes written out even before the experiment was begun.[18] "We put some rocks in a glass container, poured some liquid over it, and it bubbled and stank," reported one man, while a woman recalled that "a match went out when you put it into carbon dioxide." Similar practical demonstrations characterized the introduction of something new in manual arts, manual training, and home economics.

Teachers closed the oral part of lessons by explaining and initiating the seat work which was to follow. Admonished to "keep between the lines," pupils wrote a couple of rows of "ovals," and other practice elements in handwriting. In the rooms of teachers who were writing "purists," pupils had to use H.B. MacLean's "whole arm" or "muscular movement" method of handwriting.[19] Pupils wrote a sentence to illustrate each of the spelling words or "syllabicated" the list. In primary classes children went to "number work" tables on which they manipulated such objects as blocks, pop or milk-bottle caps, or, later, Cuisinaire rods. They worked arithmetic questions that employed the new skill, or wrote out and "diagrammed" sentences in ways that showed understanding of the newest wrinkle in usage or parsing form. They wrote out dictated drills in arithmetic and spelling. They wrote friendly letters, business letters, and thank-you notes. They answered questions, *always* answered in sentences ("that were never to start with 'Because', or 'And', or 'But'"), that tested their comprehension of what they had read in their texts. They wrote short essays. One Grade Eight work sheet from the time instructed: "Study pages 94, 95, 96, 97, 98, and the first paragraph on page 99 and write ... a full account of Edward the III's reign ..."

In the upper grades, much seat work consisted of copying notes from the blackboard. Sometimes notes were so copious—"reams and reams" of them, covering board after board after board—that pupils groaned inwardly and sometimes outwardly at the sight of them, and even the recollection of them can still create a sinking feeling in some stomachs. One teacher "covered the blackboard with notes and that's how we learned English." Teachers often left blank spaces in the notes that pupils were to fill in by referring to the textbook.

Until schools permitted fountain pens and, later, ball-point ones, many found note-taking a difficult task. Straight pens with steel nibs that had to be dipped frequently in the ink-well and often blotted challenged everyone; they were particularly hard on those whose motor coordination was not very good, or whose teachers insisted on "muscular movement." "I had terrible coordination," remembered one man, "and wrote very poorly. When we did MacLean's I was even worse. There was ink from hell to breakfast."

Some teachers harassed the left-handed. "My sister was dragged to the back of the room by her hair and dunked in cold water," said one man. The teacher said, "Maybe that will teach you to write with your right hand." (It didn't.) When, in 1928, Hubert Smith entered South Park School in Grade Six, he was given special permission to remain left-handed. The principal, however, lamented, "I'll be the only principal in all of Victoria to have one of these in my school."[20] By the 1930s, British Columbia forbade teachers from making the left-handed changeover, but some teachers continued to do so right through the 1950s. For pseudo-theological reasons, many teachers in Catholic and other denominational schools forced right-handedness on all pupils, often employing corporal punishment as they did so.[21]

Pupils freed themselves from the bonds of these routines as best as they could. Some learned to talk to neighbours in such a way that they were rarely seen or heard, or to throw balls or wads of paper when the teacher was not looking. Some, as one person boasted, "mastered the skill of copying ... without ever needing to comprehend" and were thus able "to dream of outdoor matters while rarely missing a word." Others travelled to the lavatory or pencil sharpener as frequently as they felt they could get away with the practice. This latter activity was especially popular in classrooms where the sharpener was on the bookcase under a window; then one "could have a look out of the window." Many doubted that the period or the day or the week would ever come to an end. "Wednesday was usually the lowest point in the week," wrote Hugh Palmer. "By Thursday noon, however, I was ready to believe again that Saturday would really come."[22]

Pupils welcomed any small change in routine. They enjoyed health classes, in which they copied diagrams, and geography ones, in which they sketched or traced maps, recording on them the names of mountains, rivers, and cities, and then colouring the product. Occasionally pupils did history or geography "projects" on such topics as "British Columbia," or "totem poles," or the "Loyalists," or "Our New Allies, the Russians." Some recall making models, such as a fort in history class, using Plasticine and card paper, or crafting "a salt and flour map of Australia, and painting it." Most recall that they made butter in Grade One or Two: "We each took a turn shaking." One woman remembered her teacher's poetry lessons: "To this day, when I see a full moon on a windy night I still hear her reading 'the moon was a ghostly galleon tossed upon cloudy seas.'"

While the pupils worked, some teachers moved about the room, correcting questions, checking on the neatness of the work, and adding to explanations. They awarded gold, blue, and red stars or coloured stickers to those whose work reached a high standard. Other teachers increased the store of notes on the blackboard, erasing and adding new material to one panel after the other—sometimes more quickly than some pupils could copy—in what in many rooms became an endless sequence. Still others sat at or on their desks, or watched the children from a favourite position by a window. All regularly surveyed the class to ensure that heads were down, that no whispered conversations took place, and that no notes were passed. They acknowledged hands that were raised, answered questions, or permitted pupils to go to the pencil sharpener or the lavatory, one child at a time.

As the period drew to a close, teachers summarized the main points that they had tried to make in the lesson. They reminded the pupils of what was to be finished before the next period, they assigned even more material for homework, or they dispatched monitors to collect exercise books for marking. Over the course of the day, teachers collected many piles of scribblers.

Music, art, industrial arts, home economics, and physical education had welcome or unwelcome characteristics that made them different from the other subjects. First, children generally found classes in these subjects somewhat livelier than the others. Second, they often brought their competence to the classroom rather than learning it there. Finally, their competence, or lack of it, often made the children look upon them as either high or low points in the weekly routine.

Aside from a small amount of what was called "music appreciation"—that is, listening to a classical piece played by teacher or pupils, or on a phonograph record or school radio broadcast—most school music consisted of singing. Some teachers taught rudimentary music reading. William Macklon recalled, "our teachers drilled away at us until some of us ... could recite "Every good boy does fine" and "f-a-c-e" and stick'em on the lines in more or less the right places."[23] Classes began with vocal exercises using the tonic sol–fah scale. Pupils then sang such "ridiculous songs" as "Heart of Oak" and "Early One Morning" from Sir Ernest MacMillan's inaccurately titled *A Canadian Song Book*.[24] Some teachers could make this bill-of-fare enjoyable: "We had a good music program, with lots of British songs," one person recalled, and another remembered that her music teacher made it "so enjoyable we really wanted to sing for him." Other pupils enjoyed the variety provided by school music broadcasts.[25] Some youngsters, especially self-styled "crows," did not enjoy music very much but really disliked it only when they were asked to sing alone. A woman noted, "I couldn't carry a tune ... I was determined to do it, but I was no good."

In many schools teachers sorted out the best singers to prepare for the annual music festival, in Vancouver sponsored by the Kiwanis Club. Those selected to take part remember the festival as one of the "really great" days in the school year; we "got at a minimum a complete day off." Melinda McCracken, who grew up in Winnipeg, recalled that, on festival day there, children "would come to school squeaky clean, their hair shining, the runs in the girls' black stockings sewn up, the sleeves of their white shirts rolled down and buttoned, their ties neatly tied and their tunics pressed. The boys' hair was stuck down with water; they wore white shirts with ties."[26] A Halifax man whose class sang in festivals boasted: "We won the trophy three times in a row, so we kept it!"

In physical education, teachers concentrated on those who already could perform well. They paid less attention to basic skills than they did in reading and arithmetic. If the facilities were available and their parents had provided the "strip," pupils changed into white shirts, blue shorts for boys, tunics and bloomers for girls, and running shoes. If the class was conducted on a hardwood floor in a gymnasium or school auditorium, the school would insist on rubber-soled shoes as the minimum acceptable strip. There the class would line up in rows or teams and the teacher would take them through such exercises as "toe touching" and "astride jumping."

After these "physical jerks," as the children called them, the teacher would conduct activities that practised skills related to whatever sport was emphasized at the moment. In softball season, for example, pupils tossed balls back and forth, and practised batting and bunting, and teachers batted out "grounders" to be retrieved. The period then culminated in the playing of one or more games of softball. In some classes, teams would be picked to last over the season; in others, the best players were picked as captains each day and, as captains selected their teams, children received a finely honed demonstration of exactly how their peers evaluated their competence. Those who were picked towards the end still recall the sense of inadequacy, or even self-contempt, this system engendered. Sometimes, however, even the incompetent were lucky. One less-than-athletic student still has a "vivid recollection of when I was on third base and just reached out and caught the ball; what a fabulous feeling it was, just to catch a ball!"

Since the subject had neither text nor festival to ensure consistency, art programs differed more than most subjects from teacher to teacher and from school to school. Recollections of art in the primary grades focus on craft activities involving making such things as woven place-mats, bookmarks, and pen wipers out of burlap. Intermediate-grade pupils also sewed burlap, and measured, folded, and pasted cardboard, and sometimes made things out of soft wood. They also sketched still lifes, copied drawings illustrating perspective ("why a thing at the upper part of the page should *have* to be smaller than that at the bottom *always* mystified me"), made designs that "always involved a ruler," and did a variety of paintings.

Until the 1950s, tasks in art tended to be specific; there was "no freelancing at all," and "there was no freedom to draw what you wanted, so everyone [was] compared to each other." In painting many recall a misordered sequence that began with watercolours—in their "little Reeves tins"—in the early grades, and permitted only the most senior and capable to work with the easier-to-use poster paints. Some had art teachers who made the subject really exciting for the pupils; we did "all kinds of sketching, watercolours, poster paints; we put up big displays at one end of the school ground on sports day for our parents to see the work."

Most former pupils recall their home-economics and manual-training classes with pleasure. While children may not always have enjoyed these subjects, only really nasty teachers could make them actively dislike them. Those who had some practical bent often looked on them as the high point of the week and remain grateful for what they were taught. One man explained, "I figured out how many hours in the week and would count down to the time to go to carpentry." Of one teacher, a woman remembered, "She was fussy, and taught me to be fussy." Girls who had already learned some cooking or sewing at home sometimes became impatient at the slow pace of their classes, but they enjoyed the annual tea or "parade of fashion" at which they showed off their skills to their mothers. In industrial arts, one man remembered, "you got to make the occasional simple object that had a use ... So we did pencil boxes, simple stands for Mom's flower pots, some sort of wall bracket, etc. I remember spending five or six months alone remaking the lid to my pencil box until I managed one that fit snugly. Meanwhile more adept pupils finished small end tables in time for Mother's Day."

Beginning in the mid-1920s, some elementary schools made traditional classroom practices more efficient by "platooning."[27] In such "departmentalized" schools, pupils moved from room to room, some of which had special equipment, to visit specialist teachers, many of whom had some extra training leading to a provincial "specialist" certificate. Platooning also had its special set of routines. On the bell or, in those rooms in which the teacher regularly said, "The bell is for me, not for you," on his or her signal, the pupils would gather up their materials. The children then lined up in pairs to move from room to room. Although forbidden to talk in the corridors, pupils looked upon moves as pleasant breaks in the day. However, those moving to the rooms of the vicious fretted at what was ahead, and those leaving them were sometimes giddy with relief at having survived another day in their presence.

Friday brought variation in school routines. Pupils did the final draft of the week's writing exercise in their copy books or "compendiums." Teachers conducted the weekly tests. In language, pupils wrote out as exactly as they could—correctly spelled, punctuated, and capitalized, "with one mark off for each mistake from a total of ten"—the texts of such poems as "Silver," or "Sea-Fever" that they had memorized.[28] Some teachers then "read out the results of these weekly and other tests so all would know who came first and last." On those occasions, one Toronto woman remembered, "I hated the good spellers!" In the 1920s, test results could still lead to a shuffling of classroom seating based on how each pupil ranked. As a man from that era proudly recalled, "I had missed several days of schooling and when I came back I was right at the bottom ... So, anyways, this word came up and it came right down the line until it got to me and I answered correctly so I went to the top of the class!" Tests might be followed by spelling bees or games such as arithmetic baseball. Pupils in Catholic schools went to confession.

Friday afternoon brought a relaxation in the rigidity of the week's work. Teachers read stories or perhaps a chapter from *The Wind in the Willows*, or a novel by Sir Walter Scott or Charles Dickens, or a heroic account of the life of a saint—sessions recalled with special warmth. In an increasing number of schools, at least up to the 1950s, pupil officers conducted the weekly meeting of the Junior Red Cross, during which Maurice Hodgson (and likely many others) accepted as necessary "the need to care for others; not others like family or town or even country, but that truly nebulous "other" that encompasses the world."[29] In other schools, older pupils dispersed to a range of "clubs" for the last period of the day. "I enjoyed especially Grades Five and Six, perhaps because the principal and myself organized a successful stamp club," noted one man. "We had a lot of clubs," reported one woman: "stamp, science, chess, tennis, badminton, cooking, service, library; everyone had to belong to some organization, to learn to work with others."

Many schools marked the end of the week with a school assembly. After the pupils had filed, class by class, to their appropriate places, the principal or music teacher led the school in "O Canada." Two or three classes then presented items that they had prepared; a song that they would later sing in the music festival, a play taken from a reader, or some acrobatics learned in physical education. Sometimes assembly programs drew attention to talented individuals who would perform a dance, or recite an item learned in elocution lessons, or sing or play a classical piece: "The Foley kid played his violin a few times every year. He was really good." Classes that had had the best turn-out of parents at the previous Home and School or Parent-Teacher Association meeting received a banner. Those whose writing came up to standard were presented MacLean's writing certificates. ("Getting a MacLean's ... certificate was a big deal!") During the Second World War, the principal or a visitor would honour the classes which had bought the most war saving stamps, or collected the most metal or paper for the regular salvage drives. In some schools the pupils would all join together to sing a hymn, a patriotic song ("The Maple Leaf Forever!"; "There'll Always Be an England"), a Christmas carol, or a round such as "Row, row, row ...."

In nearly every school the penultimate item on the program was the principal's message: he—or, in a very few public schools, she—usually addressed some problem of school or community governance.[30] The principal explained that some pupils were "hanging around" too long after school, or that there was too much talking in the halls, or that there was too much fighting to and from school, or that the police were about to crack down on those who rode their bicycles on the sidewalk or who had not renewed their bicycle licences. Finally, the children all stood to sing "God Save the King" or "God Save the Queen," and then marched back to their classrooms.

Some events broke irregularly or infrequently into class and school routines. Pupils enjoyed those occasions when the teacher wandered, or was drawn from the subject under discussion. "The room hushed" because pupils did not want to break the thread. Some teachers recounted personal adventures or told war stories. ("He sure had an exciting time during the First War, or at least he told us he did!"; "He flew a Spitfire!") Others talked about their families; one told "about all the people in her family who had TB, and how terrible it was."

During outbreaks of such infectious diseases as measles, chicken pox, mumps, and scarlet fever, or during the seasonal visit of lice, the school nurse would inspect each of the pupils. Sometimes the teacher, or principal, or nurse would warn children about men hanging around the school grounds, admonishing them to go directly home after school and not talk to any strangers on the way. At other times individual children would be called out of class to visit the nurse, the school doctor, or the school dentist, or to attend a toxoid or vaccination clinic. Those who did well in school enjoyed receiving report cards and comparing them with friends before they took them home. Those who did badly met the occasion with bravado or tried to keep their results to themselves.

Among irregular interruptions, pupils particularly welcomed fire-drills: "Who knows, the school might really have been burning down!" They also enjoyed not only the events themselves, but also preparing for the music festival, for maypole dancing on May Day, for sports day, for a tea or fashion show in home economics, for a production of a play or operetta, and especially for the Christmas concert.[31] Those who attended one Vancouver elementary school in the 1930s remember the delight they took in their production of *The Mikado*. Valentine's Day sometimes brought a class party, but also the misery of those who received few if any valentines. ("She said, 'My mom made me bring one for everyone, that's why you got that card.'")

Occasionally, events outside of the school impinged on what went on in it. Influenza closed schools right across the country for some weeks in 1918, and a fuel shortage did so in Vancouver in 1943. Severe winter weather sometimes closed schools for a day or two. One interviewee recalls forming up to see the Prince of Wales in 1919, and giving him a cheer when he gave them the day off. Another remembers being urged to listen to the coronation of George VI on the radio, and making in class a little crown to wear while doing so. More remember how their school marked the Royal visit of 1939 or the visit of Princess Elizabeth and Prince Philip not long after their marriage. Some made scrapbooks of these events in their classes or learned to sing "Land of Hope and Glory." All classes went out to watch at the place assigned to their school, with great excitement, "as they whisked by" on their drives about the city.

During the Second World War, its major events were frequently discussed, or even more directly impinged on the classroom.[32] The war felt very real and very close to those who had relatives in the services, or who lived in such seaports as Montreal, Halifax, Sydney, St. John's, and, later, Prince Rupert and Vancouver. Sometimes teachers would explain that a classmate was away because a relative had been killed. In all parts of the country, pupils bought war savings stamps and knitted for the Red Cross. As one Powell River woman reported, "My dad made knitting needles for the whole Grade Three class and we knitted squares." In some schools that early casualty among the elements of the "new" education, the school garden, reappeared for a time as the "Victory garden." "We planted things that grew quickly;" pupils were supposed to persuade their parents to plant such gardens at home. Some school gardens had short-term and long-term effects: "I persuaded my parents to plant potatoes in our yard; ... to this day my hobby is vegetable gardening."

On a more frightening note, pupils practised what they would do in an air raid; in one school they went to the school basement, in another they filed out into the playground, where "the principal blew a whistle and we would all fall down." In another the principal gave a vivid description of just how bombers would destroy Vancouver in air raids. In a fourth the janitor added to the fear occasioned by a Japanese submarine shelling the lighthouse at Estevan Point, in June 1942, by telling the children it was "the beginning of the end." In St. John's, Helen Fogwill Porter reported, "We had regular air-raid drill on Thursday mornings in school and we had to bring tinned food to have it stored away in case we ever had to stay there."[33] In the 1950s, children learned about "fallout" and practised how to shelter from atomic blasts under their desks.

The ways in which pupils and teachers behaved towards each other were what bound them and the curriculum together to make a school. Thus recollections of what was taught, how it was taught, and who taught it led naturally into an elaboration of what is implicit therein about how elementary schools controlled their pupils, and how the pupils responded to that control. First, an overall observation. Discussions of what was "fair" and what was "unfair," usually initiated by informants themselves, often burn through with an intensity that belies the fact that the events discussed took place, not the day before, but sometimes four or more decades earlier. Here one must note that children seem to have been predisposed to accept the consequences of just about any code of conduct so long as the school administered it fairly. One teacher "was very annoyed and took four of us into the cloakroom, where she used the ruler on our knuckles. It was grossly unfair: she had watched a note go through the four people before she intervened." Another, by whom the pupils felt "cheated" and "betrayed," marked a set of tests without noting anything on the papers, returned them to the children to mark their own, asked the youngsters to call out their marks, and then excoriated those who had yielded to the temptation to pad.

One man, who believes that corporal punishment is a "beneficial" device and that schools would be better places if strapping were restored, "to this very day feels wrongly punished" on two out of the three occasions he was strapped. As a six-year-old child who emigrated to Canada in 1955, Mary di Michele had some "unpleasant encounters" before she became fluent in English. One day, "a nun dressed formally in black cloth and veil saw me standing quietly and waiting. For some reason ... the very sight of me sent her into a rage ... She dragged me into her class of senior students and strapped me soundly in front of the girls ... I discovered later that I had been standing in the wrong spot; the entrance to the school had been declared off-limits for the students ..."[34] Mass punishments were always considered unjust. Eric Adams recalled "one episode when two entire classes of boys, totalling about 80 children, some of whom had persisted in whispering during an assembly period, were lined up on the spot and 'slugged' once on each hand, I was one of them. I hadn't been whispering."[35]

People's recollections of teachers divide them into four rough categories. They give their highest rating to those teachers who emphasized fundamentals, who drilled frequently and tested often, who concentrated on having their pupils learn those things that both community and educational tradition told them were the "core" curriculum. These teachers knew their business and they taught this curriculum thoroughly and systematically. "Good" teachers also taught this curriculum in a particular way. They had dominant personalities. They conveyed a sense that what they did, and what they wanted their pupils to do, was of immense importance. They ran "no nonsense" classrooms in which routines were all-pervasive, and cast in a code that itemized many "thou shalt nots." Some pupils also knew that these were good teachers because "you *knew* you'd learned a thing. The evidence was there because you could *repeat* the learning accurately—even years later."

Good teachers often fare better in memory than they did at the time. In Powell River, one man reported, pupils "always shuddered when ... we got Miss Cedar. She was an old spinster ... but I thought she was the greatest thing. When you got out of her room, you knew you had spent a year of learning. No nonsense." Many former pupils reported that Anna B. Dunsmuir, who taught at Lord Selkirk School in Cedar Cottage from 1921 to 1950, was such a teacher. Colleen Wright Manness, for example, reported of her that "we all thought the world of her and were terrified of her. When we pleased her we felt like a million dollars. If we went back to the school, she was the one we went back to see. We loved her. We didn't know it then, though."[36]

Good teachers were also fair teachers. They dispensed their rebukes and punishments rarely, in an even-handed way, and in strict accordance with the rules. It was appropriate, it was fair, for these teachers to give special attention to the best pupils—to those who learned the rote packages, obeyed the rules meticulously, and did everything neatly—so long as these children did not receive blatant favouritism. Pupils also believed it was "fair" for teachers to ride herd on those who did not do their homework, or who were often unruly, and sometimes even on those who were not very bright, so long as the teachers did so without malice and so long as the breach in the rules was evident to all.

There is some objective evidence that such teachers had strong, positive, and lifelong effects on their pupils. One well-documented example was Iole Appugliese, who taught Grade One for thirty-four years in Montreal's Royal Arthur School, a Protestant school serving a working-class district. Pupils recalled that she gave them a "profound impression of the importance of schooling, and how one should stick to it"; that "she gave extra hours to the children who were slow learners"; a former colleague explained: "How did she teach? With a lot of love!" Although Grade One pupils in this school were randomly assigned to teachers, a far higher proportion of Miss Appugliese's former pupils eventually achieved higher adult status than did those of the school's other two Grade One teachers: of Miss Appugliese's, 64 per cent did so, of Miss "B's," 31 per cent, and of Miss "C's," only 10 per cent.[37]

A larger group of teachers were "nice." Such teachers are remembered less sharply, less vividly than the others; recollections of them tend to be enveloped in a pleasant haze. One was "always warm and friendly;" another was a "lovely person, an excellent teacher;" a third was 'a very quiet man; we kids thought he was really nice;" a fourth was "a very kind man, the first one who really challenged us; he made you think about things." When Geiri Johnson started school in 1927 near Hnausa, Manitoba, "it was a shock to both myself and the teacher that I knew only two English words—yes and no—... My teacher was Icelandic, and a very kind, understanding lady who ... kept me in while all the other kids played outside. She taught me the basics so I could learn school work."[38] In Elphinstone Elementary School on British Columbia's Sechelt Peninsula, in 1940, "Miss [Florence] Evans gave vitamin pills to a student who lived in a make-shift home where the meals were neither regular nor nutritious. She taught back exercises to a boy with round shoulders. She encouraged me with my written compositions."[39]

Such people apparently taught well and easily, they mothered or fathered their charges without all the elaborate apparatus that characterized the classroom of the "best" teachers. They did, however, use a pedagogy almost identical to that of their more overbearing colleagues. Of a Powell River teacher, one former pupil explained, "[He] was a good all-round teacher. You couldn't beat him. We could have fun, but you blinkin' well had to work ... If we started horsing around there would be a strap come down." Although few people remember them in this way, I suspect that they were probably as effective in carrying out the bread-and-butter tasks of teaching as were their more famous and martinet-like colleagues. (One person who had both kinds, however, argues that what the "nice" teacher taught didn't seem to have the same mental precision or self-evident value and worthiness as the product of the "good" teacher's efforts.)

If the above are memory's satisfactory elementary teachers, two other sorts also stand out. One was made up of teachers and principals who were mean, nasty, sarcastic, cruel, or even vicious. One woman recalled a teacher who called her, alternatively, "Dummy" and "Fatty;" another remembered a teacher who remarked, when he mispronounced a word in the reader or made some other mistake, "What else can you expect from bohunks?;" and another who described her classmate as a "filthy little pig" because she ate garlic. One teacher "plunked a kid in the waste-basket ... She said he smelt like garbage." There was also the teacher who "smiled when you stumbled, and then waited for the moment to pin the truth on you," another who announced that she was "sick and tired of calling out 'foreign' names," and a third who mocked those who stuttered until they cried. One of Cessie McLaren's teachers was "a churlish brute of a woman whose method for maintaining order was simple and effective—fear. Her humorless, disapproving demeanor bespoke the possiblity of unimaginable horrors inflicted with pointers, yardsticks or the inevitable 'strap' ... a length of leather that everyone knew lay coiled in her lower left-hand desk drawer."[40]

In the Depression, while most teachers were discreet, some drew attention to those on relief and in receipt of shoes, clothes, or school supplies. "Our school books were given to us because we were on relief," reported one man. "It was very embarrassing getting up in front of the class to get those books." When "Arlene" came to school without supplies, her teacher declared, "Oh, I know your family, they are all the same." This and other belittling remarks led to deep resentment on Arlene's part; she naively explained that the teacher "doesn't know my family. She has never met my mother and father."[41] On the really dark side, there were, as well, the principal who fondled girls and the school physician who sexually assaulted some of the boys. Such teachers usually employed a pedagogy that was not very different from that used by other teachers. They differed from their colleagues mostly in that, instead of being respected or liked by their pupils, they were feared and hated. Only in retrospect did these people achieve a dubious sort of merit; some former pupils gradually came to look upon the fact that they had "survived" these teachers as evidence that they had in their classes taken a major step towards adulthood.

Finally, pupils looked on a few teachers with contempt. These unfortunates displayed their ineffectiveness or their incompetence in a variety of ways. They could not explain things clearly. The oral parts of their lessons rambled and their notes were incoherent. They could not keep order; they sometimes broke down and wept. Some tried to bribe the children to behave with candy, or even money. While most disappeared in a year or less, a few persisted to become almost legendary objects to be scorned by class after class of pupils. Whether they stayed or left, they received no compassion or mercy from either pupils or parents.

Those who went to Catholic schools divided their teachers (usually sisters of a teaching order) into the same four groups. "We were terrified of the nuns," wrote Michael Enright, "as we had been taught to be terrified of religion. With their severely cut black robes, the starched wimples and leather belts with the rosaries hanging down, they were God's Amazons who would brook no deviation from their established orthodoxy. We ate fish or macaroni on Fridays because we would burn in hell forever if we ate meat."[42] On the other hand, one man said, "This one sister was like a second mother to us; even the bad kids really loved her." Of the nuns in his eastside Vancouver parochial school in the early 1940s, Ray Culos reported, "some of them were quite strict, and corporal punishment was a means of getting at you ... But they *did* help a group of young kids who might not have had the direction or the religious instruction that in all likelihood saved them [from] problems as they grew up."[43]

Two main themes characterize overall school discipline in this era. The first and dominant mode was that imposed by the school. It displayed itself in a continuum that at one end had the presence, the personality, the aura of the teachers and the principal, and, at the other, the strap and expulsion. School staffs held back the latent barbarism they perceived in the children with an increasingly severe range of sanctions that began with displeasure and ended with corporal punishment. Teachers joined parents, police, magistrates, and most other adults in justifying this range of measures by appealing to a very long-standing tradition; to the proverbial "Spare the rod and spoil the child." In Catholic schools, tradition held that discipline helped produce "perfect human beings according to the example and teaching of Christ." Thus bad behaviour was a sin as well as a crime.

The second mode saw some schools introducing a range of "progressive" practices through which the children were to learn "democratic self-control." Through a system of monitors, older and abler pupils joined teachers and principals in the task of teaching and maintaining appropriate standards, especially among the younger children. Democratic self-control, however, was tightly circumscribed by traditional disciplinary means, which were brought in these years to a peak of effective performance.

The presence of a seasoned teacher was clearly the first line of defence against barbarism. Teachers had presence; pupils, and their parents expected them to possess it. Teachers with this quality said, "Do this," and the children did it. All but ineffectual teachers exerted their personalities with more or less intensity on their pupils, and expected, and received, a reasonably automatic compliance with their directions. Even those who created a loving atmosphere in their classrooms did so in this broader context. The woman who now recalls that "I knew who the teacher was and did as I was told," speaks for her classmates as well as herself. Presence came with experience, but neophytes set out, self-consciously, to acquire it. Eighteen- and nineteen-year-olds stare at us from the Normal school annuals of these years with an intensity that makes them look older, more severe, and altogether more formidable than the much older beginning teachers of later years.[44]

Teachers used an armoury of sanctions to back up their demands that pupils meet certain standards of behaviour and work habits. They gave children "the ray." They gave them the cutting edge of their tongues; they spoke sharply; they made nasty, and sometimes sarcastic, remarks; they spoke more and more softly, coldly, ominously; they shouted, and even raged against their charges. ("She really lambasted us; she had a short fuse;" "I recall his scarlet face and his ferocious temper.") Many maintained full control solely through verbal means. Others made children sit or stand in a corner; they kept children in at recess, at lunch hour, and after school. One person recalls being kept in after school, asking to leave the room, being refused, and then wetting his pants: "I stayed away for three days." Teachers made pupils sit up straight, motionless, with hands behind their backs, for periods of time up to half an hour. They forced chewers to put their gum on the ends of their noses or behind their ears. As punishment, they gave extra work of an excruciatingly boring and valueless sort, such as eight- or nine-digit long-division questions and their proofs, the writing of lines—some wrote such things as "I will not chew gum," or "Silence is golden," five hundred to a thousand times—the copying of pages out of textbooks or dictionaries, and the memorization of poems.

Teachers assigned offenders to those classroom and school chores not popular with "monitors" such as picking up paper and other garbage in the school and on its grounds. In Burnaby in the late 1950s, Allan Safarik, instead of an expected strapping, "was to pick up garbage on the school ground every day after school for one week. I was thrilled ... I worked like a fiend ... Every now and then I would glance over my shoulder and see [the principal's] grey muzzle looking from an upstairs window."[45] Teachers sent offenders to school detention halls, where the duty teacher or vice-principal imposed sanctions, often with great severity of tone. Some teachers and schools kept elaborate systems of "demerit" records, through which offending pupils progressed through an increasingly severe range of sanctions. Other schools and teachers employed the opposite of this system by giving out merit points for good behaviour, and providing minor rewards—such as being dismissed first—to those pupils or rows of pupils which collected the most points.

Teachers and principals kept corporal punishment as their ultimate sanction short of expulsion. "I got the strap ten times in one year," remembered one man. "I was very inattentive ... and she tried to make me pay attention." "I wasn't a good student," reported another: "I remember being strapped three times in one day." Classroom teachers often employed less formal—and, in most provinces, unlawful—sorts of physical punishment. Former pupils recall teachers who spanked them on the bottom, or slapped them on the hands or about the shoulders and, occasionally, on the face. Other teachers pinched the upper arm or the earlobe, or hit victims on the top of the head with tightened knuckles. Still others used pointers, rulers, chalk brushes, gym shoes, or other things to hit children on their bottoms, hands, knuckles, shoulders, elbows—especially on the "funnybone"—and, less often, on their heads. A somewhat fondly remembered Grade One teacher, who that year enrolled forty-six pupils, "stepped on their toes as she hit them with a ruler." A few, carried by temper almost beyond control, sometimes dragged children from their desks to shake them, to bang them against walls, or even to manhandle them out of the classroom.

Unlike the cold, ritualized formality that characterized corporal punishment by a principal, classroom teachers sometimes struck out in a high pitch of unleashed emotion. A few teachers tried to be light-hearted, even affectionate, in their physical punishment. On these occasions the ritualized rules of the "game," especially as it was played between boys and male teachers, and in such all-boy classes as those in physical education or industrial arts, required that the victim accept, however reluctantly, that his physical punishment was part of a game. In the same jocular way, some teachers threw chalk, chalk brushes, and even textbooks at their charges.

For really serious violations of class or school codes, children were sent to, or summoned by, the school principal. Pupils found these interviews with the principal to be extremely stressful occasions; some were tongue-tied into silence. Being strapped was not an inevitable product of a trip to the "office," but it happened often enough for youngsters to be extremely wary of visiting there. "Getting THE STRAP was to us the same as going to the gallows," wrote Pete Loudon of his school in Anyox, British Columbia. "You didn't just get THE STRAP, you were sentenced to it."[46]

Once a principal decided to strap a pupil, he followed a routine—transformed into a formal and unvarying ritual in many schools—laid down by the Department of Education.[47] He summoned the required witness, explained the crime and punishment to the latter, positioned the subject carefully, administered the strokes and counted them out in a firm voice, and then recorded the event in a special book. Some principals removed their jackets and hung them up on a coat hanger. Others emphasized the formality of the occasion by buttoning their jackets. If there was more than one victim, those waiting their turn either watched or listened from just outside the door. The worst thing was when friends were there, "because then you couldn't cry." One man, recalling his first four on each hand, said, "I couldn't understand the pain, it was so intense." Another "died a thousand deaths but refused to show it [by crying] … afterwards I held my hands between my legs trying to get the fire out of them." Robert Thomas Allen, on the other hand, claimed that the strap "didn't really hurt … and when you got back to class among friends, you were able to hold your hands against the cast-iron sides of your desk, putting on a great act of cooling the unbearable heat and grinning in a worldly way at the girls."[48]

Since principals used corporal punishment as much to deter as to punish, they often permitted the sounds to carry their warning through the school; the appearance back in the classroom of a red-eyed and red-handed victim quickly reinforced the message. A few principals even prolonged the misery by administering punishment over more than one session, or by announcing it and then postponing its administration to noon hour or after school, or even to another day.[49] Although girls sometimes received corporal punishment of the informal classroom sort, they rarely took part in the ritual in the office.

Expulsion constituted the school's most serious sanction for bad behaviour. None of my informants was ever expelled or, if any was, did not admit to it. Unless the transgression was really heinous, schools did not expel pupils on a first offence; they reserved this punishment for a series of serious offences, and especially those that posed a threat to the very order of the classroom or school. In January 1951, twelve-year-old "Peter" threw a waste-basket at a teacher who "was a little abrupt" with him. "Later that week he was rude in class, the teacher kept him in after school, and Peter threatened the teacher with a baseball bat." Peter was then expelled.[50] Another "Peter" was twice expelled from elementary schools for "severe behaviour problems," including theft. In adolescence this lad embarked on a career of automobile theft and breaking and entering and, before he was eighteen, received a three-year sentence to the penitentiary.[51]

If parents and teachers often justified stern discipline and corporal punishment by appealing to proverbial wisdom, their approach was also deeply rooted in fear. On the one hand, they feared that, without severe sanctions, family, classroom, school, and society would quickly descend into disorder, and even barbarism; on the other hand, they feared for the future of the unchastened. Many still believed that the "old Adam" was very close to the surface in boys, and especially those in early adolescence. In eight-grade elementary schools, some teachers in the upper grades seem to have seen a barely suppressed violence in some of the boys; in responding to it savagely, they perhaps transformed their own fears into realities. In turn, these violent episodes communicated such beliefs and fears to the younger pupils and gave them notions of a sort of behaviour that one day they might well perform.

The school's informal communication system passed down and exaggerated stories of epic disciplinary events in the upper grades. These tales seem to have kept certain youngsters in a state of anticipatory tension over much of their school days, "feeling ... that the certainty of it occurring to you was not only high, but preordained." Many now recall the paradox in this system; it terrified the good children who only very occasionally got caught up in its machinery, but gave those who were often punished and who "could take it" a heroic status among their peers. One boy, for example, was one of those "who was strapped two or three times a year." One day he kicked a football at a school window; "it took him three kicks to get it through the window. He just stayed there until the teacher came and took him away" for the usual punishment.

By the 1920s nearly all school-aged children in English Canada spent at least a few years in school. Despite the general belief that they all would benefit from the experience, a few may actually have been worse off than their counterparts in earlier times. In the era before attendance laws were vigorously enforced, fractious boys—and, occasionally, girls—who fell behind because of large classes, poor teaching, irregular or poor attendance, or with little or no disposition or perhaps ability to learn, dropped out of school and found a place in the community. Now their parents, or economic conditions, or truant officers forced them to stay in school. Some may have benefited from the extended experience; others, no better or more appropriately taught, or more able to profit from formal learning than their predecessors, were oppressed by it. Of his brother, Fraser Miles wrote: "So maybe he was a bit slow in school, but nobody is likely to learn any better sitting in class all day terrified he would beaten at the end of it. The strappings sure didn't help Lloydyboy learn any more ..."[52]

Others found their outlet in being "tough." They moved along the very edge of forbidden practices and behaviours, they dominated the cloakroom and the boys' playground, they used bad language just at the edge of earshot of the teacher, they fought each other, and they carried "rollings" or cigarettes in their pockets, which they smoked just out of sight of the school. They quit school as soon as they were old enough to do so, or when they received the school's ultimate sanction and were expelled.

What has come to be called the school's "hidden" curriculum has been an implicit part of what appears above. Learning to survive was perhaps its most important element. Pupils had first of all to learn how to deal with their fears: their fear of the other children in their own class; their fear of the bigger children who might harass them to and from school, or on the playground; their special fear of "tough" boys and girls; their fear of teachers and the principal; their fear of the strap. Others feared that they would not measure up to family expectations for them. Most children obviously learned to manage, or at least to live with, their fears.

The foundation for children's sense of themselves as persons, of who they were and who they would be, was laid in their families. When they went to school, they found both the overt and hidden curriculum taught them still more about themselves. The merit of belonging to certain ethnic groups was reinforced. Those of British background found that their history and culture formed the basis of much of what they learned. During and after both world wars, those of "enemy" origin experienced both the cultural hostility that permeated formal and informal classroom discourse and the personal hostility of some teachers and many classmates. In Gertrude Story's trenchant words, "What I call the Holy British Imperial Empire Saskatchewan School System did a heck of a lot more for the British Empire ... than it ever did for Saskatchewanians. We learned to be loyal British Empire subjects, proud as punch that the sun never set on the British Empire ... [but] you did not (indeed, you dared not) play Norwegian singing games in the schoolyard (and under pain of death, German ones)."[53]

Many children found that, so far as the school was concerned, a culture they had been taught to cherish by family and congregation did not exist. Mary di Michele "suffered from an acute sense of otherness because my home language and culture were not reflected at all in my education, nor in my reading, nor in the American dramas of film and television I liked to watch."[54] Children were also the butt of the racial and ethnic stereotypes and slurs that were part of popular culture. Norm Alexander, descendant of a pioneering black family in British Columbia, was cast as "Little Black Sambo" in a school play in Victoria in the 1930s.[55] Gloria Steinberg Harris recalled, "We were never, ever allowed to forget that we were foreign. I was born in this country, but I was 'foreign.'"[56] School subsumed other cultures into larger conglomerations; Ukrainians, Georgians, and others from that Empire found themselves labelled Russians, German-speaking Mennonites from Russia and even the Dutch and Dutch-speaking Belgians became Germans, all Eastern Europeans were "bohunks," and so on. The Second World War euphemism for refugees, "Displaced Persons," was employed pejoratively in its abbreviated form, "DPs." Teachers Anglicized pupils names or even gave them new ones: "I cant pronounce all that, so I'll call you Mary."

Schools also affected religious identities. Public schools were clearly Christian schools, and generally presented a non-denominational form of liberal Protestantism.[57] Those interviewed who attended them offered few direct comments about the religious dimension of schooling. Some mentioned hearing Bible stories and readings and saying the Lord's Prayer as part of their accounts of classroom routines. If parents so requested, children could be excused from taking part in religious exercises. Usually, these pupils waited in the hallways until this part of the opening activities was over. Such children had an intense dislike of drawing attention to themselves in this way, an attitude reinforced when teachers made derogatory comments. In Toronto in the 1950s, for example, "one teacher accused us [Jews] of being Communists because we wouldn't say the Lord's Prayer." Others who were not Christian often found the prejudice against them expressed in ethnic—Sikhs labelled "ragheads" or "dirty Hindus," for example—rather than religious terms.

Parochial and separate schools created an environment suffused with Catholic doctrine and practice. Unlike their public counterparts, wrote Harry J. Boyle, "Catholics had holidays on holy days ... But in return they had an admixture of catechism every day and a Friday afternoon grilling on matters of faith by the parish priest."[58] "We learned the catechism by heart," wrote Patrick O'Flaherty, "and it is still all there somewhere in my deepest memory, triggered now by some chance word or phrase, as when I heard someone recently say the word 'chrism.'"[59]

Schools also played a major role in developing gender identity.[60] This process began, of course, long before youngsters entered school, but in the new setting identity was presented in a more structured and systematic way. And, if gendered expectations grew out of an adult agenda, they none the less received strong support from the youngsters themselves.[61]

Schools presented a gendered physical message; there, boys and girls inhabited sharply differentiated spaces. Some schools, and especially parochial and other Roman Catholic ones, enrolled only boys or girls, as did most private schools.[62] As the next chapter will show, playgrounds and play patterns of large schools were sharply segregated by deeply rooted custom, often reinforced by administrative fiat. Although play on the grounds of small rural schools was often more coeducational than on large urban ones, each also had a boys' and a girls' area, often on the way to or near the widely separated privies. Many schools had separate entrances for girls and boys. Once inside, children went to girls' classes or boys' classes, or to the boys' side or the girls' of cloakrooms and classrooms.

Schools insisted that pupils, and especially girls, dress appropriately. As one woman explained (among many we point out), "If we wore slacks in cold weather, we had to put them under our dresses or skirts, and take them off in class." Inside as well, children saw that women nurtured and men administered. If the former provided adult role models for girls, the latter did not always do so for boys. Some men, for example, recalled their male teachers in elementary school as "wimps," and a couple referred to their principals as "men among boys, but boys among men."

Classroom discourse and behaviour reinforced the messages of the setting. On the one hand, teachers seem to have demanded, and usually received, more docile conduct from girls than they did from boys. "We had a very fine teacher," reported one man, "and he would have stayed; but he wouldn't use the strap on a girl, and the girls simply took advantage of him; and ... he resigned." On the other, the culture of childhood itself structured much of the different ways that boys and girls came to behave. Most beginners of both sexes probably came to school disposed to conduct themselves in a way designed to please teachers. However, as they got to know other children; as they formed same-sex friendships, groups, and gangs; as they integrated themselves into the playground pecking order, the sexes came to have different norms as to how they should behave towards each other and how to conduct themselves in the classrooms. Responding to both sorts of expectations, girls tended to work more conscientiously, to complete tasks more expeditiously and neatly. They did the major share of classroom housekeeping. Their work became the classroom model; their answers were more likely to conform to teacher expectations. Since neither parents or teachers questioned these differences, both boys and girls came to see them as being rooted in the natural order of things.

Curricula and texts strengthened gendered messages, prescribing both childhood and adult roles. In the 1957 version of the British Columbia primary curriculum, the "desired outcomes" for the first grade included:

An understanding of the dependence of the family upon father.
An appreciation of the various kinds of work fathers do.
An appreciation of mother's contribution to our welfare, comfort, and happiness.[63]

Primary readers became more gender-specific over these years. In the first-grade reader prescribed in British Columbia from 1923 to 1934, nursery rhymes, poems, and a miscellaneous collection of stories made up most of the content. When "Mother Goose" had a tea party, she asked, "Is the table set, Boy Blue? Please get the bread, Miss Muffett. Please bring the cake, Jack Horner." [64] In 1935, this reader was replaced with one dealing with a single cast of characters, six-year-old twins Jerry and Jane, their sibling Baby, their parents, and their pets. In the late 1940s, this family in turn gave way to that of Dick and Jane. Both series focused on middle-class family life of a traditional sort. As well, the teachers' guides and optional workbooks for the latter series structured class discussion along traditional gender lines. [65]

In fact, in all the subjects in the elementary grades, children studied content that looked on the world from a male perspective and emphasized traditional patterns of work and play. In geography, they learned that, in all sorts of societies all over the world, men worked and mothers nurtured. In the late 1940s, J.M. Dent brought out a new, "postwar" series of readers for the intermediate grades that was used for nearly two decades in the schools of British Columbia, Alberta, and Ontario. In the one prescribed for Grade Five, thirty-eight stories had a clearly identified protagonist. In 29, the protagonist was a male human, in eight, a male animal, and in one a teenaged girl. [66] Further, notions that one sex or the other was "better" at, or "needed," particular fields of study, often learned outside of school, were confirmed in the upper elementary grades. Language and literature became "girls" subjects, and mathematics and science "boys". "When I came home from school all excited about a science class, Mom would say, 'What does a girl need to know about that for?,'" declared one woman who came herself to accept the opinion.

Children's experience of schooling is obviously more than its parts. It is important to reiterate that most of those whom we interviewed reported that, overall, they enjoyed their schooling. In the words of one, "I sure enjoyed my days at school, even if I wasn't good at it," and another stated, "The years in grade school were the best in my life." Fredelle Bruser Maynard wrote: "In many respects my early education was narrow, repressive, unimaginative," but the "curious truth, though, is that I *liked* school and acquired there a love of learning." [67] For those from large families, school provided a setting in which their individual characteristics could be recognized and developed. As the sixth in a family of eight children, Max Braithwaite found that, in school, "I soon discovered that I was pretty quick to learn, and this gave me status. I was in a new pecking order now, not one governed by age or sex or rotundity, but by ability." [68] For those from both rural and urban families, in which children had lots of hard work to do, school provided a some relief from their labours. For those frightened, harassed, or even persecuted by other children, the classroom provided some sanctuary. For those from extremely poor, crowded, abusive, or disrupted families, school provided a warm, ordered, and structured environment. As Percy Janes's protagonist explained, he was "glad" to start school, "for here I began to feel that I had at least some small measure of control over the things that happened to me, in a violent and bewildering world. By close attention and diligence I could influence and therefore predict my rulers' behaviour toward me ..."[69]

Other children were less fortunate. Someone who did well enough to complete high school reported that visiting his elementary school at a recent reunion gave "a bad feeling even now... I have bad memories of that place." Another, hearing about my research through a radio interview, telephoned to insist I talk to him: "I know things you have to know." When we met, and after he had savagely criticized his own schooling, he asked what sort of alternatives to the public system I could suggest for his own child.

In the context of this overall assessment, I want to make two final comments about schooling in this era. First, it is clear that the whole community—pupils, teachers, parents, employers—believed that the "learning out of a book" sort of schooling described in this chapter was the way it ought to be. In particular, parents of all social classes shared in this common viewpoint as to the nature and value of elementary schooling. They knew what children should learn, they knew how teachers should teach it, and they knew how principals and teachers should maintain order. They were sceptical of anything new. ("Why learn to cook on those [electric] stoves if you'll never afford one, anyway?"; "We didn't have any of that colouring nonsense when I went to school—we learned proper drawing.") Indeed, because parents and employers lacked the daily empirical testing of their expectations against the real world of the classroom, they often held the most rigid of formalistic expectations of what school should be like.

That working-class parents apparently held the same views on elementary education as did their middle-class counterparts may seem somewhat surprising. As other chapters show, the lives of children outside of school clearly displayed differences based on class. Recollections of school are surprisingly similar, however, whatever the neighbourhood or class background of the children. Schooling sorted children within rather than between schools.[70] Thus, all schools encouraged the "bright," and told those who were not as able as their peers that they were not going to climb very far up the educational ladder.

None the less, formal schooling met, in a rough and ready way, somewhat different class needs. At the political level, organized labour supported free public education, and, in Vancouver at least, working-class people ran for, and were elected to, school boards.[71] At the personal level, in a city composed of people born elsewhere, or the children of those born elsewhere, parents took seriously their role as educational strategists for their children.

My second closing comment is to note how far classroom practice was from educational theory. The "new" education—by the 1930s often called "progressive" education—embodied notions of learning by doing, and of building child-centred curricula out of the interests of children. In the context of these ideas, most provinces gradually introduced a series of what were really administrative reforms. They standardized curricula and time allotments for each subject, adopted the notion of the junior high-school, eliminated high school entrance examinations, tightened standards for admission to Normal schools, and promoted school consolidations. In British Columbia in the 1930s, for example, the province undertook a major revision of the curriculum. By 1937, the Department of Education had produced a new course of study that was more than 1,600 pages long. In the words of one of its chief architects, H.B. King, the philosophy characterizing this new curriculum "may be briefly expressed as the promotion of individual growth and social adjustment through purposeful activity."[72] None the less, if my informants are to be believed, then all of the changes that took place in education outside of the classroom had very little effect on what went on behind its doors. For children, their schooling was still epitomized in the time-honoured response of their teachers: "Yes, neatness counts!"[73]

NOTES

1 For affectionate accounts of rural schooling, see Joan Adams and Becky Thomas, *Floating Schools and Frozen Inkwells: The One-Room Schools of British Columbia* (n. p., 1985); and John C. Charyk, *The Little White Schoolhouse* (Saskatoon, 1968); *Pulse of the Community* (Saskatoon, 1970); and *Those Bittersweet Schooldays* (Saskatoon, 1977).

2 For a contemporary perspective on elementary schooling in the 1950s, see Joseph Katz, ed., *Elementary Schooling in Canada* (Toronto, 1961).

3 Jessie Mifflen, *A Collection of Memories* (St John's, 1989), 1.

4 Roy Bonisteel, *There Was a Time ...* (Toronto, 1991), 193.

5 "Chicken Little," appeared in *The Canadian Readers: Book One: A Primer and First Reader* (Toronto, 1922), 74-80. I have not been able to find out from which books the first two sentences came, but the person who recollected the third is obviously recalling an early story in the reader by Henrietta Roy, Elsie Roy, P.H. Sheffield, and Grace Bollert, *Highroads to Reading: Jerry and Jane: The Primer* (Toronto, 1932). "Spot" was a pet in the famous American "Dick and Jane" series, introduced in Canada after the Second World War. The first "pre-primer" in the series was William S. Gray, Dorothy Baruch, and Elizabeth Montgomery, *We Look and See* (Toronto, n.d.).

6 Evelyn Huang with Lawrence Jeffery, *Chinese Canadians: Voices from a Community* (Vancouver, 1992), 93.

7 School architecture in Canada is surveyed and illustrated in a series of Parks Canada research bulletins. Although they deal only with years up

to 1930, because so few schools were built during the Depression and the war, these publications in fact show school design as it was, except for the new buildings of the 1950s. See, for example, Ivan J. Saunders, "A Survey of British Columbia School Architecture to 1930," *Research Bulletin* no. 225, Parks Canada, November 1984.

8 Victoria *Times-Colonist*, 22 May 1994, M4.

9 The wording is taken from a copy now in the possession of Jean Barman. See also Vancouver School Board, *Report, 1940*, 55. Mildred Young Hubbert recalled that the same words appeared in a reader she used in Ontario in the early 1930s: *Since the Day I Was Born* (Thornbury, ON, 1991), 79.

10 E.A. Harris, *Spokeshute: Skeena River Memory* (Victoria, BC, 1990), 115.

11 See British Columbia, Department of Education, *Report*, 1943-4, B30; British Columbia, *Statutes*, 1944, c. 45.

12 In 1930, 3.9 per cent of Vancouver pupils had goiter. By 1936, this had declined to 1.1 per cent: Vancouver School Board, *Report, 1937*, 31-2.

13 Mary Thomson, "The Social Worker in the School: An Experimental Study of the Liaison and Service Functions of the Social Worker in a Vancouver Elementary School," unpublished MSW thesis, University of British Columbia, 1948, 49.

14 *Vancouver Sun*, 29 August 1981, A5.

15 Hubbert, *Since the Day I Was Born*, 88.

16 *Vancouver Sun*, 14 March 1995, A3.

17 Ibid., 12 January 1994, A3.

18 See George H. Limpus and John W.B. Shore, *Elementary General Science* (Toronto, 1935), 11-12.

19 H.B. MacLean, *The MacLean Method of Writing: Teachers" Complete Manual: A Complete Course of Instruction in the Technique and Pedagogy of the MacLean Method of Writing for Teachers of Elementary Schools, Junior and Senior High Schools, Commerical Schools, and Normal Schools* (Vancouver, 1921). The note at the foot of the title page of the thirty-first edition says that it is authorized for use in British Columbia, Quebec, Nova Scotia, Prince Edward Island, New Brunswick, and Newfoundland.

20 Victoria *Times-Colonist*, 22 May 1994, M4.

21 Stanley Coren, *The Left-Hander Syndrome: The Causes and Consequences of Left-Handedness* (New York, 1992), ch. 1.

22 Hugh Palmer, *Circumnavigating Father* (Surrey, BC, 1990), 64.

23 William C. Macklon, *The Fledgling Years* (Saskatoon, 1990), 32.

24 Sir Ernest MacMillan, ed., *A Canadian Song Book* (Toronto, 1937). The first edition of this text appeared in 1928.

25 The nature of school music and other broadcasts are described in Laurie Elizabeth Ion, "Over the Airwaves: School Broadcasts in British

Columbia, 1960-1982," unpublished MA thesis, University of British Columbia, 1992. Ion reports that teachers used music broadcasts more frequently than those on other subjects.

26 Melinda McCracken, *Memories Are Made of This* (Toronto, 1975), 54.

27 Lord Tennyson School pioneered platooning in Vancouver in 1924. By 1938, all elementary schools in the city employed some form of specialist teaching: Vancouver School Board, *Report, 1925,* 11-12; ibid., 1937-8, 64-5. The American origins of platooning are described in Raymond E. Callahan, *Education and the Cult of Efficiency: A Study of the Social Forces That Have Shaped the Administration of the Public Schools* (Chicago, 1962), 128-36.

28 Both poems, the first by Walter de la Mare, the second by John Masefield, appeared in E.G, Daniels, T.R. Hall, and H.H. MacKenzie, *Dominion Language Series,* Book 2 (Toronto, 1932), 68 and 179.

29 *Vancouver Sun,* 26 August 1995, A3. A "demonstration" Junior Red Cross meeting conducted by a class at Tecumseh School in Vancouver in May 1936 is described in "Practical Citizenship," *B.C. Teacher,* June 1936, 17-19. See also Nancy M. Sheehan, "The Junior Red Cross Movement in Saskatchewan, 1919-1929: Rural Improvement through the Schools," in *Building Beyond the Homestead: Rural History on the Prairies,* ed. David C. Jones and Ian MacPherson, (Calgary, 1985), 66-86.

30 In the 1920s, one woman in Vancouver, one woman in Point Grey, and nine women in South Vancouver held school principalships for one or more years. By the school year 1930-1, and after the three districts had amalgamated, only one woman—a former South Vancouver principal—still held the role. After Miss E.M. Dickieson retired in 1934, all forty-nine Vancouver elementary schools had male principals: British Columbia, Department of Education, *Report, 1935-36,* H165-82. The next female principal was appointed in 1969. In Catholic schools, however, a sister often served as principal.

31 Christmas concerts are fondly recalled in John C. Charyk, *The Biggest Day of the Year: The Old-Time School Christmas Concert* (Saskatoon, 1985).

32 See Charles M. Johnson, "The Children's War: The Mobilization of Ontario Youth During the Second World War," in *Patterns of the Past: Interpreting Ontario's History,* ed. Roger Hall, William Westfall, and Laurel S. MacDowell, (Toronto, 1988), 356-79; Emilie Montgomery, "'The War Was a Very Vivid Part of My Life': The Second World War and the Lives of British Columbian Children," in *Children, Teachers and Schools in the History of British Columbia,* ed. Jean Barman, Neil Sutherland, and J. Donald Wilson, 161-74 (Calgary, 1995); Patricia Roy "'Due to Their

Keenness": The Education of Japanese Canadian Children in the British Columbia Interior Housing Settlements during World War Two,' in ibid., 375-92; Norah Lewis, "'Isn't This a Terrible War?': Children's Attitudes to Two World Wars," *Historical Studies in Education 7/2* (Fall 1995), 193-215.

33 *Books in Canada,* 22. The minutes of a staff meeting held at Vancouver's Charles Dickens School on 5 October 1942 note: "Re Air Raids—(1ˢᵗ) If there is time—Send class home. (2ⁿᵈ) If there is only a little time, send pupils to the basement. (3ʳᵈ) If there is no time, pupils and teachers under their desks. N.B. If you hear any anti-air craft fire, there is no time to go home."

34 Mary di Michele, "Writers from Invisible Cities," *Canadian Woman Studies/Cahiers de la femme* 8 (Summer 1987), 37.

35 Toronto *Globe and Mail,* 13 September 1986, D7.

36 Seymour Levitan and Carol Miller, eds., *Lucky to Live in Cedar Cottage: Memories of Lord Selkirk Elementary School and Cedar Cottage Neighbourhood, 1911-1963* (Vancouver, 1986), 46.

37 Robert Collins, "Miss Apple Daisy," *Reader's Digest* (Canadian edition), September 1976, 144. A research study on the effects of Miss Appugliese's teaching, involving both a study of school records and interviews with former pupils then in their thirties, is reported in Eigel Pedersen, Thérèse Annette Faucher, with William W. Eaton, "A New Perspective on the Effects of First-Grade Teachers on Children's Subsequent Adult Status," *Harvard Educational Review,* 48 (February 1978), 1-31.

38 Geiri Johnson, *My Compass Points North* (Arnes, MN 1994), 4.

39 Mary Razzell, "Tribute to a Teacher," Bank of British Columbia's *Pioneer News,* April/May 1988, 15.

40 Toronto *Globe and Mail,* 31 August 1985, A6.

41 Mary Thomson, "The Social Worker in the School: An Experimental Study of the Liaison and Service Functions of the Social Worker in a Vancouver Elementary School," unpublished MSW thesis, University of British Columbia, 1948, 105.

42 Michael Enright, "Notes of a Native Son," *Quest,* March 1984, 24.

43 Daphne Marlatt and Carole Itter, eds., *Opening Doors: Vancouver's East End* (Victoria, BC, 1979), 164.

44 John Calam drew my attention to what old annuals and class photographs tell us about the determined maturity of beginning teachers of earlier eras. Perhaps this characteristic reinforced the view of many pupils that all their teachers, as one man put it, "were as old as the hills." One woman, recalling a teacher of the 1930s who "wore her hair in a bun and had dark clothes," was really surprised, thirty years later, to read that this teacher had just retired.

45 *Vancouver Sun,* 1 February 1992, D5.

46 Pete Loudon, *The Town That Got Lost: A Story of Anyox, British Columbia* (Sidney, BC, 1973), 41.

47 Corporal punishment was rooted in the Canadian Criminal Code. Statutes, precedents, and reported cases for this era are discussed in Peter Frank Bargen, *The Legal Status of the Canadian Public School Pupil* (Toronto, 1961), 125-33; see also *Manual of the School Law and School Regulations of the Province of British Columbia* (Victoria, BC, 1944), 127-8. For a more contemporary summary, with a focus especially on Ontario, see Jeffrey Wilson and Mary Tomlinson, *Children and the Law,* 2d ed. (Toronto, 1986).

48 Robert Thomas Allen, *Your Childhood and Mine: Happy Memories of Growing Up* (Toronto, 1977), 37.

49 Mordecai Richler reported that postponement to after school, or even the next day, was also the practice at the Montreal school he attended: *Saturday Night,* March 1969, 49-50.

50 Jack Macdonald Cobbin, "Treatment of Emotionally Disturbed Teen-Age Boys in (a Group Living) Residence: An Examination of Children's Aid Society Wards, with Special Reference to Movement Shown after a Period in a Group-living Institution," unpublished MSW thesis, University of British Columbia, 1955, 36.

51 Mildred May Wright, "Social and Family Backgrounds as an Aspect of Recidivism among Juvenile Delinquents: A Compilation and Review for a Group of Juvenile Delinquents Who Failed to Respond to Programmes Provided for Their Rehabilitation," unpublished MSW thesis, University of British Columbia, 1957, 42-50.

52 Fraser Miles, *Slow Boat on Rum Row* (Madeira Park, BC, 1992), 21.

53 Gertrude Story, *The Last House on Main Street* (Saskatoon, 1994), 168.

54 di Michele, "Writers from Invisible Cities," 37.

55 *Vancouver Sun,* 23 February 1994, B8.

56 Marlatt and Itter, eds., *Opening Doors,* 130.

57 Harro Van Brummelen, "Shifting Perspectives: Early British Columbia Textbooks from 1872 to 1925," *BC Studies* 60 (Winter 1983-4), 8.

58 Harry J. Boyle, *Memories of a Catholic Boyhood* (Don Mills, ON 1974), 10.

59 Patrick O'Flaherty, "Caught in the Nets: Growing Up Irish Catholic in Newfoundland," *The Canadian Forum,* March 1986, 9.

60 For an account of the gendered nature of current American schooling, see Barrie Thorne, *Gender Play: Girls and Boys in School* (New Brunswick, NJ, 1993).

61 Rosanna Tite, "Sex-Role Learning and the Woman Teacher: A Feminist Perspective," *Feminist Perspective Feministes* 7 (July 1986), shows how deeply rooted traditional notions are among contemporary children.

62 See Jean Barman, *Growing Up British in British Columbia: Boys in Private School* (Vancouver, 1984).

63 British Columbia, Department of Education, *Program for the Primary Grades* (Victoria, BC, 1957), 143.

64 *The Canadian Readers: Book One: A Primer and First Reader* (Toronto, 1933), 27.

65 This discussion is in part based on Lynne A. Saddington, "Family Life in Grade One British Columbia Primers, 1900-1985," MEd Major Paper, University of British Columbia, 1985.

66 Donalda Dickie, Belle Ricker, Clara Tyner, and T. W. Woodhead, *Gay Adventurers* (Toronto, 1947).

67 Fredelle Bruser Maynard, *Raisins and Almonds* (Markham, ON, 1973), 127.

68 Max Braithwaite, *Never Sleep Three in a Bed* (Toronto, 1969), 37.

69 Percy Janes, *House of Hate* (Toronto, 1970), 140.

70 This statement is supported both by my interviews and by an examination of such data as class size and teacher qualification for selected schools from different neighbourhoods in the city.

71 Jean Barman, "'Knowledge Is Essential for Universal Progress But Fatal to Class Privilege:' Working People and the Schools in Vancouver During the 1920s," *Labour/Le Travail* 22 (Fall 1988), 9-66.

72 British Columbia, Department of Education, *Report, 1939-40*, B32.

73 For an analysis of the dichotomy between theory and practice in Canadian education at the time, see George S. Tomkins, *A Common Countenance: Stability and Change in the Canadian Curriculum* (Toronto, 1986).

* * * * *

Documents for Chapter Ten

The first document explores the attitudes of young people between 15 and 24 years of age regarding the education they had received or were receiving in 1943. A total of 1,467 (756 were female) answered the questionnaire. By occupation, 256 were still in school, 216 were in the Armed Forces, 702 were working, and 172 were in college. In general, how would you summarize young peoples' satisfaction with their education? What seemed to be their most important concerns? Using gender as your yardstick, analyze these tables, especially question 17. In which areas did the replies of French-speaking students differ from those of English-speaking students, and why? Document 37 surveys the opinions of Atlantic Canada's grade 8 students about school life in the mid-1990s. To what extent do you think these results were applicable to your school? What comments would you make on the final sentence in this survey? Summarize the findings of this study.

36) CANADIAN YOUTH EVALUATES ITS EDUCATION, 1946[1]

WHAT DOES YOUTH THINK OF ITS EDUCATION?
An Inquiry Conducted by the Canadian Youth Commission

This form is addressed to a selected group of Canadian Youth 15 to 24 years of age. Twenty-six important questions will be found on the inside pages. Please answer these as fully and accurately as you can. We want to find out what young Canadians really think about their schooling. What you say may have a definite influence on school policy in the future.

Answer each question frankly, and do not sign your name anywhere on the paper.

There followed nine routine questions as to age, sex, province in which educated, educational status achieved, present occupation (school, college, job or armed forces), and residential classification (farm, village, etc.). The questionnaire itself consists of 26 items, some of them "double-headers." This chapter is devoted to a consideration of the answers given by Canadian Youth to these questions ....

THE MOST IMPORTANT REASON FOR GOING TO SECONDARY SCHOOL

Question 1. While all may be important, which of the following do you think is the most important reason for going to Secondary School (i.e., High, Technical, Commercial, Agricultural, Vocational School)? (Check one. If you find it necessary to check more than one, number the items in order of importance.) ....

The following table indicates the number of approvals (not only firsts) given by the participants to each of the suggested reasons for going to secondary school:

Help think clearly on the problems of life 736
Help understand modern society and responsibilities of a citizen. . . 560
Enable student to get a better job 536
Help discover and develop abilities and interests 518
Increase knowledge of important subjects 306
Prepare for university entrance. 194
Improve your social position 190
Teach how to get on with other people 175
Prepare for wise use of leisure 121
Others and blank. 49

HOW WELL DID YOUR SCHOOL SERVE YOU?

The first item of the Questionnaire set the young people a serious task of evaluating educational objectives in general. Having thus put them "in the groove," the inquisitor now turns their attention upon their own experience with the following question:

Question 2. Which of the above things did your schooling do best?

The question elicited 2,488 favourable opinions which are distributed thus:

Help think clearly on the problems of life 405
Increase knowledge of important subjects 365
Help discover and develop abilities and interests 356
Enable student to get a better job 356
Help understand modern society and responsibilities of citizenship . 267
Prepare for university entrance. 243
Teach how to get on with other people 232
Improve social position 142
Prepare for wise use of leisure 122

Question 3. In which of the above things was your schooling least adequate?

There were 1,747 unfavourable opinions, which are distributed thus:

Help discover and develop abilities and interests 269
Prepare for wise use of leisure 268
Help understand modern society and responsibilities of citizenship . 264
Improve social position 205
Teach how to get on with other people 190
Enable student to get a better job 167
Prepare for university entrance. 166
Help think clearly on the problems of life 117
Increase knowledge of important subjects 101

Question 4. Can you suggest any ways in which your schooling might have prepared you better than it did for what you have had to do since leaving school?

Although many respondents did not answer this question, those who did have provided us with 1,023 suggestions, which may be grouped conveniently as follows:

THEY WOULD LIKE TO HAVE HAD MORE (OR BETTER)

Agriculture—instruction in soils, animal care and breeding,
practical field work, accounting, etc. 41

Aptitudes and Interests—discovery and development of 35

Business Training—typing, shorthand, bookkeeping,
commercial law, store organization, use of money, etc 48

Choice of Subjects—freedom to follow interests and aptitudes
and omit courses of no direct utility or appeal 20

Clubs—for discussion of public affairs, for promoting hobbies
and leisure pursuits, for providing social training 20

Cultural Subjects—only art (7) and music (16) are mentioned 23

English—more instruction in, desired by Quebec young people 25

Home Economics—sewing, cooking, budgeting, interior
decoration, home nursing; housekeeping at low income level 55

Language Training—English instead of foreign or dead
languages (11), better grammar grounding (2),
stress on oral mastery of French, etc 33

Life—instruction in facts and problems of—moral guidance,
religious training (5), a philosophy of life, character training 56

Mathematics—more thorough; better courses in high school
arithmetic, practical arithmetic instead of so much algebra, etc 23

Physical Education—frequent emphasis on field and team sports
as a character discipline. 30

Practical Instruction—this plea comes in every conceivable form and
connection—housekeeping, child care, mechanical skills etc.,
merging naturally with the demand for vocational training 88

Public Affairs—current events—civics, mechanics of government
—modern economic problems and theories—
different political philosophies, etc 65

Public Speaking—training in participation in debate, overcoming
stage fright, thinking on the feet, etc 34

Responsibility and Leadership—training in—development of
initiative; how to take hold of a proposal and carry it through, etc. . . . 27

Scientific Studies—key to modern technological, medical and
other forms of progress; more individual laboratory training 22

Sex Training—no explanatory expressions 18

Social Training—important points of etiquette; practice in mixing
with crowd, overcoming bashfulness; easy conversation, etc 39

Study Habits—instruction in the how and why of—greater
thoroughness and more pressure to study 21

Teachers—with greater understanding of pupils (9)—better trained
and more skilful (19)—give more attention to individual (7) 50

Vocational Guidance—what jobs and professions there are—
required schooling and college training—necessary aptitudes—
economic status, etc . . . . 60.

Vocational Training—all sorts of specific references which might
have been included under "Business," "Home Economics" or
"Practical" but were associated with the word "vocational" by
the respondent 42

Others—spelling, writing, geography, thinking, co-operation, etc. 152

WHAT YOUTH THINKS OF ITS SCHOOL SUBJECTS

Question 5. Which subjects of your high school course would you say have
been most valuable to you since leaving school? **Question 6.** Which subjects, if
any, have you found to be of little value?

Subject	Most Valuable	Of Little Value
French (as mother tongue)	94	0
English	650	68
Shop Work	40	4
Health	29	3
Commercial	171	20
Sociology or Psychology	50	10
Geography	144	38
Physical Education	15	4
Economics	73	21
Mathematics	601	250
Home Economics	64	29
Dramatics	6	3
Science	291	154
Vocational Guidance	6	4
History	200	229
Arts and Crafts	12	14
Art or Music	44	60
Languages (modern)	113	262
Languages (ancient)	71	256

[Questions 7 and 8 revealed that young people considered schools to be either "the most important institution in the community," or "an integral part of community life."]

Question 9. Has (or had) your high school adequate facilities?

	Yes	No
For physical training and games?	865	455
For social gatherings of adults and children	724	593
For musical education and musical concerts?	713	593
For household economics training?	593	667
For technical education?	420	832
For adult education?	347	910
Other (specify)	38	10

[Question 10 revealed that less than 3% thought compulsory school age should be under 16. In Question 13, more than one-half replied that they secured their present job through their own efforts.]

Question 14. Do you think that the modern high school should take responsibility for:

	# Checked
Guiding its pupils in their choice of jobs?	1,132
Placing its graduates in jobs?	308
Neither of these	175
(No answer, 31)	

Question 16. It is said that we lack the kind of all-absorbing passion for our country and its way of life which Russian and German youth have shown. Which of the following methods do you think would be *most effective* in giving young Canadians a compelling belief in our way of life? (Number in order of preference. Put an X against any that you would consider ineffective.)

(a) More teaching in the schools of pride in and loyalty to our country.
(b) Patriotic demonstrations with band music, parades, singing of national songs, inspirational speeches, etc.
(c) The establishment by the government of a national youth organization through which young people are trained for citizenship.
(d) One or two years of service in youth work programmes sponsored by the government through which young people of all classes perform useful labour for their country.

(e) Improving economic and living conditions for all Canadians.

(f) Giving pupils a chance to experience democracy by co-operating with the teaching staff in running the affairs of the school.

(g) Other (specify).

The first choices of 1,096 young people who responded affirmatively are distributed as follows:

(e) Improve economic and living conditions 324
(a) Patriotic teaching in schools 216
(c) Government citizenship youth programme 188
(f) Democratic participation in school 176
(b) Patriotic demonstrations, parades, etc 0
(d) Youth labour programmes 43
(g) Other 15

Question 17. Did your schooling lead to any of the following results in your case? (Check one or more.)

	Male	Female	Total
(a) Habitual reading of books and magazines	376	475	851
(b) Participation in dramatics	133	139	272
(c) Study of music (actual performance)	92	139	231
(d) Appreciation of music	199	296	495
(e) Leadership of youth groups	183	178	361
(f) Interest in making things	168	200	368
(g) Interest in drawing or painting	78	123	201
(h) Skill in household arts	20	173	193
(i) Intelligent interest in public affairs	283	271	554
(j) Participation in team games (specify)	316	192	508
(k) Participation in individual sports	153	103	256
(1) Interest in mechanical or scientific hobbies (specify)	144	39	183

[1,383 youth answered in the affirmative to Question 22 that asked if all schools should provide physical training after the war was over; 611 wanted schools to provide military training.]

Question 23a. It is held by some people that religious training should be a part of everyone's education. Do you agree?

Answers. Yes, 868; No, 175; Don't know or no answer, 124,
        (Figures for French-speaking Quebec not tabulated.)

Question 23b. (If yes) Which of the following methods would you advocate for schools to follow? (Number in order of preference. Put an X against any to which you would be opposed.)

(a) Conduct Bible reading and prayers in school.
(b) Teach prescribed passages of scripture.
(c) Teach Bible history as a course, or part of a course.
(d) Introduce religious principles incidentally in the teaching of courses like English and Social Studies.
(e) Demonstrate religious principles through the way the school is run, by the personal example of the teaching staff, etc.
(f) Provide a course for the teaching of religious principles and their relation to life.
(g) Other (specify).

The answers here have been tabulated separately for French-speaking and English-speaking youth.

ENGLISH-SPEAKING REPLIES

The *first choices* and *rejections* (marked X) totaled as follows:

Item	First Choices	Rejections
(a)	169	142
(b)	19	170
(c)	104	118
(d)	76	105
(e)	98	154
(f)	136	73
(g)	3	8

FRENCH-SPEAKING REPLIES

	First Choices	Rejections
(a) Bible reading and prayers in school	159	13
(b) Teach prescribed passages of scripture	121	13
(c) Teach Bible history as a course, or part of course	81	29
(d) Introduce religion incidentally in other subjects	136	40
(e) Demonstrate religious principles by the way the school is run, by ...... example of teachers, etc.	106	37
(f) Provide a course on religious principles and their relation to life	220	9

[Questions 24a, 25, and 26 revealed that 1,207 of 1,467 youth believed that many people were prevented from continuing their education because of their parents' lack of money. The suggested solutions were government assistance, lower fees, and federal grants to the provinces. 92% were willing to pay higher taxes for better educational opportunities.]

*　*　*　*　*

37) ATLANTIC CANADA STUDENTS GRADE THEIR EDUCATION, 1996[2]

Satisfaction

The satisfaction of education stakeholders (i.e., students, parents, teachers, post-secondary institutions, business, community) can provide valuable insight into the relevance of the education system. In an effort to begin accessing this information, this report includes the results of the Quality of School Life Survey of Grade 8 students in the Atlantic provinces.

It is intended that future reports will assess the satisfaction of other education stakeholders.

How do Grade 8 students in Atlantic Canada feel about the quality of their school life?

How do students rate the quality of their school lives? How interested are students in learning? How do they view their school work, quality of teaching and school climate? Do students perceive the school as a secure place to learn? There are few current indicators of student satisfaction with school, even though Canadian students are spending more than one-fifth of their lives in grade school, post-secondary institutions and other forms of training.

To begin to provide answers to some of these questions, in November 1995, all Grade 8 students in the Atlantic provinces participated in the Quality of School Life (QSL) attitude assessment administered by the provincial departments of education. This survey was designed to gather information about the attitudes of students toward their schooling experience. Students were asked to respond to a series of statements that began with "School is a place where . . ." by indicating on a four-point scale whether they agreed or disagreed with each statement. The statements can be classified into the following attitude dimensions: student satisfaction; student dissatisfaction; *student perception of their school work, interest in learning, peer relationships; student perception of their own status;* and *student perception of teachers.* An additional four items designed to assess the extent to which students felt *safe* and *secure* in school were added to the survey.

The QSL survey instrument emanated from research conducted in Australia for IEA, an international assessment organization. It was recently refined and further field-tested by researchers at Memorial University of Newfoundland and the Newfoundland Department of Education and has been administered at various grade levels in that province since 1989. The *safety and security of students* dimension was first added this year.

Table 4.1.1 provides results on 15 survey items selected to represent the eight attitude dimensions of the survey. Results for each item are reported as the combined percentage of students who agreed or strongly agreed with the statement.

On items that measure *student satisfaction and dissatisfaction* (items 1, 2 and 3) results are mixed. Although most students in the Atlantic region agreed with the statement "school is a place where I like to be" (62%), only 42% agreed that "school is a place where I really like to go." The range of results across provinces, from lowest to highest, was about six percentage points. The survey also asked that students respond to the statement "school is a place where there is nothing exciting to do." Thirty-nine percent of Atlantic students agreed with this statement. Except for New Brunswick (francophone) students (29%), results for different provincial populations were generally similar.

The results from items designed to reflect *student perception of their school work* and *interest in learning*, suggest that students in the Atlantic provinces are generally motivated. Seventy-five percent of students agreed that they "feel good about their work at school" (item 4) while 74% agreed that "the work I do is important to me" (item 5). Responses on item 4 were very similar among provinces, within a range of six percentage points. On item 5, however, larger differences were evident. Students in Nova Scotia, at 69%, were least positive in their responses, while New Brunswick (francophone) students, at 81%, were the most positive. This pattern was also apparent for items 6 and 7.

The differences in the overall results for items that reflected interest in learning are worthy of mention. Eighty-five percent of students in the Atlantic region agreed they "like to learn new things," while only 61% said they were "genuinely interested in [their] work." This discrepancy raises questions about the relevance of the educational program as perceived by a large segment of the young adolescents in our schools. Although the vast majority of students report that they like to learn new things, less than two-thirds agree they are interested in their work.

TABLE 4.1.1
Quality of School Life Survey results for Grade 8 students in Atlantic Canada, by province, (1995-96)

School is a place where:	Atlantic Avg.	NB (a)	NB (b)	NF (f)	NS	PEI
(1) I like to be	62	65	63	61	59	63
(2) I really like to go	42	44	47	42	39	41
(3) there is nothing exciting to do	39	39	29	39	42	40
(4) I feel good about my work	75	73	75	79	73	76
(5) the work I do is important to me	74	72	81	80	69	71
(6) I like to learn new things	85	85	88	87	83	84
(7) I am genuinely interested in my work	61	59	72	65	57	58
(8) I learn to get along with other people	86	85	87	88	85	88
(9) I can along with most of the students even though they may not be my friends	83	82	80	86	82	85
(10) I know that people think a lot of me	62	61	73	59	62	67
(11) people think I can do a lot of things	68	68	70	68	68	71
(12) teachers treat me fairly in class	77	78	66	80	76	80
(13) teachers help me to do my best	78	77	82	83	73	78
(14) I feel safe from personal harm	69	66	74	73	64	73
(15) students pick on each other all the time	55	56	45	48	62	58

All values are percentage of students agreeing with statements.

Items designed to elicit responses on *peer relationships* show that the vast majority of students are positive about their relationships with other students. There was very little difference among populations on these items (8 and 9). The results clearly indicate that students believe school helps them learn to get along with others. All groups had at least 80% of students who agreed with both selected items. Populations were very comparable, with the greatest difference between groups being six percentage points.

Although the *peer relationships* items show that most students believe school helps them learn to get along, responses to the *safety and security* items indicate that many students in the region are concerned about their personal safety. Almost one-third of the students, regionally, did not agree that "school is a place where I feel safe from personal harm" (item 14). Moreover, more than half the Grade 8 students in the four provinces agreed that "school is a place where students pick on each other all the time" (item 15). As shown in Table 4.1.1, these findings show some interprovincial differences. The percentage of students who agreed they felt safe from personal harm ranged from 64% in

Nova Scotia to 74% for New Brunswick (francophone) students; at 73%, results were the same for Newfoundland and Prince Edward Island. The pattern of responses to item 15 was analogous in that fewer New Brunswick (francophone) students and more Nova Scotia students agreed that "students pick on each other all the time" as compared with the other populations.

Items selected from the *student perception of their own status* dimension are believed to be indicators of student self-esteem. The results show that, in the Atlantic region, 62% of students agree that "school is a place where I know that people think a lot of me" (item 10) while 68% agree that "school is a place where people think I can do a lot of things" (item 11). Differences were seen among provinces within the region. For item 10, percentages of students who agreed with the statement ranged from 59% in Newfoundland to 73% among New Brunswick (francophone) students. On item 11, the percentages among provinces did not vary appreciably, hovering around 69%.

The overall results for items that asked about *student perception of teachers* show that more than three-quarters of the students viewed their teachers positively. A large majority of students in the region agreed that they are treated fairly by teachers (77%) and that teachers help them to do their best (78%).

Gender Differences

The Grade 8 data were analyzed to determine whether there were gender differences in responses. Generally, females were more positive in their responses on all dimensions, as shown in Figure 4.1.1. In terms of student satisfaction, for example, 70% of females indicated that "school is a place [I] like to be" as compared with 54% for males, a difference of 16 percentage points. On item 2, more females than males agreed that "school is a place I really like to go," by 14 percentage points. On the *student dissatisfaction* item, 44% of male students in Grade 8 reported that "there is nothing exciting to do" in school, compared with 34% of females.

On the other dimensions, a similar pattern is apparent to a greater or lesser degree. For example, only 57% of the boys surveyed agreed with the statement, "I am genuinely interested in my work," compared with 66% of girls. Moreover, 80% of girls agreed with the statement, "the work I do is important to me," compared with 69% of boys. These differences, combined with the differences in levels of achievement, overall attainment and participation between males and females, are cause for concern. Based on these data and the indicators reported in the "Achievement and Attainment" and "Participation" chapters of this report, it is evident that our male students are underparticipating, underachieving in certain areas and have a more negative attitude toward their schooling experience. These data point to a need for more focused attention on identifying the reasons for these attitudinal differences and improving poor attitudes toward school among male students as a group.

Although, at this time, no causal link can be established between the attitudes of male students and their levels of participation, graduation and achievement, the possibility that these are related requires examination.

How the survey was administered and scored?

The survey was administered to the full population of Grade 8 students through the provincial departments of education and their school districts during the first two weeks of November 1995. Survey items were printed on a machine-scoreable answer form, and students responded to items by shading one of four response options for each item ranging from *strongly agree* to *strongly disagree*. Although items on the surveys were later classified as falling into one of several different dimensions, for the purposes of survey administration, items were mixed. The surveys were confidential, and students were not required to provide their names or any identifying information on the forms. The surveys took about 20 minutes to complete but students were allowed as much time as they needed to complete the form. Forms were then collected by students, packaged and forwarded to the department of education in each province. All forms for the four provinces were scanned in a single location.

For each statement the proportion of students who strongly agreed were pooled with the proportion who simply agreed. Data gathered by the survey is therefore expressed as the percentage of students who agreed with each individual statement.

---

*   *   *   *   *

---

151 *Youth Challenges the Educators* (Toronto: The Ryerson Press, 1946). Prepared for the Canadian Youth Commission. Questions 1, 2, 3, 4, 5, 6, 8, 9, 14, 16, 17.
152 "Satisfaction: How do Grade 8 Students in Atlantic Canada feel about the quality of their school life?" *Education Indicators for Atlantic Canada* (Human Resources and Development Canada, 1996), pp. 42-45.

Chapter Eleven:
Teaching Teachers

In 1949 the Canadian Education Association sampled 589 teachers and non-teachers regarding teachers' qualifications. Given the choice of Grade XI, Grade XII, or two years of university, approximately one-half of the respondents believed that elementary school teachers should have at least a Grade XII education. Twenty-seven percent of the non-teachers voted for two years of university, compared to sixteen percent of the teachers. At that time, most elementary school teachers had graduated from Grade XII with one year professional training.[119]

The previous year, another CEA survey revealed that 80% of a heterogeneous group thought that the teaching profession lacked prestige. "The public believes," it concluded, "that students with initiative, ambition, drive, and personality turn to business and industry rather than to teaching .... One imagines his new friends saying, "He's a good sort with plenty of ability. I wonder why he doesn't get out of teaching?" ... Classroom teachers are respected, but as a group they have not the social status of more prosperous professional folk. They stand on a social par with civil servants, below business managers and bankers." The 1953 *Year Book of Education* argued that "if teacher training were everywhere the responsibility of the universities, standard of entrance and training would be higher than at present and teaching might be given recognition as a profession."[120]

Half a century later, two academics involved in teacher education reported that university faculties of education had become dangerously separated from "the world of schools," and that the typical prospective teacher was "a white, monolingual, middle-class female who hopes to teach children in a community like her own." They called upon faculties of education to strengthen the public education system to meet the demands of the changing ethno-cultural society and the requirements of rapidly changing information technologies.[121]

Earlier chapters touched briefly on various aspects of teacher education. Here, Nancy Sheehan and Donald Wilson offer a perspective on this topic by detailing the history of teacher education in British Columbia. Other useful sources include: Mark Holmes, *The Reformation of Canada's Schools: Breaking the Barriers to Parental Choice* (Montreal, 1998); K.A. Hollihan, "'Willing to Listen Humbly': Practice Teaching in Alberta Normal Schools, 1906-44," *Historical Studies in Education*, vol. 9, no. 2 (Fall/Autumn, 1997); John Calam, "Teaching Teachers on Campus: Initial Moves and the Search for UBC's First Professor of Education," *Historical Studies in Education* 6, 2 (Fall/automne 1994); John W. Chalmers, "Development of Alberta's First Faculty of

Education," *Alberta History* 40, 1 (Winter, 1992); Patrick J. Harrigan, "The Development of a Corps of Public School Teachers in Canada, 1870–1980," *History of Education Quarterly* 32, 4 (Winter 1992).

* * * * *

FROM NORMAL SCHOOL TO THE UNIVERSITY TO THE COLLEGE OF TEACHERS: TEACHER EDUCATION IN BRITISH COLUMBIA IN THE 20TH CENTURY[122]

ABSTRACT *This article examines the history of teacher education in the Province of British Columbia, Canada over this century. It argues that from subject-based examinations to the development of Normal Schools to the transfer of all teacher education to the universities, British Columbia's system for the education and certification of teachers was much like that found in most Anglo-Saxon countries. The enactment of the* Teaching Profession Act *in 1987, establishing the BC College of Teachers as a professional body with jurisdiction over certification and discipline, challenged this unified approach. The authors review the College's efforts to establish itself and exercise its legislative mandate. They conclude that despite problems the College has raised the awareness and importance of teacher education in BC and may help forestall the move to school-based and/or alternative certification practices found in Britain and in the United States.*

Introduction

In 1983 a publication appeared entitled *Historical Inquiry in Education* sponsored by the American Educational Research Association (Best, 1983). Of the 15 chapters devoted to various topics in educational history, not one was concerned with the history of teachers or teacher education. Significantly, just 6 years later the same association sponsored another 15-chapter publication devoted this time exclusively to the history of teachers and teaching in the US (Warren, 1989). The last several years have seen a similar development in Canada of interest in the subject of the history of teachers and teacher education (Abbott, 1986; Calam, 1986; Patterson, 1986; Wilson, 1989, 1991; Wilson & Stortz, 1988). This paper is an attempt to extend this historical interest to Canada's west coast province, British Columbia, and to focus particular attention on the creation of an institution unique to Canada and the US, namely the BC College of Teachers. Since 1988 this latter body has had the authority to exercise control over the certification, discipline and professional development of teachers in this Province in a fashion similar to that of other professional bodies operating in the interests of doctors, lawyers, and engineers. The presence of the College of Teachers has had immediate effects on teachers themselves, their professional association (the British Columbia Teachers'

Federation), and the provincial universities which, for close to 40 years, had operated teacher education programs with little involvement from the profession.

Early Developments—The Normal Schools

It may be wise to begin our story with some historical background. Significantly, one of the first acts to pass the new British Columbia legislature after the Province entered the Confederation in 1871 was the Public Schools Act of the following year. Wherever a handful of settler children could be gathered together, a free nondenominational public school was to be opened and operated. Despite this generous state provision for universal schooling, no institution was created for training teachers until some 30 years later when the Province's first normal school opened its doors in 1901. Thus during that intervening time to become a teacher it was only necessary to pass a knowledge-based examination set by the Superintendent of Education of the Board of Education in Victoria, and with subject matter roughly equivalent to that taught in the high school. The passing mark for a certificate good for one year was 30%. Higher grades earned a longer-term certificate. Even those trained in other provinces had to take this examination. The "opportunity cost" to be a teacher was thus not great because there were no classes to attend and one could continue with one's regular occupation while studying for the examination. There was no screening or weeding out process as found in Ontario or the Maritime provinces, each with its own normal school (Prentice, 1990). There was no formal induction of the teacher-to-be, something on which Egerton Ryerson had put great stock in mid-19th century Ontario. To become a teacher in this era was largely a matter of self-selection.

Before 1901 very few teachers from elsewhere came to British Columbia specifically to teach (Barman, 1990). More frequently, they were men and women simply looking for better opportunities, as the first Superintendent John Jessop himself had done when he arrived from Ontario in 1860 to seek his fortune (Johnson, 1971). From 1872 to 1901 and especially after 1886 with the arrival in Vancouver of the transcontinental railway, the number of elementary schools rose dramatically and thus the corresponding need for teachers (Dunn, 1980). Since the supply never quite met the demand, it was not difficult to secure a position, even for a year or two. Using a number of diaries, letters and reminiscences and the letterbooks of the Superintendent of Education, Jean Barman has identified five categories of individuals who became teachers before 1901: girls just out of school, often filling the transition period between school and anticipated marriage; young men determined to get ahead and seeing teaching "as a stepping stone toward what they really wanted out of life", such as law, medicine or the church; females forced to fend for themselves as a result of unforeseen circumstances, for example, death of parents, widowhood; men in need of ready cash, who moved in and out of teaching as need dictated, or who combined teaching and farming; and experienced teachers, those who had made some lifelong commitment to teaching. For almost all men and for a considerable proportion of the women, Barman concludes the motivation to be a teacher was economic, "the necessity to earn a living or to contribute to the family economy in geographical and socioeconomic circumstances where the range of possible occupations was limited" (Barman, 1991-92). That teaching was seen as a legitimate goal for a certain class of young women to aspire to is underlined by the fact that females could become teachers at age 16 while males had to wait to age 18. For most girls, however, marriage remained their true and ultimate vocational aim.

With the inauguration of the normal school in Vancouver in 1901, professional educational credentials became accepted in lieu of provincial examinations held annually in Victoria. Local boards still did the hiring of teachers, but the Province, through its licencing standards, defined those people qualified to teach in the Province. Providing teachers for the ever-expanding population of school-aged children made it difficult to improve the education qualifications of teachers. For example, it was not until 1922 that the lowest qualification, a third class certificate (3 years of high school and 4 months of normal school) was abolished. An oversupply of teachers in the depression years of the 1930s, however, allowed the Department of Education to raise the minimum requirement for admission to one of the two provincial normal schools to senior matriculation (4 years of high school). All this changed in the war years as normal school enrolments dramatically declined and by 1942-43 a teacher shortage resulted in lower standards of admission (back to 3 years of high school) (Johnson, 1964).

The introduction of contracts for teachers had the desirable effect of providing a measure of security of employment. On the other hand dozens of responsibilities, such as janitorial duties, and proscriptions against certain behaviour were made part of the contract. Typically female teachers were restricted in their social contacts with men, they were prohibited from marrying, and were obliged to terminate their employment once they married. Exceptions to this last provision occurred but were not at all common, and were most often found in rural areas where a widow might be hired or a female teacher married to a local resident might be employed in preference to an unknown stranger. Both the community and the individual female teacher believed, with some exceptions, that married women and mothers belonged in the home not in the classroom. Single women teachers might well play an important role in building the nation and the province through their teaching efforts, but once married they were expected first to build their own families. Their prime and true vocation was in the home not the school. The right of married women to continue teaching in British Columbia schools was not confirmed until 1950 (Bruneau, 1979).

In early twentieth century British Columbia, about the time that the British Columbia Teachers' Federation came into being in 1917, it was difficult to tell whether teaching was a profession or not. The pay was certainly poor and teachers' work was highly supervised. In that sense teaching was hardly "professional". One might even argue that teaching resembled more a working class job with low status, little autonomy, strict supervision and few educational requirements. Manual tasks such as lighting the fire and cleaning the school were often expected of teachers. Paperwork grew and much of this was purely mechanical and clerical and not the sort of work done by other professionals. Teaching, at least at elementary school, was not exactly "mental" work either. Much of it was routinized around standardized textbooks and classroom procedures, and supervision from male principals, inspectors and school trustees continued to increase as the educational bureaucracy became firmly established (Danylewycz & Prentice, 1986).

The undeveloped nature of the teaching profession in the interwar period is perhaps best summed up by reference to the critical appraisal of BC teachers in the Putman-Weir *Survey* of British Columbia education done at government behest in 1925:

> Too many unmarried male teachers; the immaturity of the teachers, especially in rural schools; lack of vision and professional pride; deficient academic and professional qualifications, unwillingness to take additional professional training beyond the legal minimum; lack of experience; inability adequately to profit from experience; tendency to change schools too frequently …

Ironically, the path which British Columbia teachers took to try to improve their professional status was to form a teachers' union in 1917. Thus the most prevalent instrument of class consciousness at the time, the trade union, became the means by which teachers sought to achieve a sense of definition for their work and to better their working conditions. The debate over whether the BCTF should play by the rules of the trade union or the professional association was to extend over close to three decades before the Federation formally affiliated with the Trades and Labour Congress in 1943. But support for labour affiliation within the Federation was always precarious, divided as it was between those who favoured unionism as such and those who preferred to develop a professional association. The Federation thus broke with the TLC in 1956. In the mid-1970s renewed efforts were made to re-affiliate with the trade union movement but they proved unsuccessful (Bruneau, 1979). As late as March 1992, the BCTF in its Annual General Meeting voted against a resolution calling for affiliation with the Canadian Labour Congress.

Mid-Century—Transfer to Universities

By the end of World War II, the normal pattern of teacher education across Canada was as follows. Secondary school teachers were expected to have a bachelor's degree followed by a 1-year post-baccalaureate course leading to certification. Elementary school teachers, for the most part, took a one-year course following high school graduation in what was called a normal school. Following US practice, in some provinces the name "teachers' college" came to replace the latter. Also following the lead of the US, in one province after another responsibility for the training of elementary school teachers was assumed by the universities; in Alberta in 1945, in Newfoundland in 1946, in British Columbia in 1956, in Saskatchewan in 1964, and in Manitoba in 1965. By 1970 the transfer to universities either had been accomplished or was about to be in all other provinces with Quebec and Ontario being the last to make the change. Most elementary teachers were by then receiving at least 2 years of university education and the goal of a BA or BEd for all teachers was within sight. Thus, we see that British Columbia was among the first Canadian provinces to transfer all teacher education to the university. In 1961-62, British Columbia led the provinces in the proportion of its teachers holding university degrees at (37%). In 1962 3 years' study toward the BEd degree became the requirement for a permanent certificate for elementary school teaching (Johnson, 1964).

It is worth noting that the supply of and demand for teachers had a continuing effect on certification requirements. In the two decades after the war the demand for teachers across Canada severely outstripped the supply as the effect of the "baby boom" ran its course through the schools. Whereas the teaching profession advocated lengthening the period of teacher preparation, the provincial departments of education, concerned about putting teachers in classrooms, delayed the introduction of longer training periods and more stringent certification requirements. To this end, some provinces, such as Ontario, introduced emergency short courses requiring only two summers of teacher education with an intervening year of "supervised" teaching at full salary. By these arrangements the various provincial departments of education managed to direct and exert control over both the training and licensing of teachers in the various public school systems. This situation contrasted sharply with other professions in Canada, such as law, medicine and dentistry, where both education and self-regulation were supervised by their respective professional bodies. If the notion of a profession involves the use of a professional organization, belief in public service, sense of calling, belief in self-regulation, and a large degree of autonomy in its day-to-day operation, then teaching in Canada had some way to go at least with respect to the last two points (Hall, 1972; Haskell, 1984).

In 1960, in a wide-sweeping critique of public education for being overburdened by politics and the state, the political scientist, Frank MacKinnon, in a book entitled *The Politics of Education*, advocated delegating more responsibility and freedom to Canadian public schools and teachers. His criticism may be summarized as follows:

To the schools the state gives no power of their own; and the teaching profession is a kind of low-drawer civil service, trained, licensed, hired, inspected and directed by the state. No other activity, institution, or profession is in this extraordinary position; education in North America is now the most completely socialized activity in modern society.

In place of this situation which he roundly deplored, MacKinnon advocated granting a large amount of local control to the public schools, even down to the individual school, and recommended that teachers should become a true profession by virtue of being allowed to regulate themselves as to certification, discipline and professional development in much the same way as Canadian doctors, engineers and lawyers were able to do. "Most institutions and professions which serve the public," he continued, "are able to do so largely on their own terms and with some protection from political interference." Why not teachers? MacKinnon centred his critique on the fact that at that time teaching was the only profession where the State controlled both training and licensing. He contrasted this with the other professions where "the requirements are set and administered jointly by a university and the professional organization concerned, and the licence is given by the profession after certification by the university". For teaching, however, the teacher's licence was "a State permit, not a professional diploma." It was not until the late 1980s that MacKinnon's recommendations were to be seriously addressed, and this occurred in the Province of British Columbia.

By the 1980s, despite the lack of autonomy accorded other professions, teachers—both men and women—had made great strides. The development of the British Columbia Teachers' Federation enabled teachers to focus on both economic and working condition issues and on professional development. Decent salaries, pensions, benefits and contracts became commonplace; negotiating on working conditions, class size, preparation time and extracurricular activity gave teachers some control over their day-to-day lives. At the same time professional issues received attention and membership on ministry curriculum committees, educational commissions and task forces were demanded and accepted. The establishment of professional specialist associations enabled teachers to work together to improve their own professional development (BCTF Members' Guide, 1978).

The transfer of all teacher education to the universities also helped professional development. In many ways this transfer was akin to a shot-gun marriage and it has taken many decades for both parties in this marriage—teachers and universities—to come to appreciate one another. There is no question that despite many difficulties the move to universities has been beneficial to teacher education and to the professional development of the teaching force in the

Province. First of all, virtually all teachers now have degrees and can be said to have a broad liberal education as well as a grounding in the professional aspects of teaching, learning and education generally. Second, because research is integral to the university and separates it from colleges, institutes and normal schools, research on teaching and teacher education, as well as on other areas such as the curriculum, has developed to the extent that it is having an influence on teacher education programs, policy decisions at the Ministry level, and the development of curricular and resource materials. Third, the emphasis on graduate studies has helped develop a cadre of career professionals—administrators, counsellors, curriculum developers, specialists of all kinds. The theoretical knowledge base, professional understanding, and skill development that these teachers and specialists bring to their school and classroom practice ensure that teaching in British Columbia has attained a professional status recognized by parents and the public generally (Fullan & Connolly, 1987; Clifford & Guthrie, 1988; Stapleton, 1988; Houston, 1990).

Despite this progress, criticisms of faculties of education in Canada have remained fairly strong. It is difficult to support or refute such criticisms since there has been no comprehensive study done of university faculties of education in Canada over the last three or four decades. For the US, William R. Johnson has concluded that during this time period, "first, university schools of education have tended to distance themselves from the training and concerns of classroom teachers; second, the research agenda has not often produced knowledge useful to the practitioner nor has it often gained respect among members of the traditional academic disciplines; third, university schools of education have produced no permanent, durable models of teacher training (Johnson, 1989). Clifford & Guthrie (1988), in *Ed School*, an insightful and critical look at schools of education in the US, agree with the conclusion of a committee in California which stated: 'Education schools have been unable either to establish the degree of academic prestige enjoyed by schools such as law and medicine, or to obtain a perception of indispensability on the part of the education profession." The Carnegie Report, *A Nation Prepared: Teachers for the 21st Century* (1986), the report of the Holmes Group (1986), and John Goodlad's trilogy (1990), all conclude that schools/colleges/faculties of education need reform.

In Canada the Fullan/Connolly Report on Teacher Education in Ontario, produced in 1987, was quite damning, "The qualifications of most faculty members presently teaching is a serious concern. In the perception of their critics, many of them lack the training or desire to engage in research, some of them do not keep up-to-date with the research that is being done, and others do not fully appreciate the value of educational research." On the other hand a good number of education professors have learned to play the academic game. The 1988 Birch/Robitaille (1988) Canada-wide study documents the refereed journals, grant proposals and research teams that have been established. As education professors felt obliged to establish academic credentials and to forge academic careers, that is succumb to "publish or perish," their research became more and more sophisticated methodologically and theoretically and thereby, less and less acceptable to practitioners. A chasm opened between theory and practice.

Professors of education, members of research institutions but with a professional commitment to schools and teachers, have found themselves pulled in opposite directions. Unlike other professional faculties—medicine, law, business, engineering—faculties of education have not been as successful in gaining the respect of either the university or the professional community (Clifford & Guthrie, 1988; Dill, 1990). One reason for this may be the history of the move from the normal school to the university; another may be the lack of professional autonomy including control by teachers over certification and discipline.

Recent Developments:
The British Columbia College of Teachers

In 1987, without warning, the British Columbia Government led by a right-of-centre party gave teachers professional autonomy, i.e. control over who may become and continue to be teachers. Bill 19, *The Industrial Relations Act* (1987), gave teachers the right to strike, bargain collectively for wages and working conditions, put principals and vice-principals on contract as managers and therefore not eligible for membership in the BCTF, and legislated either independent local teacher associations or unions within the BCTF. Bill 20, *The Teaching Profession Act* (1987), created the British Columbia College of Teachers. The legislation was developed without consultation with teachers, the universities or other members of the education community. Although it is unclear why the Government acted as it did, there is some speculation. For several decades and increasingly in the 1980s, the BCTF had an agenda which many have argued has been at odds with the agenda of the Government. Each approached education from a very different ideology resulting in growing antagonism between the two (Ungerleider, 1991). It has been suggested with much plausibility that Bill 20, in creating a second body of teachers, and Bill 19 which allowed independent local teacher associations, was intended as a way of undermining the control and authority of the BCTF. A second conjecture suggests that the Socred Government had already adopted a policy of privatizing many government services. By creating an independent College with control over certification and discipline the Government decreased its costs. The price of professional control was the institution of fees. Accordingly teachers now pay for a certification service formerly supplied by government.

The enabling legislation established the College (BCCT) as a professional body of teachers with a College Council of 20 individuals as the governing body. Membership on the Council comprised 15 teachers elected by teachers in each of the 15 zones in the Province, two members appointed by cabinet, two appointed by the Minister of Education, and the last a representative of the Deans of the Faculties of Education in the Province appointed by the Minister but selected by the Deans.[1] *The Teaching Profession Act* was proclaimed in August 1987, elections were held in the fall, and the College and the Council began operations in January 1988. Control over certification, discipline and professional development was henceforth to be in the hands of the teaching profession. To teach in the public schools of British Columbia membership in the College was made mandatory.

All 15 teacher members first elected in the fall of 1987 had been supported by the British Columbia Teachers' Federation. Many had at one time or another held executive positions in either a local branch or the provincial association. The Chairperson of the council elected at the first meeting was Bill Broadley, a former President of the BCTF. The BCTF announced it had control over the Council of the College and believed that it had circumvented the legislation which had created a second body of teachers (BCTF, 1987 and *Teacher*, 1988).

The Council members had a difficult first term as they struggled to clarify the meaning of the Act and determine their responsibilities. The College of Teachers was the first attempt, certainly in North America but possibly (except for Scotland) world-wide, to put control of teacher certification, discipline and professional development in the hands of the profession. Therefore, it had no precedent upon which to base its decisions.[2] It had authority over certification of teachers in BC and yet it had no officers, no registrar, no system in place to handle certification. The College had authority to approve the programs for teacher certification at the three universities and yet it had no way of establishing whether these programs should be accredited. It had by legislative authority control over teacher discipline and yet it had no disciplinary by-laws and did not have a system in place to handle either new discipline cases or those turned over to it by the Ministry. It had control over professional development and yet it was cognizant of the fact that the BCTF and the Provincial Specialists' Association of the BCTF had been involved in professional development for some time. In its first 6 months of operation the College of Teachers gave interim approval to the teacher education programs at the three provincial universities, hired a registrar, rented space, designed membership and service fees, developed a budget and proceeded to establish committees which would produce by-laws.

The creation of the College of Teachers has produced a number of issues affecting teacher education in the Province. Although the College has had to deal with many questions connected with membership and discipline and with reactions from the Government, other education groups and the public, in this paper we shall concentrate only on those which affect teacher education. It is noteworthy that on a Council of 20 individuals who have authority over the approval of teacher education programs for certification purposes, only one member is a teacher educator.

The legislation gave the College control over professional development. However, as noted, the BCTF had exercised a professional development mandate since its founding and numerous provincial specialist associations operated under the banner of the Federation. The College made the decision not to exercise its mandate in this area and appealed to the Government to change the legislation, mandating a Standing Professional Development Committee as one of three standing committees. The Government agreed and, in 1993, substituted a Teacher Education Programs Committee. Professional development for teachers in BC is thus separated from pre-service. This has caused some discomfort among those who see teacher education as a continuum of pre-service, induction and in-service professional development.

The certification process and the approval of programs for initial teacher certification at the three universities have provided interesting challenges for the College. In the initial months of its operation the College adopted the certification practices of the Ministry and gave interim approval to the three universities' teacher education programs. Over time it has developed certification policy, by-laws and appeals procedures. One of the areas of some contention and the source of many appeals has been the qualification of teachers from out of province, especially teachers who don't meet the academic requirements but who have many successful years of classroom teaching experience.[3] Another issue has been the more stringent requirements of the three faculties in the Province compared to requirements in other universities in Canada and whether it is iniquitous to BC graduates to certify out-of-province candidates whose qualifications are less stringent. In some instances the practices of the College in reviewing nominations for certification from BC universities have been more specific and the interpretation of certification criteria more literal than Ministry practice had been. This poses problems for admission decisions of the Faculties as they attempt to judge whether an applicant's previous academic work meets the College's specific criteria. The Universities believe that they should be able to exercise their academic and professional judgment as teacher-educators on such matters as the waiver of a particular course, or the substitution of one course for another, without constant referral to the College Registrar's staff for approval and decision. Traditional university autonomy has been challenged.

Another issue that has affected the Universities has to do with the establishment in the Province of University Colleges which, in association with a university, offer degree programs.[4] The students attend the colleges where they register, pay their fees, and receive student numbers. The courses they take are university courses. At issue is that only the programs at the universities have been approved for certification by the College and a university transcript is required as evidence. The students at the university colleges are registered as college students and receive a *college* transcript. The question of how to grant BC certification to these students and not violate the policy that only the universities have received approval for programs has been a difficult one to resolve.

A third issue causing some contention among Council members and the BCTF is the request by the Universities to have some students do the major portion of their practicum in independent schools. Schools in question are government funded, use the BC curriculum, and have teachers who are members of the College. This issue has been before the Council for 2 years without appreciable movement toward a solution. The ability of the faculties to exercise judgment on suitable placements for practica is being challenged as is the right of students who wish a career in independent schools to get some practice and exposure in them.

The major effort of the College affecting the faculties of education in BC has been a review of the universities' pre-certification programs. In 1989 the College requested that each of the three faculties of education produce a self-study; asked for briefs from all education partners in BC; surveyed practising teachers, cooperating teachers who worked with the practicum teachers, faculty advisors and students; held two forums on teacher education; and conducted on-site visits by a three member team: one teacher-educator, one teacher chosen by the BCTF and the Chair of the College of Teachers, Bill Broadley, also a teacher. This work was facilitated by a consultant, Jim Bowman, a former teacher and BCTF staff officer, who coordinated and summarized the briefs and other documentation and wrote a report, *Teacher Education in British Columbia*, which was circulated for discussion and considered at a third forum (1991). From this forum and other feedback the College established criteria for approval of new teacher education programs and approved on an on-going basis those currently in existence. It also established an on-going process for working collaboratively with the Faculties for the improvement of teacher education.

The review process and the report presented to the College engendered much discussion. The meaning and purpose of the review were viewed differently by College members and by members of the university who deal with various kinds of accreditation bodies. Issues such as the nature of autonomy versus the authority of the College, the desire to make specific recommendations against the need for flexibility, idealistic suggestions which in practical terms could not be implemented, and the relative emphasis given to pre-certification programs by the faculties, have all been part of the debate.

Heated discussions have taken place on the role of faculties of education in the university community, and the place and prestige of teacher education in faculties which serve purposes other than the provision of teacher education programs, such as graduate and diploma programs and fundamental and applied research. These are important issues to faculties of education which are part of the university community and must play by its rules not only those of the College of Teachers. They are also important issues for the teaching profession in its search for status, improved practice and the knowledge to handle its increasing social, as well as educative, role in society. Moreover, many practising teachers have a vested interest in that they engaged in some form of graduate study. Finally, suggestions which would seem to separate pre-service from the full continuum of teacher education have caused much comment, with overwhelming support among practitioners as well as faculty members for the continuum of pre-service and in-service including a central but not a separate role for pre-certification teacher education programs.

The College is struggling to establish its approaches and its methodologies. The review of programs provided one example of the tasks. There is no question that, without precedents in place, it will take some time for the College to develop an effective accreditation process. A willingness by all parties involved to recognize this and work together should help to facilitate the process and enable the College to gain its own sense of maturity.

Conclusion

This brief look at teacher education in British Columbia suggests several conclusions. First, if one looks back over the century from the pre-normal school days when almost anyone could teach provided they passed a written examination, to today's very explicit by-laws and policies of the BCCT, the change is profound. However, almost all jurisdictions in Canada moved from a written subject-based examination, to normal schools, to university or college control of teacher education. Most jurisdictions also moved from very short programs of four months to one or two years following junior matriculation, to the requirement of a degree, either a BEd degree or a first bachelor's degree followed by a certification program. Most jurisdictions have also changed from a concentration on school subject-based knowledge to a combination of liberal arts, professional courses and an extended practicum. The difference in British Columbia is not in the content or length of programs; it is in the locus of legal authority for these matters and the ways that legal authority is exercised.

For the greater part of this century in BC and in most other jurisdictions the legal authority for teacher education and certification has been with the government of the particular province or state. When teacher education was transferred to the university that legal authority did not change. However, in practice governments accepted the recommendations of the universities without question. Faculties of education, in making curriculum and/or program changes, were bound by the regulations of the Senate of the University. The government, at least in British Columbia, did not review such changes and did not establish a mechanism to approve program requirements. *De facto*, the universities controlled who received certification within the province. Clearly that has changed with the establishment of College by-laws and Policies and the exercise by the College of its authority. It will be unfortunate if the bureaucratic and minute attention to detail practised by the College prevents or delays university attempts to change teacher education programs. Change is always difficult and faculties of education now have two hurdles to overcome in making change— the traditional university mechanism of faculty and senate approval, and now as well the mechanisms for approval established by the College.

A second point involves the review of teacher education and the Report prepared by Jim Bowman. The results of this are equivocal. Certainly, members of the Council learned quickly how complex a matter it is to design and prepare programs to educate teachers for the classrooms of the nineties. They were unprepared for the variety of courses that individuals and groups argued should be included in pre-service teacher education programs. The critical role that classroom teachers have in the success of the practicum and the cavalier attitude that many principals and teachers displayed toward this task became evident. The lack of relevant knowledge, attitudes toward faculties of education based on out-dated information and the prevalence of biases and assumptions all played a part in this review.

For the faculties, the requirement to articulate their programs, the need to justify the balance between theory and practice, and the results of surveys of both practising teachers and pre-service students on various aspects of the programs resulted in numerous committees being set up in the faculties to look at and analyse the program components and their delivery. Nonetheless, despite thirty-two recommendations in the Bowman Report, the courses and programs of the three faculties of education have not changed as a result of this review.

Third, the enactment of *The Teaching Profession Act* (Bill 20) creating the BC College of Teachers has served to focus more attention on teacher education than has heretofore been the case in British Columbia. The review, with its numerous surveys, questionnaires, site visits and forums, has raised the level of interest in the faculty programs, the supporting role of the school and classroom teachers, and some awareness of the complex nature of the task. Teachers, administrators, Ministry personnel, trustees and faculty members had debated with good humour and a genuine interest in each other's point of view. The BCTF has elevated the attention given to teacher education and produced a revised position paper for approval by its membership. At the same time, however, the College and the BCTF are in conflict over control. At its Annual General Meeting in March 1992, the BCTF adopted a motion calling for the repeal of the Teaching Profession Act and the closure of the College created by Bill 20. In place of the College, a Teachers' Professional Certification Council was proposed composed of fifteen members appointed by the BCTF and five members appointed by the provincial government. In addition, the new council would be financed by the Ministry of Education instead of the teachers themselves. To date the Government has not dealt with this request. Although there is disagreement around the issues of control and financing, the level of interest in the education community is healthy, and one which, if nourished appropriately, should provide a basis for continuing dialogue and the improvement of professional practice in the education system.

Finally, although it may have been unintentional, the Government, in creating the College, may have helped prevent a trend, prevalent in some states of the US and in Britain, from gaining a foothold in BC. In the US alternative certification practices put individuals in schools without professional courses or practicum, relying instead on academic preparation in the subject field (Stein, 1990; Gideonse, 1992). In Britain the move of teacher education out of the institutions of higher education and into schools would seem to put emphasis on practice as opposed to theory (Gutteridge & Milburn, 1992). The acceptance of the College as a strong player in education in BC, the heightened awareness of teacher education in the ultimate success of schools and the willingness of all parties to work together may be the antidote necessary to resist such developments. In the final analysis it is important that the BC College of Teachers thrives and succeeds in giving the teaching profession control over certification and discipline. To fail may indicate that teachers cannot manage their own affairs and that would be devastating to teachers, teacher educators and the profession generally.

NOTES

1 To date, the two members appointed by the Cabinet have been political appointments; of the two appointed by the Ministry of Education one has been a Ministry official and the other an individual from the independent schools sector; the Deans' appointee has been Dr. Nancy Sheehan, Dean of Education at the University of British Columbia.

2 The only other jurisdiction to give substantial control over who should be admitted to the Register of Teachers and, therefore, entitled to teach, is Scotland, where the General Teaching Council for Scotland was established in 1965. This Council has a much broader membership and, although teachers are in the majority, there is substantial representation from the teacher education institutions. The Council and the institutions are also subject to decisions by the Scottish Education Department in such areas as policy, course approval and degree stipulations (Kirk, 1988).

3 Certification requirements specific to individual provinces have been a

source of dissatisfaction in Canada for all of this century. There are a few reciprocal agreements on certification between Canadian provinces at present but none involving British Columbia.

4 The Government's Access Program was developed in 1988 with a goal of creating 15 000 new places for university students. One aspect of this program was the creation of university colleges at three of the Province's colleges. In association with a university these colleges are granting certain degrees and, over time, hope to become autonomous degree-granting institutions.

REFERENCES

Abbott, J. (1986) Accomplishing a man's task: rural women teachers, male culture, and the school inspectorate in turn-of-the-century Ontario, *Ontario History*, 78, pp. 313-330.

Barman, J. (1990) Birds of passage or early professionals? Teachers in late nineteenth-century British Columbia, *Historical Studies in Education*, 2(1), p. 19.

Barman, J. (1991-92) Pioneer teachers of British Columbia, *British Columbia Historical News*, 25, pp. 15-18.

BCTF Newsletter (1987), 27(4) (Nov.) and 278(5) (Dec.).

Best, J.H. (Ed.) (1983) *Historical Inquiry in Education: a research agenda* (Washington, AERA).

Birch, D.R. & Robitaille, D.R. (1988) Canadian educational research: an assessment and strategies for achieving excellence, in: H.A. Stevenson & J.D. Wilson (Eds) *Quality in Canadian Public Education*, pp. 67-84 (Philadelphia, Falmer Press).

Bowman, J. (1991) *A Report to the College of Teachers on Teacher Education in British Columbia* (Vancouver, BC, College of Teachers).

Bruneau, W.A. (1979) "Still pleased to teach:" a study of the British Columbia Teachers' Federation, 1917-1978, unpublished, p. 31.

Calam, J. (1986) Teaching the teachers: establishment and early years of the BC Provincial Normal Schools, in: N.M. Sheehan, J.D. Wilson & D.C. Jones (Eds) *Schools in the West: essays in Canadian educational history*, pp. 75-97 (Calgary, Detselig).

Carnegie Task Force on Teaching as a Profession (1986) *A Nation Prepared: teachers for the twenty-first century* (New York, Carnegie Forum on Education and the Economy).

Clifford, G.J. & Guthrie, J.W. (1988) Eds. *School: a brief for professional education* (Chicago, University of Chicago Press).

Danylewycz, M. & Prentice, A. (1986) Teacher's work: changing patterns and perceptions in the emerging school systems of nineteenth and early twentieth century central Canada, *Labour/Le travail*, 17, pp. 59-80.

Dill, D.D. (1990) Transforming schools of education into schools of teaching, in: D.D. Dill *et al.* (Eds.) *What Teachers Need to Know: the knowledge, skills and values essential to good teaching*, pp. 224-239 (San Francisco, Jossey Bass).

Dunn, T.A. (1980) The rise of mass public schooling in British Columbia, 1900-1929, in: J.D. Wilson & D.C. Jones (Eds) *Schooling and Society in Twentieth Century British Columbia*, p. 26 (Calgary, Detselig).

Fullan, M. & Connolly, F.M. (1987) *Teacher Education in Ontario: current practice and options for the future* (Toronto, Ministry of Colleges and Universities, Ontario).

Gideonse, H.D. (1992) *Teacher Education Policy: narratives, stories and cases* (Albany, State University of New York Press).

Goodlad, J.I. (1990) *Teachers for Our Nation's Schools* (San Francisco, Jossey Bass).

Goodlad, J.I., Soder, R. & Sirotnik, K.A. (Eds) (1990) *The Moral Dimensions of Teaching* (San Francisco, Jossey Bass).

Goodlad, S. & Sirotnik, K.A. (Eds) (1990) *Places Where Teachers are Taught* (San Francisco, Jossey Sass).

Gutteridge, D. & Millburn, G. (1992) Forward: to the Canadian reader, in: J. Wilson (Ed.) *Reflections and Practice: teacher education and the teaching profession* (London, Althouse Press).

Hall, R. (1972) Professionalization and bureaucratization, in: R. Hall (Ed.) *The Formal Organization* (New York, Basic Books).

Haskell, T. (Ed.) (1984) *The Authority of Experts: studies in history and theory* (Bloomington, Indiana University Press).

HOLMES, GROUP (1986) *Tomorrow's Teachers: a report of the Holmes Group* (East Lansing, MI, Holmes Group).

Houston, W.R. (Ed.) (1990) *Handbook of Research on Teacher Education*, a project of the Association of Teacher Educators (New York, Macmillan).

Industrial Relations Act (1987) Statutes of British Columbia.

Johnson, F.H. (1964) *A History of Public Education in British Columbia* pp. 213-214 (Vancouver, UBC Publications Centre).

Johnson, F.H. (1971) *John Jessop: gold seeker and educator* (Vancouver, Mitchell Press).

Johnson, W.R. (1989) Teachers and teacher training in the twentieth century, in: D. Warren (Ed.) *American Teachers: histories of a profession at work*, p. 243 (New York, Macmillan).

Kirk, G. (1988) Persistence and change in teacher education, in: S. Brown & R. Wake (Eds) *Education in Transition: what role for research?* (Edinburgh, Scottish Council for Research in Education).

Mackinnon, F. (1960) *The Politics of Education: a study of the political administration of the public schools* (Toronto, University of Toronto Press).

Members' Guide to the BCTF (1978-79) (Vancouver, BCTF).

Patterson, R.S. (1986) Voices from the past: the personal and professional struggles of rural school teachers, in: N.M. Sheehan, J.D. Wilson & D.C. Jones (Eds) *Schools in the West: essays in Canadian educational history*, pp. 91-111 (Calgary, Detselig).

Prentice, A. (1990) "Friendly atoms in chemistry:" women and men at normal school in mid-nineteenth century Toronto, in: D. KEANE & C. READ (Eds), *Old Ontario: essays in honour of J.M.S. Careless*, pp. 285-317 (Toronto, Dundurn).

Province of British Columbia News Releases (March 21, 1989) Ministry of Advanced Education and Job Training, and Ministry Responsible for Science and Technology. "Hagen provides details on university degree programs in Kelowna;" "Hagen provides details on university degree programs in Kamloops;" "Hagen provides details on university degree programs in Nanaimo."

Putman, J.H. & Weir, G.M. (1925) *Survey of the School System*, p. 174 (Victoria, King's Printer).

Stapleton, J.J. (1988) Preparing teachers for more complex classrooms: an overview of the pressures for extension and/or reform in teacher education programs, in: *Extended Programs of Teacher Education*, pp. 2-23 (Ottawa, Canadian Teachers' Federation).

Stein, S.E. (1990) *Teacher Education Policy in the States: a 50-state survey of legislative and administrative actions* (Washington, American Association of Colleges for Teacher Education).

Teacher: Newsmagazine of the BC Teachers' Federation (1988) March, pp. 8-9.

The Teaching Profession Act (1987) Statutes of British Columbia.

Ungerleider, C. (1991) Power, politics and professionalism: the impact of change in British Columbia on the status of teachers and their professional conduct, presented to the *Teacher Development: Key to Educational Change Conference*, Vancouver, BC.

Warren, D. (Ed.) (1989) *American Teachers: histories of a profession at work* (New York, Macmillan).

Wilson, J.D. (1989) The visions of ordinary participants: teachers' views of rural schooling in British Columbia in the 1920s, in: P. E. ROY (Ed.) *A History of British Columbia: selected readings* (Toronto, Copp Clark Pitman).

Wilson, J.D. (1991) "I am ready to be of assistance when I can:" Lottie Bowron and rural female teachers in British Columbia, in: A. Prentice & M. Theobald (Eds.) *Women Who Taught: perspectives on the history of women and teaching*, pp. 239-255 (Toronto, University of Toronto Press).

Wilson, J.D. & Stortz, P.J. (1988) "May the Lord have mercy on you:" the rural school problem in British Columbia in the 1920s, *BC Studies* 79, pp. 24-58.

∗ ∗ ✳ ∗ ∗

Documents for Chapter Eleven

Teacher training is a contentious topic. How and what should teachers be taught in university? What qualifications should they possess? Document 38 explorers the following questions: who became teachers immediately after the Second World War, what were societal attitudes towards the teaching profession, and how successful were teacher training programmes. The final document analyzes what a sample of 629 teachers between 1957 and 1963 stated they liked the most and the least about their occupation. Compare these responses to Sutherland's finding in Chapter Ten. Other topics to explore include: should teachers control licensing and disciplining as do other professions? Should faculties of education concentrate on teaching content or skills? Should high school teachers be required to have some sort of content qualifications before teaching specific courses? And should the training and licensing of teachers be a federal government responsibility (thus allowing ease of movement among provinces)?

38) CANADIAN TEACHERS, 1953[1]

Approximately 4,000 trainees register each year in the normal schools and schools of education to train as teachers. In 1948, accurate information was gathered regarding the home backgrounds of 3,577 students registered in teacher training classes. Thirty-seven per cent of these future teachers came from farm homes, this occupational group being the largest in each province. In second, third, and fourth places were those whose fathers were in the skilled labour, clerical, or civil service and merchant-retail groups, from which respectively 10, 8, and 8 per cent, of the students came. Although the 3,577 trainees represented twenty-six nationality backgrounds, 47 per cent were of Anglo-Saxon and 9 per cent of French descent.

Teaching, though not a well-paid vocation, appears to be an avenue by which students from the lower and middle socioeconomic groups can improve their social and financial standing. Many students who do not intend to make teaching their life-work use teaching as a stepping-stone to professions and vocations more remunerative than teaching. Because fewer than 30 per cent of those who train as teachers ever intend to continue in the profession, it is not surprising that the average period of service of all teachers is less than ten years ....

What steps are taken to interest capable high school students in teaching as a career? How are prospective teachers selected? The growing teacher-shortage has resulted in more emphasis on recruitment than upon selection. Several Departments of Education have distributed to the high schools vocational-guidance bulletins with titles such as, "Should I Teach?," "Teaching as a Career," and "To Teach or Not To Teach," in the hope of interesting senior students in teaching. It may be, however, that the attitude of staff members towards teaching has more influence upon student choice of vocation than have the bulletins.

Many teachers are apparently advising their best students to select some vocation other than teaching, because of the few opportunities the latter offers for social, economic, or professional advancement. The attitude of the teachers may be inferred from the fact that although 75 per cent of the children of professional folk generally choose the professions of their fathers, only 23 per cent of teachers' children select their fathers' vocation. Students in the training colleges report that many of their teachers advised them against selecting teaching.

Besides distributing guidance bulletins to students, a few provincial Departments of Education are reducing or abolishing fees in the training colleges, giving scholarships of $200 or $300 per year to all who agree to teach for at least three years after graduation, reducing entrance requirements, shortening training periods, and lowering standards of training. Few attempts are being made to select, from those applying for admission to teacher training schools, those who give promise of becoming successful teachers. With the exception of the Ontario College of Education, which interviews all candidates wishing to register in candidacy for high school certification, the writer does not know of any school or college that does not accept all applicants who meet minimum entrance requirements, which, unfortunately, have been lowered in some provinces as a "short-term" method of coping with the shrinking teacher supply. Although positive, controlled measures of selection are not being applied, there are many factors at work determining who do and do not wish to be teachers.

Entrance requirements for the normal schools are lower than for Matriculation into the universities, except in a few instances when Junior Matriculation admits to either institution. Ordinarily there are more electives in the first-mentioned programmes with the privilege of substituting non-academic subjects such as shop, home economics, music, and art for foreign languages, mathematics, and science courses.

In Alberta, where the university is responsible for all teacher training, candidates are required to present complete Senior Matriculation if registering for a two-, three-, or four-year programme in education. Until very recently candidates for temporary licences were permitted to register for a one-year programme if they held a high school graduation diploma with Senior Matriculation credit in two subjects. Candidates permitted to register with these low qualifications were, on the average, of lower ability than others. On the 1945 edition of the Thurstone Psychological Examination the median score of the 144 senior matriculants was 122.7; that of the temporary licence group, 90.2. The ninth decile score of the latter group was 118.6. In this single instance where reliable data are available, the students attracted to teaching by the lower entrance requirements were inferior not only in educational attainments but also in intellectual capacity.

There is evidence that at least 25 per cent of the present normal school student body would not be accepted for training if elementary screening techniques were used. When 1,767 of these students were asked why they enrolled in the teacher-training programme, 26 per cent said they "liked working with young people"; 28 per cent, that they thought they would be successful teachers; 14 per cent, that they had been advised by teachers or parents to take the course; while 22 per cent said that they were candidates for the profession because "Salaries are high," "Teaching is easy," "Holidays are long," "It's easy to get a certificate," and "I wanted to earn a little money before getting married."

* * * * *

39) TEACHERS' FEELINGS ABOUT THEIR JOB, 1967[2]

Background of the Study

For a number of years a course entitled "Mental Health in the School" was offered at the Macdonald College Summer School of Education. During lectures and conference periods, consideration was given to the question of the mental health of the teacher and to factors in the teaching situation which contributed either positively or negatively to mental health. Some of the factors discussed were as follows:

1) What aspects of teaching do I as a teacher enjoy and find stimulating (thereby contributing positively to mental health)? What aspects of teaching do I dislike (thereby contributing negatively to mental health)?

2) What about the nature of interpersonal relationships within the school— relations with principals, supervisors, and inspectors? In what respects do these associations contribute positively or negatively to mental health?

3) What are the characteristics of the "best" and "worst" teacher in the school? Although there will be exceptions, it could be hypothesized that, in general, the "best" teachers will have a higher level of "teacher" mental health than their "worst" colleagues, and will also make a greater positive contribution to the mental health of their pupils.

Since the discussions produced some interesting points of view, it was decided to examine the above topics more comprehensively. As a result, a "Personal Relations Questionnaire" was prepared and distributed among students attending the Summer School course.

The questionnaire requested the teachers to express their opinions about the following statements: (1) What do I most like (or dislike) about teaching; (2) Characteristics of my principal, supervisors, and inspectors which I like (or dislike); (3) Characteristics of the "best" (and "worst") teacher in our school. Space was provided for three responses to each statement. The questionnaires were unsigned and a frank expression of opinion was encouraged.

The Sample of the Study

Between 1957 and 1963 inclusive (with the exception of 1961), completed questionnaires were obtained from a total of 629 teachers of whom about 90% were female ....

1. What I most like about teaching

In general, the respondents tended to produce rather uniform reasons for their enjoyment of teaching. Whether such uniformity is the result of a stereotype representing the way one *should* react, or whether it represents a genuine attitude is a matter upon which there might be a difference of opinion.

TABLE 2
RESPONSES TO THE STATEMENT:
"WHAT I MOST LIKE ABOUT TEACHING"

Response	*Number of Responses*
Working with children	457
Seeing results of helping children; sense of accomplishment	333
Helping children	104
Holidays and hours; vacations	101
Variety of work	92
Independence; my own boss	73
Stimulation; challenge of work	60
Pleasant relationships with other teachers	58
Proud to be member of the profession; prestige	44
Pleasant working conditions	34
Learning about children	19
Chance to study; travel; keep up with the world	16
Pleasure in teaching a particular subject	16
Feeling of authority	16
Meeting new people	12
Miscellaneous* (responses which occurred less than 10 times)	54
Total	1489

*Regular pay, meeting parents, extra-curricular activities, feeling of security, general enjoyment of the work, learning about subjects taught, seeing former students become good citizens.

2. What I most dislike about teaching

Because of numerous "no dislikes" comments, there were fewer responses than in the previous section. On the other hand, the number of categories is considerably greater.

TABLE 3
RESPONSES TO THE STATEMENT:
"WHAT I MOST DISLIKE ABOUT TEACHING"

Response	Number of Responses
Clerical duties—making up records, reports; "paper-work"	150
Parent-teacher difficulties—lack of co-operation; "disinterest"	138
Correcting books and examinations	128
Excessive and/or ineffective supervision by principals, inspectors, and supervisors	95
Non-academic duties—e.g., noon, recess, and playground Supervision	86
Inadequate salary	82
Difficulties in discipline—"problem" children	68
Rigid and unsatisfactory curriculum	58
Unsatisfactory relationships with principal and/or colleagues	55
Community interference and indifference	48
Frustrations as the result of a sense of non-accomplishment—e.g., inability to help slow child	47
Large and unstreamed classes	47
Inadequate supplies and equipment	42
Making lesson plans—preparing lessons	36
General tension of the work	36
Interruptions of classroom work	22
"After hours" demand on time	17
Collecting money—Red Cross, school supplies	17
Dislike of certain subjects	16
Lack of recognition by public	16
School board interference	14
Monotony	13
Need for evaluation—examinations	10
Miscellaneous*	45
Total	1286

*Home and School demands, staff meetings, attending Summer School, inefficiently-run school, extra-curricular activities, inflicting punishment, commuting to school, boarding house, poor social life.

[Tables 4-9 dealt with characteristics of principals, inspectors, and supervisors.]

9. Characteristics of the best teacher in our school

From the large number of responses to this section of the questionnaire, it was obvious that the teachers felt prepared to identify and describe the teacher whom they recognized as the "best in the school." (No criteria for evaluating the "best" and the "worst" teacher were provided.) It was also apparent that a particular teacher was being portrayed—not a hypothetical person built up by combining the best features of several individuals.

TABLE 10
RESPONSES TO THE STATEMENT:
"CHARACTERISTICS OF THE BEST TEACHER IN OUR SCHOOL"

Characteristic	Number of Responses
Good discipline	194
Kindly; understanding; patient	158
Well-organized; efficient	142
Helpful to pupils and new teachers	135
Likes and knows children; interested in them	120
Liked by children, fellow teachers, and parents	92
Friendly	83
Creative; variety of activities; A/V aids; "has ideas"	81
Conscientious	78
Cheerful	61
Co-operates with others	56
Responsible; hard worker	54
Good sense of humor	47
Knows curriculum	45
Fair	35
Calm, quiet manner	34
"Personality"	32
Interested in everything	29
Gets subject matter across	26
Personally interested in pupils	23
No screaming	22
Minds own business; no gossip	19
Enjoys teaching	19
Attractively dressed; well-groomed	16
Miscellaneous*	47
Total	1648

*Well informed, high moral standards, cultured, kept attractive classroom, punctual, sincere, generous, enthusiastic, confident.

10. Characteristics of the worst teacher in our school

TABLE 11
RESPONSES TO THE STATEMENT:
"CHARACTERISTICS OF THE WORST TEACHER
IN OUR SCHOOL"

Characteristic	Number of Responses
Lazy: irresponsible; "gets by"	214
Poor discipline	205
Inefficient in work; disorganized; poor or no planning	120
Screams at pupils; a "yeller"	105
Not interested in children; dislikes them	90
Tells stories; gossips	83
Not interested in teaching	81
Not co-operative; poor relationship with colleagues	68
Sloppy and inappropriate dress and appearance	57
Egocentric and selfish	50
Impatient; hot tempered; mean	49
Congenital complainer; very critical	45
Domineering; bossy	39
Doesn't understand children	32
Dull	27
Shows favoritism	25
Nervous and fussy	23
Dull and drab classroom	19
Sarcastic	17
Inconsistent	15
Conceited	13
Insincere	12
Immature	10
Miscellaneous*	79
Total	1478

*Troublemaker, bad voice, poor English, too conscientious, questionable morals, never smiles, plays up to principal, no sense of humor, too familiar with pupils, shows racial and religious prejudices, doesn't teach beyond text, unfriendly, doesn't get along with parents ....

*   *   *   *   *

1 "Who Are Canada's Teachers? How Are They Recruited and Selected?" *The Year Book of Education, 1953* (London, England: University of London Institute of Education, 1953), pp. 230-233.

2 J.E.M. Young, "A Survey of Teachers' Attitudes toward Certain Aspects of Their Profession," *Canadian Education and Research Digest* (June, 1967), tables 2, 3, 10, 11, pp. 115-117, 126, 128.

Chapter Twelve:
The Ideal Curriculum

Until the 1960s, history courses were compulsory and were assigned approximately the same classroom time as mathematics and language. Canadian and British history courses were at the core of the curriculum in both elementary and secondary schools. Historian Ken Osborne has identified five crises in the teaching of history in the last one hundred years.[123] At the end of the nineteenth century, educators became concerned that history was not sufficiently national and patriotic. Subsequently, the Dominion Education Association sponsored a competition to produce an acceptable nation-wide textbook. The second crisis emerged in the 1920s when it was discovered that students knew more American than Canadian history, and that students considered Canadian history to be boring. As a result, political and constitutional history was de-emphasized in favour of biographical, narrative, and social history. During the Second World War, the divisive conscription crisis resulted in the modification of the history curriculum to promote greater understanding between Anglophone and Francophone Canadians. In the late 1960s, students were once again discovered to be woefully ignorant of Canadian history and to have little interest in it. The Canada Studies Foundation emerged in 1970 to correct this situation. Thirty years later, historian Jack Granatstein ignited the fifth crisis when he declared that Canadian history was dead.[124]

The common thread in these crises was the debate regarding the role of history in fostering national identity—an identity that was seen to be threatened. Osborne noted that Canadians are now asking such questions as: "Should the teaching of history be related to the practice of citizenship and, if so, how should citizenship be defined? Should history be, at least in schools, a vehicle for the formation of national identity? Can national identity be defined—and should it be and by whom? ... What is the appropriate balance among historical knowledge, skill, and understanding ...? Should a national curriculum or national standards be imposed on schools?"[125] Keep these questions in mind as you read the following article.

Ken Osborne has expanded on the topic of citizenship in: "Education Is the Best National Insurance: Citizenship Education in Canadian Schools, Past and Present," *Canadian and International Education*, vol. 25, no. 2 (December 1996); and *In Defence of History: Teaching the Past and the Meaning of Democratic Citizenship* (Toronto, 1995). Also see: Rosa Bruno-Jofre, "Citizenship and Schooling in Manitoba, 1918-1945," *Manitoba History*, vol. 36 (Fall 1988/Winter 1999); and Veronica Strong-Boag, "Claiming a Place in the Nation: Citizenship Education and the Challenge of Feminists, Natives, and Workers in Post-Confederation Canada," *Canadian and International Education*, Special Issue (1997).

* * * * *

Education for Citizenship[126]

When the Manitoba Minister of Education made school attendance compulsory in that province in 1916, he did so in terms of citizenship. Boys and girls, he said, were the citizens of the future and they must attend school to learn how to perform the duties of citizenship. A much later Minister, in that same province, spoke a very different language, explaining a new policy direction in 1991 with these words: "The workforce will demand highly skilled and adaptable workers who have the ability to upgrade existing skills and develop new skills, who can help create and participate in a climate that encourages entrepreneurship, innovation and economic growth; and who can understand the complex dynamics of a competitive global environment."[1]

Here is another juxtaposition covering roughly the same years. In 1925, the influential Putman-Weir inquiry into education in British Columbia concluded that "The development of a united and intelligent citizenship should be accepted without question as the fundamental aim of our schools." In 1987 the Radwanski inquiry into dropouts in Ontario described education as "the paramount ingredient for success in the competitive world economy" and essential to "our very survival as an economically competitive society."[2]

It seems that a world has passed away in education. We no longer see students as citizens but as workers. We value not citizenship and the society that sustains it, but economic success in the global economy. The week before I wrote these words, my local newspaper featured statements from 39 candidates in elections for surrounding school boards. It is perhaps not surprising that, of the 39, the great majority spoke of computers, high-tech, the global economy, excellence, and the other educational buzz words of the moment, and only two even mentioned the word citizenship. It is in this climate that schools are urged to form partnerships with business, that literature is downgraded to literacy, that history disappears from the curriculum, that knowledge and appreciation are abandoned for skills, that understanding is reduced to performance standards, attainment targets, and intended learning outcomes.

Until the last 10 or 15 years, the Canadian public school system cohered around the concept of citizenship. Schools existed, and children were compelled to attend them, for the purpose of producing citizens. Definitions of citizenship and approaches to citizenship education changed over the years, but that citizenship was the central goal of schooling was never in doubt.

Initially, in the years before and immediately after the First World War, citizenship was seen in harsh and coercive terms. It was the code word for the assimilation of immigrant children, the First Nations, religious and linguistic minorities, to a unitary and homogenizing view of what it meant to be Canadian. Outside Quebec, educationists were convinced that Canada was either already a nation, or was well on the way to becoming one, and that the task of the public schools was to educate the young for national citizenship, English-speaking, British in allegiance, able to cast an informed vote, subscribing to more or less the same social values, and suitably temperate in thought and deed. This notion of citizenship has been described by some historians as the embodiment of Anglo-conformity, and though this characterization is both too simple and too sweeping, it does catch the essence of citizenship education in those early years.

Despite its assimilationist and coercive elements, however, citizenship also carried within it some very different possibilities. If, on the one hand, it threatened forced uniformity in a narrowly defined Canadian nationality, on the other, it offered the promise of democracy, respect for rights, and the chance to participate in public life regardless of personal background. Citizenship has always been a flexibly protean word. It was and is used by conservatives, liberals, radicals, and even revolutionaries, to press their various claims. Citizenship is not static but dynamic. It is shaped by debate and discussion, struggle and conflict. Women fought their way into the citizenship tent, as they won the right to vote, to hold public office and to be constitutionally recognized as persons, as did workers when they won the right to organize, to bargain and to strike, and as now are the First Nations as they negotiate for equity and justice. The rights of citizenship can never be taken for granted. They are won and preserved, and sometimes lost, through struggle and their definition changes with each new generation. The quality of citizenship, which is so vital to the health of democracy, depends on the energy and commitment of citizens.

As a result of this continual process of debate, redefinition, and struggle, definitions of citizenship over the years became more generous and inclusive. Assimilation gave way to multiculturalism; unilingualism to bilingualism; uniformity to diversity—to the point that some commentators today worry that Canada is in danger of falling apart. As ideas of citizenship changed over time, so did approaches to citizenship education. By the 1970s, Canadian citizenship education had come to consist of six principal elements. It aimed to give students, first, a sense of identity as Canadians but also as citizens of the world; second, an awareness of and respect for human rights; third, an acceptance of the responsibilities and obligations of citizenship; fourth, a reflective commitment to broad social values; fifth, the capacity to participate in public life; and, sixth, the ability to think about and act intelligently on the implications of all five of these elements.[3]

This is not to say, of course, that Canadian schools acted as one cohesive force to implement this version of citizenship education, or that all schools saw all six elements as equally valuable. No school system is that tightly organized, least of all in Canada. Teachers have a good deal of autonomy in their classrooms when they care to use it and they often have more immediate things to worry about than teaching citizenship. Today, for example, they have to worry about the physical safety of their students; to see that they are fed; to prepare them for exams and tests. Increasingly, teachers' working conditions force them to think in terms of sheer survival, not of educating citizens. One of the weaknesses of citizenship education over the years has been its inability to penetrate the classroom, to turn its rhetoric into actual practice. Nonetheless, citizenship was, until recently, at the heart of educational policy making.

A moment's thought shows that the six elements of citizenship education that have just been described raise as many questions as they offer answers. It is easy, for example, to say that education should result in students having a firmer sense of Canadian identity than they otherwise would have, but just what does this mean? Is identity the same as national pride or patriotism? In the 1970s the Canada Studies Foundation spoke of "pan-Canadian understanding" and Professor Tom Symons spoke of "knowing ourselves," but what is it that students should know and understand? What vision of Canada lies at the heart of these questions? Is John Ralston Saul right to say that Canada is not a nation-state in the orthodox European and American sense and that our organizing principle is complexity?[4] Are we one nation, or two, or three or more? Just what does it mean to be a multinational state if that is in fact what we are? Whatever we are, what do we want to be and how do we get there? And in the world of the twenty-first century, how do we combine our sense of national identity with a wider global awareness? Are there limits to national sovereignty and if so, where do we place them and what do we concede and to whom?

These are obviously tough and complex questions, but at the same time they are questions that face all Canadian citizens. They faced us in Meech Lake, in the Charlottetown Accord, in NAFTA, in the Quebec referendum, in negotiating with the First Nations, in the debate over the Multilateral Agreement on Investment, and will undoubtedly continue to face us in the future. They remind us that citizenship in Canada, perhaps more than in most countries, is a matter of continuing debate. It is not a matter of learning the answers to the age-old questions, as when one learns the catechism, but of being able and willing to join in a continuing conversation. Political theorists have long said that dialogue and debate lie at the heart of democracy and nowhere is this more true than in Canada.

As with identity, so with the other elements of citizenship education. All raise difficult and continuing questions which constitute the very essence of citizenship in Canada. We all agree, for example, that citizenship confers certain rights, but just what are they and what should they be? To some extent, they are enshrined in the 1982 *Charter of Rights and Freedoms*, but the Charter does not cover everything and is in any case open to challenge. Is health care a right, for example? Is a job? What is the balance between individual and group rights? And even when we agree about rights in the abstract, we can easily disagree on their application in concrete cases, as in the controversies over abortion, assisted suicide, censorship, discrimination, and so on. As in the case of identity, the rights of citizenship are not once-for-all givens, but matters of continuing debate.

The same is true of all the elements of citizenship education listed above, most obviously in the cases of social values and of the duties and obligations of citizenship, but this dynamic fluidity of citizenship is what makes education so important. The quality of life in Canada, and even its political integrity, depends in large part on the ability of its people to act as citizens, to take an intelligent and informed interest in public affairs, to participate in those affairs, to accept disagreement and difference, to understand that there are often no easy or agreed answers to common problems. This means that citizens must possess what philosophers have identified as the democratic virtues. Carol Gould, for example, has identified these as reciprocity in dealing with other people, openness to diverse viewpoints, respect for human rights, mutuality, flexibility, open-mindedness, concern for community, ability to work with others, capacity for rational activity and initiative. The Manitoba Department of Education put it very simply in 1948, describing the responsible citizenship as openness to other viewpoints, respect for the rights of others, realizing that every right brings a corresponding responsibility, understanding the democratic process, respect for the law, and participation in public affairs.[5]

We are not born with these qualities. We have to learn them. And school is where much of our learning should take place, especially in an age where powerful voices convey a contrary message. For the most part, the media do not preach a message of citizenship. Instead, they teach our children far more about the United States than about Canada, and generally emphasize personal gratification, withdrawal from public life, political apathy and cynicism. Citizenship requires the schools to teach knowledge as well as skills. Despite the urging of futurists, knowledge is not obsolete. Citizens need it in their heads, not in their computers. They also need the skills to analyze and use it. And, as is obvious from all that has been said so far, citizenship is also a matter of values.

Citizenship education is far more than a course in civics or a training in good behaviour. It draws on all the subjects in the curriculum, and on extracurricular activities. It is shaped by the way teachers teach and interact with students and by the overall atmosphere of the school. A good general education is in many ways the best preparation for citizenship, provided that teachers show students how what they are learning applies in the world as it exists. The nineteenth-century poet and literary critic, and school inspector, Matthew Arnold, said that education should introduce us to the best that has been known and written, not so much because this was good for its own sake, but because this kind of knowledge and understanding helps us see our contemporary affairs, what Arnold called "our stock of received", in perspective and gives us some standards against which to judge them.[6]

To argue that we should make citizenship the centrepiece of education policy is not to call for the training of heel-clicking, flag-waving patriots. In 1937 the Principal of McGill University made this statement: "The path to a better community lies before us, open but not clear. As I see it, the task of education is to give us the wisdom to see that path, hope to believe in our goal, and the will to pursue it".[7] A few years earlier, in 1932, the Principal of the Manitoba Normal School had said much the same thing: "The only hope for curing the ills of the world is that young people may picture a better one and strive to realize it. To frame this picture and to cultivate this ambition is the greatest duty of the school."[8]

It is a vision of education and of the demands of citizenship that is far more attractive and far more worthwhile than our present concern for training workers who will adapt to the imperatives of the global economy.

NOTES

1 *Building a Solid Foundation for our Future: A Strategy Plan*, 1991-96 (Winnipeg: Manitoba Education and Training, 1991), p.1. For the remark of the Minister of Education in 1916, see R. Henley & J. Pampallis, "The Campaign for Compulsory Education in Manitoba," *Canadian Journal of Education*, 7 [1], 1982, pp. 59-83.

2 J.H. Putman, & G.M. Weir, *Survey of the School System* (Victoria: King's Primer, 1925), p. 38. The Radwanski quotations can he found in G. Radwanski, *Study of the Relevance of Education and the Issue of Dropouts* (Toronto: Ontario Ministry of Education, 1987), p. 11.

3 For the development of citizenship education in Canada, see K. Osborne, "Education is the Best National Insurance: Citizenship Education in Canadian Schools, Past and Present," *Canadian and International Education*, 25 [2], 1996, pp. 31-58. For two expressions of concern that multiculturalism has gone too far, see N. Bissoondath, *Selling Illusions: The Cult of Multiculturalism in Canada* (Toronto: Penguin, 1994); and J. Granatstein, *Who Killed Canadian History?* (Toronto: Harper Collins, 1998). For a defence of multiculturalism in the context of citizenship, see W. Kymlicka, *Multicultural Citizenship* (Oxford: Clarendon Press, 1995); and C. Taylor, *Multiculturalism and the Politics of Recognition* (Princeton: Princeton University Press, 1992).

4 John Ralston Saul, *Reflections of a Siamese Twin: Canada at the End* of *the Twentieth Century* (Toronto: Penguin, 1998). For the idea of pan-Canadian understanding, see P. Gallagher & A.B. Hodgetts, *Teaching*

Canada for the 80s (Toronto: Ontario Institute for Studies in Education, 1978) For Symons, see T.H.B. Symons, *The Symons Report* (Toronto: McCelland and Stewart, 1978).

5 C. Gould, *Rethinking Democracy: Freedom and Social Cooperation in Politics, Economy and Society* (Cambridge: Cambridge University Press, 1992), pp. 283-299. The 1948 statement is taken from The Manitoba School Journal, X [2] October, 1948, p. 4. Other formulations of democratic values can be found in W. Galston, *Liberal Virtues: Diversity and Values in the Liberal State* (Cambridge: Cambridge University Press, 1991), pp. 220-227; and D.T. Sehr, *Education for Public Democracy* (Albany: State University of New York Press, 1997), pp. 78ff.

6 On Matthew Arnold's educational ideas, see G. Sutherland, *Arnold on Education* (Harmondsworth: Penguin, 1973). Also M. Arnold, *Culture and Anarchy*, edited by Samuel Lipman (New Haven: Yale University Press, 1994).

7 A.E. Morgan, "Education and Democracy," *The Western School Journal* XXXII [6], June, 1937, p.168.

8 W. A. MacIntyre, "The School Preparing for Life," *The Western School Journal*, XXXVII [2], 1932, February, 1932, p. 45.

*   *   *   *   *

Documents for Chapter Twelve

As many of the previous chapters and documents revealed, the purpose of education has always been to mould good citizens. However, as Ken Osborne outlined above, society's definition of a good citizen is constantly changing. In the first document, The Canada and Newfoundland Education Association Report for 1943 outlines its recommendations for an ideal curriculum. Document 41 by Larry Booi, president of the Alberta Teachers' Association, examines this issue from the viewpoint of a practising teacher and offers a response. Based upon the survey results for questions 1, 2, 3, and 5 in Document 36 in Chapter Ten, to what extent did students' answers support the conclusions presented by The Canada and Newfoundland Education Association Report (Document 40)? Assume that Ken Osborne's research did not uncover Document 40: to what extent does this 1943 report prove and/or disprove Osborne's conclusions for the period before and shortly after the Second World War? To what extent do you agree with Booi's arguments?

40) VIEWS ON CURRICULUM, 1943[1]

In a modern democracy it is readily agreed that everyone should be able to read, write, spell fairly well and do simple Arithmetic. It is fundamental that the principles of morality should be firmly established. That good social customs should loom large in the standard curriculum is becoming increasingly recognized. Pupils must be taught to be open-minded, tolerant, co-operative, respect constituted authority and learn to become good citizens. They should study Nature in all its aspects and become acquainted at first hand with the factors that constitute their environment. It is essential that they secure a knowledge of the rights and practices of healthful living. They must be given opportunities to appreciate the finer things of life through Literature, Art, Music, Craft and Religion. Facility in expressing themselves is desirable. Such an education is essential if society is to be improved, and if people are to live more cultural and satisfying lives.

The school curricula in a democracy are thus showing a tendency to break away from their former single track and to afford cultural, vocational and avocational, social, and character forming educational experiences suitable to the demands of individual lives. In the schools, pupils should be given an opportunity to grow in such a way that they will constantly be able to make adjustments in an environment that changes, perhaps with some rapidity. They should learn to understand and appreciate their environment, selecting the elements that are most worthwhile, cultivating attitudes and sharing experiences so that they will be able to enjoy their surroundings and appreciate their fellow men. Pupils should be encouraged to understand themselves better through the great variety of experiences they meet and thus discover their own best interests and aptitudes.

At the same time it is becoming rather widely recognized that children must prepare themselves in some way to make a living and that the school can play its part in the process. The day has probably dawned when no person should reach adulthood without having become skilled in at least one art or craft. An education that leads towards such a goal would be revolutionary in Canada. This objective is being acknowledged freely by all Canadian provinces in connection with the revision of the school curricula, to the dismay of many and the joy of others, by the general introduction of such practical subjects as Household Science for girls and Industrial Arts for boys. If schools are to fulfill their mission in the future it is essential that, in some part, they prepare youth to do the work of the world. Probably the best method of doing this is by providing occupational orientation and vocational guidance. Instruction in all vocations from shoemaking to hairdressing is not necessary, but schools must teach children the dignity of manual labor, and endeavour to give them a fondness for work.

Many people object to the introduction of manual and occupational subjects in schools on the ground of the inappropriateness of such training at public expense. They must be reminded that the schools have always been pre-occupational centres. The three R's have been taught that pupils might grow up to be instructed citizens who can take their place in the business of the world. Education on the American continent in its early days was fostered particularly that a supply of men might be provided for the ministry. A large percentage of the men who went through the colleges for many years after their establishment were thus prepared. Later the Liberal Arts colleges offered courses in preparation for admission to the other professions ....

If we wish to have pupils profit in large measure from their studies, the curricula must be reasonably attractive to them. It is the business of the school to make them so, even by indulging in some explanations and by propaganda if necessary, and by having pupils sample courses so that they may discover those best suited to them and be able to assimilate the knowledge gained. Neglect or enforced idleness following the period of schooling because pupils have not been able to make the necessary adjustments to life must be strenuously avoided. This does not mean that courses must be made unduly easy or that serious sacrifices must be made to make interest the predominating factor in the learning process. It simply means that the creation and maintenance of pupil interest is a factor of great concern to the curriculum builder and the teacher.

School programmes must not only conform to the needs of the day; they must also meet the needs of the community in which they are carried out. Though the essential factor of population migration must be considered in Canada, the salient characteristics of each community should largely determine the type and kind of educational offerings to be provided. Schools that are to serve farming communities should contain elements fitted to the needs of those who are likely to make their homes there. Industrial populations should be served in a similar manner. Herein lies the strength of the educational freedom laid down in the Confederation pact. The sons and daughters of professional men should likewise be provided with curricula that will benefit them. These offerings should not be so rigid, however, that they will condition children too greatly and prepare them only for restricted occupations in one location. The tastes of children may not be those of their parents, and their desires may be for life beyond the confines of their communities. Consequently, while providing liberal opportunities for entering into community activities subsequent to the completion of school life, the offerings in schools must be such that they will provide a rich background for future citizenship no matter in what kind of community the graduate may eventually settle.

Hitherto school offerings have remained similar both for boys and girls. When girls were allowed to enter secondary schools it was thought that they should follow the boys' curriculum. Provision for some differentiation, however, is inevitable if boys and girls are to be trained along lines that will fit their needs. As girls may be expected to be more domesticated than boys, they should have their tastes cultivated along useful home lines. Many women have more time for reading than men. This fact of life should be recognized in the schools to the extent that girls' tastes in literature should be nurtured with great care, and the encouragement given to them to read the treasures of the past should be enormous. They should be well schooled in reading materials for every age, as they will probably be expected to care for their children, their parents and grandparents, as well, perhaps as younger and older brothers and sisters.

Musical tastes and abilities should be fostered in all girls who are capable of profiting thereby. Girls so trained are of great value in their homes and in their communities. Today clubs play important parts in community living and they will be much more numerous and influential in the future. Girls should be so educated that they will be able to take their places in clubs and community centres. This means that, during their school days, they should be instructed in those arts that will serve them in good stead in community and club life. As the greatest potentialities for the training of future generations lie in the hands of women, it is the duty of school authorities to see that basic good tastes are established and that these are largely developed during school days.

Art should likewise be taught to all girls who can profit by it. Too often the tastes of young people are criticized adversely by critics whose thinking does not run so far as to ask why tastes are unrefined and what opportunities should be provided in order that they may be developed.

Household Science or Home Economics cannot be overlooked for any girl who is to perform the functions that can naturally be expected of her. Taste in dress is essential for every woman who wishes to make the most of herself and her family. Attractiveness in home furnishings, decorations and appointments must be taught if men and women are to be surrounded with beauty. The choice, preparation and manner of serving of food should be learned by every girl from experts who have studied the science and art of balanced diets and other food requirements. A knowledge of the rules of etiquette is needed by all.

It may be urged that some of these subjects do not demand the rigorous discipline of the academic courses which have furnished the mental stamina of the past. No apology need be offered on this score both on account of the urgency of the demand for this type of learning in the technological age that is before us and also because the above subjects will not consume all the school hours of the pupils. There will still be time for one or more languages, history, mathematics or other offerings. Moreover, whether all the virtues claimed for the academic subjects are justifiable is debatable. It has never been proved that the traditional subjects contain needed elements of a disciplinary nature that are lacking in some of the newer school subjects. Instrumental Music, for example, requires ability to read Music, an accomplishment that is certainly at least equal to that of reading ordinary type and script. The musical score has to be read vertically as well as horizontally, in two clefs, must be comprehended, held in the mind for at least a second or two, interpreted, and executed correctly. Much of it, moreover, must be memorized by the artist and recalled on the instant for subsequent performance.

A similar case may be made for other subjects that have had wide popular appeal hitherto. When so analyzed, one wonders whether the psychological elements in many of the school subjects are not somewhat similar and is tempted to contend that, from the point of view of mental discipline, it perhaps matters little what subject a person studies so long as he works at the height of his capacity.

The taste and abilities of boys should similarly be developed in the English language. As they will perform much of the business of the world they should be trained in the technical perfections of the language. For this purpose a Printing Shop has advantages. There the boy learns the importance of spelling, punctuation, spacing, size and kinds of type, and what is useful and ornamental in lettering. The actual manipulation of type has practical advantages that cannot be gainsaid. As the cost of operating a Printing Shop is comparatively small, these advantages should be sought for boys.

The appreciation of Music and Art is by no means confined to girls, nor is the performance, but their appeal to boys is perhaps less widespread and general. Those whose tastes lie along these lines should be given the opportunity for developing them.

Most boys like to use the typewriter, but stenography is not employed by them so much as by girls. Whether a boy is to work in a garage or an office, is to become a professor or a statesman, he will probably find a knowledge of typing of great benefit. As a time saver it is invaluable. Duplicate copies of letters, accounts, etc., are essential and are easily made on the machines. Letters that are well typed bespeak for themselves a good reception.

Consideration must be given to the fact that all pupils do not have the same ability, and that many have left school because its activities have not appealed to them, the academic subjects in particular having been beyond their grasp or unsuited to them. In a true democracy all tastes should be met and provision made for all both in quantity and quality of offerings.

In view of these facts, a large and growing body of opinion is moving towards the relaxation of the requirements that certain traditional subjects be compulsory for high school graduation and admission to higher institutions of learning, and is tending to allow pupils who so desire to choose those that have a greater functional value. Though the voices in favour of retaining the old are numerous and influential it is probably true that, if as large a percentage of Canadian pupils is to remain in school as in the United States, the old emphasis on certain compulsory academic requirements for all must be relaxed as it has been there. Some pupils will always want to follow academic courses, but many a boy and girl would stay in school, for example, to study English,

French, Art, Music, Stenography and Typewriting, Domestic Science or Industrial Arts and Bookkeeping, who have no taste for, and little ability in, Latin, Greek, Algebra, Geometry and Physics.

The high rate of elimination from the high schools of the provinces suggests that all that is possible is not being done to keep pupils in school. There is a falling away that becomes marked in some provinces as early as the fifth grade. Frequently the school does not attract, the courses are not considered practical enough, the rewards for staying in school are not sufficiently large.

In spite of all the changes that have been made during recent years, many problems remain unsolved. Though the administrators may know the improvements that should be made, they are unable to introduce them largely because the public wishes to adhere to tradition, and legislators and others with influence hesitate to go too far ahead of public opinion.

For many years, progressive thinkers have maintained that the high school should not be merely a college preparatory institution. This is a commonsense position because it is well known that the majority of high school graduates do not now wish to go to college. There has been, however, a great deal of weight attached to the completion of matriculation requirements, and this has become almost a fetish to many.

Tradition has also supported the idea that Latin and Mathematics are of paramount importance for mental training. It was originally planned to give public education to pupils in the elementary grades only. Such limited facilities were, however, soon found to be inadequate. Since the turn of the century there have been increasing demands for high school education. These have grown enormously during recent years. In many provinces the high school population has more than doubled during the present decade. With the advent of increased numbers have come demands for diversified curricula that will meet the needs of all. As the compulsory age limit goes higher the adjustment of the high school must be greater, and new standards for high school leaving and matriculation must be adopted. A great advance would be made if all educational authorities throughout the Dominion would accept, for such standards, the completion of any approved provincial high school curriculum extending over four years after the completion of the elementary school. Such a programme should be accepted without other restricting academic qualifications for admission to any university, normal school, technical school, agricultural college, or other institution of higher learning. Based on such standards, institutions themselves could set up their own methods of selection for continuation and graduation.

Due to tradition, the large percentage of pupils in Canadian high schools are in those that offer only academic subjects. Many circumstances tend to maintain the traditional. Teachers have almost all been trained under the traditional offerings, qualified teachers of special subjects are hard to find, small accommodation is needed in which to teach the academic subjects, large rooms are necessary for the so-called vocational, industrial and commercial subjects, little equipment is needed for teaching the academic subjects, but for the others the equipment is expensive and some of it requires much space. Moreover, there is a prejudice against the vocational school, and a similar bias in favour of the academic school, though, strangely enough, one can often reach his goal in the latter by persistence and tenacity. Those who are aware of the facts, however, know that every boy is better for some "practical" education, and can profit from the knowledge and training obtained therein. When he is receiving this practical education he is usually enjoying it, working towards a definite standard, exercising self-control, and submitting to a discipline similar to that which will be demanded of him in the business and industrial world.

In spite of all these handicaps, however, the time has come when the call for the more practical subjects has reached the irresistible stage. It has been helped by the demands of the war which has revealed the necessity for men and women skilled in the use of machines in business and shop. The technical expert, indeed, and his machines, have saved the day for civilization several times during the course of the war and it is likely that they will do so many times more. This call is going to be continued and increased after the cessation of hostilities. The manual labourer also will emerge from the war with an added dignity—a condition which will be retained in the generations to come, for both national needs and social demands will require it. Never again must personal interest or prejudice be allowed to throw out of balance the needs of many for occupational training of a manual character. Moreover, with the close of the war, Labor will demand for all demobilized men the right to work, and the opportunities for the employment of boys and girls of school age will be diminished. Young people, therefore, should be encouraged to stay in school. The best inducement that can be offered them is curricula which will meet their needs.

* * * * *

41) HOW WELL ARE OUR STUDENTS PREPARED TO BE CITIZENS?[2]

"Choosing a type of education means choosing a type of society."
—JACQUES DELORS

"You are the last best hope for democracy," American political theorist Benjamin Barber told more than 300 Alberta social studies teachers at their annual conference in Calgary three years ago. "You have a sacred task."

Barber is one of North America's most passionate and articulate advocates for a reinvigorated democracy. His view is that public education is the vital vehicle for developing citizens of a democratic society and that social studies teachers have the main role to play in this regard.

At a time when accountability dominates discussions of education, it is certainly fair to ask how Alberta's social studies teachers are doing in their efforts to develop future citizens for a democratic society. It is also fair to raise more fundamental questions regarding citizenship. To what extent should the task of fostering citizenship be a function of the schools? What roles do families and communities have to play? And within schools, is citizenship education the sole preserve of social studies? We need to ask, "What kind of citizens, and for what kind of democracy?"

To some, a "good citizen" is a person who obeys the laws, respects authority, and votes whenever an election is called. On this basis, there would probably be general agreement that our system is working reasonably well in that most Albertans tend to be law-abiding and respectful of authority, and also participate in voting. (At least, they do so at a higher rate than Americans.)

But surely these criteria set the bar at an unreasonably low level. Political scientists sometimes refer to this limited view of the citizen's role as "liberal democratic minimalism," characterized by ongoing disengagement punctuated at long intervals by the relatively hollow ritual of voting. University of Manitoba's Ken Osborne, social studies specialist and professor emeritus in the faculty of education, says that Canadian schools have tended to see citizenship in these passive terms, emphasizing obedience and conformity, producing "responsible" citizens— "those who do what they are told and do not ask too many awkward questions."

There is another, higher sense in which being a citizen is very different from being a consumer, a client, a customer, a tax-payer or a "subject." This second sense of citizenship is based on action, involvement, engagement—on "being in charge." It is centred not on the question, "Who governs?" but rather, "Who acts?"

This view of citizenship implies a very different conception of the democracy we should be advocating. Barber argues for a commitment to a "strong democracy" based on three key features: *participation* (active, ongoing involvement on the part of citizens), *deliberation* (widespread debate and discussion of issues by citizens) and *agency* (the belief that citizens, individually and collectively, can make a difference in their communities and society).

This disagreement over the nature of citizenship and democracy is part of a wider debate over the nature and purpose of social studies education. Some provinces even reject the concept of "social studies," opting instead for various combinations of history, geography and civics. Readers are probably familiar with an annual survey, widely picked up in the media, which purports to reveal a dismal lack of historical knowledge on the part of Canadian citizens. Each year, when this survey is released by the Dominion Institute as part of its efforts to sell a very traditional view of studying the past, debate over the proper role of history once again rears its head. While it might appear to be relatively easy to agree on what should be taught in mathematics or chemistry, social studies has always been more contentious and problematic.

The debate is by no means confined to Canada. A recent American study reported that social studies teachers there held four different perspectives on social studies' role, ranging from "critical thinking" to "assimilationism." Despite their differences, however, all shared the view that cultivation of "good citizenship" was a central purpose and overriding concern. The U.S. National Council for the Social Studies, in 1994, defined the primary purpose of social studies as that of "help[ing] young people develop the ability to make informed and reasoned decisions for the public good as citizens of a culturally diverse, democratic society in an interdependent world."

The problem is that this apparent general agreement quickly breaks down into arguments over what and how to teach. As University of Alberta philosophy professor David Kahane points out, "Everyone supports good citizenship, and there will be broad consensus on pieties regarding tolerance, multiculturalism, social justice and so on. We need to recognize, however, that this agreement on pieties usually hides deep division over the proper shape of a just society and the citizenship skills that are important. When we turn from abstract pieties to concrete details of teaching materials, lesson plans, outcomes and so on, disagreement reemerges."

The difficulty is clear: How can we hold social studies teachers accountable for outcomes in citizenship education if there is no consensus on the outcomes desired? Those who favour Barber's view of an active, engaged citizenry would be deeply disappointed if our schools produced passive, obedient subjects; the reverse is undoubtedly true as well.

Responsible citizenship is the ultimate goal of social studies, according to the Program Rationale of Alberta's social studies curriculum. The social studies program "assists students to acquire basic knowledge, skills and positive attitudes needed to be responsible citizens and contributing members of society." This citizenship education is to be based on "an understanding of history, geography, economics, other social sciences and the humanities as they affect the Canadian community and the world."

The constant emphasis on producing *responsible* citizens raises Osborne's concern about passivity, conformity and obedience, but the curriculum does refer to the need for a more critical and active component. It clearly states that the development of critical thinking is basic to the goal of citizenship, that knowledge is changing rapidly, that issues will result in significant disagreement and that a key element of citizenship involves "participating constructively in the democratic process by making rational decisions."

However, a different picture emerges when we consider the actual content of specific courses. In Social Studies 10, for example, Grade 10 students are to examine important issues facing Canadians—a wonderful opportunity to foster discussion, debate, critical thinking and decision making. But, for teachers, the more imposing reality is 10 pages of highly specific knowledge objectives, as compared to the very small section on skills and attitudes. The same pattern prevails in the rest of Alberta's social studies courses: a general commitment to the importance of engagement, decision making and critical thinking, combined with a highly detailed, daunting specification of knowledge objectives. (Readers can consult Alberta Learning's website for details of social studies courses at http://ednet.edc.gov.ab.ca)

"The curriculum has lost sight of the goals of teaching effective participatory citizenship as a result of pressure to cover what seems to be a limitless amount of knowledge." This comment is from a survey of social studies teachers commissioned by the social studies council of the Alberta Teachers' Association in 1997. The perspective of concerned teachers is instructive: "Over the years, I have become increasingly concerned with the quantitative knowledge my students must possess to achieve acceptable standards. I find that, as a whole, I am spending less and less time engaging in skill-building activities such as oral debates or simulation/role-plays—I am constantly concerned about time, as are my colleagues in other subject areas;" and, "There is way too much stuff! We have been told not to worry about the stuff or content in the guide, but if we don't cover it, especially in Grade 12 courses, the students are at a great disadvantage."

These comments reflect the frustration of many social studies teachers with the seemingly contradictory messages: "Foster the skills and dispositions of active citizenship" and "Cover enormous amounts of specific content." Teachers surveyed overwhelmingly agreed with the goals of the curriculum. Ninety five per cent agreed that "the main goal of social studies should be to prepare students for active citizenship." They also agreed that social studies should emphasize the skills of decision making (84 per cent), that it should emphasize the development of critical thinking (98 per cent), and that the study of current events should be an essential element (92 per cent). They cannot focus on these goals and at the same time cover endless content in preparation for narrow, knowledge-based tests.

The Alberta Provincial Achievement Test for Social Studies, administered to all Grade 9 students, consists of 55 multiple-choice questions. Obviously, only what is easily quantified and measured is tested; objectives are narrowly knowledge-based. The difficulty, of course, is that key outcomes such as critical thinking, creativity, decision making, rational judgement and democratic attitudes are hard to measure in this simplistic manner; they require a more sophisticated, qualitative approach. We measure what doesn't matter much, and don't measure what matters a great deal. And, unfortunately, the old adage holds—"What gets tested is what gets taught"—particularly when achievement test results are used to evaluate schools, and when some newspapers publish misguided "rankings" of schools based solely on these multiple-choice tests. In addition, these achievement tests cover only the four core subject areas (mathematics, science, language arts and social studies). As a result, the importance of fine arts, languages, health and physical education and career/technology studies is diminished, and student learning is further narrowed, rather than broadened.

This heightened emphasis on high-stakes testing linked to narrow and measurable "standards" reflects a growing tendency of governments to look for a cheap "quick fix," such as external testing, rather than to make the necessary investments in public education. Such trends have narrowed curriculum and instruction, precisely when we need the opposite—innovative, creative, critical thinkers who can express themselves proficiently and work well with others in the highly touted new "knowledge society in a globally competitive world." Such qualities are also clearly consistent with the development of the critical, engaged citizens essential to participatory democracy. University of Michigan professor Gary Fenstermacher says: "We hear a great deal about readying the next generation of workers for global competition, about being first in the world in such high status subjects as math and science, and about having world class standards for what is learned in school. We hear almost nothing about civic participation or building and maintaining democratic communities, whether these be neighborhoods or governments at the local, state or federal level."

We need to "make some space" for the things that matter most, for the "big outcomes" related to citizenship. As one junior high school teacher stated in the 1997 survey, "To create good middle school activities, students must have the time to ... present information in many ways. These types of activities take time, more time than is now available given the breadth of knowledge we are now expected to cover. We need more time to teach reading and writing skills in relation to social studies ... to differentiate between fact and opinion, to find bias, and to write using facts and examples for support."

But in order to make the time and create the space, we will need to cut back on the overwhelming number of knowledge objectives teachers are required to "cover." In other words, if we want more emphasis on fostering the skills and attitudes of active democratic citizenship, we have to have less of something else.

Our students will be far better off as a result. Knowledge is vital, and positions not founded on evidence are weak. But internalizing countless "facts" will not result in lasting or useful knowledge. In truth, this "drill-and-kill" approach probably has most to do with turning students off social studies and history. Specific knowledge is better learned in the consideration of larger, more important issues. Students are far more likely to remember information about Canada's involvement in the wars if it is placed in the context of the larger, ongoing debates related to our role in the world. And they are far more likely to develop their abilities to make judgments as citizens if they have continual opportunities to make decisions as students.

In order to become active, engaged citizens as adults, students need systematic, structured activities that develop the skills and disposition to think critically as well as make judgments and decisions. These activities are necessary, but not sufficient. If nothing changes in our assessment practices—that is, if achievement tests and common examinations stay focused on narrow knowledge objectives—then teachers will continue to emphasize these objectives in classrooms, at the expense of more important outcomes. So either the external examinations must change their focus to higher-end objectives (probably unlikely, given the government's desire for cheaper, multiple-choice testing) or we must permit and support more teacher-based assessment. We can't have it both ways. There is no "Canadian Creativity Index," no "Alberta Critical Thinking Scale" and no "Citizenship Skills Growth Inventory."

Despite these concerns, there are reasons for optimism. For a start, Alberta has a social studies curriculum that at least reflects a recognition of the importance of goals related to active citizenship. It also has a committed community of social studies teachers, more than 500 of whom met in October 2000 in Banff at their annual social studies conference, where a high level of concern and dedication was demonstrated in the plenary sessions related to the future of social studies. We have options for change that could make a real difference.

We need to support teachers in their efforts to incorporate issues, critical thinking and decision-making skills more systematically. In their preparation, teachers need to be encouraged to ask questions about their learning plan:

1. *What decisions am I asking students to make today?*
2. *In what ways are we dealing with current issues?*
3. *How are we connecting events to larger developments?*

Teachers also need assistance with materials and methods for fostering critical thinking. Too often, critical thinking has been associated with a vague conception of "higher order thinking" or with "mental puzzles." Missing is the concept of critical—that is, criticism or "critique." This does not imply "being negative;" a critical review of a movie can be overwhelmingly positive. But it does require making judgments based on criteria, arguments and evidence.

A "tool kit" of critical questions for examining any suggested public policy includes the following: What assumptions underlie this position/policy? What values underlie the position? Whose interests are served by this policy? What are the gains/losses/costs/benefits—and for whom? For what problem is this policy a suggested solution? What is the evidence that it is a problem? What evidence is there that this policy will help to solve this problem? How is power involved? How are factors such as gender, race and income involved? Citizens who systematically raise such questions are more likely to come to informed conclusions on issues. Students trained to use this "tool kit" are much more likely to develop into reflective, engaged and informed citizens.

Simon Fraser University Professor Roland Case says critical thinking skills must not be dealt with in isolation; rather, they must be embedded in the curriculum and daily activities in classrooms. Case and his colleagues in British Columbia have worked with teachers to produce *Critical Challenges in Social Studies*, an excellent series of books that systematically integrate the development of critical thinking skills into the required content at each grade level. We need to follow this lead in Alberta.

Such materials also help students see the reasons for the diversity of opinion in a democratic society. They foster understanding of why there cannot be simple answers to complex questions, how and why people might reasonably disagree and what makes some answers stronger than others. They help students become more comfortable with ambiguities and uncertainties, while fostering committed engagement in ongoing, informed dialogue on public issues in democratic communities.

Social studies classrooms are crucial for understanding our selves, communities and society, as well as in nurturing critical capacities and engagement. But, if we are really serious about fostering the development of active, involved citizens, we can't leave the task entirely to social studies teachers. It's clear there are enormous opportunities and obligations in other subject areas. Language arts classes deal with competing values, opinions, arguments and evidence. They also offer crucial opportunities in media literacy and critique. Science courses can involve students in compelling issues in science, technology and society. Young people also can be involved in general decision making in our schools, including school policies and operations.

But, above all, if we communicate the view that citizenship is merely a school subject, why would students continue their involvement once graduated? The final test of "creating citizens" is not the last social studies examination of students' high school careers, but rather the degree to which they become engaged, informed citizens afterward. To that end, schools can benefit in many ways from the support of families and communities. In discussing public issues at home, parents foster citizenship and also help students do well in school.

More specifically, parents can encourage their daughters and sons in junior and senior high school to read one newspaper editorial and column every day. They will, in effect, be reading short "policy judgments" by editors and columnists on current issues. Parents should encourage students to look for three things: the position, the arguments and the evidence. Such reading can provide a basis for regular discussion between parents and students. Too, if a student develops the habit of investing a mere 10 or 15 minutes per day in reading an editorial and column, by the end of the year, he or she will have read more than 700 short essays on social studies topics. The potential positive effects on a student's ability to read and write effectively, as well as on knowledge, are obvious. But, more important, the student will be building a habit of engagement in public issues, with the active support of the parents.

The Internet offers unparalleled opportunity, in some ways, to create an educated and informed citizenry because information and other citizens are within easy access. But there are some important cautions.

U.S. author Theodore Roszak points out that an increased volume of information is not always a blessing, nor is it necessarily what we need most. In his book *The Cult of Information*, he argues that what students need is not more information, but rather "ideas, values, taste and judgment, without which information is worthless." In other words, our problems have more to do with the processes by which we draw conclusions and make decisions than with obtaining information. Once again, we return to the need for fostering skills, competencies and dispositions rather than simply acquiring information.

We need to get good at the Internet because it is used increasingly for information—in our schools and communities. How can we help students sort high-quality information from "the bad and the ugly?" How should we deal with increasingly sophisticated attempts at commercial marketing to children through the Internet? What about online privacy and safety, particularly with respect to children? In effect, these bespeak the skills of developing citizenship in the information age. Fortunately, one of the best resources on these issues for both teachers and parents is readily available online. Canada's Media Awareness Network, at www.media-awareness.ca, endorsed by the Canadian Teachers' Federation and the Alberta Teachers' Association, believes the new technologies must be used to foster the growth of active citizenship. They offer first-rate resources for teachers, students, parents and community members on their websites.

In the end, "democracy is a discussion," Benjamin Barber reminds us, emphasizing the importance of face-to-face interaction among citizens: "There is no simple or general answer to the question "Is the technology democratizing?" until we have made clear what sort of democracy we intend. Home voting via interactive television might further privatize politics and replace deliberative debate in public with the unconsidered instant expression of private prejudices, turning what ought to be public decisions into private consumer-like choices.... If democracy is to benefit from technology, then we must start not with technology but with politics. Having a voice, demanding a voice .... Will virtual community heal the rupture of real communities? Will we do on our keyboards what we have notably failed to do face to face?"

Barber's words should remind us of several important points as we struggle with how to "create citizens" in our homes, schools and communities. First, in order to be successful, it must be a shared responsibility. Teaching about government in school will not create democratic tendencies in young people. If we want a democracy based on participation, deliberation and agency, we will have to consciously structure our schools to do so. Michael Apple and James Beane, in *Democratic Schools*, suggest that schools will need to become "living models of democratic principles in action" if they are to foster active citizenship and sustain and enrich democracy. We also will need the support of parents and the community, particularly through their example of engagement in public issues and civil society.

Barber also reminds us that democracy is, by definition, often messy and uncomfortable, involving disagreement and debate, requiring patience and hard work. Canadian thinker John Ralston Saul refers to "the slow, complex, eternally unclear continuity of democracy, and all the awkwardness of citizen participation." Why should it surprise us if the same is true of education for democracy?

Czech President Vaclav Havel once said people tend to misunderstand democracy, seeing it as "the light at the end of the tunnel." Both Havel and John Dewey suggest instead that democracy is not an end, but rather a way of doing things, a vehicle by which we work things out together, a way of living. As we make decisions about social studies, schools and communities, we need to keep these thoughts in mind.

*   *   *   *   *

1 "Curricula," in *Report of the Survey Committee* (Canada and Newfoundland Education Association, 1943), pp. 37-43.
2 Larry Booi, "Citizens or Subjects? How well do Alberta's social studies classes prepare our kids for citizenship?" *Alberta Views* (March/April, 2001), pp. 28-33.

Chapter Thirteen:
Assessment and Accountability

D
o teachers earn too much money and have too many holidays? Should teachers be held more accountable to society? Are Canadian students receiving an education that is appropriate for the twenty-first century? Should teachers be subject to testing every five years or so? Should students be regularly tested by outside educators to ensure that they meet the intended expectations for their grade? In the past few years these have become common questions or concerns across Canada. The following article by Lorna Earl outlines the history and some of the major concerns with external testing and teacher accountability. The documents focus on the issue of inclusion.

Other useful sources include: Bob Davis, *What Ever Happened to High School History?* (Toronto, 1995); R.D. Gidney, *From Hope to Harris: The Reshaping of Ontario's Schools* (Toronto, 1999); Mark Holmes, *The Reformation of Canada's Schools: Breaking the Barriers to Parental Choice* (Montreal, 1998).

* * * * *

Assessment and Accountability[127]

In uncertain times, education inevitably comes under scrutiny. When people feel anxious and concerned about the future for themselves and their children, they look to schools and teachers for reassurance, and they worry about whether schools are fulfilling their responsibilities. Educators are under pressure to show the public that what they are doing is working, and governments everywhere have seized on education as a cornerstone for their political agendas. Government response has been fairly consistent across countries: more centralized curricula and formal student testing.

A number of dilemmas are embedded in this blend of accountability and large scale assessment—dilemmas that are often unexamined and sometimes unacknowledged.

A Brief History of Large-Scale Assessment in Education

External tests and examinations have always existed in schools, with a clear and singular purpose: making decisions about the educational status of individual students. They have been seen as a fair way to identify the best candidates for scarce resources, and they have been the vehicle for directing students into various programs or into the world of work. Most Canadian provinces have had provincial examinations over the years. In other countries, centralized assessment programs have meant examinations at key junctures or decision points for students, like the General Certificate of Secondary Education (G.C.S.E.) exams and A-levels in England, the Baccalaureate in France, and the public examinations in Hong Kong.

Beginning in the 1970s most states in the U.S. and a few districts in Canada expanded their standardized testing programs in elementary and secondary schools to help teachers make decisions about individual children, particularly where teacher judgement might be questioned, like entrance to special education programs or academic scholarships. However, although provincial or national assessments get the "sound bites" in the media, daily classroom assessments have always had the greatest influence in Canadian schools. Teachers have designed their own techniques for assessing student achievement based on provincial curriculum, made judgements about the quality of student work, determined student placement, promotion and program, and explained their decisions to parents.

A Change of Purpose

Recently, large-scale assessment has become the vehicle of choice for accountability around the world, and testing has changed from an instrument for decision-making about students to a lever for holding schools accountable.[128] In most Canadian provinces, only three grades (usually 3, 6, 9 or 4, 7, 10) are tested, and in a number of provinces or territories the testing is done with a provincial sample of students (e.g., Saskatchewan, British Columbia). Several provinces have graduation examinations, as well. Some, like Alberta, use multiple choice items exclusively; others, like Ontario, Manitoba, New Brunswick, and Quebec, include a mixture of multiple choice, open-ended items, and tasks that require the student to produce a response, often to real life problems that require higher-order thinking and problem-solving.

Most provinces also participate in the School Achievement Indicators Program, a cyclical national assessment program in language, mathematics and science, operated under the auspices of the Council of Ministers of Education, Canada. Several provinces have also opted to participate in international assessment programs like the Third International Mathematics and Science Study, where they are included separately, as if they were countries.

So, what is educational accountability all about in 1999? Why has large-scale assessment of student achievement come to dominate educational reform policy? A close look at the field of accountability and assessment reveals a tangle of anxiety, enthusiasm, politics, values, truths, half-truths and misconceptions.

Is Education in Crisis?

After many years in the comfort of general public trust, education has come under scrutiny, and everyone has an opinion about how to reform it. Think tanks, royal commissions, business forums and government reviews have decried the state of public education and prophesied grave futures unless dramatic change is undertaken. Schools are viewed as failing to produce the kinds of learning that students will need for the world that awaits them. The rhetoric describing this perceived crisis portrays a sense of urgency. The political realm has been swift to answer with a plethora of education reforms.

An alternate view holds that public unhappiness with education has been "manufactured" by politicians, the media, and the business roundtable to strengthen their political agendas. Berliner and Biddle are blunt about the results of their investigations, going so far as to claim that: "Organized malevolence might actually be underway .... Claims attacking the conduct and achievements of America's public schools are contradicted by evidence."[129]

As is often the case, the reality probably lies somewhere in between. Nevertheless, public and political "eyes" are on education and on the findings of large-scale assessments.

Improvement or Surveillance?

In theory, accountability sounds wonderful. In practice, it raises a host of thorny issues, not the least of which is philosophical. What does accountability mean? No blueprint defines accountability, and a number of very different understandings prevail.

For some, schools are like businesses, with accountability reflected in the bottom line. How good is the "product"? Which schools are best? Education is like a horse race with winners and losers. Accountability rewards the winners and exposes the losers. Assessments sort the schools (or students) into categories just as quarterly profit reports describe the financial status of one company in relation to others.

For others, schools are accountable for the learning and progress of all students, and assessment is part of the learning process—a tool to provide the detailed information educators and policy makers need to make good decisions and to identify areas for future actions. The relative position of schools is irrelevant. Instead, the focus is on continuous improvement in all schools, and the nature of the assessments is as important as the results, because they are a starting point for discussions about how to enhance learning.

Blaming or Capacity Building?

There is general agreement that large-scale assessment should have an impact on schools and on changing education. There are, however, two quite different views about how these changes might occur. Linda Darling Hammond describes them this way:

One view seeks to induce change through extrinsic rewards and sanctions for both schools and students, on the assumption that the fundamental problem is a lack of will to change on the part of educators. The other view seeks to induce change by building knowledge among school practitioners and parents about alternative methods and by stimulating organisational rethinking through opportunities to work together on the design of teaching and schooling and to experiment with new approaches. This view assumes that the fundamental problem is a lack of knowledge about the possibilities for teaching and learning, combined with lack of organisational capacity for change.[130]

This dichotomy is evident in many reform agendas and the large-scale assessment that goes with them. According to one view, teachers have both the capacity and the ability to act differently, but are unfocused, lazy and recalcitrant. Those holding this view use testing as the impetus for change, to "name and blame" offending teachers or to reward successful ones. According to the other view, educational change is an internal process requiring time, learning and reflection. Its proponents advocate for creating opportunities for teachers to rethink their assessment and teaching practices and learn new ones. Policymakers often try to appeal to both camps by embracing common standards and individual variation, numerical comparability and descriptive sensitivity, assessment to improve student learning and to placate demands for system-wide accountability.[131]

Statistical Illiteracy

Using assessment results and other indicators of quality has moved education into the world of statistics, resulting in misuse and misinterpretation because of the deceptive simplicity of numbers.

Statistics and assessments do not have a life of their own. They are tools, designed to provide consistent measurements. But unlike a metre stick, they measure things that are invisible and not easily checked. Tests and statistical procedures have been developed to provide estimates of invisible human qualities like learning and achievement, and there are extremely important conventions and rules for the measurement of student achievement, especially when the results are being used to make significant decisions. Too often, the symbolic representations of quality have been accepted as objective and unassailable descriptors of student achievement or of school or school system quality. Statistics and test scores may give the illusion of accuracy and objectivity, but the numbers are only as good as the way in which the test was developed and the results interpreted. Most people fail to recognize that some margin of uncertainty in the scores is an inevitable part of measuring any human characteristic that we can't see directly.

So, tests provide an estimate of student achievement, but never give a perfect measurement. When that uncertainty is taken into account, many—sometimes most—differences in raw scores between schools or districts disappear. With small schools, the uncertainty can be very large. And yet, raw score differences continue to be treated as if they were real and used to form opinions and make decisions about schools, even to reward or punish them. Educators have a responsibility to become statistically literate and to use statistics appropriately, so that their interpretations of assessment results are not misguided or misleading.

Consequences: Anticipated and Unanticipated

Experience has shown both expected and unexpected, both positive and negative consequences of large-scale assessment. While the misinterpretation and misuse of test results is sometimes due to a limited understanding of statistical concepts, it is sometimes due to the "high stakes" attached to them. When they are very important to individuals and institutions, or when they are associated with rewards or sanctions, test results are very susceptible to manipulation. This is less a testing issue than a political or moral issue. Any test can be corrupted.

When teachers are held responsible for their students' scores, test scores may go up, but often learning doesn't change.[132] Fewer curricular activities are undertaken while instructional time is spent preparing for the test. Teaching methods become more test-like, often at the expense of good instructional practice (e.g., multiple choice identification of misspelled words rather than spelling correctly from dictation or in composition). Other areas of the curriculum are neglected and instruction is focused on memorization at the expense of thinking.[133] Some studies have even found cheating.

Because of these unanticipated consequences, researchers, educators and measurement specialists have worked hard to align the testing process more closely with classroom activities. Many jurisdictions have adopted assessment strategies that make "teaching to the test" desirable. For example, when the test items and tasks change for each administration and are designed to push students beyond recall of facts and algorithms to higher order thinking and problem solving, the best strategy for preparing the students is good teaching of all of the curriculum.

Educational assessment is an emotional issue. In some jurisdictions (largely in the United States), individuals and groups have challenged test fairness, test validity, test use, standards, or the accountability of the testing organizations in the courts. Competency tests have been challenged when opportunities to learn have been denied or there is evidence of bias. Some cases have addressed the use of assessment results for purposes that were not intended when the assessment was developed; others have arisen as a challenge to the process and the result of setting a cutscore or a standard of performance.[134]

Accountability and assessment are also very political. The national assessment in England originally combined teacher-assigned and externally-set assessment tasks, reported as student profiles. Its central purpose was to strengthen pupils' learning and teachers' professional role, while at the same time satisfying legitimate demands for public accountability.[135] Over the years, it has become the measurement of a standard product for consumers; its purpose has shifted from influencing school practice to providing a currency for accountability. In Ontario, there is evidence of major changes in pedagogy, assessment and curricular focus as a result of the Grade 3 assessment.[136]

Surveying the Landscape

Clearly, there are no simple answers in the realm of accountability and assessment. There are, however, some fairly clear issues that warrant attention—socio-political issues and technical issues.

Socio-Political Issues

What is the purpose of large-scale assessment? Is it a gate on the road, providing access or privilege for some and punishment or blame for others, or is it a road map for planning the future? This is a real choice. It is possible to serve both purposes, but very tricky because of an interesting paradox in the world of assessment. When the stakes are not high, large-scale assessments, in conjunction with other measures, can be reasonably accurate indicators of learning and provide clues about avenues to improve learning. When the stakes are high, however, assessment results become less accurate and sometimes downright invalid. Why? Because when the scores matter in life-changing ways, people will invariably move their focus away from enhancing learning towards increasing scores. So, a precondition of using assessments for improvement is that they be seen as important, but not as instruments of public judgement. Rather, they should be vehicles for developing action plans to improve school organization, instruction, staff development, resources and community engagement—as ways of adding value to students' lives and ensuring that all students receive a high quality education.

Technical Issues

If educators or politicians are going to rely on sophisticated measurement techniques and use them to make serious decisions about people or policy, it is their business to understand what the numbers mean and to ensure that they are being used and interpreted appropriately. There is a whole industry to analyze, interpret, and monitor the financial world around us. Why rely exclusively on newspaper reporters and politicians to assess schools? The technical requirements in educational measurement need to be monitored, challenged, and developed. If we ignore them, we run the risk of making important decisions using the Mad Hatter's logic, and justifying them by pointing at the Emperor's new clothes.[137]

Dr. Lorna Earl is an Associate Professor in 'the Theory and Policy Studies Department and Associate Director of the International Centre for Educational Change at the Ontario Institute for Studies in Education/University of Toronto. Her primary interest is the wise application of research, assessment and evaluation knowledge to the realities of schools and classrooms. In 1994, she was named a "Distinguished Educator" by O.I.S.E. in recognition of contributions which served to stimulate and enrich education in Ontario.

*   *   *   *   *

Documents for Chapter Thirteen

Analyze the data in Document 42 by age, occupation, and province. To what extent do the provincial policies on "special education" in Document 43 reflect the findings of Document 42? Research the current policies on inclusion in your province.

42) EDUCATORS' THOUGHTS ON STREAMING AND IQ, 1968[1]

Many of the problems confronting elementary and secondary schools stem from the fact that their input student populations are heterogeneous. Students vary with respect to social background, ability, physical and emotional maturity, and a host of other characteristics. Such variation complicates curriculum planning as well as the process of teaching itself.

The present paper presents the views of Canadian secondary school principals, teachers and counsellors regarding various organizational ways of coping with students' differences in two crucial areas—ability and sex [for the data on gender see document 26 in Chapter Six].

The data utilized derive from a national survey of public secondary schools carried out in the fall and spring of 1965-66. The sample was designed as a stratified probability sample, and included academic, composite, vocational and technical, and academic and commercial schools ....

[It] is based on the results of the "Career Decisions of Canadian Youth" project, a study of the educational and occupational plans of a national sample of Canadian high school students conducted by the Federal Department of Manpower in cooperation with the Provincial Departments of Education. Roughly 150,000 students from 360 schools were surveyed, as well as teachers, counsellors and principals from these schools ....

VARIATION IN STUDENT ABILITY
Ability Grouping

Measured mental ability plays a central role in determining a high school student's academic career. Indeed, 88.2% of Canadian secondary schools administer some form of test of mental ability.

Along with this large-scale acceptance of IQ testing, there has developed a concern over the best educational environment for students of different ability levels. The issue is generally formulated in terms of the relative merit of heterogeneous versus homogeneous classes. To explore the opinions of Canadian school personnel on this issue, the respondents were asked whether or not they were in favour of ability grouping ....

TABLE I

PERCENTAGE OF PRINCIPALS, TEACHERS AND COUNSELLORS IN FAVOUR OF ABILITY GROUPING BY PROVINCE AND AGE, AND ACTUAL ABILITY GROUPING

Principals:
"Do you think that students should be separated into 'bright' and 'slow' classes in certain subjects?"

Teachers and Counsellors:
"Do you think that students, at each grade level should be 'streamed' into separate classes according to ability?"

In Favour	CAN	PROVINCE										AGE		
		NFL	P.E.I.	N.S	N.B	QUE	ONT	MAN	SASK	ALTA	B.C.	Under 35	35–49	50+
Principals	85.6	93.1	34.6	77.1	94.2	90.5	75.1	86.9	81.4	69.3	100	96	87	79
Teachers & Counsellors	73.8	76.6	56.5	63.6	70.3	78.7	75.4	69.5	71.4	55.8	73	77	70	71

Principals:
"Is there any 'streaming' in your school based on ability, that is, are students of different ability placed in separate classes for one or more subjects?"

Yes	38.4	26.5	12	48.2	29.7	26.4	73.5	45.4	45.4	38.9	95.5			

Acceleration versus Enrichment

With widespread concern over detecting and encouraging the "gifted child," various ways of coping with such students have been suggested and experimented with. One long-standing debate centers around the advisability of permitting the very bright student to complete his high school program in less time than the average student. This policy is often called "skipping" or "acceleration." Those who support the practice argue in terms of the waste of time and the loss of interest characteristic of those bright students forced to maintain the same pace as their less gifted classmates. Those who are opposed to acceleration point to the possible negative psychological consequences of placing physically and emotionally immature students with those who are older and relatively more mature. The alternative is some form of "enrichment," whereby the bright student covers additional material while still remaining with his peers. The opinions of Canadian school personnel regarding acceleration and enrichment are presented in Table 2 [deleted].

IQ and Program Allocation

There is some evidence that the program of study in which the student is placed in high school is greatly dependent on his IQ. For example, a recent paper on occupational preferences of Canadian students reports a strong correlation between IQ and program of study. The same result also appears in a 1961 study of Toronto secondary schools.

When IQ is the main criterion for allocating student to programs of study, it is perhaps inevitable that certain students will be dissatisfied with their placement. That is, the more a student's interest deviates from the program of study to which he was assigned on the basis of his IQ, the more likely his dissatisfaction....

Indicate the importance of the following in assigning students to each of the programs or courses of study:

	CAN	NFL	P.E.I.	N.S	N.B	QUE	ONT	MAN	SASK	ALTA	B.C.
1) IQ important or very important in assigning students to programs	85.4	66.7	94.5	96.3	89.5	96.5	74.4	73	93.6	92	65
2) Interest important or very important in assigning students to programs	95.0	89.3	94.5	100	100	94.4	96.5	98.3	74.2	100	100
3) Relative importance of IQ and interest	+9.6	+22.6	0	+3.7	+10.5	-2.1	+22.1	+25.3	-19.4	+8	+35

*   *   *   *   *

43) SPECIAL EDUCATION AND INCLUSION, 1980[2]

Public policy on special education in Canada can at best be described as fluid. Nearly every Minister of Education indicated that their province was at present drafting legislation that would change policy concerning special education or was studying special education with a view to recommending changes.

The summaries presented start in the east and work across the country to British Columbia.

Newfoundland and Labrador

The Newfoundland Task Force on Education[178] submitted its report to the Minister of Education in June, 1979. Basically the report recommends increased integration, increased services, increased expenditures on a per pupil basis and rearrangement of the administrative services for the administration of special schools and classes.

On December 14, 1979, Section 12 of the Schools Act was amended by adding the following with respect to school boards, for whom it is now mandatory to: "(a.1) organize the means of instructing children who for any physical or mental cause require special classes, either by the establishment of special classes in its schools or by making arrangements with another school board or with any educational body or authority within Canada for the education of such children."

The Division of Special Services, which was established in 1969, is responsible for meeting the needs of handicapped children. The education of special students rests with the school boards but the education of trainable retarded children, visually impaired and hearing impaired rests with the Division of Special Services.

The general position of special education in Newfoundland is under review. An Advisory Committee on Special Education was formed by the Minister of Education in 1977. The Committee meets on a regular basis and recommends changes in the field to the Minister.

In 1974, the Province of Newfoundland signed an agreement with the other three Atlantic Provinces for the joint education of multi-handicapped children under the Atlantic Provinces Special Education Authority.

Newfoundland has accepted in principle the position of integration and has taken steps in that direction by having local school boards assume responsibilities for a number of classes for the trainable mentally retarded which were under the jurisdiction of the Department. Many such classes will now be situated in the regular school setting.

Prince Edward Island

The main policy on special education in Canada's smallest province is to provide free school privileges for every child from 6-20 years of age who has not graduated from high school. Special children are not singled out in any section of the Education Act but it is the belief of the Department of Education that as far as it is possible and appropriate, the special child should be educated "among and with his peers."[179]

The Department does have special classes available for retarded and deaf children but all such classes are integrated into regular schools and to the degree possible and beneficial, the children take part in some regular classes. The PEI Department of Education does not favour segregated classes for emotionally disturbed and learning disabled children but prefers that they remain in regular classes with additional individual help.

Nova Scotia

In Nova Scotia,[180] mandatory legislation makes it necessary for school boards to provide schooling for physically and mentally handicapped, auditorily and visually impaired children between the ages of 5 and 21. However, the provisions of the legislation are not always implemented because Section 92 of the Education Act states in part that a child shall not have to attend school if his physical condition is such as to render his attendance or instruction at school inexpedient or impractical. Other parts of this Section of the Act allow school boards to exclude a handicapped child if there is not sufficient accommodation in the school that the child should attend or his mental condition is such that it would be inexpedient or impractical to require attendance.

Special education is included in the Nova Scotia foundation program. This program distributes the educational funds of the province in such a way as to enable all districts to provide acceptable standards of education. The education of hearing and visually impaired children is funded under the Atlantic Provinces Special Education Authority.

New Brunswick

In 1974 a White Paper entitled "Opportunities for the Handicapped"[181] was published and this document has since provided the major impetus for special education in New Brunswick.

The special education component of the paper is worded in such a way as to include all handicapped children who are in need of educational programs and services regardless of the handicapping condition or the geographical location of residence. One of the major components of the provincial philosophy is the right of all children to receive an education.

The stated philosophy of the New Brunswick Department of Education aligns with the principles of normalizaton initially presented by the Canadian Association for the Mentally Retarded. An expanded operational model of this principle is being drafted and it will include all handicapped children in New Brunswick.

In terms of the White Paper, handicapped children are to be educated by local school districts wherever possible. Where only a small number of children with a particular handicap exist in a district, there should be co-operation between districts to provide for the educational needs of such children. Government departments and school districts should also share services when possible and suitable. In some cases, services may have to be purchased outside the province.

Educable mentally retarded, learning disabled and emotionally disturbed children should remain in the regular classroom if possible. Hearing and visually impaired children are educated under the Atlantic Provinces Special Education Authority but the White Paper recommended that local school districts become more involved at the preschool level and with regular classroom and residential programs.

The Government of New Brunswick recognizes that the Department of Education can provide the stimulus, coordination and overall leadership but only a sensitive and enterprising local citizenry can insure that the handicapped child will receive a fully worthwhile educational experience.

Quebec

The Green Paper on Primary and Secondary Education in the Province of Quebec (1977) contained many components, one of which concerned special education. When this document was analyzed and consultation carried out, the Government of Quebec summarized the official position with the 1979 publication of a document entitled, *Schools of Quebec: Policy Statement and Plan of Action—Children with Difficulties in Learning and Adaptation.*

The first aspect of this paper deals with terminology to be used with children who had previously been described as exceptional or maladjusted. These children would now be referred to as "children with difficulties in learning and adaptation" which the province viewed as a positive change in the perception of children with difficulties. A general aim of the new education policy for Quebec (1979) is:

> to insure that children with special needs have access to quality educational services, all appropriate to their needs, within a regular school environment, in order to enable them to function effectively in the community as adults. In order to attain this objective, the ministère d'education will be obliged to act in close collaboration with other departments of government, particularly with the ministère des Affaires sociale.[182]

This statement seems to state quite succinctly the educational objective for children with special needs in Quebec. Children have a right to education and must have access to a public system of education. It is the basic responsibility of a school board to provide appropriate educational services for all school-age children residing in its territories and, insofar as possible, the school board should provide these services in its own schools. If a board does not have the resources it should enter into an agreement with another board or a private institution to provide the required services.

The policy statement recognizes that education in the full sense of the word is to provide the optimum integral development and social integration of the child. Education must pay particular attention to the potential of the child with difficulties and not his limitations.

Early identification and prevention play important roles in the new program in Quebec. In addition, the Green Paper expresses the need to extend schooling to young adults 16-21 who need the extra years to complete their training and to facilitate their social integration. Particular attention is paid to the idea of the child having access to an education in as near "normal" a setting as possible. This setting is initially the family which nurtures the child's physical growth and personality; for the school-age child, attendance at the school his brothers, sisters and peers attend. Thus, integration is clearly the preferred mode of educating the child with educational difficulties.

Ontario

Special education in Ontario has been undergoing many changes within the past year. The Minister of Education, The Honourable Bette Stephenson, M.D., made a statement in the Legislature in December 1978 introducing legislative and policy changes concerning special education.[183]

The Minister began her statement by indicating that every child in Ontario should have the opportunity to excel to reach his or her potential. However, according to her statement, the right had not been extended to all children having special educational needs. She outlined a three-part plan to rectify the situation:

1. All boards will be required to offer an Early Identification Program to ensure that the learning needs of every child entering schools will be identified so that remedial programs can be provided promptly.
2. All boards will be directed to provide educational programs for children with learning disabilities. Disabilities are defined as "disorders in one or more of the basic processes involved in understanding or using symbols or spoken language: these disorders result in a significant discrepancy between academic achievement and assessed intellectual ability."
3. The Ministry is establishing residential schools for severely learning disabled children in Milton for Anglophone children, and in Ottawa for francophone children because boards will be unable to offer programs due to the severity of the disability. These schools will also provide in-service training for board-employed teachers to equip them to conduct programs for learning disabled children in their schools.

In addition, amendments to the Education Act are to be introduced. The most notable change concerns Section 147(1) 40 of the Act which at present makes special education programs optional. The Act will be amended to set out each school board's responsibility to insure that all children within its jurisdiction are provided with appropriate educational service.

Another major change concerns trainable retarded children. Boards will be required to follow formalized procedures if they wish to exclude such children from elementary, secondary or special schools.[184] The amendment will require that a board take all reasonable steps to assist the parents or guardians of the child to obtain non-educational services when a child is excluded. Prior to this change, trainable mentally retarded could be excluded from school from the outset. With the new legislation such children would have to be admitted and placed in a program before formal exclusion could be initiated. In essence, they will have the same access to schools as other school-age children.

At present, as many exceptional children as possible are taught in the regular classroom and in many cases consultation services are provided for the teacher. Some children receive supplementary instructional services. Children who have more severe difficulties are enrolled part-time in a special class or special school. For children who cannot be taught within the regular school, home or hospital instruction is provided by board employed teachers. There are some residential schools, residential treatment centres, and in extreme cases only, hospital residence. The aim is to move in the direction of regular class placement as soon as possible.

Manitoba

Manitoba, like other provinces in Canada, is in state of transition regarding current policy related to special education. It is recognized by the province that many former policy statements are outdated but new policies have not been completely formalized.

In 1975 the legislative assembly passed Bill 58, an Act to amend the Public Schools Act. Section 465(22) of this Act reads as follows: "Every school board shall provide or make provision for the education of all resident persons who have the right to attend school and who require special programs for their education." However, in order to provide the necessary time for appropriate implementation of the Bill, this legislation was not proclaimed mandatory at that time.

The intent of the Bill was expressed in a draft statement by the Working Group on the Education of Children and Youth with Special Needs:

> To the maximum extent practicable handicapped children shall be educated along with children who do not have handicaps and shall attend regular classes. Physical and mental impediments to normal functioning of handicapped children in the regular school environment shall be overcome by the provision of special aids and services

rather than by separating schooling for the handicapped. Special classes, separate schooling or other removal of handicapped children from the regular educational environment shall occur only when, and to the extent that, the nature or severity of the handicap is such that education in regular classes, even with the use of supplementary aids and services cannot be accomplished satisfactorily.[185]

Manitoba's legislative assembly is considering a general revision of the Public Schools Act which contains Bill 58. It is hoped that when the new Act is passed the Department of Education will change both the level and method of funding for special education and draw up appropriate regulations and guidelines. It is expected that a detailed *Manual of Legislation Regulations, Policies and Guidelines for Special Education in Manitoba* will be soon available.

Saskatchewan

Saskatchewan attempts to provide handicapped children with educational opportunities relevant to their needs. It is the government's policy that "all handicapped children can be educated or trained for more complete and productive lives."[186] Handicapped children include those with sensory defects, mental retardation, communication disorder, neurological or physical impairment or behavioural disorders.

According to present policy each board should make available appropriate educational services for handicapped pupils in the least restrictive program. Integration of the handicapped child in a regular class setting is stressed; placement in a special class is provided only when absolutely necessary. There should, even then, be as much integration with the rest of the school population as possible.

Although school boards are expected to provide educational services to such pupils at no cost to parents, boards may in certain instances exclude a pupil from a particular program. Pupils so severely handicapped that they could not benefit from existing services provided by the board may be excluded. With this, the board must help in arranging other suitable services or provide the necessary services in other facilities or by agreement with another board, agency, institution or person capable of providing appropriate services.

In Saskatchewan, the emphasis is on normalization for special education students. If they remain in a regular classroom setting they are provided with special instructional materials and equipment. There are itinerant and tutorial programs and resource rooms for children who require assistance additional to regular class instruction. Also, there are special classrooms and, where necessary, special schools. Homebound, hospitalized or institutional instruction is provided only when absolutely necessary with the understanding that the movement toward normalization is the goal.

The province feels that early intervention is necessary to enhance opportunities for self-realization. Screening of pupils is accomplished by an annual school system survey. Each pupil so screened is individually assessed by specialized personnel and appropriate placement is made with parents' consent. A child so placed is subjected to continual evaluation, his case being reviewed annually.

It is recognized that teachers of the handicapped should have special training in addition to the general requirements for teacher certification. A Bachelor of Education degree with a special education major is preferred with the minimum qualification being certification and three courses in special education. A course work concentration in the particular area of exceptionality in which the teacher is working is considered desirable.

Alberta

Alberta recognizes that there are many different possible arrangements for educating handicapped pupils. Handicapped children are considered to be those who require special provisions for their education. School boards are required to accept every pupil whose parents reside in the district or division. If this is not possible, because an appropriate program is not available, the pupil must be directed to a school in another district or division; the home board assumes responsibility for the costs involved.

Special provisions may include accommodation in the regular classroom with the necessary individual assistance provided. In some instances individual assistance may be in the form of a special, individualized program. Assistance in carrying out the programs may be provided by the regular classroom teacher, a resource teacher, a teaching aide, or some other person. Special materials and equipment to assist learning may be necessary. When the handicapped child is accommodated in the regular classroom, he is removed for special programs to a resource room or education clinic and then returned to the regular classroom once the special program is completed for the day.

Those children who cannot benefit by instruction in the regular classroom remain the responsibility of the segregated classroom teacher but the child is permitted and encouraged to join the regular program whenever it is feasible. A variation on this theme is to have the pupil remain full-time in the special class if he requires very specialized services and a protective, supportive environment.

Further arrangements allow the child who is homebound or hospitalized to receive educational service on an individual basis—either short—or long term depending on the condition. Finally, there is the situation where the handicapped pupil, because of noneducational reasons, requires a special setting in a home, hospital or institution which may offer active treatment, custodial services or detention facilities. Education services are available in these settings as well.

The province recognizes the normalization principle as being a good principle but one which must be applied with a great deal of forethought and planning. Before a pupil is integrated, criteria for integration must be carefully prepared and followed to insure both the handicapped pupil and the people with whom the handicapped pupil will associate meet established criteria. In addition, active and ongoing support must be immediately available to the pupil, teacher and parents. "While integration or normalization is an objective of special education it is not a panacea for the problems of all handicapped children."[187]

British Columbia

The special education program is currently in a state of reorganization in British Columbia. A new statement on integration is close to acceptance and the guidelines for the operation of the Special Programs Branch are undergoing revision. A Task Force has begun work in the field to assess the efficacy of the special approvals under which the Ministry of Education assists school districts to finance their special education programs.[188]

At present British Columbia has no mandatory legislation that guarantees the right of all children to an appropriate, free education. Handicapped children wishing to enrol in a school district are analyzed in relation to their ability to benefit from an education program. They are accepted if they can be served in a regular school by regular teachers, aides and other resources.[189]

If the child's needs cannot be met through existing resources, he is referred to the local or regional Children's Committee. The Committee usually arranges for the additional resources required. If additional help cannot be arranged, the case is sent to the Inter-Ministry Children's Committee to be resolved.

Education of the handicapped is paid for by the school boards. The policy of the B.C. Ministry of Education is to see that educational services per se are available to all children regardless of the handicap. The Special Programs Branch assists school boards in seeing that appropriate educational services are provided in the home, institution or other settings.

The Ministry of Education does not, at present, provide additional finances to meet the cost of the additional services required for mainstreaming handicapped pupils.

It is apparent from the brief summaries that all provinces are concerned about special education and at present are studying the situation with a view to making appropriate changes. The changes may not be fast enough in coming for some, but the knowledge that the provinces are striving to cope with the various problems and issues is somewhat comforting.

* * * * *

1 Stephen Richer, Raymond Breton, "School Organization and Student Differences: Some Views of Canadian Educators," *Canadian Education Research Digest*, (March, 1968), pp. 21-27. The first half of Richer's and

Breton's article was reproduced in Document 27, Chapter Six.

2 Leslie D. Karagianis, Wayne C. Nesbit, "Special Education: Public Policy in Canada," *Education in Canada* (Summer, 1980), pp. 5-10, 29. Karagianis was then head of the Department of Educational Psychology at Memorial University, and Nesbit was co-ordinator of special education at Memorial.

3 R.K. Crocker and F. Riggs, *Improving the Quality of Education: Challenge and Opportunity* (St. John's: Government of Newfoundland and Labrador, 1979).

4 Personal correspondence with F. MacLellan, Prince Edward Island Department of Education, 1979.

5 T. Cushing. *Canadian Public Policy Committee Reports,* presented at 3rd Canadian Congress of Council for Exceptional Children, Winnipeg, 1978.

6 *White Paper: Opportunities for the Handicapped* (Fredericton, N.B. Department of Education. 1974.

7 *The Schools of Quebec: Policy Statement and Plan of Action: Children with Difficulties in Learning and Adaptation* (Quebec: Quebec, Ministry of Education, 1979), p. 15.

8 B. Stephenson, *Legislative and Policy Changes concerning Special Education,* statement in the Ontario Legislature, December 1978.

9 Personal correspondence with G. Bergman, Ontario Ministry of Education, 1979.

10 Cited in personal correspondence (1979) from W.C. Lorimer, Manitoba's former Deputy Minister of Education.

11 *Special Education: A Manual of Legislative Regulations, Policies and Guidelines* (January 1977) *Supplement* (Regina, Saskatchewan, Department of Education, 1978).

12 *Guidelines for the Payment of Special Education Teaching Position Grants under Section 5 of the School Grants Regulations* (Edmonton: Alberta Department of Education, 1978), p. 3.

13 Personal correspondence with Dr. P. McGeer, former B.C Minister of Fducation, Science and Technology, 1979.

14 L. Krywanuik, *Canadian Public Policy Committee Reports,* presented at the 3rd Canadian Congress of Council for Exceptional Children, Winnipeg, 1978.

ACKNOWLEDGEMENTS

The publisher gratefully acknowledges permission to reprint the materials listed below (in order of their appearance in the text) by the individuals or organizations named.

Nadia Fahmy-Eid, "The Education of Girls by the Ursulines of Quebec during the French Regime," tr. Sarah Segev and Norma Scotcher, in Wendy Murchison et al., *Canadian Women: A Reader* (Toronto: Harcourt Brace, 1996); permission of the author.

Charles Bilodeau, "Quebec Education," in *The Year Book of Education, 1951* (London, Eng.: University of London Institute of Education, 1951, by permission of London: Institute of Education, University of London.

Robert D. Gidney, "Elementary Education in Upper Canada: A Reassessment," first published in *Ontario History*, vol. 65, no. 3, September 1973 and reprinted by permission of the Ontario Historical Society.

Marilyn Färdig Whiteley, "Annie Leake's Occupation: Development of a Teaching Career, 1858-1886," *Historical Studies in Education* 4, no. 1 (Spring 1992); permission of the author.

Susan E. Houston and Alison Prentice, "What One Might Teach and Another Learn," from Houston and Prentice, *Schooling and Scholars in Nineteenth-Century Ontario* (Toronto: University of Toronto Press, 1988); reprinted by permission of the publisher.

Robert S. Patterson, "Voices From the Past: The Personal and Professional Struggle of Rural School Teachers," in Nancy M. Sheehan, J. Donald Wilson, and David C. Jones, eds., *Schools in the West: Essays in Canadian Educational History* (Calgary: Detselig Enterprises, 1986); by permission of Detselig Enterprises Ltd.

Barbara Riley, "Six Saucepans to One: Domestic Science vs. The Home in British Columbia, 1900-1939," in *Not Just Pin Money: Selected Essays on the History of Women's Work in British Columbia*, Barbara Latham, Roberta Jane Pazdro, eds., (Victoria: Camosun College, 1984); by permission of the editors.

Mary Kinnear, "'Mostly for the Male Members': Teaching in Winnipeg, 1933-1966," *Historical Studies in Education* 6, no. 1 (Spring 1994); permission of the author.

Morris Mott, "Confronting 'Modern' Problems Through Play: The Beginning of Physical Education in Manitoba's Public Schools, 1900-1915," in Nancy M. Sheehan, J. Donald Wilson, and David C. Jones, eds., *Schools in the West: Essays in Canadian Educational History* (Calgary: Detselig Enterprises Ltd., 1986); by permission of Detselig Enterprises Ltd.

Robert C. Goode, "The Physical Fitness of Our School Children," *Education Canada* (Winter 1976); copyright Canadian Education Association 2000 ISSN 0013-1253, *Education Canada* Vol. 14 (4). Reprinted with permission.

Cynthia Comacchio, "Inventing the Extracurriculum: High School Culture in Interwar-Ontario," first published in *Ontario History*, vol. 93, no. 1 (Spring 2002), 33-56 and reprinted here by permission of the Ontario Historical Society.

A.E. Ault, "A Survey of Examinations," in Harley V. Usill; ed., *The Year Book of Education, 1938* (London: The University of London Institute of Education: Evans Brothers, 1939); by permission of London: Institute of Education, University of London.

John W. Friesen and Virginia Lyons Friesen, *Aboriginal Education in Canada: A Plea for Integration* (Calgary: Detselig Enterprises, 2002), pp. 99-117; by permission of Detselig Enterprises Ltd.

"Education of the Native Peoples of Ontario," (Toronto: Union of Ontario Indians, 1971), pp. 4-7; by permission of the Union of Ontario Indians.

John Taylor, "Non-Native Teachers Teaching in Native Communities," reprinted with permission of the publisher from *First Nations Education in Canada*, edited by Marie Battiste and Jean Barman, University of British Columbia Press, 2002. All rights reserved by the publisher.

Neil Sutherland, "Children in 'Formalist' Schools," in Sutherland, *Growing Up: Children in English Canada from the Great War to the Age of Television* (Toronto: University of Toronto Press, 1997); reprinted by permission of the publisher.

"Satisfaction: How do Grade 8 Students in Atlantic Canada feel about the quality of their school life?" in *Education Indicators for Atlantic Canada* (Human Resources and Development Canada, 1996); by permission of the Atlantic Ministers of Education and Training.

Nancy M. Sheehan and J. Donald Wilson, "From Normal School to the University to the College of Teachers: Teacher Education in British Columbia in the 20th century," in *Journal of Education for Teaching*, vol. 20, no. 1 (1994); by permission of Taylor and Francis Ltd.

"Who Are Canada's Teachers? How Are They Recruited and Selected?" in *The Year Book of Education, 1953* (London, Eng.: University of London Institute of Education, 1953); by permission of London: Institute of Education, University of London.

Ken Osborne, "Education for Citizenship," *Education Canada* vol. 38, no. 3 (Winter 1998-99); copyright Canadian Education Association 2000 ISSN 0013-1253, vol. 38 (3). Reprinted with permission.

Larry Booi, "Citizens or Subjects? How well do Alberta's social studies classes prepare our kids for citizenship?" in *Alberta Views* (March/April 2001); permission of the author.

Lorna Earl, "Assessment and Accountability in Education: Improvement or Surveillance?" in *Education Canada* vol. 39, no. 3 (Fall/Autumn 1999); copyright Canadian Education Association 2000 ISSN 0013-1253 vol. 39 (3). Reprinted with permission.

ENDNOTES

1 E.H. Carr, *What is History?* (London, 1964), 23

2 Charles E. Phillips' pioneering text for teachers' colleges and faculties of education, *The Development of Education in Canada* (Toronto, 1957), is an excellent example of this school of writing.

3 Nadia Fahmy-Eid, "L'éducation des filles chez les Ursulines de Québec sous le Régime français," in Nadia Fahmy-Eid and Micheline Dumont, eds., *Maîttresses de maison, maîttresses d'école: Femmes, famille et education dans l'histoire du Québec* (Montreal: Boreal Express, 1983), 49-76. Nadia Fahmy-Eid, "The Education of Girls by the Ursulines of Quebec during the French Regime," translated by Sarah Segev, Norma Scotcher, in Wendy Mitchinson et al., *Canadian Women: A Reader* (Toronto: Harcourt Brace, 1996), pp. 33-49.
*Translators' Note: Unless otherwise indicated, direct quotations are our translations. For full references consult the original article in French.

4 Francis Parkman, *The Old Regime in Canada* (Boston: Little, Brown & Company, 1874), 365.

5 Joyce Marshall, translator, *Word from New France-The Selected Letters of Marie de l'Incarnation* (Toronto: Oxford University Press, 1967), 94.

6 Marshall, 90.

7 Ibid., 74.

8 Ibid.

9 Ibid.

10 Ibid., 89.

11 Ibid., 334.

12 Reuben Gold Thwaites, *The Jesuit Relations and Allied Documents— Travels and Explorations of the Jesuit Missionaries in New France, 1610-1791* (Cleveland: 1896-1901), vol. 23, p. 51.

13 *An Ursuline of Quebec, the Life of the Venerable Mother Mary* (France: C. Paillart, 1813), 85.

14 Marshall, 341.

15 Ibid., 216.

16 Ibid., 222.

17 Ibid., 336.

18 Ibid., 72.

19 Ibid., 72-3.

20 Ibid., 73.

21 Ibid., 131-2.

22 Ibid., 71-2.

23 Ibid., 336.

24 Ibid., 73.

25 Ibid., 336.

26 Ibid.

27 *An Ursuline of Quebec*, 82.

28 Ibid.

29 Ibid., 83.

30 Marshall, 335.

31 Ibid.

32 Ibid.

33 Ibid., 204.

34 Ibid., 335.

35 Ibid.

36 Ibid., 336.

37 Thwaites, vol. 36, p. 173.

38 Thwaites, vol. 51, p. 211.

39 Ibid., 336.

40 R.D. Gidney and W.P.J. Millar note that applying the terms "primary schools," and "secondary" or "high schools," to the grammar schools and common schools is not strictly accurate. The grammar school was not conceived as the second stage in the education process, but as a classical school that accepted boys after they had learned the basic ABCs and gave them both an "elementary" and a "secondary" education. The common school taught both the three Rs and more advanced subjects. Not until the 1880s was the present vertically integrated system of primary and secondary schooling completed. R.D. Gidney, W.P.J. Millar, *Inventing Secondary Education: The Rise of the High School in Nineteenth-Century Ontario* (Montreal, 1990).

41 R.D. Gidney, "Elementary Education in Upper Canada: A Reassessment," *Ontario History*, 65, 3 (September 1973), pp. 169-85.

42 Marilyn Färdig Whiteley, "Annie Leake's Occupation: Development of a Teaching Career, 1858-1886," *Historical Studies in Education*, 4, 1 (Spring, 1992), 97-112.

43 Susan E. Houston, Alison Prentice, "What One Might Teach and Another Learn," the first section of chapter 8 of their *Schooling and Scholars in Nineteenth-Century Ontario* (Toronto: University of Toronto Press, 1988), 237-253, 385-89.

44 This incident is discussed in J. Donald Wilson, "Lottie Bowron and Rural Women Teachers in British Columbia, 1928-1934," in Gillian Creese, Veronica Strong-Boag, eds., *British Columbia Reconsidered: Essays on Women* (Vancouver: Press Gang, 1992).

45 Robert S. Patterson, "Voices From the Past: The Personal and Professional Struggle of Rural School Teachers," in Nancy M. Sheehan, J. Donald Wilson, David C. Jones, eds., *Schools in the West: Essays in Canadian Educational History* (Calgary: Detselig Enterprises, 1986), 99-111.

46 Barbara Riley, "Six Saucepans to One: Domestic Science vs. the Home in British Columbia, 1900-1939," in *Not Just Pin Money: Selected Essays on the History of Women's Work in British Columbia*, Barbara Latham, Roberta Jane Pazdro, eds., (Victoria: Camosun College, 1984).

47 *Daily Colonist*, 6 September 1903.

48 *Daily Colonist*, 2 February 1904.

49 Vancouver *Province*, 7 April 1904.

50 Correspondingly, local dissatisfaction could also undermine domestic science at the local level. British Columbia, *Annual Report of the Public Schools of the Province of British Columbia* (hereafter *Annual Report*), 1916-17, p. A40; *Annual Report*, 1918-19, p. A31.

51 *Annual Report*, 1925-26.

52 The interviewees, born between 1897 and 1916, were located by the "snowball" method. The interviews have been deposited with the Provincial Archives of British Columbia as numbers 4088.1-4088.42.

53 Provincial Archives of British Columbia (hereafter PABC), nos. 4088.29, 4088.42, 4088.11.

54 See Neil Sutherland, *Children in English-Canadian Society: Framing the Twentieth Century Consensus* (Toronto: University of Toronto Press, 1976) for an analysis of the new social and educational ideas, their proponents, and their influence.

55 *Annual Report*, 1900-01: 251.

56 Annual Report, 1919-20: C48, quoting from the Report of the Royal Commission on Technical Education and Industrial Training (Ottawa: King's Printer, 1913-14).

57 Annual Report, 1917-18: D68.

58 *Daily Province*, 6 March 1915; Timothy A. Dunn, "The Rise of Mass Public Schooling in British Columbia, 1900-1929," in J. Donald Wilson and David C. Jones, eds., *Schooling and Society in Twentieth-Century British Columbia* (Calgary: Detselig Enterprises, 1980).

59 *Annual Report*, 1918-19: A78.

60 *Annual Report*, 1917-18: V43.

61 6 March 1915.

62 *Daily Colonist*, 20 January 1926. Racist appeals based on Anglo-Saxon supremacy sometimes figured in the rhetoric supporting the teaching of domestic science. See, for example, "Domestic Science Should Not Be Considered a Frill," *Daily Colonist*, 3 August 1924.

63 J. H. Putnam and G. M. Weir, *Survey of the School System* (Victoria: Province of British Columbia, 1925): 339.

64 Political Equality League, *The Champion* (October 1912): 5-6. See also "The Labour Question and Women's Work and its Relation to Home Life," in National Council of Women of Canada, comp., *Women*

Workers of Canada (Ottawa, 1898): 254-62, reproduced in Ramsay Cook and Wendy Mitchinson, eds., *The Proper Sphere: Woman's Place in Canadian Society* (Toronto: Oxford University Press, 1976); *Daily Province*, 19 April 1907; a reference to the solution of the "Chinese problem" with respect to domestic labour, *Daily Colonist*, 9 June 1898.

65 See section on home economics in *Annual Report*, 1925-26: R58.

66 *Annual Report*, 1916-17: A73; Department of Education, *Courses of Study for the Public, High, and Normal Schools of British Columbia*, 1921: 52, 55; Department of Education, Programme of Studies for the High and Technical Schools of British Columbia, 1928-29: 59; Department of Education, *New Programme of Studies for the High and Technical Schools of British Columbia*, 1930: 98.

67 "Resolution arising from the findings of a special committee on home economics, appointed by the executive of the provincial Parent-Teacher Federation," printed in Putnam and Weir, *Survey*: 540.

68 Victoria *Daily Times*, 20 October 1926; *Daily Province*, 6 October 1926.

69 *Daily Times*, 26 March 1927; Vancouver *Morning Star*, 30 September 1926. See also Robert M. Stamp, "Teaching Girls their God Given Place in Life," *Atlantis* 2, no. 2 (Spring 1977): 18-34.

70 Interview 4088.5; Putnam and Weir, *Survey*, chapter 6; *Daily Times*, 24 March 1924; *The Agricultural Journal* 3, no. 8 (October 1918): 201; Vancouver *Province*, 7 April 1904; *The Islander* 1, no. 6 (August 1920): 15; *Daily Times*, 26 March 1927.

71 *Daily Province*, 21 October 1926; *Morning Star*, 30 September 1926; Helen Cameron Parker, "Technical Schools for Women," *The Canadian Magazine* 1 (1893): 634-7, reproduced in Cook and Mitchinson, *The Proper Sphere*.

72 Putnam and Weir, *Survey*: 91.

73 *Vancouver World*, 12 January 1916.

74 See Dunn, "Rise of Mass Public Schooling" for the impact of this approach on British Columbia's school system.

75 *Daily Province*, 21 October 1926. References to the scientific care of children and the role of domestic science in improving child welfare were noted in the 1920s (Annual Report, 1923-24: T75; *Vancouver Sun*, 5 and 6 October 1926; *Morning Star*, 7 October 1926).

76 Annual Reports, 1915-16: A81; 1923-24: T75.

77 Annie B. Juniper, *Girls' Home Manual of Cookery, Home Management, Home Nursing and Laundry* (Victoria: King's Printer, 1913).

78 Olive Dean, "Domestic Science Notebook," Modern History Division, British Columbia Provincial Museum (BCPM).

79 Lois Kinley, "Domestic Science Notebook," Modern History Division, BCPM.

80 A.M. Ross, "The Romance of Vancouver's Schools," *B.C. Magazine* 7, no. 6 [n.d.], 45. Insistence on proper methods extended to all domestic science subjects. The Annual Report for 1924-25 noted that "good habits in sewing are also a necessity; perpetual vigilance is required on the part of the teacher against the child's tendency to work without a thimble, to hold the work the wrong way, and to dream over it" (p. M55).

81 26 January 1912.

82 *Nelson Daily News*, 8 June 1912. Shortly after this account the Nelson school board had to deal with criticism of the extravagant cost of the equipment (*Daily News*, 21 June 1912). I am grateful to Patricia Roy for bringing these references to my attention.

83 Annual Report, 1918-19: A79.

84 See, for example, references to educational exhibits featuring class work and the activity of domestic science teachers in the war effort. (*Annual Reports*, 1905-06: A18; 1911-12: A48; 1917-18: D66.)

85 See Sutherland, *Children in English-Canadian Society*, for a thorough examination of the "new education."

86 *Annual Reports*, 1915-16: A81; 1918-19: A78.

87 *Annual Report*, 1920-21: F47.

88 *Annual Reports*, 1917-18: D66; 1918-19: A78-A79; 1926-27: M64.

89 Putnam and Weir, *Survey*: 534.

90 *Annual Reports*, 1911-12: A48; 1918-19: AT9; 1924-25: M55.

91 *Annual Reports*, 1923-24: T75; 1924-25: M55; 1926-27: M63-M64; PABC, nos. 4088.38, 4088.40; British Columbia, Department of Education, *Recipes for Home Economics Classes*. Home Economics Circular No. 1 (Victoria: King's Printer, 1927).

92 This was true for both boys and girls. However, while girls were often expected to participate in the same chores as their brothers, for example, filling the woodbox or cutting grass, the reverse was seldom the case.

93 Other foods were produced at home: twenty-one mothers made their own bread, fifteen families kept laying hens, and five kept a cow.

94 Commercial cookbooks, published by brand name companies such as Fleischmann's, Blue Ribbon, and Crisco, were the most common.

95 One woman described the impossibility of making her mother's recipes because the verbal instructions started with "a jugful of sour cream" (PABC, no. 4088.23).

96 PABC, no. 4088.6.

97 Putnam and Weir, *Survey*: 339. By contrast, some interviewees stressed that it was their fathers who insisted on acquiring the latest household equipment, and in their own households, their husbands (PABC, nos. 4088.25, 4088.26, 4088.31).

98 British Columbia, Department of Education, *Manual of School Law and*

School Regulations, 1912, p.77.

99 *Nelson Daily News*, 8 June 1912; *Vancouver Sun*, 13 June 1912; PABC, GR457, DS III, 1915, correspondence between G. H. Deane and Mrs. M. Andison, Secretary of Burnaby School Board, 8 July 1915, 23 July 1915, 5 August 1915. In Armstrong the enamel drainboards were included in the original tender to furnish the domestic science centre, though these would have cost more than wooden drainboards (GR457, DS IL 1915, Supervisor of Technical Education to MacPhail-Smith Hardware Company, Armstrong, B.C., 9 August 1915.

100 PABC, nos. 4088.16, 4088.12.

101 GR457, MT III, 1915, Deane to J. M. Wright, Armstrong School Board, 14 August 1915. Deane's enthusiasm for electrical stoves may also have been dampened by continuing problems with the Canadian Westinghouse stoves installed in the Mission, Bridgeport, Ladner, and Chilliwack domestic science centres. See GR457, correspondence from 31 March 1915 (micro B2031) to 28 December 1915 (GR457, DS I, 1915).

102 GR457, DS I, 1916, Deane to W. D. Vance, Prince Rupert, 7 March 1916.

103 Micro B2032, 1816-19, Mr. Kyle, Inspector's Reports.

104 GR4S7, Box 1, file 10, Winnifred May Townsend to John Kyle, 25 May (1916).

105 GR457, Miscellaneous 1915, Supervisor of Technical Education to Singer Sewing Company, 9 August 1915.

106 GR457, DS III, 1915, McClary Manufacturing Company to the Supervisor of Technical Education, 21 June 1915.

107 GR457, Box 2, File 3, letter and printed material from Hotpoint Electric Heating Company to George Deane, 2 August 1915.

108 GR457, DS III, 1915, Deane to Andison, 23 July 1915; DS I, 1916, John Kyle, Organizer of Technical Education to W.A. McKenzie, Penticton School Board, 27 July 1916.

109 GR457, micro B2032, John Lillico, Ridgeway's Tea, to John Kyle, Organizer of Technical Education, 5 October 1916.

110 *School Days*, 1919-27. The magazine's Advisory Committee consisted of Vancouver's Municipal Inspector and the principals of several Vancouver schools.

111 *Annual Report*, 1928-29: 253. In 1919 the first year high school Household Science course included visits to market, grocery, and meat stores, dairies, and manufactures (British Columbia, Department of Education, *Courses of Study for the Public, High, and Normal Schools of B.C,* 1919: 47). Provincial government departments also recognized the opportunity presented by home economics classes. Brochures and recipe

booklets extolling the virtues of British Columbia fruit and potatoes were distributed to teachers and students as a result of cooperation between the Provincial Horticulturist and the Organizer of Technical Education, who also invited the donation of crates of fruit which home economics classes could preserve for the Horticulturist to use in exhibitions (GR457, DS I, 1915, R. M. Winslow to John Kyle, 20 October 1915, 23 October 1915; Bessie N. Allan to John Kyle, 12 December 1915; Elizabeth Berry to John Kyle, 14 December 1915). Elaine Fisher, "Images of Angels and Whores: Wedding Women to Consumerism," paper presented at the Canadian Research Institute for the Advancement of Women, Annual Conference, Vancouver, November 1983.

112 The information in this introduction was derived from Steve McNutt, "Shifting Objectives: The Development of Male Physical Education in Nova Scotia from 1867 to 1913," *Canadian Journal of History of Sports* vol. 22, no.1 (May, 1991), pp. 32-51.

113 Morris Mott, "Confronting 'Modern' Problems Through Play: The Beginning of Physical Education in Manitoba's Public Schools, 1900-1915," in Nancy M. Sheehan, J. Donald Wilson, David C. Jones, eds., *Schools in the West: Essays in Canadian Educational History* (Calgary: Detselig Enterprises Ltd, 1986), pp. 57-71.

114 By 1934, attendance was compulsory up to age 15 in Saskatchewan, Alberta and British Columbia; to age 16 in Ontario and Manitoba; to 13 in Prince Edward Island; and to 14 in rural Nova Scotia and to 16 in urban areas.

115 Cynthia Comacchio, "Inventing the Extracurriculum: High School Culture in Interwar Ontario," *Ontario History*, vol. XCIII, no. 1 (Spring 2002), pp. 33-56.

116 John W. Friesen, Virginia Lyons Friesen, *Aboriginal Education in Canada: A Plea for Integration* (Calgary: Detselig Enterprises, 2002), pp. 99-117.

117 H.L. Willis, Gerald Halpern, "A Survey of How Students Perceive their High Schools," *Education Canada* vol. 10, no. 2 (June, 1970).

118 Neil Sutherland, "Children in 'Formalist' Schools," in his *Growing Up: Children in English Canada from the Great War to the Age of Television* (Toronto: University of Toronto Press, 1997), pp. 186-219, 304-309.

119 Quoted in M.E. LaZerte, "Canada," *The Year Book of Education, 1953* (London, England: University of London Institute of Education, 1953), pp. 237.

120 Ibid., p. 248.

121 Stan M. Shapson, Neil Smith, "Transformative Teaching: An Agenda for Faculties of Education," *Education Canada* vol. 39, no. 1 (Spring, 1999).

122 Nancy M. Sheehan, J. Donald Wilson, "From Normal School to the

University to the College of Teachers: Teacher Education in British Columbia in the 20ᵗʰ Century," *Journal of Education for Teaching*, vol. 20, no. 1 (1994), pp. 23-37.

123 "'Our History Syllabus Has Us Gasping': History in Canadian Schools—Past, Present, and Future," *Canadian Historical Review*, vol. 81, no. 3, (September, 2000), pp. 404-435.

124 J. L. Granatstein, *Who Killed Canadian History?* (Toronto, 1998).

125 Ibid, p. 405.

126 Ken Osborne, "Education for Citizenship," *Education Canada*, vol. 38, no. 3 (Winter, 1998-99), pp. 16-19.

127 Lorna Earl, "Assessment and Accountability in Education: Improvement or Surveillance?" *Education Canada*, vol. 39, no. 3 (Fall/Autumn 1999), pp. 4-6, 47.

128 W. Firestone, D. Mayrowetzand, J. Fairman, "Performance-based assessment and instructional change: the effects of testing in Maine and Maryland," *Educational Evaluation and Policy Analysis,* (20), no. 2 (Summer 1998): 95-113.

129 D. Berliner and B. Biddle, *The Manufactured Crisis: Myths, Fraud and the Attack on American Public Schools*, (Reading, MA.: Addison Wesley, 1998).

130 L. Darling Hammond, "Performance-based assessment and educational equity," *Harvard Educational Review*, 64 (1994):23.

131 A. Hargreaves, L. Earl, and M. Schmidt, "Four perspectives on classroom assessment," forthcoming.

132 L. Earl, "Assessment and accountability in Ontario," *Canadian Journal of Education*, 20 (1) (1995): 45-55.

133 L. Shepard, "Psychometricians' beliefs about learning," *Educational Researcher* (October, 1991): 2-16.

134 L. Darling-Hammond, J. Ancess and B. Falk, *Authentic assessment in action: Studies of schools and Students at work* (New York: Teachers College Press, 1994).

135 W. Mehrens and J. Popham, "How to evaluate the legal defensibility of high stakes tests," *Applied Measurement in Education* 5 no. 3 (1992): 265-283.

136 P. Black, "Performance assessment and accountability: The experience in England and Wales," *Educational Evaluation and Policy Analysis* 16 no. 2 (1994): 191-204.

137 L. Earl and N. Torrance, "Impact of EQAO Assessments On School and Classroom Practices," forthcoming.